WHERE MEN WIN GLORY

ALSO BY JON KRAKAUER

Eiger Dreams

Into the Wild

Into Thin Air

Under the Banner of Heaven

WHERE MEN WIN GLORY

The Odyssey of Pat Tillman

Jon Krakauer

DOUBLEDAY
New York   London   Toronto   Sydney   Auckland

CD
DOUBLEDAY

Copyright © 2009 by Jonathan R. Krakauer

All rights reserved. Published in the United States by Doubleday, a division of Random House, Inc., New York, and in Canada by Random House of Canada Limited, Toronto. www.doubleday.com

DOUBLEDAY and the DD colophon are registered trademarks of Random House, Inc.

Book design by Caroline Cunningham
Maps by Matthew Ericson

Library of Congress Cataloging-in-Publication Data
Krakauer, Jon.
Where men win glory : the odyssey of Pat Tillman / Jon Krakauer. —1st ed.
p. cm.
1. Tillman, Pat, 1976–2004. 2. Football players—United States—Biography.
3. Soldiers—United States—Biography. 4. Afghan War, 2001—United States.
5. Afghan War, 2001—Casualties. I. Title.
GV939.T49K73 2008
796.332092—dc22
[B]
2008023155

ISBN 978-0-385-52226-7

PRINTED IN THE UNITED STATES OF AMERICA

10 9 8 7 6 5 4 3 2 1

First Edition

TITLE PAGE PHOTO: Looking down at the Pakistani firebase known as the Gray Castle from the Afghan side of the border, near Forward Operating Base Tillman. Photo by Jon Krakauer.

For Linda;

and in memory of Sergeant First Class Jared C. Monti, killed in action on June 21, 2006, near Gowardesh, Afghanistan

Who among mortal men are you, good friend? Since never before have I seen you in the fighting where men win glory, yet now you have come striding far out in front of all others in your great heart . . .

—HOMER, *The Iliad*

MAPS

DRAMATIS PERSONAE

April 22, 2004
Convoy from Magarah to Mana, Spera District, Khost Province, Afghanistan
Second Platoon, Alpha Company, Second Battalion, Seventy-fifth Ranger
 Regiment

SERIAL ONE

Vehicle 1: Humvee (GMV) with Mk 19 mounted on top turret
Lieutenant David Uthlaut, platoon leader, right front seat
Staff Sergeant Matt Weeks, Third Squad leader, driver
Specialist Ryan Mansfield, gunner in top turret
Specialist Jade Lane, radio operator, right waist seat
Specialist Donald Lee, forward observer, left waist seat
Private First Class Bryan O'Neal, M4 rifleman, rear seat
Specialist Mark, 84-millimeter Carl Gustav gunner, left rear seat
Specialist Jay Lamell, assistant gunner, right rear seat

Vehicle 2: Toyota Hilux King Cab
Specialist Brandon Farmer, mechanic, driver
Specialist Kilpatrick, M4 rifleman, right front seat
Specialist Pat Tillman, acting team leader, SAW gunner, left rear seat

Vehicle 3: Up-armored Humvee, no gun mounted on top turret
Sergeant Mel Ward, team leader, driver
Specialist Will Aker, M4 rifleman, right front seat
Specialist John Tafoya, right waist seat
Specialist Douglas Ping, left waist seat

Vehicle 4: Toyota Hilux King Cab
Sergeant Bradley Shepherd, team leader, driver
Specialist Russell Baer, SAW gunner, right front seat
Private First Class Josey Boatright, backseat
Specialist Jean-Claude Suhl, 240 Bravo machine gunner
Specialist Alvin Fudge, forward observer

Vehicle 5: Toyota Hilux King Cab
Sayed Farhad, Afghan Militia Forces soldier
Three other Afghan Militia Forces soldiers (names unknown)

Vehicle 6: Toyota Hilux King Cab
Three Afghan Militia Forces soldiers (names unknown)

SERIAL TWO

Vehicle 1: Afghan jinga truck, towing non-operable Humvee
Afghan driver (name unknown)
Jamal, Afghan interpreter
Sergeant First Class Jeffrey Jackson, Second Squad leader
Staff Sergeant Jonathan Owens, weapons-squad leader

Vehicle 2: Humvee (GMV) with .50-caliber M2 on top turret, M240B on right rear
Staff Sergeant Greg Baker, First Squad leader, right front seat
Sergeant Kellett Sayre, M4 rifleman, driver
Specialist Stephen Ashpole, gunner in top turret
Specialist Chad Johnson, M4/203 rifleman and grenadier, right waist seat
Specialist Trevor Alders, SAW gunner, left waist seat
Specialist Steve Elliott, 240 Bravo machine gunner, right rear seat
Private First Class James Roberts, M4/203 rifleman and grenadier, left
    rear seat
Wallid, Afghan interpreter, rear seat

Vehicle 3: Cargo Humvee
Specialist Stephen McLendon, driver
Sergeant First Class Steven Walter, mortars platoon sergeant, right front
    seat
Specialist Miltiades Harrison Houpis, sniper, left rear seat
Specialist Josh Reeves, sniper, right rear seat

Vehicle 4: Cargo Humvee
Sergeant Brad Jacobson, mortarman, driver
Master Sergeant John Horney, right front seat
Command Sergeant Major Alfred Birch, regimental sergeant major, right
    rear seat
Specialist Dunabach, left rear seat

Vehicle 5: Humvee (GMV) with Mk 19 mounted on top turret
Sergeant Jason Parsons, team leader, driver
Sergeant First Class Eric Godec, platoon sergeant, right front seat
Specialist Kevin Tillman, gunner in top turret
Specialist Pedro Arreola, right waist seat
Private First Class Kyle Jones, left waist seat
Sergeant Jason Bailey, rear seat
Private First Class Marc Denton, rear seat
Specialist James Anderson, medic, rear seat

PROLOGUE

If David Uthlaut was still angry when the convoy finally rolled out of Magarah, Afghanistan, the young lieutenant kept his emotions hidden from the forty-four Army Rangers under his command. Certainly he had reason to be steamed. For the previous six hours his platoon had been stopped in the middle of Taliban territory while he argued with headquarters over what to do about a wrecked Humvee. When the discussion finally concluded, Uthlaut was on the losing end of the debate, and he was ordered to complete a series of problematic tasks before nightfall—even though there wasn't nearly enough time to meet the deadline without taking dangerous chances.

The date was April 22, 2004. For eight straight days Uthlaut and his men had been combing the rough backcountry of Khost Province for Taliban insurgents. The Rangers had slept in the mud, been soaked by freezing rain, humped up and down towering escarpments with inadequate rations. At one point they got so hungry that one of the platoon's machine gunners had resorted to rooting in a garbage dump for edible morsels. But none of these tribulations had kept the elite Special Operations unit from executing its mission.

At 11:30 that morning, however, the gnarly terrain delivered a terminal blow to one of the platoon's eleven vehicles, bringing the Rangers to a halt in Magarah, a ramshackle hamlet where the Taliban held sway. Both of the Humvee's tie-rods had broken off, leaving its front wheels flopping uncontrollably in opposite directions. After the platoon mechanic determined that repairing the damage in the field was impossible, Uthlaut radioed headquarters to request that a helicopter be dispatched to hook a sling to the vehicle and airlift it back to their base, an operation considered routine for a CH-47 Chinook—a jet-powered, tandem-rotor behemoth that brings to mind an immense titanium insect.

Earlier in the day the Rangers had observed Army Chinooks lumbering purposefully across the sky, but headquarters told Uthlaut that no helicopter would be available to extract the crippled Humvee for at least ninety-six hours.

With a sling-load operation ruled out, someone in the platoon suggested they simply pull the .50-caliber machine gun from the Humvee's turret, yank its radios, blow the damn thing up with C-4 explosives so the Taliban couldn't salvage it, and abandon the smoldering wreckage where it lay. Uthlaut knew from a prior tour in Afghanistan, however, that destroying a vehicle, even a fubar* vehicle, was strictly forbidden without approval from the commander of the Seventy-fifth Ranger Regiment. Because the colonel in question happened to be on the opposite side of the planet at Fort Benning, Georgia, such approval was unlikely to be granted anytime soon, if ever. Some other solution to the problem would be required.

At 4:00 p.m. headquarters provided one. Uthlaut was ordered to split his platoon into two elements. Half his unit was directed to immediately begin towing the damaged Humvee toward the only paved road in all of Khost, which lay on the far side of a high massif. Concurrently, the other half of the platoon was supposed to proceed to a village called Mana, situated four roadless miles from Magarah in the opposite direction, to complete the day's mission: search every building in the settlement for caches of enemy weapons. Word came down the chain of command, moreover, that "this vehicle problem better not delay us any more." The platoon leader was admonished to quit wasting time and "put boots on the ground" in Mana before nightfall.

---

* A military acronym dating from World War II that is frequently used in the modern Army, "fubar" stands for "fucked-up beyond all recognition."

Khost Province was the home turf of Jalaluddin Haqqani, a short, scrawny man with Coke-bottle eyeglasses and a beard like black steel wool that hung to his belly. Although his physical stature was unimpressive, he was legendary throughout Afghanistan for his bravery and military acumen. Commander of Taliban forces in much of the country's eastern region, Haqqani was one of Osama bin Laden's most trusted associates. The enemy fighters the Rangers had been hunting were part of the so-called Haqqani Network—a loose amalgam of Taliban militias and tribal insurgents. Mana was the last village in the area that the Rangers needed to search for Haqqani's forces, and headquarters was adamant that they clear it at the earliest possible opportunity in order to conform to a schedule established weeks earlier by deskbound officers at a distant base.

Uthlaut and his men were no less eager than headquarters to finish their business in Mana, because as soon as it was completed they could return to Forward Operating Base Salerno, where they'd be able to shower off the stink and grime, repair their battered vehicles, re-zero their weapons, and spend a night or two on honest-to-God cots before heading back outside the wire. But the Rangers on the ground weren't keen to take unnecessary risks simply to meet an arbitrary bureaucratic timeline set by "fobbits": officers who seldom ventured beyond the security of the forward operating base (the FOB, in military-speak), and therefore, from the grunts' perspective, had no clue what it was actually like to fight a war in this unforgiving country.

Uthlaut sent a series of e-mails that respectfully but vigorously registered objections to the orders he'd received. The twenty-four-year-old platoon leader pointed out, among other shortcomings, that the mountainous topography would make communication between the divided elements problematic, and that embarking for Mana with just half a platoon, in his view, "was not safe."

One of the most highly regarded young officers in the Army, Uthlaut had graduated at the top of his class at West Point as first captain of the Corps of Cadets. When George W. Bush was sworn in as president in 2001, Uthlaut was the guy chosen to lead the Army's procession down Pennsylvania Avenue in the inaugural parade. After leaving the academy and becoming a platoon leader in the Second

Ranger Battalion, he quickly earned the admiration of the enlisted men and noncommissioned officers who served under him. Uthlaut was a disciplined soldier who seldom questioned orders, and never without a compelling reason. But his urgent requests to reconsider the directive to split the platoon elicited this brusque reply from headquarters: "Reconsider denied."

"Nobody on the ground in Magarah thought it was a good idea to split the platoon," recalls Specialist Jade Lane, who, as Uthlaut's radio operator, had been privy to the entire extended debate between headquarters and the platoon leader. "The PL didn't want to do it. But in the Army you obey orders. If somebody with a higher rank tells you to do something, you do it. So Uthlaut split the platoon."

———

Less than an hour of daylight remained by the time Uthlaut had finished dividing the platoon into two elements. After placing himself in charge of the element bound for Mana (designated Serial One, it consisted of two Humvees and four Toyota pickup trucks carrying twenty Rangers and seven Afghan Militia Forces), he hurriedly rolled out of Magarah in the lead Humvee at 6:00 p.m. Absent a road, Uthlaut's convoy drove down an intermittently dry riverbed, followed closely by the second element's convoy, designated Serial Two. A few minutes outside the village they reached a fork in the wadi. Uthlaut's convoy turned downstream, to the left. Serial Two, towing the trashed Humvee, turned upstream, to the right.

A British soldier named Francis Leeson, who battled a fierce tribal insurgency in this same area in the late 1940s, wrote a book in which he characterized the terrain as "frontier hills [that] are difficult of access and easy to defend. When one speaks of them as hills, rolling downs on which tanks and cavalry can operate are not meant, but the worst mountain-warfare country imaginable—steep precipices [and] narrow winding valleys." Six decades after Leeson's tour of duty, this remains a chillingly accurate description of the landscape that confronted Uthlaut's Rangers.

Half a mile west of the junction where the convoys had separated and gone in opposite directions, Serial One entered the mouth of a spectacularly narrow canyon. It was 6:10 p.m., and the lower flanks of the gorge already lay in shadow. The afternoon's warmth had been supplanted by the chill of the advancing evening, prompting the Rangers to don Gore-Tex jackets beneath their body armor. The air smelled of sage, dust, and wood smoke rising from cooking fires in a nearby village.

Ahead, the route snaked through a deep, crooked slot the river had gouged into the bedrock of the surrounding mountains. In places the passage was only a foot or two wider than the Humvees and was constricted by vertical limestone cliffs that reduced the sky overhead to a pale blue stripe. Only by sharply craning their necks could the soldiers see the canyon rim. Up there on the heights, far above the gloom of the valley floor, the otherwise barren slopes were dotted with graceful Chilgoza pines still washed with sunlight, their silver bark and viridescent needles glowing in the fleeting rays.

The magnificence of the setting was not lost on the Rangers as their vehicles lurched over gravel berms and limestone ledges. This canyon was the most dramatic landform they'd seen since arriving in Khost: the sort of geologic wonder one might encounter in Utah's Zion National Park, or the Mogollon Rim of northern Arizona. One soldier remarked that it would be "an awesome place to go rock climbing." But most of the Rangers were less interested in the natural splendors than in the unnatural hazards that might be lurking somewhere above them.

Specialist Russell Baer was in the convoy's fourth vehicle, a Toyota Hilux pickup. Turning to Sergeant Bradley Shepherd, who was driving the truck, Baer declared, "This looks like those movies they showed us before we deployed. Back in the 1980s the Afghans used to ambush the Russians in places just like this. They slaughtered them in these canyons from above. It's how they won the war." Shepherd pondered the obvious implications of this comment, nodded soberly, then pulled out his camera and documented their passage through the dirty windshield as he drove.

For the next twenty minutes the convoy crept through the claustrophobic rift, forced by the severity of the terrain to move at an excruciatingly slow pace. The slot was so tight that the Humvees' fenders sometimes scraped against its sheer walls. The Rangers remained twitchy and anxious, expecting to be attacked from the high ground at any moment. According to Private Bryan O'Neal, a rifle-man, "The canyon was very rough, there were large boulders every-where, and the walls were at least a hundred feet high on each side. I actually had to lay on top of the vehicle to be able to pull security"— the cliffs rose so precipitously that O'Neal had to lie flat on his back in order to scan the canyon's ledges for Taliban through the scope of his M4 carbine.*

After twenty minutes, Uthlaut's Humvee emerged from the west-ern end of the slot. The valley opened, and the canyon floor broad-ened into a relatively flat gravel channel some thirty yards across. Corn and poppies grew in terraced plots of cultivated earth on both sides of the wadi. Clustered on a dun-colored hillside just outside the mouth of the narrows, eight or nine mud-walled buildings stood above the opium fields. Young Pashtun boys in filthy clothing ran up to the convoy as it rolled by, waving and laughing. The danger of an ambush appeared to have passed.

A moment later, a series of loud explosions echoed from the nar-rows behind them. "I turned toward where we had just come from," says Baer, "and all of a sudden it looked like *Star Wars* back there. Red tracer rounds were flying up out of the canyon, lighting up the sky." Tracers are special bullets manufactured with a pyrotechnic charge that ignites as each projectile exits the barrel of a weapon, making the bullet's trajectory appear as a bright red streak, enabling the shooter to more easily adjust his fire toward the intended target. Every fifth bullet loaded into the machine guns used by American forces in Afghanistan was a tracer round; the Taliban in that area didn't use tracer ammunition. Baer understood instantly, therefore, that the red streaks flashing through the canyon's shadows were bul-lets from American soldiers returning fire against an enemy ambush. "I knew it was our guys getting hit," he says. "It was the other half of the platoon."

The platoon's other element, Serial Two, was supposed to be miles away by then, towing the derelict Humvee in the opposite direction. Uthlaut and his men had no idea why Serial Two would impulsively reverse course and follow them, but apparently their counterparts in

* The M4 is a lighter, more compact version of the Vietnam-era M16 rifle.

the other element had done precisely that, and were now caught in the middle of what looked and sounded like an intense firefight half a mile away.

Serial One skidded to a halt and the soldiers jumped out of their trucks and Humvees. The element's highest-ranking Ranger under Uthlaut was a self-possessed staff sergeant named Matthew Weeks who had been awarded a Bronze Star for his valorous actions during a firefight in Iraq the previous year. He assigned a half-dozen soldiers to stay with the six vehicles and then ordered most of the rest to move with him up the north slope of the canyon toward the cluster of mud buildings they'd just driven beneath. Weeks informed Uthlaut, "I'm going to try to push past the village and see if I can overwatch [Serial Two's] movement out of the ambush zone," explaining that his squad would move no farther than a brow of high ground above the settlement.

A Ranger platoon is typically organized into three squads, each consisting of two "fire teams" of six or fewer men. When Uthlaut was forced to hastily divide his platoon back in Magarah, he put Third Squad (commanded by Weeks) in Serial One and assigned the bulk of First and Second squads to Serial Two. Because the two convoys needed to be of more or less equal size, however, Uthlaut pulled two men from Second Squad and added them to Serial One. These two soldiers were Private O'Neal, a baby-faced eighteen-year-old who was the youngest, greenest member of the entire unit; and Specialist Patrick Tillman, the leader of O'Neal's fire team.

Tillman—twenty-seven years old, previously employed as a strong safety in the National Football League—was unquestionably the most famous enlisted man in Afghanistan. When the World Trade Center came crashing to earth on September 11, 2001, he had been a star player with the Arizona Cardinals, renowned for patrolling the defensive backfield with riveting intensity. But Tillman came from a family with a tradition of military service that went back several generations, and he believed that as an able-bodied American he had a moral obligation to serve his country during a time of war. He didn't think he should be exempt from his duty as a citizen simply because he played professional football. So after the 2001 NFL season he walked away from a $3.6 million contract and volunteered to spend the next three years of his life as an infantryman in the U.S. Army. His brother Kevin, fourteen months younger than Pat, had enlisted at the same time and was a member of Uthlaut's platoon as well.

When the platoon was split in Magarah, Kevin had been assigned to Serial Two. Now, as Pat listened to the exploding mortar shells and the pop-pop-pop-pop of rifle fire, he was hyperaware that his little brother was somewhere back in the confines of the canyon getting hammered. The moment Sergeant Weeks directed the Rangers to move up the hill, Tillman sprang into action. "Pat was like a freight train," says Private Josey Boatright, recalling how Tillman sprinted past him. "Whoosh. A pit bull straining against his leash. He took off toward the high ground, yelling, 'O'Neal! On me! O'Neal! Stay on me!' "

According to O'Neal, Pat told him, " 'Let's go help our boys,' and he started moving. And wherever he went, I went."

The route to the village ascended a steep gully, the bottom of which was six thousand feet above sea level. Between his weapons, body armor, night-vision optics, CamelBak water bladders, grenades, and extra ammunition, each Ranger was carrying more than sixty pounds of dead weight. Thus burdened, within seconds of leaving the vehicles, everyone was gasping for air, but the sounds of the nearby battle—moving noticeably closer by the minute—kept the Rangers pushing upward despite the pain. When they reached the village, the Rangers performed a "hasty clear," passing quickly through the settlement without pausing to search inside any of the buildings, and then hurried toward the crest of a spur that rose above the village.

Tillman was among the first to arrive atop the spur, which was devoid of trees or other cover. After pausing for a few seconds to assess the lay of the land, he continued over the crest and scurried down the other side to a pair of low boulders, accompanied by O'Neal and a twenty-seven-year-old Afghan soldier named Sayed Farhad. These rocks afforded only minimal protection from enemy fire but provided an excellent view of the wadi where Tillman expected Serial Two to emerge from the mouth of the gorge.

A few minutes later two vehicles came speeding out of the canyon and stopped ninety yards beneath the boulders. Several Rangers climbed out of a Humvee and gazed up toward Tillman and O'Neal, who waved to let their buddies know they were up there and had them covered. It appeared as though Serial Two had escaped the ambush and everything was copacetic. And then, without warning, hundreds of bullets began to pulverize the slope around Tillman, O'Neal, and Farhad.

———

Ever since *Homo sapiens* first coalesced into tribes, war has been part of the human condition. Inevitably, warring societies portray their campaigns as virtuous struggles, and present their fallen warriors as heroes who made the ultimate sacrifice for a noble cause. But death by so-called friendly fire, which is an inescapable aspect of armed conflict in the modern era, doesn't conform to this mythic narrative. It strips away war's heroic veneer to reveal what lies beneath. It's an unsettling reminder that barbarism, senseless violence, and random death are commonplace even in the most "just" and "honorable" of wars. Consequently, and unsurprisingly, when soldiers accidentally kill one of their own, there is tremendous reluctance to confront the truth within the ranks of the military. There is an overwhelming inclination to keep the unsavory particulars hidden from public view, to pretend the calamity never occurred. Thus it has always been, and probably always will be. As Aeschylus, the exalted Greek tragedian, noted in the fifth century B.C., "In war, truth is the first casualty."

When Pat Tillman was killed in Afghanistan, his Ranger regiment responded with a chorus of prevarication and disavowal. A cynical cover-up sanctioned at the highest levels of government, followed by a series of inept official investigations, cast a cloud of bewilderment and shame over the tragedy, compounding the heartbreak of Tillman's death.

Among the several thousand pages of documents generated by military investigators, some baffling testimony emerged from the Ranger who is believed to have fired the bullets that ended Tillman's life. In a sworn statement, this soldier explained that while shooting a ten-round burst from his machine gun at the hillside where Tillman and O'Neal were positioned, he "identified two sets of arms straight up" through the scope of his weapon. "I saw the arms waving," he acknowledged, "but I didn't think they were trying to signal a cease-fire." So he pulled the trigger again and sprayed them with another ten-round burst. How was one supposed to make sense of this?

Or this: in July 2007, the Associated Press published an article reporting that the Navy pathologist who performed Tillman's autopsy testified that the forensic evidence indicated Tillman had been shot three times in the head from a distance of thirty-five feet or less. The article prompted widespread speculation on the Internet and in the mainstream press that he had been deliberately murdered.

Many other details about the fatal firefight that found their way into the public domain were similarly perplexing. Perhaps the greatest mystery, however, surrounded not the circumstances of Tillman's death but the essential facts of his life. Before he enlisted, Tillman was familiar to sports aficionados as an undersized, overachieving football player whose virtuosity in the defensive backfield was spellbinding. But during the four years he spent in the NFL, Tillman played for the Arizona Cardinals—a mediocre small-market team that was seldom in the limelight—so his name wasn't widely recognized beyond the realm of hard-core football fans.

Although it wasn't Tillman's intention, when he left the Cardinals to join the Army he was transformed overnight into an icon of post-9/11 patriotism. Seizing the opportunity to capitalize on his celebrity, the Bush administration endeavored to use his name and image to promote what it had christened the Global War on Terror. Tillman abhorred this role. As soon as he decided to enlist, he stopped talking to the press altogether, although his silence did nothing to squelch America's fascination with the football star who traded the bright lights and riches of the NFL for boot camp and a bad haircut. Following his death on the battlefield, the public's interest in Tillman shot through the roof. The posthumous media frenzy shed little light on who he really was, however. The intricate mosaic of personal history that defined his existence was obscured by the blizzard of hype.

Unencumbered by biographical insight, people felt emboldened to invent all manner of personae for Tillman after his passing. Most of these renderings were based on little more than rumor and fantasy. The right-wing harridan Ann Coulter claimed him as an exemplar of Republican political values. The left-wing editorial cartoonist Ted

Rall denigrated him in a four-panel comic strip as an "idiot" who joined the Army to "kill Arabs."

Neither Coulter nor Rall had any idea what motivated Pat Tillman. Beyond his family and a small circle of close friends, few people did.

PART ONE

Earlier times may not have understood it any better than we do, but they weren't as embarrassed to name it: the life force or spark thought close to divine. It is not. Instead, it's something that makes those who have it fully human, and those who don't look like sleep walkers. . . . It isn't enough to make someone heroic, but without it any hero will be forgotten. Rousseau called it force of soul; Arendt called it love of the world. It's the foundation of eros; you may call it charisma. Is it a gift of the gods, or something that has to be earned? Watching such people, you will sense that it's both: given like perfect pitch, or grace, that no one can deserve or strive for, and captured like the greatest of prizes it is. Having it makes people think more, see more, feel more. More intensely, more keenly, more loudly if you like; but not more in the way of the gods. On the contrary, next to heroes like Odysseus and Penelope, the gods seem oddly flat. They are bigger, of course, and they live forever, but their presence seems diminished. . . . The gods of *The Odyssey* aren't alive, just immortal; and with immortality most of the qualities we cherish become pointless. With nothing to risk, the gods need no courage.

—Susan Neiman, *Moral Clarity*

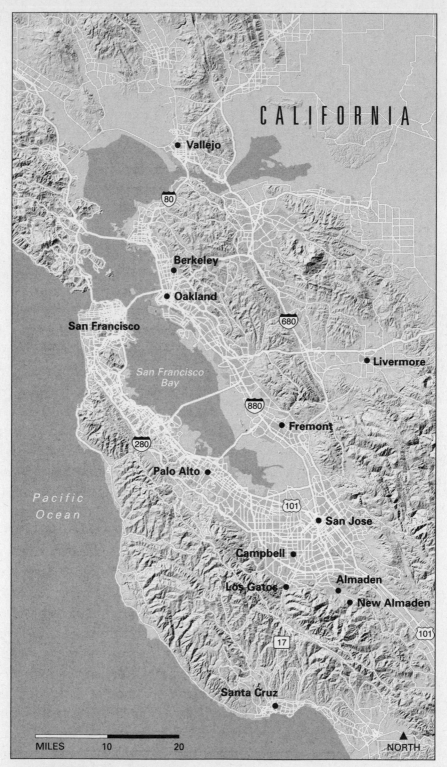

CALIFORNIA

● Vallejo

80

● Berkeley

● Oakland

San Francisco

680

San Francisco
Bay

● Livermore

880

● Fremont

280

Pacific
Ocean

Palo Alto ●

101

● San Jose

Campbell ●

Los Gatos ●

Almaden ●
● New Almaden

17

101

Santa Cruz ●

MILES   10   20   NORTH

SAN FRANCISCO BAY AREA

CHAPTER ONE

During Pat Tillman's stint in the Army he intermittently kept a diary. In an entry dated July 28, 2002—three weeks after he arrived at boot camp—he wrote, "It is amazing the turns one's life can take. Major events or decisions that completely change a life. In my life there have been a number." He then cataloged several. Foremost on his mind at the time, predictably, was his decision to join the military. But the incident he put at the top of the list, which occurred when he was eleven years old, comes as a surprise. "As odd as this sounds," the journal revealed, "a diving catch I made in the 11–12 all-stars was a take-off point. I excelled the rest of the tournament and gained incredible confidence. It sounds tacky but it was big."

As a child growing up in Almaden, California (an upscale suburb of San Jose), Pat had started playing baseball at the age of seven. It quickly became apparent to the adults who watched him throw a ball and swing a bat that he possessed extraordinary talent, but Pat seems not to have been particularly cognizant of his own athletic gifts until he was selected for the aforementioned all-star team in the summer of 1988. As the tournament against teams of other standout middle-school athletes got under way, he mostly sat on the bench. When the coach eventually put Pat into a game, however, he clobbered a home run and made a spectacular catch of a long fly ball hit into the outfield. Fourteen years later, as he contemplated life from the perspective of an Army barracks, he regarded that catch as a pivotal moment—a confidence booster that contributed significantly to one of his defining traits: unwavering self-assurance.

In 1990, Pat matriculated at Almaden's Leland High School, one of the top public schools in the San Francisco Bay Area, both academically and athletically. Before entering Leland he had resolved to become the catcher on the varsity baseball team, but the head coach, Paul Ugenti, informed Pat that he wasn't ready to play varsity baseball and would have to settle for a position on the freshman-sophomore team. Irked and perhaps insulted by Ugenti's failure to recognize his potential, Pat resolved to quit baseball and focus on football instead, even though he'd taken up the latter sport barely a year earlier and had badly fractured his right tibia in his initial season when a much larger teammate fell on his leg during practice.

With a November birthday, Pat was among the youngest kids in Leland's freshman class, and when he started high school, he was only thirteen years old. He also happened to be small for his age, standing five feet five inches tall and weighing just 120 pounds. When he let it be known that he was going to abandon baseball for football, an assistant coach named Terry Hardtke explained to Pat that he wasn't "built like a football player" and strongly urged him to stick with baseball. Once Tillman set his sights on a goal, however, he wasn't easily diverted. He told the coach he intended to start lifting weights to build up his muscles. Then he assured Hardtke that not only would he make the Leland football team but he intended to play college football after graduating from high school. Hardtke replied that Pat was making a huge mistake—that his size would make it difficult for him ever to win a starting position on the Leland team, and that he stood virtually no chance of ever playing college ball.

Pat, however, trusted his own sense of his abilities over the coach's bleak predictions, and tried out for the Leland football team regardless. Six years later he would be a star linebacker playing in the Rose Bowl for a national collegiate championship. Twenty months after that he began a distinguished career in the National Football League.

Midway between San Jose and Oakland, the municipality of Fremont rises above the eastern shore of San Francisco Bay, a city of 240,000 that's always existed in the shadow of its flashier neighbors. This is where Patrick Daniel Tillman was born on November 6, 1976. Not far from the hospital where Pat entered the world is a commercial district of pharmacies, chiropractic clinics, and fast-food restaurants bisected by a four-lane thoroughfare. Along three or four blocks of this otherwise unremarkable stretch of Fremont Boulevard, one finds a concentration of incongruously exotic establishments: the Salang Pass Restaurant, an Afghan carpet store, a South Asian cinema, a shop selling Afghan clothing, the De Afghanan Kabob House, the Maiwand Market. Inside the latter, the shelves are stocked with hummus, olives, pomegranate seeds, turmeric, bags of rice, and tins of grapeseed oil. A striking woman wearing a head scarf and an elaborately embroidered vest inlaid with dozens of tiny mirrors stands at a counter near the back of the store, waiting to buy slabs of freshly baked naan. Little Kabul, as this neighborhood is known, happens to be the nexus of what is purportedly the highest concentration of Afghans in the United States, a community made famous by the bestselling novel *The Kite Runner*.

By loose estimate, some ten thousand Afghans reside in Fremont proper, with another fifty thousand scattered across the rest of the Bay Area. They started showing up in 1978, when their homeland erupted into violence that has yet to abate three decades later. The chaos was sparked by accelerating friction between political groups within Afghanistan, but fuel for the conflagration was supplied in abundance and with great enthusiasm by the governments of the United States and the Soviet Union as each maneuvered to gain advantage in the Cold War.

The Soviets had been lavishing billions of rubles in military and economic aid on Afghanistan since the 1950s, and had cultivated close ties with the nation's leaders. Despite this injection of outside capital, by the 1970s Afghanistan remained a tribal society, essentially medieval in character. Ninety percent of its seventeen million residents were illiterate. Eighty-five percent of the population lived in the mountainous, largely roadless countryside, subsisting as farmers, herders, or nomadic traders. The overwhelming majority of these impoverished, uneducated country dwellers answered not to the central government in Kabul, with which they had little contact and from which they received almost no tangible assistance, but rather to local mullahs and tribal elders. Thanks to Moscow's creeping influence, however, a distinctly Marxist brand of modernization had begun to establish a toehold in a few of the nation's largest cities.

Afghanistan's cozy relationship with the Soviets originated under the leadership of Prime Minister Mohammed Daoud Khan, a Pashtun with fleshy jowls and a shaved head who was appointed in 1953 by his cousin and brother-in-law, King Mohammed Zahir Shah. Ten years later Daoud was forced to resign from the government after launching a brief but disastrous war against Pakistan. But in 1973 he reclaimed power by means of a nonviolent coup d'état, deposing King Zahir and declaring himself the first president of the Republic of Afghanistan.

A fervent subculture of Marxist intellectuals, professionals, and students had by this time taken root in Kabul, intent on bringing their country into the twentieth century, kicking and screaming if need be, and President Daoud—who dressed in hand-tailored Italian suits—supported this shift toward secular modernity as long as it didn't threaten his hold on power. Under Daoud, females were given opportunities to be educated and join the professional workforce. In cities, women started appearing in public without burqas or even head scarves. Many urban men exchanged their traditional *shalwar kameezes* for Western business attire. These secular city dwellers swelled the ranks of a Marxist political organization known as the People's Democratic Party of Afghanistan, or PDPA.

The Soviets were Daoud's allies in the push to modernize Afghanistan, at least initially. Aid from Moscow continued to prop up the economy and the military, and under an agreement signed by Daoud, every officer in the Afghan Army went to the Soviet Union to receive military training. But he was walking a perilous political tightrope. While welcoming Soviet rubles, Daoud was an impassioned Afghan nationalist who had no desire to become a puppet of the Soviet president, Leonid Brezhnev. And although Daoud was committed to modernizing his nation, he wanted to move at a pace slow enough to avoid provoking the Islamist mullahs who controlled the hinterlands. In the end, alas, his policies placated few and managed to antagonize almost everyone else—most significantly the Soviets, the urban leftists, and the bearded fundamentalists in the country-side.

At the beginning of his presidency, Daoud had pledged to reform the government and promote civil liberties. Very soon after taking office, however, he started cracking down hard on anyone who resisted his edicts. Hundreds of rivals from all sides of the political divide were arrested and executed, ranging from antimodernist tribal elders in far-flung provinces to urban communists in the PDPA who had originally supported Daoud's rise to power.

For millennia in Afghanistan, political expression has all too often been synonymous with mayhem. On April 19, 1978, a funeral for a popular communist leader who was thought to have been murdered on Daoud's orders turned into a seething protest march. Organized by the PDPA, as many as thirty thousand Afghans took to the streets of Kabul to show their contempt for President Daoud. In typical fashion, Daoud reacted to the demonstration with excessive force, which only further incited the protesters. Sensing a momentous shift in the political tide, most units in the Afghan Army broke with Daoud and allied themselves with the PDPA. On April 27, 1978, MiG-21 jets from the Afghan Air Force strafed the Presidential Palace, where Daoud was ensconced with eighteen hundred members of his personal guard. That night, opposition forces overran the palace amid a rain of bullets. When the sun came up and the gunfire petered out, Daoud and his entire family were dead, and the surrounding streets were strewn with the bodies of two thousand Afghans.

The communist PDPA immediately assumed power and renamed the nation the Democratic Republic of Afghanistan. Backed by the Soviet Union, the new government moved ruthlessly to establish control across the country. During the PDPA's first twenty months at the helm, twenty-seven thousand political dissidents were rounded up, transported to the infamous Pul-e-Charkhi prison on the outskirts of Kabul, and summarily executed.

By this point the violence had instigated a wholesale exodus of Afghans to foreign lands. Because those targeted for elimination by the PDPA tended to be influential mullahs or members of the intellectual and professional classes, many of the refugees who sought sanctuary came from the elite ranks of Afghan society. Two years after Pat Tillman's birth in Fremont, California, Afghans began flocking to the city where he was delivered.

————

Back in Afghanistan, the brutality of the PDPA inspired a grassroots insurrection that rapidly escalated into full-blown civil war. At the forefront of the rebellion were Muslim holy warriors, the Afghan mujahideen, who fought the communist infidels with such ferocious intensity that in December 1979 the Soviets dispatched 100,000 troops to Afghanistan to quell the rebellion, prop up the PDPA, and protect their Cold War interests in the region.

Nations throughout the world sternly criticized the Soviets for the incursion. The strongest rebuke came from the United States. Expressing shock and outrage over the invasion, President Jimmy Carter called it "the most serious threat to peace since the Second World War," and initiated first a trade embargo and then a boycott of the 1980 Moscow Olympics.

But Carter's righteous indignation was more than slightly disingenuous. Although the U.S. government claimed otherwise in official statements, the CIA had begun purchasing weapons for the mujahideen at least six months *before* the Soviet invasion, and this clandestine support was intended not to deter Moscow but to provoke it. According to Carter's national security adviser, Zbigniew Brzezinski, the purpose of arming the Afghans was to stimulate enough turmoil in Afghanistan "to induce a Soviet military intervention." Brzezinski, the most fervent cold warrior in the Carter administration, boasted in a 1998 interview that the intent of providing arms to the mujahideen was specifically to draw "the Soviets into the Afghan trap" and ensnare them in a debilitating Vietnam-like debacle.

If that was the plan, it worked. Almost immediately upon occupying the country, the legendary Soviet Fortieth Army found itself neck deep in an unexpectedly vicious guerrilla war that would keep its forces entangled in Afghanistan for the next nine years.

Before the Soviet invasion, Afghanistan was riven by so many intransigent political and tribal factions that the nation had been for all intents and purposes ungovernable. In reflexive opposition to the Soviet occupation, virtually the entire country spontaneously united—a degree of cohesion no modern Afghan leader had ever come close to achieving.

This newly unified opposition was characterized by extraordinary violence. The mujahideen seldom took prisoners in their skirmishes with the invaders. They made a habit of mutilating the bodies of the Soviets they killed in creatively gruesome ways in order to instill terror in those sent to recover the bodies. When the mujahideen did take prisoners, according to Soviet survivors, the infidel soldiers were often gang-raped and tortured.

The Afghans quickly figured out that fighting the Soviets by conventional means was a recipe for certain defeat. Instead of confronting Soviet forces directly with large numbers of fighters, the mujahideen adopted the classic stratagems of insurgent warfare, employing small bands of ten or fifteen men to ambush the enemy and then vanish back into the landscape before the Soviets could launch counterattacks. Soviet soldiers began to refer to the mujahideen as *dukhi*, Russian for "ghosts." The Afghans took brilliant advantage of the mountainous terrain to stage devastating ambushes from the high ground as Soviet convoys moved through the confines of the valley bottoms. The Soviet cause wasn't helped by a policy designated as "Limited Contingent": Moscow decided to cap the number of Fortieth Army troops in Afghanistan at 115,000, despite the fact that before the invasion Soviet generals had warned that as many as 650,000 soldiers would be needed to secure the country.*

The pitiless style of guerrilla combat waged by the Afghans had an unnerving effect on the Soviets sent to fight them. Morale plummeted, especially as the conflict dragged on year after year. Because opium and hashish were readily available everywhere, drug addiction among the Soviet conscripts was rife. Their numbers were further ravaged by malaria, dysentery, hepatitis, tetanus, and meningitis. Al-

---

* U.S. defense secretary Donald Rumsfeld received strikingly similar admonitions from American generals during their planning for the invasions of Afghanistan in 2001 and Iraq in 2003.

though there were never more than 120,000 Soviet troops in Afghanistan at any given time, a total of 642,000 soldiers served there throughout the course of the war—470,000 of whom were debilitated by disease, addicted to heroin, wounded in battle, or killed.

The tenacity and brutality of the mujahideen prompted the Soviets to adopt ruthless tactics of their own. As they came to realize that it was much easier to kill unarmed civilians than to hunt down the fearsome and elusive mujahideen, the Soviets increasingly focused their attacks on the rural tribespeople who sometimes harbored combatants but didn't shoot back, rather than assaulting the mujahideen directly. Jet aircraft bombed whole valleys with napalm, laying waste to farmland, orchards, and settlements. Helicopter gunships not only targeted villagers but massacred their herds of livestock as well. These calculated acts of genocide went virtually unnoticed outside of Afghanistan.

The shift toward scorched-earth tactics intensified after Konstantin Chernenko became the Soviet general secretary in February 1984 and initiated a campaign of high-altitude carpet bombing. Taking off from bases within the Soviet Union and flying as high as forty thousand feet, safely beyond the range of mujahideen antiaircraft weapons, squadrons of swept-wing, twin-engine Tu-16 Badgers annihilated entire towns.

Under the Chernenko regime, the Soviets also increased the use of antipersonnel mines. Bombers sprinkled the countryside with tens of thousands of miniature booby traps made to resemble brightly colored toys. Such mines were specifically created to attract very young Afghans; when the kids picked them up they would explode, maiming and killing the children. Toward this same end, Soviet Badgers also randomly scattered hundreds of thousands—some reports say millions—of so-called butterfly mines over vast areas. Designed to flutter gently to earth and then arm upon impact, these camouflaged plastic devices wouldn't detonate until Afghan herders happened to step on them. The mines' relatively small size was intended to blow off limbs but not necessarily cause fatal injuries, in the belief that forcing Afghan villagers to take care of gravely injured countrymen would cause more hardship than killing them outright.

The Soviets' genocidal strategy inflicted terrible casualties on the

Afghan people, but it also hardened their resolve. Despite all they had suffered, the mujahideen showed no sign of abandoning their fight, which must have given Moscow pause. By the time the Soviet politburo elected Mikhail Gorbachev general secretary on March 11, 1985, following the death of Chernenko, the war in Afghanistan had degenerated into a stalemate. One wonders if the new Soviet leader perhaps pondered the famous tenet voiced sixteen years earlier by Henry Kissinger in reference to the American experience in Vietnam: "We lost sight of one of the cardinal maxims of guerrilla war: the guerrilla wins if he does not lose. The conventional army loses if it does not win."

Although the mujahideen were doing the actual fighting against the Soviets, the CIA under President Ronald Reagan was supporting the Afghan holy warriors with billions of dollars in armaments and cash (support matched dollar for dollar by Saudi Arabia, and delivered to the mujahideen by Pakistan's Directorate for Inter-Services Intelligence—the shadowy ISI). A disproportionate share of that bounty was directed to Jalaluddin Haqqani—a man who would have a notable impact on world affairs over the ensuing decades. Early in the Soviet-Afghan War, Haqqani had emerged as a fearless combatant and a brilliant leader of men, which is how he came to receive so much American largesse. As the war intensified throughout the 1980s and the mujahideen demonstrated amazing steadfastness, many in the CIA came to regard him as the most effective commander in the entire Afghan resistance. The Americans thought so highly of Haqqani that at one point he was reportedly brought to the United States and feted at the White House.

The base of operations for Haqqani and the fighters under his command was the mountainous terrain of what is now Khost Province.* In 1984 a wealthy young engineer from Saudi Arabia, name of Osama bin Laden, arrived in Khost to assist Haqqani's forces. When the Soviets invaded Afghanistan in 1979, bin Laden had been an idealistic college student receiving an annual allowance of $1 million from his family. At the time he showed up in Khost, he had yet to discover

---

* Khost was part of Paktia Province until 1995, when it was split off as a province unto itself.

his calling, but this skinny, self-serious Arab was about to assume a much larger role on the world stage, thanks in part to what he experienced in Afghanistan.

Initially, bin Laden's role in Khost was limited to providing cash to the mujahideen and overseeing the construction of supply roads, training camps, and fortified underground bunkers. He quickly developed an uncommonly close relationship with Haqqani, however, who was fluent in Arabic and had an Arab wife. Before long, bin Laden was inspired under Haqqani's tutelage to take up arms and personally engage in combat against the Soviets. Although a bumbling foot soldier, bin Laden participated in several firefights, displayed courage under fire, and at one point was even wounded—all of which bolstered his stature tremendously among Muslims across the globe when, shortly thereafter, he began beating the drum for global jihad.

Before his initial visit to Afghanistan, according to Lawrence Wright's book *The Looming Tower*, "bin Laden did not . . . make much of an impression as a charismatic leader. . . . 'He had a small smile on his face and soft hands,' a hardened Pakistani *mujahid* recalled. 'You'd think you were shaking hands with a girl.' " Following bin Laden's exposure to combat, Wright reports, "one can hear for the first time the epic tone that began to characterize his speech—the sound of a man in the grasp of destiny." In the summer of 1988, bin Laden and Ayman al-Zawahri founded al-Qaeda. Significantly, when bin Laden established the first al-Qaeda training camps, he situated several of them in the mountains of Khost, Haqqani's homeland. According to an interview bin Laden gave to a journalist from Al Jazeera in 2001, the name al-Qaeda—which means "the training base" in Arabic—in fact owes its origin to these camps in Khost. "The name 'al-Qaeda' was established a long time ago by mere chance," bin Laden explained. "We used to call the training camp 'al-Qaeda.' And the name stayed."

Two years before the emergence of al-Qaeda, the CIA provided the mujahideen with a weapon that began to tip the balance of the war in their favor: a thirty-five-pound, shoulder-fired, antiaircraft missile known as the FIM-92 Stinger that cost about $65,000 apiece. The heat-seeking Stingers, which would lock automatically onto a fast-moving airborne target, proved to be tremendously effective. More than two thousand Stingers were given to the Afghans, many of which went to Haqqani. As the mujahideen figured out how to use them, fear spread through the Soviet forces. By 1987 their once invulnerable Hind attack helicopters were being shot down on an almost daily basis. The Soviets' dominance of the skies above Afghanistan—their great advantage—was over.

In 1988, Moscow belatedly acknowledged that victory against the insurgents would never be achieved at any cost, and Gorbachev began to systematically withdraw the Soviet forces from Afghanistan. On February 15, 1989, when the last Soviet soldier retreated back across the Amu Darya—the broad, glacier-fed river that delineated the border between Afghanistan and the Soviet republics of Uzbekistan and Tajikistan—the war had claimed the lives of an estimated twenty-five thousand Soviet soldiers and well over a million Afghans, 90 percent of whom were civilian noncombatants. Another five million Afghans—nearly a third of the prewar population—had taken flight from the ravaged nation, mostly to dismal refugee camps in neighboring Pakistan and Iran, although some fled to places as far away as California.

On the face of it, the trap set for the Soviets by the Carter administration in 1979 seemed to have worked. Nine months after Gorbachev pulled his troops from Afghanistan, the Berlin Wall came down, heralding the imminent dissolution of the Soviet empire—a collapse indubitably hastened by the staggering cost of the Afghan conflict. The climactic battle of the Cold War had been won without the American military even having to get off the couch. Acting as a proxy army, the mujahideen had given the United States a free ride. Or so it seemed at the time.

In the summer of 1989, an essay titled "The End of History?" was published in the journal *National Interest* by a young State Department official named Francis Fukuyama. The essay, which catapulted Fukuyama from obscurity to overnight fame (and was later expanded into an even more widely read book, *The End of History and the Last Man*), argued that history is properly regarded as the progress of ideas rather than merely a record of human events, and that the end of the Cold War signaled the permanent victory of modernity—the apotheosis of which was the Western idea of liberal capitalist democracy. "The triumph of the West, of the Western idea," wrote Fukuyama, "is evident first of all in the total exhaustion of viable systematic alternatives to Western liberalism. . . . What we may be witnessing is not just the end of the Cold War, or the passing of a particular period of postwar history, but the end of history as such: that is, the end point of mankind's ideological evolution and the universalization of Western liberal democracy as the final form of human government."

The Soviet Union managed to hang together for another two and a half years after its army left Afghanistan, and during the interim the CIA delivered several hundred million additional dollars to the mujahideen just to make sure the Kremlin didn't change its mind about causing further mischief in South Asia. But in the final days of 1991, when the Council of Republics of the Supreme Soviet officially dissolved the Soviet Union, the CIA concluded that the Afghan freedom fighters were no longer of any use to it and immediately cut off all support. Without a second thought, the United States forgot about the mujahideen and turned its attention to other foreign adventures, in the manner of a lothario who's gotten what he wants and doesn't bother to call the morning after.

Regrettably, the men and women running things in Washington also seemed to forget that Haqqani and bin Laden still controlled large numbers of fanatical holy warriors and possessed massive stockpiles of weapons that the CIA had graciously purchased for them. Beyond the borders of the United States, a great many people— Haqqani and bin Laden prominent among them—begged to differ with Fukuyama's assertion that the game was over and Western liberal democracy had won.

CHAPTER TWO

Although Pat Tillman was born in Fremont, for all but two years of his childhood he lived thirty minutes down the freeway in a neighborhood known as New Almaden—a tranquil, closely woven community tucked alongside the narrow seam of Los Alamitos Creek, where the Tillman family occupied a tidy thirteen-hundred-square-foot cottage surrounded by shade trees. The slopes of the Santa Cruz Mountains, redolent of Scotch broom and manzanita, jutted directly from their backyard. Thanks to the serenity of the setting and the proximity of so much open space, New Almaden still feels like it's at a distant remove from the hyperthyroidal sprawl of greater San Jose, even though the latter begins less than two miles down the valley.

The hills immediately west of the Tillman abode are honeycombed with mine shafts that once yielded a bounty of mercury ore. It was the most valuable mine in California during the latter half of the nineteenth century, but the diggings were shut down in 1975, after which the site was designated a forty-two-hundred-acre recreational area and thirty-five miles of hiking trails were built across its sun-parched ridges. Mary Lydanne Tillman—known as Dannie to her friends and close acquaintances—spent countless hours walking these trails with Pat on her back when he was a baby.

In her book, *Boots on the Ground by Dusk: My Tribute to Pat Tillman,* Dannie acknowledged that her eldest son "was not a cuddly infant." Animated and adventurous right out of the womb, Pat started walking at eight and a half months, and when he was awake he was constantly in motion. The Tillmans owned a television, but the walls of the Alamitos canyon restricted reception to a single channel, and sometimes not even that, so Pat and his younger brothers, Kevin and Richard, almost never watched TV as children. Instead, they spent most of their free time playing outdoors, scrambling up the ravines and outcrops of the Almaden Quicksilver County Park, where they acquired a lasting appreciation of untamed landscapes. When the boys had to be indoors, they engaged in clamorous discussions about current events, history, and politics with their parents and each other. Almost no subject was off-limits. Encouraged to think critically and be skeptical of conventional wisdom, Pat learned to trust in himself and be unafraid to buck the herd.

From the time he was two years old, Pat was a nonstop talker, yakking all the time, and this verbosity—his insatiable appetite for spirited dialogue—would, like his confidence and the immutability of his will, turn out to be one of his signature traits. When Pat was in middle school, according to *Boots on the Ground by Dusk,* he was "conscientious about learning and generally well-behaved in class," but Dannie regularly received calls from administrators concerned about Pat's roughhousing between classes: "He was getting referrals for chasing people, wrestling in the quad, climbing on the bleachers, and talking while walking to assembly." He was a loud, happy, rambunctious youth whose exuberance could not be contained.

Pat inherited superlative athletic genes, as did his brothers, and he began playing in an organized soccer league at the age of four. Thereafter, Tillman family life was organized to no small extent around the sports played by Pat, Kevin, and Richard. In Pat's case, by the time he was in high school, the sport that he cared most passionately about was football.

For reasons having to do with safety and liability, students were not allowed to play on the varsity football team until they were fifteen years old, so Pat didn't join the varsity squad until November 1991, when he was added to the roster for the playoffs during his sophomore year. By the time the 1992 football season got under way he had become Leland's star player. Despite his diminutive size, the coach used him on offense as a running back and wide receiver; on defense as a linebacker and strong safety; and on special teams as a punter, punt returner, and kick returner. Pat excelled at every position. Late in a crucial game near the end of the season, he ran the ball ninety yards down the field for a come-from-behind touchdown that earned Leland a berth in the playoffs.

———

Not long after Pat was killed, a remote Army firebase seven miles south of the hillside where he perished was named in his honor: Forward Operating Base Tillman. In the winter of 2007 a small contingent of American soldiers was stationed here, along with a company of Afghan National Army recruits and a handful of fighters from the Afghan Security Guard. The latter, known as the ASG, is a paramilitary militia under contract to the U.S. Army to provide additional security around the base and to accompany American patrols on missions into the surrounding countryside, which is still controlled by Taliban who belong to the Haqqani Network. FOB Tillman—squatting less than two miles from the Pakistan border, encircled by a seven-foot-thick blast wall constructed from earthen HESCO barriers topped with razor wire—is attacked frequently by Haqqani's forces.

Recruited and trained by American Special Forces, members of the ASG are courageous, highly skilled fighters who have earned the esteem of their American counterparts. Like members of most other Afghan armed forces—whether the Afghan Army, the Taliban, al-Qaeda, or independent militias—from the time they wake up until they go to sleep at the end of the day, the majority of the ASG are under the mild narcotic influence of hashish and/or *naswar,* a sticky brown powder, placed between the lip and the gum, concocted from tobacco, slacked lime, lavender, and opium. "Far as I can tell, they're baked pretty much 24/7," confirms a young American specialist as he looks through a stack of counterfeit DVDs being offered for sale by a pair of local tribesmen just beyond the gate to the base. "But they're good to have on your side. The ASG we go outside the wire with, most of them would lay down their life for you. Ain't that right, Snoop?"

Snoop, a skinny twenty-seven-year-old Pashtun who happens to be walking past with his AK-47 slung over his right shoulder, commands the ASG garrison attached to FOB Tillman. In lieu of a reply, he looks impassively at the specialist and says nothing, even though he understands English quite well. American soldiers at the base started calling the commander "Snoop" a couple of years previously because he bears an uncanny resemblance to the rapper Snoop Dogg, but his actual name is Abdul Ghani, and at the moment he is clearly less than pleased to be addressed so informally by a lowly specialist—a rank just above private. After staring icily at the soldier for several seconds, Commander Ghani spots someone he apparently has been looking for and strides briskly away to speak with him. The specialist, oblivious to Ghani's scorn, continues perusing the bootleg DVDs. "Check it out," he exclaims to nobody in particular. "*Rocky Balboa*—the new Stallone flick. I don't think it's even in theaters yet back in the States, but these hajjis already got it for sale here in east bumfuck, Afghaniland."

After walking away, Ghani approaches three Pashtuns who work as manual laborers at the base, and without warning raises his rifle stock and strikes one of them in the side of the head. The man cries out and staggers, but remains on his feet, which prompts Ghani to grab him by the shoulders, throw him to the muddy ground, and begin cursing at him in Pashto. When the tribesman stands up, Ghani knocks him down again and continues yelling at him. Then the commander turns and walks back toward the base, muttering in English, "I swear, I should go back there right now and really kick his ass." Noticing the shocked expression of the American journalist walking beside him, he bristles at the reproach implied by the reporter's reaction: "That guy, he has done some bad things against me. If someone is bad to me, I must be bad to them. You know why? Because if you didn't, that guy will think you are a pussy guy. And then he will be bothering you all the time. You have to go against him back, you know?" When the journalist expresses skepticism, Ghani only becomes more adamant: "I am telling you, if the guy does something wrong, and you didn't do something back against him, after this he will have no respect for you. He will think you are a pussy motherfucker. And then he will be bothering you. Every time he sees you, he will give you a hard time."

Commander Ghani* has just provided a vivid summation of the Pashtun principles of *nang* (honor), *ghairat* (pride), and *badal* (revenge), which—along with a fourth concept, *melmastia* (hospitality)—account for the most important tenets in an unwritten, overarching code of behavior known as *Pashtunwali* that has shaped culture and identity in this part of Central Asia for centuries. There are an estimated fifteen million Pashtuns living in Afghanistan's southern and eastern provinces; they constitute that nation's largest ethnic group. Another twenty-six million Pashtuns live just across the border in western Pakistan, and to a great degree *Pashtunwali* dictates how these forty-one million people conduct their lives.

The tenets of *Pashtunwali* are fluid, highly nuanced, and occasionally contradictory. According to the precept of *melmastia,* a Pashtun is obligated to show hospitality to all visitors, especially strangers. Guests are to be fed, sheltered, and protected from harm; if they request it, even mortal enemies must be given sanctuary. According to the precept of *badal,* any injustice—no matter how slight—must be avenged. If a man suffers even the relatively minor insult of a personal taunt, for example, the insulted party must shed the taunter's blood; if the taunter flees before justice can be carried out, the blood of his closest male relative must be shed in his stead. Endeavoring to uphold this stricture, families sometimes engage in deadly feuds that have been known to drag on for decades. At their root, most aspects of *Pashtunwali* are about preserving honor and respect. And in Pashtun society, respect ultimately derives from demonstrations of strength and courage.

When Americans or Europeans hear accounts of entire families wiped out in the name of *badal,* or one Pashtun beheading another to redress a seemingly inconsequential insult, the typical reaction is shock and revulsion. The tenets of *Pashtunwali* are hardly unique to

---

* On April 12, 2007, the U.S. Army captain Dennis Knowles sent an e-mail to this author from FOB Tillman in which he reported, "Today was a very sad day as Snoop took the brunt of a mine and didn't make it. I know you had spent some time with him. He was well respected by all sides. . . . Snoop hit a double-stacked, pressure-plated anti-tank mine with his Toyota Hilux. Not good. He had his right leg gone below the waist, his left leg was a mangled mess, and his right arm was gone. There was nothing we could do but ease his pain. It hit everyone hard."

Central Asia, however. In American cities, for instance, it is not uncommon for adolescents to be gunned down for showing disrespect to gang members. And if a Red Sox pitcher beans a Yankee batter, nobody is the least bit surprised when the Yankee pitcher hurls a fastball at the head of a Red Sox batter as payback in the next inning.

———

Pashtunwali certainly wouldn't have struck Pat Tillman as an alien concept. The notion of personal honor, and the imperative of upholding it, were things he was taught at an early age, and he took them very seriously.

Pat's father—also named Patrick, albeit with a different middle name—grew up in Fremont, married Pat's mother a couple of years after graduating from high school, and then attended both college and law school while working full-time to support his new family. He had been raised according to traditional masculine values, and he passed along those same old-fashioned ideals to his sons. Young Pat and his brothers were instructed to tell the truth, to respect their elders, to stand up for the vulnerable, and to keep their promises. Tillman père also impressed upon the boys the importance of defending their honor, with their fists if necessary.

When Pat started playing high-school football as a thirteen-year-old, he understood that he would need to block and tackle with exceptional intensity to compensate for his small size, and that he couldn't afford to show fear or vulnerability if he hoped to win the respect of coaches, teammates, and adversaries. He therefore adopted an intimidating, cast-iron demeanor on the field, although beneath the armor was a sensitive kid who was easily moved to tears in private.

Pat sometimes found it advantageous to flaunt his toughness off the gridiron as well. When larger boys menaced him, Pat responded by instantly going on the offensive, forcing the aggressors to either throw down or back away. Caught off guard by the puny kid's utter lack of fear, sometimes his adversaries would elect to retreat, but when they wouldn't, Pat wasn't shy about exchanging blows. This willingness to engage in fisticuffs when challenged was fostered by the culture of high-school football, in which members of the tribe were expected to demonstrate their courage and establish their place in the masculine hierarchy by fighting. As a consequence, Pat and many of his teammates got in numerous scraps involving kids from other schools, with whom they would scuffle at malls and outside movie theaters on weekend evenings. None of this struck any of the participants as odd or aberrant; to them it was just what high-school football players did, a time-honored rite of passage. They regarded the brawling as little more than an extension of the game carried beyond the field of play.

Despite Pat's quickness to resort to his fists, he was in many ways the antithesis of a bully. As a matter of principle, he fought only with kids who were bigger than he was, and on several occasions he intervened to rescue nerdy classmates who were being hassled by older, larger tormentors. But when Pat fought, he fought to win and never capitulated, which earned him the reputation at Leland and beyond as a guy not to be trifled with. In the pack he ran with, there was no question in anyone's mind that he was the alpha male.

CHAPTER THREE

More than a quarter century after the Soviet invasion, great swaths of central Kabul still exist as bombed-out heaps of rubble. Although foreign visitors commonly take it for granted that this extensive destruction occurred during the Soviet-Afghan War, such assumptions are mistaken. During most of the Soviet occupation, Kabul remained a bustling, functional metropolis. Children filled the schools. Business flourished. The arts were vibrant. Basic services such as water and electricity continued to be provided. The war's horrors were myriad and savagely real, but they were generally visited on the countryside; Kabul dodged the worst of the violence. Life in the capital carried on much as it had before the conflict, by and large.

The devastation of Kabul didn't actually come about until long after the infidel occupiers had departed. And it wasn't caused by the Soviets. The wreckage that blights Afghanistan's principal city was the fruit of mujahideen wreaking havoc on mujahideen: Afghans doing their best to kill other Afghans.

During Pat's high-school years, as he was celebrating his youth, asserting his masculinity, and winning admirers on the football field, Afghanistan was sinking to new depths of misery—although most Americans remained oblivious to what was happening in this part of the world. When the Soviets pulled out, there had been anticipation within the Afghan diaspora, including many of the expatriates living just up the road from Pat in Fremont, that their nation was on the cusp of a new era of peace and renewal. There were reasons to believe that millions of Afghan refugees might soon be able to go home. Such hopes evaporated with cruel speed, however, as the nation instead slid deeper into anarchy and fratricidal violence.

Two years before the Soviets began withdrawing their troops, they installed a thirty-nine-year-old Pashtun named Mohammed Najibullah as president of the Democratic Republic of Afghanistan (DRA), their puppet government in Kabul. Before he was made president, Najibullah had run the country's feared secret police, an agency known as KHAD. In that role he had imprisoned, tortured, and executed tens of thousands of Afghans. Eyewitnesses have testified that Najibullah personally brutalized and murdered numerous political prisoners, in some instances by stomping them to death.

After the last Soviet soldier left Afghanistan in February 1989, the CIA predicted that Najibullah's regime would fall to the mujahideen within three to six months. But even after their departure, the Soviets continued to provide Najibullah with sophisticated arms and more than $3 billion in annual support. Moreover, American intelligence analysts badly underestimated Najibullah, a shrewd leader who was as ruthless as any of the mujahideen commanders. As it became clear that the DRA under his leadership was not simply going to roll over and surrender, the CIA—working in conjunction with Pakistan's intelligence service, the ISI—decided to hasten the process by pressing the mujahideen to attack the city of Jalalabad, a crucial DRA stronghold near the Pakistan border, eighty miles northeast of Khost City. Some ten thousand holy warriors under the leadership of nine different mujahideen commanders assembled outside of Jalalabad in March 1989 to launch the assault. Among them was Osama bin Laden, leading a contingent of two hundred Arab fighters.

The attack on the city commenced on March 5, 1989. The mujahideen quickly captured the Jalalabad airfield and some of the surrounding suburbs. But the DRA counterattacked with tanks, Scud-B missiles, and jet bombers, bringing mujahideen progress to a halt. Over the next three months the attackers managed to advance no farther into the city, and the battle for Jalalabad became a bloody standoff. Compounding the mujahideen's woes, their forces were

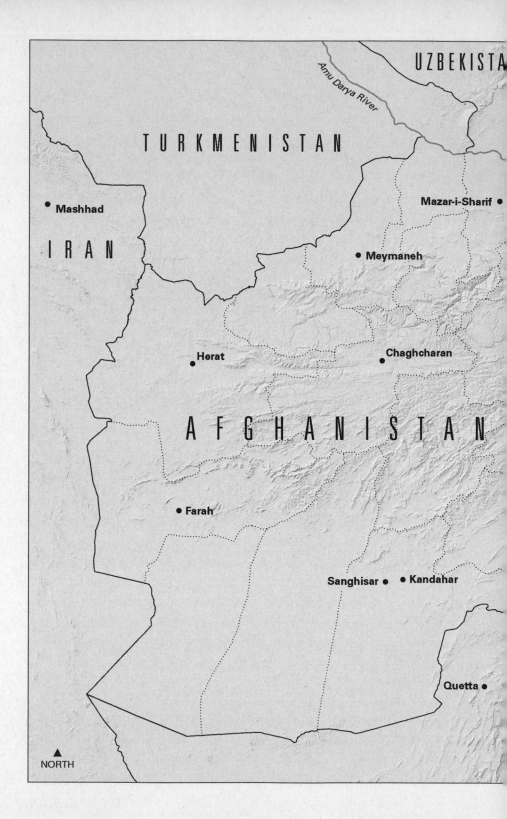

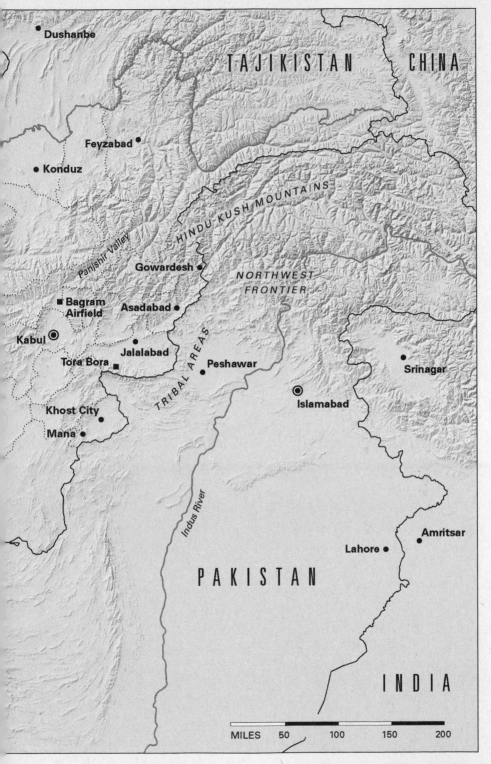

AFGHANISTAN

comprised of rival factions that despised one another. Not only were they incapable of fighting in concert against Najibullah's DRA forces, but mujahideen commanders sometimes seemed to intentionally undermine the efforts of their putative allies. By July, after having lost three thousand fighters (including approximately a hundred of bin Laden's forces), the mujahideen abandoned the fight and withdrew from Jalalabad in an atmosphere of bickering and recrimination. It was a humiliating defeat.

Ever since Afghanistan emerged as a nation in 1741, the country has been cobbled together from a shaky union of stubbornly autonomous fiefdoms. In Afghan society, individual loyalty belongs foremost to the family and then—in rapidly descending order—to one's extended clan or tribe, one's ethnic group, and one's religious sect.

The central government had never provided much in the way of support or services to the 85 percent of Afghans who lived outside of Kabul or other major cities. In the chaos of the Soviet-Afghan War, as this support dwindled to nothing, rural Afghans looked exclusively to their mullahs, village elders, and the mujahideen commanders for protection and governance. With the national economy in ruins, these commanders and their followers turned to the cultivation of opium poppies as their primary source of revenue. By the early 1990s, Afghanistan was well on its way to supplying the lion's share of the world's heroin. Although the mujahideen factions continued to regard Najibullah and the DRA as their main enemy, they increasingly began fighting each other for control of the drug trade, and for weapons supplied by Pakistan, Saudi Arabia, Egypt, and the CIA. Increasingly as well, they appeared to direct their efforts at least as much toward looting and pillaging as liberating their country. In important ways they started to resemble the Latin American drug cartels—except the mujahideen had a much greater penchant for brutality and carried out their depredations in the name of God. With some justification, Western journalists began referring to mujahideen commanders as warlords. Meanwhile, even though the Soviet Army had evacuated the country, the CIA continued to provide the Afghan holy warriors with about $250 million per year as a counterbalance to the billions spent to prop up the DRA by the Soviets.

Discouraged by the infighting among the mujahideen, in 1990 bin Laden left Afghanistan and returned to Saudi Arabia—even as tens of thousands of Arab *jihadis* he'd inspired flocked to the conflict, and numerous al-Qaeda training camps established by bin Laden continued to instruct young zealots in the art of guerrilla warfare.

Najibullah and the DRA Army held their own against the squabbling mujahideen for the better part of two years. But in April 1991 holy warriors under the command of Jalaluddin Haqqani overran DRA defenses and captured Khost City. The victory exacted a gruesome toll on the local populace Haqqani had "liberated," thousands of whom had their homes destroyed by indiscriminate mujahideen shelling or were killed outright in the crossfire. Nevertheless, Khost City became the first major Afghan urban center to come under mujahideen control since the Soviet invasion.

Six months later, the Soviet Union imploded and ceased to exist, bringing an abrupt end to Najibullah's font of money and weapons. Without Soviet backing, his regime was doomed. The DRA ran so low on fuel that the entire Afghan Air Force was forced to remain on the ground. Soon thereafter it couldn't even provide its soldiers with food, causing DRA soldiers to desert in droves and join the mujahideen militias that until then had been trying to kill them. Smelling blood in the water, the mujahideen warlords began jockeying for position to capture Kabul, the seat of Najibullah's government.

Shifting ethnic divisions and alliances have long played a central role in Afghanistan's chronic dysfunctionality. Although no single ethnic group makes up a majority, Pashtuns are the largest with approximately 40 percent of the national population. They are followed by ethnic Tajiks, who constitute some 30 percent; Uzbeks, with about 9 percent; Hazaras, a Shiite minority, also with about 9 percent; and a number of smaller groups such as Turkmen, Baluchis, Nuristanis, and Ismailis.

The most prominent of the mujahideen warlords were Abdul Rasul Sayyaf, a Pashtun with close ties to bin Laden; Gulbuddin Hekmatyar, a Pashtun based along the Pakistan border who had received hundreds of thousands of dollars from the CIA, and who commanded the loyalty of Haqqani and his network of hardened fighters; and Ahmad Shah Massoud, an ethnic Tajik whose base of power was in the Panjshir Valley north of Bagram Airfield. In early 1992, as these distrustful allies plotted to overrun Kabul, an important commander of a DRA Army regiment named Abdul Rashid Dostum—an ethnic Uzbek from northern Afghanistan who for thirteen years had been viciously fighting against the mujahideen on behalf of the Soviets and Najibullah—abruptly turned on his communist benefactors. Bringing along DRA tanks, aircraft, and forty thousand disciplined soldiers, Dostum joined forces with Massoud's mujahideen against Najibullah and the DRA.

The moment Dostum defected from the communists, Najibullah recognized that his regime was doomed. He held a press conference in which he made a desperate appeal to the United States to curb the forces of jihad it had done so much to nurture, lest the holy warriors bite the hand that had so recklessly fed them. As recorded by a reporter for the *International Herald Tribune*, Najibullah declared, "We have a common task—Afghanistan, the U.S.A., and the civilized world—to launch a joint struggle against fundamentalism. If fundamentalism comes to Afghanistan, war will continue for many years. Afghanistan will turn into a center of world smuggling for narcotic drugs. Afghanistan will be turned into a center for terrorism."

Upon making these observations, which would soon turn out to be disturbingly prescient, Najibullah offered to step down as president and work with the United Nations to effect a peaceful transition of power. A few senior officials in President George H. W. Bush's administration argued that the United States should seize this opportunity to help install a moderate coalition government that would establish order and prevent rabid *jihadis* such as Hekmatyar from seizing control of the country. But a Cold War mind-set still prevailed in Washington, particularly within the CIA. According to such thinking, now that the Soviet Union was defunct, America no longer had any reason for remaining involved in Afghan affairs. No effort was made to thwart a takeover by the holy warriors, and the moment passed. The United States determined that it was time to wash its hands of Afghanistan and walk away.

By announcing his willingness to resign, Najibullah had abdicated the last of his influence and credibility. His government disintegrated on the spot as a consequence, and Kabul was for all intents and purposes left undefended. Mujahideen factions moved on the city from all points of the compass, playing cat and mouse with one another to determine who would seize the capital and assume power. The main contenders were Hekmatyar, approaching from the south; and Massoud, supported by Dostum, approaching from the north. Across the border in Peshawar, Pakistan, representatives of the Pakistani ISI and Saudi Arabia frantically worked to negotiate a last-minute power-sharing arrangement between Hekmatyar and Massoud, and thereby forestall a violent confrontation between them. According to Steve Coll's superb history of this period, *Ghost Wars,*

> Even Osama bin Laden flew to Peshawar and joined the effort to forge cooperation between Hekmatyar and Massoud. He contacted Hekmatyar by radio from Peshawar and urged him to consider a compromise with Massoud.
>
> Bin Laden and other Islamist mediators arranged a half-hour radio conversation directly between Massoud and Hekmatyar. The essential question was whether the two commanders would control Kabul peacefully as allies or fight it out.

Although Massoud was willing to share power, Hekmatyar ignored bin Laden's repeated entreaties to do so, calculating that he could defeat Massoud in battle. Hekmatyar went to bed that night certain that he would roll into Kabul on the morrow, victorious. But the obstinacy displayed by Hekmatyar convinced Massoud that negotiating with him was a pointless exercise, so he ordered Dostum's forces to launch a preemptive strike. Getting a brief albeit crucial jump on Hekmatyar, Massoud and Dostum stormed into the city from the north. When Hekmatyar's fighters arrived from the south a few hours later, ferocious block-by-block combat ensued. Massoud had moved quickly to seize strategic positions throughout Kabul, however, and Hekmatyar wasn't able to overcome the advantage. After a week of intense fighting, the latter's soldiers withdrew from the city and retreated whence they came, although without conceding victory to Massoud. Instead, Hekmatyar, in a senseless rage, began firing barrage after barrage of rockets into the city from afar, inflicting death and ruin without regard for whom or what they might strike.

The battle for Kabul ignited a catastrophic civil war. As Coll
wrote,

> Kabul plunged into violence and deprivation during 1993. Hekmat-
> yar pounded the city indiscriminately with hundreds of rockets from
> his ample stores, killing and wounding thousands of civilians. The
> old mujahideen leaders realigned themselves in bizarre temporary
> partnerships. They fought artillery duels along Kabul's avenues, di-
> viding the city into a dense barricaded checkerboard of ethnic and
> ideological factions. Shi'ite militia fought against Hekmatyar around
> Kabul's zoo, then switched sides and fought against Massoud.
> Sayyaf's forces allied with his old Islamic law colleague [Burhanud-
> din] Rabbani and hit the Shi'ites with unrestrained fury, beheading
> old men, women, children, and dogs. Dostum's Uzbek militias car-
> ried out a campaign of rapes and executions on Kabul's outskirts.
> Massoud hunkered down in the tattered defense ministry, a decaying
> former royal palace, and moved his troops north and south in run-
> ning battles. The electricity in Kabul failed. . . . Roads closed, food
> supplies shrank, and disease spread. About ten thousand Afghan
> civilians died violently by the year's end.

At least 40 percent of Kabul was reduced to rubble by the fighting and shelling, but the effects of the civil war extended far beyond
the capital. As a bulwark against anarchy, people in the provinces retreated beneath the relatively benign tyranny of their clans, where the
mullahs and commanders of local militias provided a semblance of
security and order. This atomization of the nation—the hunkering of
the population into a thousand premodern fiefs—proved to be ideal
conditions for incubating a singularly virulent strain of terrorism that
would shortly capture the attention of the world, and most especially
the United States.

———

At 9:18 Pacific standard time on the morning of February 26, 1993,
as Pat was attending class at Leland High School, a fifteen-hundred-
pound bomb improvised from fertilizer, fuel oil, nitroglycerin, sul-
furic acid, and sodium cyanide packed into the back of a rented

Econoline van was detonated three thousand miles across the country from Almaden, in a parking garage beneath the north tower of the World Trade Center in lower Manhattan. The explosion blasted a hundred-foot-wide cavity through six stories of steel-reinforced concrete and created a seismic shock wave felt more than a mile away. Although more than a thousand New Yorkers were injured, only six people (who had the bad luck to be eating lunch in a cafeteria directly above the blast) were killed. Because the death count was relatively low and there was scant visible damage to the exterior of the building, the attack didn't raise a durable concern among most Americans. The bombers were generally portrayed as inept amateurs who had come nowhere close to bringing down the massive tower. Much was made of the fact that one of the perpetrators was so dim-witted that after the attack he attempted to retrieve his deposit for the destroyed van from the Ryder agency in New Jersey where he'd rented it.

A close examination of the facts, however, suggests the attack came shockingly close to succeeding. The van had been parked along the southern edge of the underground parking facility with the intent of causing the north tower to crash into the south tower as it toppled, destroying the entire World Trade Center in one fell swoop and thereby annihilating upwards of a quarter-million people. Although a calamity of such magnitude didn't occur on that Friday in 1993, it wasn't dodged by much: the architect of the World Trade Center later testified that if the vehicle had been positioned closer to the building's foundation, the blast could have brought down both towers.

The bomb had been assembled, delivered, and detonated by a Kuwaiti named Ramzi Yousef, under the supervision of his uncle Khalid Sheik Mohammed, who would later be identified as "the principal architect" of the attack against the same buildings on September 11, 2001. Yousef had learned the art of making bombs from a manual written by the CIA for the mujahideen to use in their struggle against the Soviets. He was given the CIA instruction booklet while attending an al-Qaeda training camp in Khost, Afghanistan, in 1991 or 1992.

CHAPTER FOUR

Although Pat Tillman remained relatively small for his age through most of high school, he was the beneficiary of a belated growth spurt at the end of eleventh grade. During the spring and summer of his sixteenth year he underwent a rapid transformation from a short, wiry child to a young man who stood five feet eleven inches tall and weighed 195 pounds. The new Pat had massive legs, a narrow waist, and an upper body sculpted by a weight-lifting regimen that he pursued with near-obsessive zeal. He was an exceptional football player even before the spurt, but the added heft allowed him to distinguish himself as one of the best players in the nation when his senior year at Leland commenced in September 1993.

California is so big that its high-school football program is divided into fourteen geographic sections, each of which includes more students and more schools than some entire states. Leland is one of 117 schools in the Central Coast Section, or CCS, among the most competitive sections in all of California.

On September 3, in its first game of the 1993 season, Leland played Bellarmine College Preparatory, a highly regarded Jesuit school that won the CCS championship in 1990 and had been runner-up in 1992. When the game began, Pat took the opening kickoff and returned it to the Bellarmine thirty-five-yard line. Eight plays later he ran the ball into the end zone on fourth and goal to score the game's first touchdown. In the third quarter he carried the ball on a dazzling sixty-eight-yard scramble from scrimmage that set up another touchdown. Leland dominated Bellarmine from start to finish, and the final score was 33–7. Kevin Tillman, a sophomore, booted three extra points as the team's kicker.

At the conclusion of the regular season, Leland had won nine of its ten games and earned a spot in the CCS playoffs as the number-three seed. Pat deserved a significant share of the credit for the team's success. Over the course of the season he caught twenty-seven passes, twelve of which were for touchdowns, and averaged 25.7 yards per reception. He ran the ball into the end zone for another fourteen touchdowns and averaged 10.9 yards per carry as a rusher. With three kicks and an interception returned for touchdowns, and a fumble recovered in the end zone, he scored a total of thirty-one touchdowns. On defense he was credited with 110 tackles, ten sacks, and three interceptions. In a highlight reel of Leland's 1993 season, Pat looks like he's moving in fast-forward while everyone else is functioning at regular speed.

When the playoffs commenced, Leland was matched in the first round against Andrew P. Hill High School, a giant public institution that drew students from the poorest, roughest part of San Jose. In the first half, Pat got his hands on the ball exactly six times, and on four of those occasions scored a touchdown. By halftime Leland was ahead, 55–0. Terry Hardtke, who had become Leland's head football coach at the beginning of the 1993 season, didn't want to humiliate Hill by continuing to run up the score, so he decided to bench Tillman and most of the other starters for the second half. Hardtke explained what happened next when he eulogized Pat at the latter's memorial service in 2004:

I went up to Pat and said, "Pat, you're done for the day, and I don't want you playing any offense or to play defense." He looked at me with this real quizzical look and he said, "OK."

And as I'm getting prepared for the second-half kickoff, my offensive coordinator turns to me and says, "You know, Pat's back there ready to take the kickoff." And I looked in astonishment and saw him back there. And he got the kickoff, and of course ran it back for a touchdown. As he came off the field, I looked at him. . . . And he came over to me very confidently and said, "You mentioned nothing about special teams."

To avert any further semantic confusion that might tempt Pat to go back onto the field to attempt a sixth touchdown, Coach Hardtke immediately confiscated his helmet and shoulder pads. With Pat and the other first-stringers sitting out the remainder of the game, Leland won, 61–14. On December 4, two weeks later, Leland routed Milpitas High School, 35–0, to win the CCS championship.

————

Pat Tillman was a conspicuously handsome young man, with chiseled features and a magnetic smile. But his eyes were his most arresting feature: greenish brown and angular, narrowly set, they were framed between high cheekbones and a dark, forceful brow that emphasized their intensity. Depending on his disposition, they could look impish, or intimidating, or wildly exuberant, but whatever emotion his eyes conveyed, there was no mistaking it. By Pat's mid-teens the white-blond hair of his infancy had darkened to a wheat-colored thatch with sun-bleached streaks, and he often wore it trimmed short across the temples with shaggy bangs down to his eyebrows, augmented by a long mare's tail that flapped across his upper back as he ran.

His good looks, cocky deportment, and status as a football star led some people to assume that he was a stereotypical jock—entitled, self-absorbed, intellectually shallow, incurious about the world beyond football. Actually, Pat was none of these things. A diary he kept as a sixteen-year-old reveals an introspective youth who mourned the death of a beloved cat, opined that religion was inadequate to elucidate the mysteries of existence, and ruminated on the downside of his empathetic nature. "I can't even be an asshole to someone anymore," the journal sardonically notes, "without feeling bad. I'm too conscious of their feelings."

Despite his sensitivity, Pat didn't have a girlfriend until his senior year at Leland. The girl with whom he finally connected, however, turned out to be someone he'd known since they were both four years old, when he started playing in a kids' soccer league. One of the teams he played against included a girl named Marie Ugenti. As they were growing up, Pat and Marie went to different elementary schools and middle schools, says Marie, "but Almaden had the character of a small town. Our families knew each other, our brothers played sports together, and our lives kept intersecting in various ways throughout our childhood." Pat and Marie thus remained more or less on each other's radar, although they spent little time interacting face-to-face until September 1990, when they both entered Leland High School as freshmen.

Marie was slender and fine featured, with blue eyes and long blond hair. The Leland yearbook notes that she was voted the girl with "the best smile" by her classmates. In contrast to Pat—who was loud and mischievous, a swinger of birches for whom achieving academic excellence wasn't the highest priority—Marie was decorous in her behavior, and her grades were outstanding; she excelled in the sciences in particular. As Benjamin Hill, an inseparable friend of Pat's since kindergarten, puts it, "Marie was a very smart, very good girl. It was a classic case of opposites attracting." Pat came home from his first day of classes at Leland with an unshakable crush on her, yet he failed to act on it for the next three years—at least in part, according to some sources, because she was taller than he was until their senior year.

Nevertheless, says Marie, "We shared the same group of friends, so we hung out together a lot. And things just sort of evolved from there." This despite the fact that Marie's father happened to be Paul Ugenti, Leland's head baseball coach—the man who'd nixed Pat's bid to make the varsity baseball team as a freshman, motivating him to switch sports and focus on football instead. But Pat held no grudge against the coach or his progeny, and in the autumn of 1993 the star of the Leland football team mustered his courage and finally asked Marie out on a date.

With one of the nation's most vibrant cities just forty-five miles north, it would be easy to assume that as soon as Almaden kids became old enough to drive, they would head into San Francisco at every opportunity. But the kids in Pat and Marie's crowd weren't much inclined to go there as teenagers. When they were in the mood to escape their local haunts and blow off steam they usually drove down to Santa Cruz—a seaside community known for its surf culture and progressive politics—which was thirty miles in the other direction. This is where Pat took Marie on their first date, to a restaurant called the Crow's Nest overlooking the Pacific Ocean.

"We sat outside on the deck upstairs," Marie remembers. "It was the beginning of October, and it was a little cold out. Pat hadn't dated much, and I could tell he was nervous. Besides his mom, he hadn't really spent much time around girls. And Dannie told me that raising all boys, she downplayed her feminine side a lot and did things outside with them, teaching them to play sports, that kind of thing. His idea of what girls were all about was not typical. But it wasn't a big problem. All three Tillman brothers always had a lot of respect for their mom. From her they learned how to treat women."

Despite Pat's inexperience with affairs of the heart, he and Marie established what would turn out to be an enduring bond. Throughout Pat's youth, his mother—a warm, expressive, tolerant woman—anchored his existence with a steadfast and unconditional love. Like most kids, Pat took this maternal devotion for granted; he was largely oblivious to the degree to which Dannie's unwavering gravitational field kept his hyperkinetic young life securely in its orbit. Although Dannie and Marie are different in significant ways—Dannie is extroverted and loquacious, for example, while Marie is demure and emotionally reserved—in Marie he encountered another smart, stalwart woman possessed of prodigious forbearance, and he must have recognized on some unconscious level that he had found his soul mate. After their first date in Santa Cruz, as Marie describes it, "We pretty much just stayed together." In fact, they would remain committed partners until Pat's death eleven years later.

All of Pat's high-school friends say that once they became a couple, Marie was a civilizing influence who helped knock off some of his sharper edges. Nevertheless, she acknowledges, "Shortly after we started dating, he got in big trouble." An apologetic grimace furrows her unlined face. "He was in that fight at Round Table."

CHAPTER FIVE

The incident to which Marie refers took place on November 13, 1993, exactly a week after Pat's seventeenth birthday, on a Saturday evening. Earlier in the day, Pat had played in the final football game of Leland's regular season, which the team won to earn a berth in the CCS playoffs. Following the game he celebrated the victory with friends and teammates at the birthday party of a girl whose parents had rented a banquet room at a swanky hotel in downtown San Jose. "I arrived late at the party," Marie remembers. "People had been drinking, but not a lot." Around nine o'clock, or maybe slightly later, Pat, Marie, and many of the other revelers decamped for a Round Table Pizza restaurant at a nondescript strip mall in Almaden. "It's right off the Almaden Expressway," says Marie. "Round Table is where everyone went on weekends." Among the kids who showed up at the pizza joint was one of Pat's closest friends, a football teammate named Jeff Hechtle.

Shortly after the Leland students had been seated in the crowded restaurant, a nineteen-year-old graduate of a rival school, Mike Bradford, walked in with six companions, ascertained that no tables were available, and departed. As this group headed for the door, Hechtle, who was drunk, got up from the table and followed them outside.

Bradford; his girlfriend, Erin Clarke; his best friend, Darin Rosas; and four other buddies—Ryan Stock, Scott Strong, Kemp Hare, and Eric Eastman—were all sitting inside their vehicles or standing next to them, preparing to drive away, when Hechtle approached the group. "I was just opening the door to get into my truck," Bradford says, "when Jeff Hechtle comes up behind me and asks, 'Hey, are you Mike Bradford?' So I turn around and say, 'Yeah, I'm Mike.' " Bradford vaguely recognized Hechtle from church; at one time both had been members of the same Mormon ward, as had Clarke, Rosas, and Strong. "I sort of knew who he was," Bradford says of Hechtle, "but couldn't really place him."

A couple of years earlier Bradford had dated a girl named Jody who had dumped him for another guy. According to several witnesses, Hechtle began taunting Bradford by claiming to be the guy who had stolen Jody's heart. It was a transparent attempt on Hechtle's part to provoke Bradford, but Bradford failed to rise to the bait. "I just started laughing," Bradford recalls. "I had moved on from that girl, so his comments were no big deal. But I razzed him back a little bit with some comments of my own, which kind of offended him. And then he said, 'So you want to do something about it?' I just looked at him like, 'Whatever, dude.' Jeff isn't very big. To me, he wasn't the kind of guy I needed to fight. . . . He'd made some comments about a girl I was dating years before. What do I care?"

Unlike Hechtle, neither Bradford nor any of his friends were inebriated. "It was early, around 9:30," Bradford says. "We were planning on getting primed up, but we hadn't started drinking yet. All of us were sober."

Hechtle, who is only five feet six inches tall, "just kept going on and on," recalls Darin Rosas. "It was obvious he wasn't leaving until he started something. Mike totally did not want to go down this road, but all the smack-talk finally got to be too much for our friend Ryan, who yelled, 'Kick the shit out of him, Mike!' or something like that." The mists of time have obscured who threw the first punch, but a moment later the fight was on. Bradford grabbed Hechtle's arm and swung him into a concrete pillar. Hechtle pushed Ryan Stock up against one of the restaurant's front windows, delivered a couple of punches to his face, and put him in a headlock as Bradford began pummeling Hechtle with his fists. As the melee unfolded in front of them, Rosas, Clarke, Strong, Hare, and Eastman hung back at a safe distance and watched with a mix of alarm and fascination.

No more than fifteen seconds after the fight commenced, one of Hechtle's Leland compadres poked his head out of the restaurant door and observed Hechtle getting his ass kicked by two much bigger strangers. "Go get Pat!" Hechtle yelled. "Go get Pat!" Unaware that Hechtle had incited the altercation, the kid ducked back inside and shouted to Pat and the rest of the Leland kids that Hechtle was getting beaten up by a mob just outside the restaurant door.

Pat was the first of at least ten Leland football players who came bursting out of Round Table Pizza to rescue Hechtle. The instant Rosas, Strong, Hare, and Eastman saw the fury on the faces of Pat and his friends, they bolted across the parking lot, running for their lives.

Pat's inner circle at Leland included perhaps a dozen kids. He was extremely close to several of them, but nobody was more important to him than Jeff Hechtle. Moreover, Hechtle had a serious health condition that made Pat feel especially protective: he was born with a rare, poorly understood affliction known as a hairy nevus, which caused immense moles to grow over much of his body. When he was born, his parents were told he wouldn't survive. The largest of the lesions covered most of his head. Hechtle underwent a series of exceedingly complex, very painful surgeries, leaving most of the left side of his head covered in scar tissue. Because it is fragile and lacks the elasticity of normal skin, such tissue is easily torn.

Sprinting from the pizza joint into the suburban night, Pat assessed the situation unfolding in front of him, mistakenly concluded that Hechtle was being assaulted by a pack of thugs, and made a split-second decision to right this grievous wrong by taking out the largest of the apparent attackers, who appeared to be a tall guy now fleeing the scene of the fight. The tall guy was Darin Rosas, and Pat, says Erin Clarke, "made a beeline for Darin."

"Pat saw Darin running away," Scott Strong speculates, "and probably thought he was running because he'd done something to his friend."

"All these guys came rushing out," says Rosas. "I had no idea who any of them were. All I knew is they were football players, and they were big. I was a surfer. I wasn't into contact sports. So I just started running. Others did, too, but I was the one who got caught.

I ran probably about six or seven steps before somebody hit me in the back of the head and knocked me out." The blow, which came from one of Tillman's fists, dropped Rosas to the asphalt like a sack of potatoes.

Much of Pat's brilliance on the football field derived from his uncanny ability to anticipate the moves of opposing players, react without hesitation, and tackle the ballcarrier with a tooth-rattling hit. But Pat had just turned seventeen, and like that of other kids that age, his dorsal lateral prefrontal cortex—the region of the brain that weighs consequences—was far from fully developed. In this instance, his dubious adolescent judgment was further distorted by both alcohol and his conviction that one of his duties in life was to be the protector of the vulnerable, the guardian of his friends and family. The upshot was that Pat flattened the wrong guy. Rosas was just a spectator who had nothing to do with the fight.

Although he was approximately three inches taller than Pat and more than two years older, Rosas was a skinny nineteen-year-old who hadn't grown into his body yet. According to Mike Bradford, "He was not a fighter, absolutely not. And I'm not saying that just to stick up for him. If he was a fighter, I'd tell you. I mean, out of our group of friends, I was known as the guy who would go hit someone if I needed to, but Darin wasn't like that. He wasn't the aggressive type."

Pat didn't know any of this, however, and in his frenzied state he didn't pause to inquire. Overreacting to the perceived threat to Hechtle, Pat went berserk.

When Pat delivered that first punch to Rosas's head, Rosas was knocked cold, but for only a few seconds. When he regained a semblance of consciousness, he was lying on his side in the parking lot undergoing an extended assault from Tillman. "What Pat did to Darin was more than just, like, 'I'll hit you until you're down and then move on,'" says Scott Strong. "It kept going. Pat was taking care of him."

"I felt like I was in a washing machine," Rosas says, "getting spun around and hit from all directions—punches and kicks and punches and kicks. . . . Then Erin jumped in and tried to stop him. There were a lot of people just standing there watching Tillman kick the shit out of me, and she was the only one who was brave enough to do anything. I was so grateful to her."

"I remember Pat had a white shirt on, and slacks, and was wearing dress shoes, like he had just come from a dressy occasion," Erin Clarke recalls. "Darin was on the ground and Pat was kicking him, so I jumped in between them to try and stop it. I was touching Pat's arm, yelling, 'He didn't do anything! He didn't do anything!' but Pat looked right through me like I wasn't there. He was just so aggressively set on hurting Darin that he seemed like he didn't even see me.

"Darin was sort of curled on his side in a fetal position," Clarke continues,

> and Pat kept kicking him in the face and chest and stomach. He was enraged, absolutely enraged. I tried to stand between them, and I kept saying, "He didn't do anything!" but Pat grabbed me by the upper arms and just tossed me aside, at which point one of his friends grabbed me and held me back. I remember this person repeating over and over, "Just let him do it. Let him do it." Now, so many years later, I'm willing to give this guy the benefit of the doubt—that he was just trying to protect me from getting in the middle of a fight—but at the time I was so angry. I kept yelling at these football players to let me go and to stop hurting Darin. They yelled back at me, calling me the "B-word," which was very hurtful.

Because the Redmond Plaza shopping center was a popular weekend hangout for adolescents, there was an off-duty policeman working security every Friday and Saturday night; the cop's base of operations was a 7-Eleven at the other end of the strip mall, a hundred yards away. Within minutes of the start of the brawl, the officer hustled across the parking lot to break it up, and additional police arrived soon thereafter.

Pat ceased his assault as soon as the cops showed up. Rosas was lying on the pavement, dazed and bleeding from his mouth and left eye. Mike Bradford kneeled beside his head and tried to comfort him. "He looked horrible," says Kemp Hare, who was observing from a few feet away. "His equilibrium was totally out of whack. He couldn't walk."

When he saw the police, Pat snapped out of his enraged trance and immediately seemed to recognize that he'd done serious harm to Rosas. "He told the officers that he was sorry," says Erin. "He acted very concerned, explained to the cops that he'd thought Darin was hurting his friend, said that he couldn't believe he'd made such a serious error in judgment. His demeanor completely changed. All of a sudden he was very respectful."

According to Rosas, "Someone eventually pulled me up off the ground and tried to walk me around, but I was dizzy and completely out of it, so they sat me down on the curb. I remember sitting there with my head down, just spitting out blood and chunks of teeth. . . . I tried to talk, but there was just so much blood and so many little pieces of teeth. As I was sitting there with my head between my knees, that's when Pat Tillman came over. He said, 'I'm so sorry. It was a case of mistaken identity. I made a bad mistake. We'll take care of this.' He was apologizing profusely."

Pat gave his contact information to Rosas, whose friends then put him into Eric Eastman's car and drove him to nearby Good Samaritan Hospital, where Rosas was treated in the emergency room. Very early Sunday morning, after Rosas was released from the hospital, Eastman drove him to his home in Folsom, a suburb of Sacramento. During the three-hour drive they had to pull over twice to let Rosas vomit—a symptom of the concussion he'd suffered. When Rosas arrived home, says his mother, Carol Rosas, "I came downstairs and looked at him and I just couldn't believe what I saw. His one eye was swollen shut, and his teeth had been kicked in. He was hurt so bad we took him back to the emergency room." Twenty-four hours later, Darin also received emergency dental care, the first of five visits he would make to the dentist over the following weeks.

CHAPTER SIX

The Sunday morning after the Round Table brawl, Bob Rosas, Darin's father, called Pat's father at home and said, "My son got hurt by your son. What are you going to do about it?" Pat's father explained that he wasn't aware Darin had been seriously injured. Then he took Mr. Rosas's phone number and said he would get back to him.

According to Dannie Tillman's book, *Boots on the Ground by Dusk,* when she told Pat about the phone call from Darin's father, Pat became visibly upset, walked outside, and climbed a eucalyptus tree behind the family home in New Almaden. Dannie followed him into the yard and said they needed to talk, whereupon Pat came down from the tree and tearfully explained how he had mistakenly beaten up Rosas. Dannie suggested to Pat that they drive up to Sacramento, apologize to Rosas and his family, and offer to pay his medical bills with some money she'd recently inherited from her grandmother. When Dannie told her husband about what they had resolved to do, however, he expressed serious reservations. Speaking from an attorney's perspective, he explained that the actions they proposed might be perceived as an admission of guilt that could leave them vulnerable not only to criminal charges but to a civil claim as well. So Dannie agreed, reluctantly, that she and Pat would not contact Rosas or his family. The next communiqué the Tillman family received regarding the matter was a notification from Santa Clara County law enforcement officers that Pat had been charged with a felony: assault with a deadly weapon.

Felony assault is a serious criminal charge. Were Pat to be found guilty, the conviction would have an enormous impact on his future. But because the first hearing wasn't scheduled until March 1994, four months later, there was little to be done about it for the time being. "Pat appreciated the seriousness of the charge," Marie remembers, "but he tried not to worry too much about what might happen because it was such a long process and he wasn't the type to sit there and brood and get all twisted around something. He was sort of like, 'Okay, I'll deal with the trial when it happens.' "

————

After Leland won the CCS championship in December 1993, Pat was voted one of two "CCS players of the year." This honor, reflecting the extraordinary statistics he'd tallied over the season, seemed to ensure that he would be offered a scholarship to play college football at one of the nation's premier Division I-A programs. He especially hoped to win a scholarship to attend Stanford, which was just twenty-five miles from his home, or the University of Washington, because Seattle's misty climate and coffee culture captured Pat's imagination. To better his chances of getting a full ride with a competitive football program, he decided to present himself as a defensive specialist rather than a jack-of-all-trades who excelled on offense, defense, and special teams—even though that's precisely what he had done in high school.

Despite Pat's strategizing, as the recruiting period ran its course only three schools indicated any real interest in him: Arizona State University, San Jose State University, and Brigham Young University. The problem was that on paper, Pat's size and speed weren't exceptional. For example, he ran the forty-yard dash (considered one of the most important benchmarks for evaluating wide receivers, running backs, defensive backs, and linebackers) in 4.55 seconds—which was mighty damn fast, but not quite as fast as the premier football prospects in the country.* College coaches who had never witnessed

————

* By comparison, Randy Moss, the star receiver of the NFL's New England Patriots, has run forty yards in 4.25 seconds. Deion Sanders was officially clocked at 4.17 in his prime, and once ran a forty-yard dash *backward* in 4.57 seconds.

the ferocity of Pat's tackles, or observed the intelligence with which he dissected the offensive schemes of his opponents, assumed he was too small to play linebacker at the elite college level, and too slow to play cornerback or safety.

Pat was crushed. But he was also pragmatic. Assessing his remaining options, he didn't think his freewheeling personality was a good fit with the restrained, straitlaced Mormon culture of BYU, and he couldn't muster any enthusiasm for the relatively undistinguished San Jose State football program. By default, therefore, he set his sights on ASU.

According to Marie, if the Sun Devils failed to offer him a scholarship, "Pat said he would have quit playing football altogether. He would have just transitioned into the next phase of his life. He didn't think football was all he had going for him."

In January 1994, Tillman traveled to Tempe, Arizona, to tour the ASU campus and meet head coach Bruce Snyder. Pat's no-bullshit candor and forthright demeanor made an impression on Snyder. Acting on little more than a hunch, he offered Pat the last of the twenty-five scholarships available for ASU football recruits. On February 2, Pat signed a formal letter of intent committing him to play for ASU. He didn't mention to Snyder or anyone else at the university that he would soon be standing trial for felony assault.

Pat knew, however, that were he to be convicted of a felony, the scholarship would certainly be rescinded. "There's always a moral turpitude clause in those scholarship agreements," explains Dan Jensen, the San Jose attorney hired by the Tillmans to represent Pat in juvenile court. The judge assigned to Pat's case, says Jensen, "was a strict, tough judge. But we showed her that he had a scholarship and he was definitely going to lose it if he got convicted of a felony. So on her own, over the objections of the district attorney, she reduced the charges from felony assault to misdemeanor assault. And Pat wasn't required to disclose a misdemeanor to the school." The judge sentenced Pat to be incarcerated for thirty days in the county lockup for juveniles and to fulfill 250 hours of community service. He would be allowed to complete his last year of high school before reporting for jail.

Darin Rosas, his family, and his friends were extremely upset that the judge had reduced the charges. "I was angry," Erin Clarke remembers. "At the time I didn't agree with the sentence at all. It seemed like the judge was more worried about Pat losing his scholarship than what happened to Darin. I felt like, 'Darin is the victim here. Why isn't anyone worried about Darin?' It didn't seem like justice had been served." Fourteen years after that day in court, however, Clarke has come to see things differently.

In April 2004, she says, "I was driving my daughter to school one morning when I heard on the radio that Pat Tillman had been killed. I remember the air being sucked out of my lungs. It was like a punch in the stomach. . . . He was the first person I knew who had died in the war, and that morning the war suddenly became very real to me." Later, from the flood of news about Tillman, Clarke learned about the decision he made to join the Army after 9/11, and the sacrifices he'd made to do it, and she was profoundly moved. She lamented that her only personal knowledge of Tillman revolved around one of the most regrettable incidents in his life. "What I take from Pat Tillman is that you are not who you are at your worst moment. After what Pat did to Darin, it seems like he really turned his life around and became quite an honorable person."

Reflecting on the Round Table brawl and its aftermath, Clarke muses, "That judge held Pat's future in her hands. She had the power to send him down one path or another, and she decided to make what turned out to be a really good decision. She said, 'I'm going to believe in you—I'm going to believe you're going to take this opportunity and do the best you possibly can with it.' And you know what? It sounds like that's what he did. I don't think there are many people on this planet who would have done as well with that kind of second chance."

CHAPTER SEVEN

Sanghisar is a village of fortresslike, mud-walled homes rising from a flat expanse of opium fields in the Panjwayi District of Kandahar Province. In most regards it resembles a hundred other crumbling hamlets in this arid corner of southeastern Afghanistan. But in the spring of 1994, as Pat was contemplating his impending incarceration, this particular community altered the course of history when the village mullah—a devout but unsophisticated thirty-five-year-old Pashtun named Mohammed Omar—gave birth to the Taliban in Sanghisar's one-room mosque.

Civil war was raging in the wake of the Soviet withdrawal. Although the worst of the violence was focused in and around Kabul, chaos afflicted the entire nation. Much of the fighting was between rival ethnic groups: Tajiks led by Ahmad Shah Massoud and Burhanuddin Rabbani; Ghazi Pashtuns led by Gulbuddin Hekmatyar and Jalaluddin Haqqani; Uzbeks controlled by the ex-communist Rashid Dostum; Hazaras led by Ismail Khan. But even in regions that were ethnically homogeneous—Kandahar, for example, was populated almost entirely by Durrani Pashtuns—the political landscape had splintered into a hodgepodge of tribal realms ruled by warlords whose militias battled each other viciously for turf and plunder.

Before the Soviet invasion, Kandahar's farmers produced an abundance of figs, melons, peaches, grapes, and pomegranates that were deservedly renowned for being the most delectable on earth. As part of the scorched-earth policy they implemented against the mujahideen, however, the Soviets not only obliterated these orchards and vineyards; they also destroyed the elaborate, centuries-old irrigation systems that had enabled the desert to bloom. To survive, the farmers started cultivating poppies instead, which needed to be watered only once every five days or so. And as the opium fields proliferated, militias vied to control the lucrative traffic in "flower oil"—a local euphemism for the gummy brown sap scraped from the plant's seed capsules to produce heroin.

Smuggling narcotics was just one among many criminal endeavors pursued by the warlords, whose entrepreneurial instincts had them constantly looking for ways to expand their sources of revenue. So-called checkpoints, for instance, sprouted like noxious weeds along every road in Afghanistan. The major thoroughfares—especially Highway A1, which formed a giant loop around the entire nation to link its principal cities—were plagued by hundreds if not thousands of such checkpoints, typically consisting of a chain or a log pulled across the road, attended by three or four bearded men brandishing AK-47s. Every time a trucker, farmer, or other traveler encountered one of these roadblocks, he would be asked at gunpoint to pay a "road tax." Refusal was not an option. Women were sometimes raped.

Sanghisar is linked to Highway A1 via a two-mile maze of crude dirt lanes. After the junction with the paved highway, twenty-three additional miles of potholed macadam lead east to Kandahar City— the provincial capital and second-largest city in Afghanistan. In 1994, during a routine trip to Kandahar, Mullah Omar was stopped and shaken down for cash at five different checkpoints on this one short stretch of highway, which made him so angry that he organized a tribal council—a *jirga*—of more than fifty mullahs to eradicate the roadblocks and halt the extortion.

The religious leaders decided to start small by pooling their weapons, forming a militia of their own, and forcefully removing a single checkpoint—the one nearest to Sanghisar. It was taken for granted that blood would be spilled, but they believed their cause was righteous and saw no other option, in any case. On the ap-

pointed day they approached the checkpoint warily with their rifles
locked and loaded, prepared for a firefight, but as they drew near, a
surprising thing happened: the hooligans manning the checkpoint
fled without firing a shot. Encouraged, the mullahs turned their attention to the next checkpoint several miles down the road, and the
outcome was similar. Before the week was out, they succeeded in removing every roadblock between Sanghisar and Kandahar. And thus
was the Taliban created. The name—a Pashto word meaning "students of Islam"—was bestowed by Omar.

The warlords of the day, unrestrained by any law or governing
body, committed reprehensible acts with impunity. Seizing young
boys and girls and forcing them into sexual slavery were routine oc-
currences. According to Ahmed Rashid's book *Taliban*, soon after
the Taliban was founded, Sanghisar residents alerted Omar that a local commander

> had abducted two teenage girls, their heads had been shaved and
> they had been taken to a military camp and repeatedly raped. Omar
> enlisted some 30 *Talibs* who had only 16 rifles between them and at-
> tacked the base, freeing the girls and hanging the commander from
> the barrel of a tank. . . .
>
> A few months later two commanders confronted each other in
> Kandahar, in a dispute over a young boy whom both men wanted to
> sodomize. In the fight that followed civilians were killed. Omar's
> group freed the boy and public appeals started coming in for the Tal-
> iban to help out in other local disputes. Omar had emerged as a
> Robin Hood figure, helping the poor against the rapacious com-
> manders. His prestige grew because he asked for no reward or credit
> from those he helped, only demanding that they follow him to set up
> a just Islamic system.

Tall and sinewy, Omar is a shy, uncharismatic man who lost his
right eye to shrapnel while fighting Najibullah's communist forces
during the mujahideen's failed assault on Jalalabad in 1989. Although a lifelong scholar of Islam, he possesses a plodding, narrow
intellect and has little knowledge of, or interest in, worldly affairs.
His interpretation of the Quran is stringently literal. But at some

point during 1994 the Prophet Muhammad came to this humble village mullah in the form of a vision, in which it was revealed to Omar that Allah had chosen him to undertake the task of bringing peace to Afghanistan. Omar, who placed great stock in dreams and apparitions, resolved to obey the Prophet's commandment. Toward that end he began recruiting students from madrassas—religious schools—to join his cause.

Although he was not a dynamic speaker, Mullah Omar made up for his lack of personal charm with earnestness and unwavering piety. His pitch to the students was well received, particularly in the numerous madrassas that had sprung up in the Pashtun tribal districts that lay just across the border in Pakistan. For nearly fifteen years more than two million Afghan refugees had been subsisting in squalid refugee camps on the Pakistan side of the frontier, and the madrassas there were teeming with the sons of these refugees—young men indoctrinated by fire-breathing Saudi clerics preaching the fundamentalist Wahhabi doctrine. These clerics instructed the Afghan youths to emulate the righteous habits of the Prophet Muhammad with the aim of reinstating the caliphate he had established in the seventh century. To restore the world to this fabled state of purity, they were urged to immerse themselves in the holy spirit of jihad. As Lawrence Wright explains in *The Looming Tower,*

> These boys had grown up in an exclusively male world, separated from their families for long periods of time. The traditions and customs and lore of their country were distant to them. They were stigmatized as beggars and sissies, and often preyed upon by men who were isolated from women. Entrenched in their studies, which were rigidly concentrated on the Quran and Sharia and the glorification of jihad, the talibs imagined a perfect Islamic society, while lawlessness and barbarity ran rampant all around them. They lived in the shadows of their fathers and older brothers, who had brought down the mighty superpower, and they were eager to gain glory for themselves. Whenever the Taliban army required reinforcements, the madrassas in Peshawar and the Tribal Areas simply shut down classes and the students went to war, praising God as the buses ferried them across the border.

The Taliban ranks expanded with astonishing speed, an indication of the craving among Afghans and Afghan refugees for a national leader who would eradicate the ubiquitous corruption, halt the depravity, and resurrect the rule of law. But the fast rise of the Taliban owed much as well to clandestine financial backing from the Directorate for Inter-Services Intelligence—the ISI, Pakistan's equivalent to the CIA—although the Taliban has never acknowledged the substantial assistance it received from Pakistan over many years (and still receives today according to credible sources).

Islamabad's reasons for supporting the Taliban were complex. Within the ISI, for example, there was (and remains today) an influential cadre of Islamists who shared Mullah Omar's fundamentalist theology. Many in Pakistan in fact viewed the Taliban and other fundamentalist *jihadis* as an effective bulwark against aggression by India, Pakistan's archenemy and nuclear rival, along the disputed border the two nations share in Kashmir. But Pakistan was also motivated to fund the Taliban for reasons that had more to do with lucre than religion or national defense: Pakistan's trucking industry had long been monopolized by a powerful transport mafia, and this organization aggressively lobbied Prime Minister Benazir Bhutto to open a reliable overland trade route across Afghanistan in order to bolster commerce between Pakistan and the Central Asia republics of Turkmenistan, Uzbekistan, and Kazakhstan. Before Pakistan's truckers could start hauling goods to and from these countries via Afghanistan Highway A1, however, the warlords needed to be brought to heel, and the Taliban appeared to offer the best prospects for accomplishing this.

On October 29, 1994, a convoy of thirty trucks organized by Pakistan's interior minister rolled west into Afghanistan to assess the security of the route through Kandahar. The convoy was led by a fundamentalist colonel in the ISI who was guided and advised by a pair of Taliban sub-commanders. The trucks were driven and guarded by eighty well-armed ex-soldiers from the Pakistan Army. Despite the size of this security force, a confederacy of local warlords brazenly hijacked the entire convoy as it approached Kandahar City.

Islamabad was outraged, and briefly considered sending a contingent of elite Pakistani commandos to rescue the convoy, but ultimately the Bhutto administration determined the plan was too risky and rejected it. Instead, it asked the Taliban to perform the rescue, and Mullah Omar obliged. On November 3, Taliban forces overran the warlords' militia, executed its commander, and liberated the trucks. That same night, taking advantage of their momentum, they attacked other militias that controlled Kandahar City and routed them as well. Within a few weeks the Taliban were in control of the entire province. By the end of 1994 their forces had swelled to twelve thousand fighters, mostly madrassa students, some as young as fourteen years old. By the middle of 1995, Omar had twenty-five thousand *jihadis* under his command, he controlled half the provinces in Afghanistan, and the Taliban were advancing steadily north toward Kabul.

Omar's impressionable young fighters believed that because they were holy warriors directed by the will of Allah, the Taliban could not lose, and this aura of invincibility affected the mujahideen they were fighting. When confronted by approaching Taliban forces, on several occasions mujahideen fighters simply surrendered en masse, without firing a shot, and then joined the Taliban themselves, at least in the case of the Pashtun mujahideen the Taliban encountered in the southern and eastern provinces. Among those who defected and came over to the Taliban was Jalaluddin Haqqani, from Khost, considered to be perhaps the most talented and effective of the mujahideen commanders.

Energized by the Taliban's victorious march north, and inflamed by religious fervor, Mullah Omar enacted his singularly draconian interpretation of Sharia, or Islamic law. By decree, every man was required to grow a beard no shorter than the span of his fist. Women were forbidden to work outside the home, or be seen in public unless accompanied by a male relative and covered head to toe in a stifling burqa. Girls were forbidden to attend school. A strict ban was enacted on such "unclean things" as satellite dishes, movies, videos, musical instruments, musical recordings, singing, dancing, dog racing, kite flying, chess, marbles, billiards, alcoholic beverages, computers, televisions, wine, lobster, nail polish, homing pigeons, firecrackers, statues, pictures, and Christmas cards.

Despite this chilling assault on education, the rights of women, and ordinary pleasures, the initial response of most countries (in-cluding the United States) to the ascendancy of the Taliban ranged from apathy to guarded optimism. Any political entity that managed to replace Afghanistan's hellish state of anarchy with some kind of order was thought to be a good thing. Or so it seemed at the time.

As Taliban forces continued to advance north and west into non-Pashtun regions, their progress slowed, and they even suffered some significant defeats. In the spring of 1995, twenty thousand Taliban fighters supported by tanks and jets advanced on Herat, adjacent to Afghanistan's western border with Iran, the stronghold of the Haz-aras—Shiite Muslims who received arms and support from Iran. When the Taliban attacked, Hazara forces led by Commander Ismail Khan slaughtered hundreds of young madrassa students and forced the Taliban to retreat all the way back to Kandahar.

Omar sent a desperate message to madrassas throughout the Pa-kistan Tribal Areas requesting reinforcements, and thousands of fresh-faced students responded without hesitation, eager to serve Allah, bearing arms provided by the ISI. Once they had regrouped, the Tal-iban counterattacked, and this time they decimated the Hazara forces and forced Khan to flee to Iran. In September the Taliban captured Herat, the five-thousand-year-old city celebrated in the writings of Herodotus, considered the cradle of Afghan civilization.

By early 1996, the Taliban had reached the margins of Kabul, threatening to overrun the nation's capital. Until then, the main mu-jahideen factions—led by Massoud, Hekmatyar, and Dostum—had continued to fight one another for control of Kabul, inflicting an ap-palling toll on the city and its inhabitants. But the arrival of Mullah Omar's army on Kabul's outskirts frightened the mujahideen com-manders into calling a hasty truce and joining forces against the Tal-iban—a coalition dubbed the Northern Alliance. Through most of the spring and summer the struggle for the capital degenerated into a bloody stalemate in which several thousand civilians were killed by Taliban rocket attacks. Then, in August, Omar persuaded Pakistan and Saudi Arabia to increase their support in order to provide the Taliban with the means to launch a decisive offensive.

In a shrewd tactical move, this offensive was not directed at Kabul itself. Instead, the Taliban skirted the capital and attacked important

Northern Alliance bases to the north and east, which were captured with ease. The Taliban were fortified in these battles by swarms of fresh recruits from madrassas across the border, whose arrival at the front lines was expedited by Pakistan. By late September the Taliban had surrounded Kabul, and had severed all lines of supply to the Northern Alliance. Ceding to the inevitable, under the cover of darkness Massoud pulled back all the way to his redoubt in the Panjshir Valley, deep in the mountains of the Hindu Kush, leaving Kabul virtually undefended.

On the night of September 26, 1996, Mullah Omar's fighters rolled into the capital without resistance, wearing their trademark black turbans and flying the white Taliban flag from their Toyota Hilux pickup trucks. The first thing they did was search out the ex-president and Soviet puppet, Mohammed Najibullah. He was found around 1:00 a.m. at his residence inside a United Nations diplomatic compound, where he had been living under house arrest since being forced from office in 1992, spending his days lifting weights, watching satellite television, and translating an English history of Afghanistan into his native Pashto. The five men who found him were led by the commander of the assault on Kabul, a Talib named Mullah Abdul Razaq. During the Najibullah regime, the Soviets had killed several members of Razaq's family, and he'd been waiting to exact revenge on Najibullah ever since.

After brutally beating Najibullah and his brother, Shahpur, Razaq and his men drove them to the Presidential Palace, where Najibullah was castrated and then dragged through the streets around the palace behind a truck, still alive. Finally he was shot to death, Shahpur was strangled, and wire nooses were twisted around the necks of both brothers. They were then strung up from a police watchtower above a traffic circle in the middle of Kabul. A mob formed around the dead men, beat their bodies with sticks, and shoved rolled-up rupees into their nostrils.

This was not the sort of "order" that had been envisioned by Western governments when they expressed the hope that Mullah Omar would prove to be the Pashtun equivalent of George Washington and become the savior of his nation—a nation that Omar had recently renamed the Islamic Emirate of Afghanistan. The Taliban now governed the country, nevertheless. The administration of President Bill Clinton issued contradictory statements about this turn of events, muddying the waters about whether the United States approved of the country's new leadership or opposed it. But some Americans were encouraged. Unocal, the American oil company, believed that with the Taliban in control it might be able to finally realize its ambition to build a lucrative pipeline across Afghanistan to carry natural gas from the former Soviet republic of Turkmenistan to Pakistan. Just weeks after Kabul was captured, Unocal opened an office in Kandahar, not far from Mullah Omar's headquarters.

To the handful of intelligence analysts who were paying close attention, however, there were many reasons to be alarmed by the Taliban victory, as well as by other recent developments in Afghanistan. During the Soviet occupation, the CIA had handed out some twenty-three hundred Stinger antiaircraft missiles to the Afghan freedom fighters. The Taliban now possessed at least fifty-three of them. Another five hundred to six hundred Stingers remained unaccounted for, but were believed to be in the hands of warlords somewhere in the country. And Sheik Osama bin Laden, who had left Afghanistan in 1990, was back.

After departing in 1990, he'd resettled in his homeland, Saudi Arabia. Not long thereafter, Iraq invaded Kuwait, prompting bin Laden to propose to the Saudi royal family that he lead thirty thousand veterans of the Soviet-Afghan War into battle against Saddam Hussein on their behalf. The Saudi leadership unceremoniously declined bin Laden's offer. Instead, they invited the United States to base 300,000 soldiers in Saudi Arabia, which bin Laden perceived as an intolerable insult. Incensed, he started mustering an army of holy warriors, which caused his family—among the most prominent in the Arab world—to disown him, and the Saudis to put him under house arrest.

In 1992, bin Laden fled to Khartoum, the capital of Sudan, where he escalated his criticisms of both the United States and the Saudi royal family, and established military training camps where hundreds of al-Qaeda fighters were taught to build bombs and conduct acts of terrorism. By this time the CIA had finally begun to pay attention to bin Laden, and the agency viewed his activities in Sudan with grow-

ing alarm. Tremendous pressure was subsequently brought to bear
on the president of Sudan to expel bin Laden, and eventually, with
sincere apologies, the former told the latter that the time had come
for him to leave. Furious, bin Laden departed but vowed to exact revenge on the United States for uprooting him. And then he contacted
some of his old mujahideen associates in Jalalabad to let them know
he was in the market for a new home. When the Afghans replied that
they would be delighted to have the sheik back among them, bin
Laden began preparations to shift his entire base of operations to
Afghanistan. Upon learning of his plans, American officials smugly
congratulated themselves for displacing him from Sudan.

Bin Laden departed Khartoum in a chartered jet on May 18,
1996, refueled in the United Arab Emirates, and landed in Jalalabad.
Two trips were required to ferry his entourage, which included three
of his four wives, several children, and approximately a hundred
bodyguards. In Afghanistan he was warmly welcomed by three commanders from the Northern Alliance, who provided him with austere
accommodations a few miles outside of the city.

At the time of bin Laden's return, Mullah Omar and most of the
Taliban leadership were extremely wary of him; among numerous
reasons for distrusting bin Laden, he had come to Afghanistan as a
guest of the Northern Alliance, with whom the Taliban were then
fighting viciously for control of the country. But bin Laden's longtime
friend Commander Jalaluddin Haqqani had recently defected to the
Taliban, and when Omar's forces captured Kabul four months after
bin Laden's arrival, bin Laden decided it would be wise to make an
overture to the man who had just driven his erstwhile hosts from
Jalalabad and now ruled the nation. Bin Laden therefore dispatched
a confidant to Kandahar and requested an audience with the Taliban
leadership.

An October meeting was arranged in Kabul between bin Laden
and one of Omar's most trusted deputies. By the time it concluded,
bin Laden had sworn an oath of loyalty to the Taliban regime, and
the Taliban had reciprocated by promising him sanctuary. The rap-
prochement seemed to please both parties very much.

The relationship was sealed a month later when bin Laden traveled to Kandahar to meet Omar in the flesh. Upon being introduced,

the Saudi sheik flattered the once-humble mullah of Sanghisar by addressing him as *Amir al-Mu'minin,* "the Prince of the Faithful"—a rarely bestowed honorific typically reserved for Islam's greatest caliphs. The flattery succeeded: Omar was charmed by bin Laden, and invited him to move his family from Jalalabad to Kandahar, where the Taliban could more easily ensure their safety. Bin Laden accepted the invitation and took possession of three compounds in and around Kandahar during the first months of 1997, whereupon he began spending much time in Omar's company. While delivering a Friday sermon at the largest mosque in the city, Omar brought bin Laden before the teeming assembly and lauded his new friend as "one of Islam's most important spiritual leaders."

The nascent partnership was not without complications, however:

- The Taliban received many millions of dollars from Saudi Arabia. But the Saudi royal family considered bin Laden a serious threat. Moreover, the Saudis maintained deep ties with the United States and were working closely with the CIA to monitor bin Laden's activities and disrupt al-Qaeda.
- The ISI, Pakistan's spy agency, had worked with bin Laden since his arrival in Afghanistan in the 1980s, when the Pakistanis and the young Saudi engineer were allied against the Soviets, and helped bring bin Laden and the Taliban together. But the ISI also received millions—perhaps billions—of dollars of clandestine aid from the Saudis, who were sworn enemies of bin Laden.
- The ISI also had a long relationship with the CIA. The latter had given billions of dollars to the Afghan mujahideen from 1978 through 1992, and most of the American support had been channeled through the ISI—which was closely allied with both the Taliban and bin Laden, who were now America's enemies.

Unquestionably, the region's politics were intricately tangled and constantly in flux. But the United States had a poor grasp of these shifting, highly nuanced dynamics and failed to appreciate the magnitude of the threat posed by the budding relationship between bin Laden and Omar. As the British journalist Jason Burke would note in the *Observer* in November 2001 (with the benefit of hindsight), the bond between the head of al-Qaeda and the Afghan leader "signified more than an alliance between the world's most wanted terrorist and the world's most reviled regime. It was the start of the final—and most critical—phase of bin Laden's development. Having secured the Taliban's protection, he was free to start building the most efficient terrorist organization the world had ever seen."

CHAPTER EIGHT

In the spring of 1994, when Santa Clara County Superior Court sentenced Pat to be incarcerated for thirty days upon his graduation from Leland High School, he was stunned and chastened. On Friday, June 17, Pat attended the Leland commencement ceremony with his classmates. He spent Saturday night hanging out with Marie and his closest friends until the sun came up, and then on Sunday morning his parents drove him to the county juvenile hall to begin serving his sentence.

When Pat's attorney had plea-bargained his original felony charge down to a misdemeanor, it kept his scholarship to Arizona State University from being automatically rescinded. But it wasn't clear what action, if any, ASU would take should Pat fail to complete his sentence before the start of the football team's summer training camp. If Pat were late to camp, or missed it altogether, he would find himself beginning his collegiate football career on shaky ground. Unproven freshman players had been cut from football teams for much less.

Pat was required to arrive in Tempe the first week of August. Serving the required thirty days behind bars by then wasn't the problem; it was doing the 250 hours of community service. Although he would spend each weekday of his imprisonment working at a job that would gradually chip away at that obligation, a parole officer explained to Pat's mother that if he relied on the juvenile hall bus sys-

tem to take him to his community service assignments, Pat was unlikely to complete the required hours before August, because the
buses were often late and sometimes didn't run at all. And the judge
was a stickler about fulfilling all 250 hours of the sentence. To get Pat
to work on time, therefore, Dannie was allowed to pick her son up
at the county lockup and drive him to his daily assignment, working
at a homeless shelter called the Julian Street Inn. A fringe benefit of
this arrangement was that on several occasions Dannie brought
Marie, or one of Pat's brothers, or one of his friends to visit with him
during the drive, which was a great consolation to him.

One of the things Pat's parents emphasized to the Tillman boys as
they were growing up was that whining wasn't acceptable behavior.
And true to the family ethos, Pat never complained about his stint behind bars. When he was released from juvenile hall in late July, he admitted that being locked up had been hard and had tested him. He
insisted, however, that he had learned more from the whole regrettable experience than from "all the good decisions he ever made," as
he later told *Sports Illustrated*.

According to Marie, "He looked around at the kids he was in jail
with and didn't see himself as that kind of person. He wasn't some
kid who was constantly in trouble and it finally caught up to him.
He'd never been arrested or even suspended from school. And now
here he was spending a month in juvenile hall with a bunch of kids
who had some pretty serious criminal records. It was definitely a
wake-up call for Pat." Although it was an expensive lesson, he'd been
shown that good intentions were not enough to ensure a positive outcome. He learned something about the perils of acting rashly, without first considering potential consequences.

If his subsequent behavior is any indication, being locked up
for thirty days was a turning point in Pat's life. The transformation would turn out to be a long, drawn-out process rather than an
overnight personality makeover, but it was nevertheless profound,
and it began to reveal itself before he was even out of jail: he started
to approach his intellectual development with the same kind of discipline he'd long applied to his athletic development. Throughout
high school Pat had received Bs and Cs with the occasional A on his
report cards. He didn't read much. When he went to juvenile hall,

however, his mother started bringing him books to pass the time, and it initiated a genuine passion for reading that persisted for the rest of his life.

———

After he was released from jail, Pat had about a week until he was due to show up at Arizona State to begin training camp. On August 2, he flew to Arizona, accompanied by Marie, his parents, and his brother Richard. When they walked out of the Phoenix airport, the temperature was well over a hundred degrees. The midsummer heat lay upon the city like a massive weight that seemed to crush the vitality in everything it touched. Being able to bear such heat for more than a few minutes was difficult to imagine, and the entire family was taken aback. Pat nevertheless accepted it as a fact of Arizona life and resolved to adapt.

As it turned out, the heat was relatively easy for him to deal with. Homesickness, though, was another matter entirely during his first months away from New Almaden. "It was an especially weird transition for him," Marie explains, "because two days after his high-school graduation he went to jail, and then when he got out, he pretty much went straight to college. He was surprised by how much he missed his family and all his friends back in Almaden. Most people don't realize it, because Pat comes across as such a tough person, but he's a homebody. He *really* depends on his friends and family."

The intensity of Pat's homesickness was exacerbated by the fact that Marie had enrolled at the University of California, Santa Barbara, five hundred miles away. "I applied to ASU," says Marie, "but I didn't really like it there. I figured it would be a mistake to make such a big decision based on some boy. So I went down to Santa Barbara instead. Both of us sort of assumed that we would stay together as a couple, even though we were going to different schools. But we also knew that when you're young, a lot can change, and that we would just have to see what happened. We always gave each other space to grow. There was an understanding that you have to do what you need to do, and if the other person decides this isn't what I want—well, then maybe you go your separate ways."

Shortly after Marie and the Tillmans bid a wrenching farewell to

Pat and returned to California, Pat accompanied the football team to the Sun Devil practice facilities at Camp Tontozona, eighty miles northeast of Tempe near the town of Payson, amid the pine forests of the Mogollon Rim. Here, in the relatively cool air fifty-four hundred feet above sea level, the team held its preseason training camp. Pat missed Marie and his family so acutely during this period that he sometimes found himself reduced to tears, and he phoned home almost every day.

During training camp, Bruce Snyder, the Sun Devils' football coach, made a point of meeting one-on-one with each new player. During his meeting with Pat he explained that incoming freshmen were typically redshirted—a designation by which they would be restricted from appearing in any games their first season but remain at ASU for five years, thereby gaining a year of training at the college level before commencing their four years of NCAA eligibility. Upon hearing from the head coach that they should expect to be redshirted, most unproven freshmen would simply nod meekly and acquiesce. But not Tillman. When Snyder told Pat that he probably wouldn't get an opportunity to play in any actual games his first year, Pat politely told Snyder, "Coach, you can play me or not play me, but I'm only going to be here four years. And then I've got things to do with my life." Although Pat desperately missed Marie, his mother, and the comforting surroundings of New Almaden, his loneliness hadn't diminished his self-assurance. Homesick or not, he didn't hesitate to let Snyder know his mind.

After seven days of grueling two-a-day practices capped by a scrimmage that drew four thousand devoted Sun Devil fans to Camp Tontozona, the team returned to Tempe shortly before the start of classes. ASU was the fourth-largest public university in the nation at that time, with more than fifty thousand students, and the campus was colossal. Because Pat was assigned to live in an athletes' dormitory far from the campus center and didn't have a car, his mother and his uncle Mike Spalding drove from California to Arizona to bring him his bicycle. When they arrived, Pat was overjoyed to see them. He slept in Dannie and Mike's hotel room during the several days they remained in Tempe, and when the academic year commenced, his mom and his uncle walked him to his first college class.

As they prepared to say good-bye and start the ten-hour drive back to the Bay Area, Pat begged them to postpone their departure until after the class was over. Seeing how sad he was, Dannie and Mike agreed. When they finally climbed into their car to leave, Pat, on the verge of bawling, gave his mom a note he'd written to both of them. As Mike steered the car west through the blistering heat of the Sonoran Desert, Dannie read the note aloud:

Mom & Mike,

    I would have just come out and said this but I know my eyes would have swelled and I would not have been able to talk. I would like to tell you that I am very glad you came to see me. I don't think you realize how much it means to me. This whole thing is a lot harder to deal with than I ever expected. It makes me feel like a woose every time I begin to cry. However, I can do nothing to change it. I'm sure I will be fine pretty soon. My moods right now change constantly from OK to sad to really sad. Your being here really helped though. It is comforting to know someone cares.

    I will call quite a bit and if either of you are bored please call, I will enjoy the company. I will probably not decide to go out and meet people for a while. . . . Thank You For Everything.

Pat

The juxtaposition of Pat's vulnerability with his fearlessness and self-assurance is not an easy thing to wrap one's mind around, but it was an absolutely central aspect of his personality. Armchair psychoanalysts might be inclined to explain his toughness as a macho pose—a protective shell he donned to disguise his insecurities. Marie strongly disagrees: "It wasn't some stereotypical tough-guy act. He really had these two opposite aspects to his personality. It was a dichotomy: he was this very tough person, but he also had this soft-hearted side, and he didn't mind showing it. And he was that way as long as I knew him. It goes back to this incredible sense he had of who he was—his self-confidence. He didn't feel the need to hide much, or pretend to be something that he wasn't. He wasn't insecure about the sensitive side, or worried that he wasn't tough. He considered both qualities important, and didn't see them as irreconcilable in any way."

CHAPTER NINE

As Pat settled into life as an ASU student, his homesickness gradually receded. Because Marie's classes at UCSB didn't begin until the end of September, she traveled to Tempe twice during that period to visit him. After starting college at Santa Barbara, she usually commuted to Arizona a couple of weekends each month to see Pat, and spoke to him on the phone every day, all of which did a lot to keep his loneliness at bay. As did the huge demands on his time made by football and classes, which left few spare moments to indulge in self-pity. Because Pat was determined to excel academically as well as athletically (as he had not done in high school), he spent almost as much time studying as he did in the gym or on the practice field—a significant change that to no small degree can be attributed to his experience behind bars. "After the Round Table incident," Marie concurs, "Pat felt he couldn't afford to be reckless and risk getting into trouble anymore." Instead, he decided to concentrate on school.

At the beginning of the semester Pat enlisted the services of a tutor to make sure he did well in his mathematics class. Two other students happened to sign up for the same tutor—his roommate and football teammate, B. J. Alford; and an uncommonly talented tennis player from Hungary named Réka Cseresnyés. Throughout the semester the three freshman athletes met with the tutor twice a week. "We studied together," says Cseresnyés, "and sometimes we would run into each other on campus or have lunch at the cafeteria. We wouldn't really hang out beyond running into each other and having these talks. But every time we'd get together, we would end up having deep conversations. So we became friends very quickly."

Cseresnyés had grown up in Budapest under a repressive communist government, witnessed the fall of the Iron Curtain as a teenager, and then leaped at the opportunity to come to the United States upon winning an athletic scholarship to attend Arizona State University. Pat was fascinated by her exotic background and barraged her with questions about life in the Soviet bloc. "I was this girl from Hungary," she recalls. "My English was rough at the time. Pretty early on, Pat became a famous athlete on campus. He had great charisma, and everybody recognized him because he had such a characteristic face. I couldn't believe he was even talking to me, someone who had a thick Hungarian accent. I was almost thinking, 'What is wrong with this guy?' "

Cseresnyés was amazed, she says, "by how friendly and down-to-earth Pat was. He was interested in other people and remembered things about them. He talked about his girlfriend so nicely. He was interested in the world beyond sports. Mostly we talked about politics and international relations. He was a critical thinker and would always challenge me—he was an amazing questioner. Which was the best way to figure out what Pat was thinking, because he didn't like to talk about himself that much. He would always turn the conversation back to whoever he was talking to: 'So what's going on with you?' " Their discussions and study sessions planted the seeds of a friendship that lasted, and strengthened, over the rest of Pat's life.

At the end of their first semester at ASU, both Tillman and Cseresnyés received As in their respective math classes, and Pat excelled in his other classes as well, earning a 3.5 grade point average. During his second semester it improved to 3.81. The semester after that, in the fall of 1995, he received an A in each of his five courses, for a perfect 4.0 GPA. "Once he got in the habit of studying, he found a lot of success," Marie says. Part of the motivation for that success, she adds, "was that most people expected football players to be kind of stupid. I think it appealed to him to go against the stereotype. He liked defying expectations."

Pat also controverted the assumptions of those who thought he was too small and too slow to play college football for a powerhouse Division I-A school. During his first year he was only put into games as a special-teams player, during punts and kickoffs, and the Sun Devils had a lackluster season with three wins and eight losses. Pat earned a varsity letter, nevertheless, and Coach Snyder characterized his play as "so smart and so aggressive." The following year Pat started just one game, but he frequently came into games off the bench to play inside linebacker, and over the course of the 1995 season recorded the sixth-highest number of tackles on the team.

That year the Sun Devils' record improved to 7-4, although there were some embarrassing defeats along the way, the most humiliating of which was inflicted by the University of Nebraska Cornhuskers. On the first play from scrimmage, Nebraska ran the football sixty-five yards for a touchdown, and the rout was under way. The Cornhuskers had scored nine touchdowns by halftime, a school record, and the final score was 77–28.

The loss was especially humbling for the Sun Devils' defense. If a football team racks up that many points, it suggests that the team being scored against has some serious defensive flaws. Nevertheless, when the 1996 season commenced the following September, Sun Devil supporters were optimistic about their prospects. Many of the team's best players from 1995 were back, most prominently the quarterback Jake "the Snake" Plummer, a leading contender for the Heisman Trophy. Although Pat was not yet considered to be of the same caliber as Plummer, the ASU coaches acknowledged that he had developed into an exceptional defensive player by designating him the starting weakside linebacker for the new season. Lyle Setencich, who coached the Sun Devils' linebackers, told *Sports Illustrated* that Pat was "the best player I've ever coached at reading body language. One game, he noticed that a tackle would look inside every time his team ran a draw, and sure enough, Pat read it and hit the fullback right in the mouth."

Pat was thrilled by his promotion to starter, and so was his family. The Tillmans were an uncommonly tight clan. Nothing was more important to Pat than Marie, his parents, his brothers, and his uncle Mike. It would be hard to overstate how much their support and company meant to him. He was thus overjoyed when his brother Kevin—who had been drafted by the Houston Astros after graduating from high school and received an offer to play professional baseball—instead accepted a baseball scholarship at Arizona State and enrolled as a freshman in the fall of 1996.

Pat and his ASU teammates won their first two football games of the 1996 season, but for their third game would face Nebraska again. After clobbering the Sun Devils in 1995, Nebraska had gone undefeated through the remainder of the year, went on to win its second consecutive national championship, and was generally considered the best team in the history of college football. When the Cornhuskers came to Tempe to play ASU on September 21, 1996, they had won twenty-six games in a row (the last time they'd lost was in 1993) and were ranked first in the nation in every significant poll.

On the evening before the game, the ASU players asked the coaches to vacate the premises and then proceeded to jack themselves up for the rematch by screaming, pounding on the walls, overturning tables, jumping on furniture, and tossing chairs around the room. When they emerged, according to one report, they brought to mind crazed animals. The next day they played with unprecedented focus and intensity.

Come Saturday afternoon it was ninety-one degrees in the shade, although there was no shade to be had on the field in Sun Devil Stadium, where seventy-four thousand screaming fans filled the seats. ASU received the opening kickoff and then moved the ball seventy yards downfield on its first five plays from scrimmage. On the sixth play, Plummer was sacked for a loss. Unfazed, after taking the next snap, he dropped back for a pass, but a Nebraska defensive end had anticipated the play and blitzed into the backfield with an unobstructed shot at him; it looked as though the ASU quarterback was about to be taken down again. Plummer, however, proceeded to give an astonishing demonstration of why he was called "the Snake": he somehow managed to wriggle out from under the tackler's grasp, scramble to his left, and sidearm the ball twenty-five yards to the receiver Keith Poole, who was standing alone in the end zone, putting ASU ahead, 7–0.

That ASU had scored first was surprising. But everyone expected

Nebraska to come thundering back: over the course of the previous season the ASU defense had ranked dead last in the Pac-10 Conference, and was widely disparaged as the team's great weakness. Nevertheless, as the Sun Devils kicked off to Nebraska, Pat and the rest of the ASU defense resolved to shut down the Cornhuskers and hold on to their lead.

Pat's primary assignment going into the game was to cover the option pitchout—to stop Nebraska from gaining big yardage on plays in which the quarterback Scott Frost tried to fool the linebackers into thinking he was going to run with the ball or throw a pass downfield and then instead tossed a lateral outside to Ahman Green, a speedy tailback who would later become a star for the Green Bay Packers. This deceptive play was one of the most effective weapons in the Nebraska arsenal, and was especially hard to defend against. It would demand astute, lightning-fast assessments by Tillman to determine how to react to the option as it unfolded.

Shortly after the Sun Devils' touchdown, with the Cornhuskers on the Nebraska seven-yard line, Frost attempted just such a play: scurrying to his right, he hucked an underhand pitchout to Green that came in unexpectedly hard, causing Green to bobble the ball and then drop it. Although Green managed to scoop it up quickly from the turf, he seemed rattled by the sight of Pat accelerating toward him, and thus never got the ball properly tucked away. It squirted out of Green's hands a second time and bounced to the ground behind the goal line. Before Green could recover it, Tillman and his teammate Mitchell Freedman converged on the loose football and swatted it out of the end zone for a safety. ASU now led, 9–0. The purportedly invincible Cornhuskers looked stunned.

In the second quarter ASU kicked a twenty-seven-yard field goal, Tillman tackled Frost in the end zone for another safety, and then ASU kicked a forty-four-yard field goal to give the Sun Devils a 17–0 lead at halftime. In the third quarter ASU scored yet another safety. In the fourth quarter the Nebraska offense finally started to play effectively, and put together a drive that moved the ball most of the way to the goal line. A Cornhusker touchdown seemed imminent. With less than two minutes remaining in the game, Green attempted to run the ball into the end zone, but he fumbled on the ASU three-yard line, and Pat dove on the loose ball to preserve the 19–0 shutout—punctuating an afternoon of brilliant play by Tillman that contributed substantially to ASU's shocking upset of the Cornhuskers. At the conclusion of the game, thousands of delirious fans swarmed onto the field, pulled down both goalposts, and carried one of them four blocks down Tempe's Mill Avenue.

As the 1996 season unfolded, the Sun Devils kept winning, suggesting that their upset of Nebraska was perhaps no fluke. On September 28, ASU defeated the University of Oregon, 48–27. A week later they beat Boise State, 56–7, and then the week after that beat UCLA, 42–34. On October 19, when the Sun Devils overcame the formidable USC Trojans in double overtime, 48–35, sportswriters began to mention the possibility that the team could go undefeated and end the year ranked number one in the country. The roll continued with wins over Stanford, Oregon State, California, and the University of Arizona. At the conclusion of the regular season ASU was a perfect 11-0, and had earned an invitation to play in the Rose Bowl on New Year's Day.

———————

The video player starts to click and whir, and an aerial shot of a gigantic football stadium fills the television screen as a familiar voice intones, "ABC Sports welcomes you to the Rose Bowl! The granddaddy! The Buckeyes of Ohio State against the Sun Devils of Arizona State! . . . Happy New Year and welcome everybody. I'm Brent Musburger with the coach Dick Vermeil. ASU—they have the ability to win it all!"

On the video it's January 1, 1997—a gray, drizzly afternoon in Anaheim, California. The entire Tillman family is present somewhere in the packed stadium to watch Pat play, as are dozens of Pat's friends. The Sun Devils are ranked second in the college polls; if they defeat the Buckeyes today, they will be the national champions.

ASU wins the coin toss and quarterback Jake Plummer, a close friend of Pat's, informs the referee that the Sun Devils will receive the kickoff. The OSU kicker boots the ball downfield as 100,645 people bellow their approval from the stands. After returning the kickoff to their own thirty-three-yard line, the Sun Devils move the ball to midfield for a first down, but then their offense sputters and they have to punt. Pat comes into the game for the first time with the punting squad, his hair spilling across the shoulders of his jersey from beneath his helmet.

The ASU kicker punts the ball, Pat hesitates for a moment to force the OSU blockers to commit, then dances around three of them and sprints furiously downfield as the pigskin arcs high into the leaden sky. Tillman's body language is so distinctive that there's no mistaking him even when he appears as a minuscule figure darting across the television screen, much too small for the number on his jersey to be visible. David Boston, the Buckeye player waiting to receive the football, catches it cleanly and dodges a tackler with a quick juke to the side. A moment later, however, a second ASU player wraps his arms around the Buckeye ballcarrier and stands him upright, and then Pat hurtles into both of them at maximum velocity, driving Boston backward for three yards before slamming him to the ground.

Two plays later the Buckeyes' quarterback, Stanley Jackson, takes the snap and tries to run with it, but Pat penetrates the OSU defense and tackles Jackson for a five-yard loss. "Jackson . . . down at the thirteen-yard line," Musburger exclaims, "as the Sun Devils brought heat right up against the middle: Pat Tillman and Shawn Swayda." On the next play Pat again gets to Jackson behind the line of scrimmage and brings him down for another loss, forcing the Buckeyes to punt from their own end zone. For the first thirty minutes, the game is a defensive standoff, and when the teams leave the field for halftime, the score is tied, 7–7.

On the first possession in the third quarter, ASU kicks a field goal, but OSU storms right back with a seventy-two-yard touchdown pass to Demetrious Stanley, and at the start of the fourth quarter the Buckeyes are up, 14–10. With less than six minutes remaining in the game, things are looking grim for the Sun Devils. OSU has the ball at the ASU twenty-one-yard line and is threatening to score again, putting the game out of reach. On third down the OSU quarterback throws a short pass to Stanley again, whom Tillman is covering one-on-one. With Stanley's tremendous speed, it should be a mismatch, but Pat anticipates the receiver's moves, stays right with him as he cuts to the inside, and slaps the pass to the ground as the ball arrives, forcing the Buckeyes to attempt a field goal on fourth down. ASU blocks the kick, recovers it, and runs the ball downfield for a touchdown. The crowd goes wild, but a penalty nullifies the score, and the ball is brought back to the ASU forty-two-yard line.

With time running out in a game in which they have had trouble moving the ball, the Sun Devils need a touchdown on this possession or they will lose. Plummer has been sacked five times. His receivers have dropped eight of his passes. But the Sun Devils have been coming from behind all season at the last minute to win, and Plummer orchestrates a thrilling drive that takes his team to the OSU nine-yard line. There, however, the OSU defense stiffens, and sacks Plummer yet again for a loss. On third down, with a minute and forty-seven seconds left to play, ASU coach Bruce Snyder calls a timeout to figure out what to do.

After the Sun Devils come back on the field, Plummer takes the snap and drops back to pass, but the Buckeyes launch a ferocious all-out blitz, and all the ASU receivers are tightly covered. As OSU tacklers converge on Plummer from all directions, he ducks and weaves and scrambles first right and then left, barely slipping away from the grasp of one Buckeye after another. "Plummer in trouble!" Musburger announces. "He steps away . . . cuts free . . . breaks loose. . . . [He's at] the five. . . . Touchdown, Sun Devils! The Snake does it again! This team won't die!" The ASU players mob Plummer in the end zone. Musburger and Vermeil start congratulating the Sun Devils' quarterback for leading the astounding comeback. With just over a minute and a half remaining, an ASU victory appears to be in the bag.

But after the Buckeyes receive the ensuing kickoff, quarterback Joe Germaine starts guiding his team efficiently down the field, pushing the ball to the ASU five-yard line with twenty-four seconds left on the clock. From the sideline, OSU coach John Cooper sends in a play designated "two left twins 240X smash." Germaine takes the snap and drops back to pass. David Boston, lined up as the Buckeye split end, smashes into his defender and then spins away to the outside. Germaine lobs him a soft pass, Boston gathers it in and prances untouched across the goal line. Ohio State wins, 20–17.

To come so close to winning the Rose Bowl and becoming national champions, only to have it all slip away in the game's final seconds, was a crushing blow to the Arizona State players and fans. Pat, however, spent little time agonizing over the defeat. He had acquitted himself well on the field, and in any case there was nothing he or anyone else could do to change its outcome. He simply accepted the loss and moved on.

CHAPTER TEN

One of the people Pat roomed with at Arizona State was a three-hundred-pound teammate named Jeremy Staat who was considered the best defensive lineman in the Pac-10 Conference when the Sun Devils began the 1997 season, eight months after their bitter defeat in the Rose Bowl. Because he was uncommonly quick for a big man and exceptionally talented, Staat attracted a great deal of attention from National Football League scouts and agents. When the University of Southern California arrived in Tempe to play ASU on October 11, an agent named Frank Bauer who hoped to represent Staat was in the stands watching the game. "I'd come to see Jeremy play," says Bauer, "when all of a sudden I see this raggedy-ass linebacker named Pat Tillman running down the field, crazy as heck. He only weighs about 208, but he's hitting the hell out of people, and he's fearless. I'm going, 'Holy cow! . . . I've gotta go talk to this Tillman kid.' I didn't even know who he was. He wasn't on anybody's radar in the NFL. Nobody had any reports on him."

Following the game, which ASU won, 35–7, Bauer went down to the locker room to say hello to Staat and then sought out Tillman. "Here's this kid with the long hair, wearing shorts and flip-flops," Bauer recalls. "I told him, 'Hey, I think you can play in the National Football League.' He looks at me with those eyes of his and he goes, 'Really?' " Actually, Pat didn't need Bauer or anybody else to tell him he could play in the NFL; he'd already made that determination on his own. But he took Bauer's card and agreed to talk again in January after the Sun Devils' football season, and Pat's college career, had concluded.

Sun Devils fans had looked forward to 1997 with high hopes, even though Jake Plummer and five other star players had graduated the previous spring. When the season ended, ASU was 9-3, finishing the year with a win over Iowa in the Sun Bowl in El Paso, Texas, on December 31—an impressive record, but a distinct letdown after competing in the Rose Bowl for the national championship the previous year. Pat had performed brilliantly, regardless: he led the team with forty-seven unassisted tackles, was credited with four sacks and three interceptions, and was voted the defensive player of the year in the Pac-10 Conference. Having attended classes during the previous two summers, Pat had accrued enough credits to earn his bachelor's degree in just three and a half years, and in December 1997 he graduated summa cum laude with a 3.84 grade point average. After receiving his diploma, he remained in Tempe in order to prepare for the NFL draft.

If he was considered a long shot for playing at the Division I-A college level after high school, even fewer people believed Tillman stood much chance of making it to the NFL. Athletes who manage to reach that rarefied stratum must survive a ruthless culling process: only 6 percent of the kids who play high-school football go on to play in college; and only about 1 percent of those college players advance to the NFL. Pat had never paid much heed to the odds, however, and his confidence in his own abilities remained undiminished.

Several of Pat's ASU teammates also aspired to play in the NFL. They spent the first months of 1998 training together in preparation for the annual NFL Scouting Combine, a weeklong event held every February at the RCA Dome in Indianapolis, wherein the most promising NFL prospects undergo a battery of rigorous trials administered by NFL scouts, coaches, and general managers. Participation in the combine was by invitation only, however, and when the invitations went out, Pat failed to receive one. The snub definitely bothered him, but other avenues of entry to the NFL remained open, and he used the brush-off as a goad.

The 1998 NFL draft was scheduled to begin on April 18. In March, ASU held a so-called Pro Day at Sun Devil Stadium for NFL scouts and coaches to evaluate ASU players who didn't attend the combine. Pat saw this as his best chance to impress a team and get drafted, so he resolved to go for broke in the tryout.

Because the Arizona Cardinals were based in Phoenix and played their home games at Sun Devil Stadium, the Cardinals organization had been paying more attention to Tillman than the other NFL teams had, and therefore understood that he possessed intangible attributes that didn't show up in the scouting reports. Cardinal general manager Bob Ferguson, defensive coordinator Dave McGinnis, and defensive backs coach Larry Marmie showed up at Pro Day to put Tillman through his paces. Having already decided that Pat was too small to play linebacker in the NFL, they asked him to try out as a safety, which demanded a significantly different set of skills, then held what was scheduled to be a fifteen-minute evaluation on the field. Pat, however, refused to let the coaches leave until he'd performed as well as possible in every drill, extending the tryout an extra thirty minutes. At the end of the evaluation, Pat was hopeful they'd seen enough to want to draft him.

The NFL draft was televised live from Madison Square Garden over two consecutive days. At the end of the first day, only two of seven rounds had been completed. Although the Pittsburgh Steelers selected Jeremy Staat (represented by the agent Frank Bauer, like Pat) early in the second round, Pat wasn't drafted by any of the thirty-two teams on day one, which didn't surprise him. By the conclusion of the sixth round, however, as the 1998 draft drew to a close, Pat still hadn't been chosen.

The Cardinals had three picks remaining in the seventh round. Staring anxiously at a television in the home of Marie's parents as this final round got under way, Pat, Marie, and their families watched as the Cardinals used two of these picks to draft other players. When their last pick came up, they selected Pat—as the 226th of 241 players chosen. The Cardinals offered him a one-year contract for the minimum NFL salary of $158,000, plus a $21,000 signing bonus. By way of comparison, the first player chosen in that year's draft, Peyton Manning, received a six-year deal from the Indianapolis

Colts worth $48 million, with an immediate $11.6 million signing bonus.

The mere fact that Tillman had signed a contract, moreover, was no guarantee that he would make the team. He would still have to compete fiercely with both veterans and other rookies at the Cardinals' training camp for a spot on the roster. If Pat failed to make the cut, he wouldn't receive a nickel of his salary.

———

Despite being one of the most lionized students at ASU—a handsome, charismatic football star over whom countless women swooned—Pat had remained devoted to Marie ever since their first date five years earlier and did not philander. Although Marie is by nature reserved, when she elects to share her thoughts she tends to speak bluntly and to the point; from the beginning, her relationship with Pat was based on such candor. "Pat was pretty straightforward," she says. "There was never a lot of game playing in our relationship, even when we were very young. We were very honest with one another; I think that's why we were able to stay together."

Pat and Marie had long intended to live together after they both graduated from college. After he was drafted by the Cardinals, she figured they would be residing in Phoenix. "Pat was confident he would make it with some NFL team," Marie remembers. "But he told me not to come to Arizona until after training camp, when he would know for sure whether he was going to play for the Cardinals."

The Cardinals held their preseason camp in Flagstaff, 120 miles north of Phoenix, on the campus of Northern Arizona University. In college, Pat's teammates called him by a variety of predictable monikers, some of which—"Goldilocks" and "Fabio" being the most prevalent—were inspired by his shoulder-length hair. But his best-known nickname was "Hit Man," for the ferocity of his tackles—not only against rivals in games, but against teammates during ordinary practice drills as well. Because Pat was expected to be one of the first players cut from the Cardinals, he knew that if he wanted to stick around, he would need to perform at full intensity at every practice and make the coaches take notice of him right out of the gate.

During their evaluation of Pat at the ASU Pro Day, the Cardinals told him that if he hoped to play safety in the NFL, he would have to lose at least five pounds in order to improve his speed when covering fleet receivers like Amani Toomer, Jerry Rice, and Randy Moss. When Pat showed up in Flagstaff already seven pounds lighter than he'd played in college, the coaches took note, but losing a little weight wasn't going to be enough to win him a spot on the roster. On the second day of camp, in the middle of a drill intended to enhance the pass coverage skills of the defensive backs, he saw an opportunity to make a more persuasive impression. After a veteran 250-pound fullback named Cedric Smith caught a short pass along the sideline, Pat—who weighed nearly 60 pounds less—launched himself at Smith like a missile, knocked the ball from his grasp, and then drilled the massive runner into the turf. It was an absolutely clean hit, and the force with which Tillman delivered the tackle impressed the coaches, but as Smith went down he tore the anterior cruciate ligament in one of his knees, ending his football career. Tillman regretted injuring the veteran, but injuries were an ever-present risk in the NFL, and as a rookie, he told a reporter for the *Arizona Republic*, "you do what you have to do to make the team. You have to let them tell you to calm down."

Ordinarily, NFL coaches try to discourage their players from playing at full speed and hitting with maximum force during practice, in order to lessen the chance of injuries like the one that removed Smith from the Cardinals' roster. But the Cardinals had won only four of sixteen games in 1997, and had been considered one of the worst teams in the league for many years. They had a reputation for playing without passion. So head coach Vince Tobin decided that an inspired rookie who raised the intensity of preseason camp might not be a bad thing, and he allowed Tillman to continue to hit aggressively during practice.

In August the Cardinals played four exhibition games, during which Pat tallied twenty-five tackles, more than any other member of the team. On August 29, in the last of these preseason games, Arizona played the Oakland Raiders in Oakland, and dozens of Pat's friends and family from the Bay Area came to watch him. Motivated by their presence, he intercepted a pass—the first of his NFL career—

that led to a Cardinals touchdown, putting them ahead, 21–14, to win the game.

Eight days later, when the Cardinals traveled to Dallas to commence the regular season against the Cowboys, the Arizona coaches told Tillman he would be starting the game at free safety, surprising almost everyone but Pat, Marie, and his family. "I always knew Patty would be a fantastic special-teams player in the NFL," says his agent, Frank Bauer, "but to be the starting safety as a rookie in his very first game—he fooled the hell out of everybody."

CHAPTER ELEVEN

Throughout high school and college, Tillman had worn the number 42 on his football jersey. When he joined the Cardinals, that number already belonged to Kwamie Lassiter, his primary rival for the free-safety position on the starting roster, so Pat was issued the number 40 instead. He'd worn this new number for the first time a month before the 1998 regular-season opener, during the first game of the preseason, back on August 7, when the Cardinals traveled to Michigan to play the Detroit Lions.

In the predawn hours on the day of that game, as Pat was asleep in his hotel room, a Toyota delivery truck appeared at the entrance to a parking lot behind the American embassy in Nairobi, Kenya. One of the two Saudis riding in the truck's cab jumped out and demanded that the guard raise the gate, and when he refused, the Saudi hurled a loud but harmless flashbang grenade toward the embassy. Several seconds later, after people inside had rushed to the windows of the six-story building to see what had caused the small explosion, the Saudi who'd stayed in the truck detonated two thousand pounds of explosives crammed into the back of the vehicle. The local time in East Africa was 10:30 a.m.

The titanic blast obliterated the entire rear side of the embassy and completely flattened a much flimsier building next door, a secretarial college. Thousands of victims were buried alive in the smoldering rubble; their screams and moans could be heard for days. The death count was 213 people. Approximately 4,500 were injured, including more than 150 who were blinded by flying glass.

Nine minutes after the attack in Nairobi, a fuel truck carrying a similar load of explosives pulled up to the American embassy in the largest city in Tanzania, Dar es Salaam—an Arabic name meaning "Abode of Peace"—and the truck was detonated by its Egyptian driver. Eleven people were killed and eighty-five wounded in this blast.

The attacks, 420 miles apart, had been carried out by members of al-Qaeda under the direction of Osama bin Laden and his collaborator Ayman al-Zawahri. Six months earlier, while Tillman was preparing for the NFL draft in Phoenix, the two al-Qaeda leaders, purportedly acting on behalf of a coalition they called the "World Islamic Front for Jihad Against Jews and Crusaders," had faxed a fatwa from Afghanistan to a London newspaper in which they declared:

> [F]or more than seven years the United States has been occupying the land of the Two Holy Places, the Arabian Peninsula, plundering its riches, dictating to its rulers, humiliating its people, terrorizing its neighbors, and turning its Peninsula bases into spearheads through which to attack neighboring Muslims. . . .
>
> All of these crimes and sins committed by America clearly demonstrate a declaration of war on God, his Messenger [the Prophet Muhammad], and Muslims. . . .
>
> On that basis, and in compliance with God's order, we issue the following fatwa to all Muslims:
>
> By the ruling, it is an individual duty for every Muslim who can do it to kill Americans and their allies—civilian and military—in any country where it is possible to do so. . . .
>
> With God's help, we call on every Muslim who believes in God and wishes to be rewarded to comply with God's order to kill Americans and plunder their money wherever and whenever they find it. We also call on the Muslim *Ulema* [Islamic scholars], leaders, youth, and soldiers to launch raids on Satan's American troops and Satan's supporters allying with them in order to displace their leaders so that they may learn a lesson.

Although the international news media had disseminated this fatwa widely when it was issued on February 23, few people paid much attention to it at the time. After August 7, bin Laden and his fatwa were regarded in an entirely new light not only by Americans but by people in other parts of the world as well—especially Muslims of a fundamentalist bent. Disaffected young men from the Arabian Peninsula, Chechnya, North Africa, Kashmir, and elsewhere began to flock to al-Qaeda camps in eastern Afghanistan to receive training in the skills necessary to wage jihad against Americans and Jews. "But to most of the world and even to some members of al-Qaeda," observed Lawrence Wright in his book *The Looming Tower,*

> the attacks seemed pointless, a showy act of mass murder with no conceivable effect on American policy except to provoke a massive response.
>
> But that, as it turned out, was exactly the point. Bin Laden wanted to lure the United States into Afghanistan, which was already being called the graveyard of empires.

President Bill Clinton and his inner circle immediately began to initiate rescue operations in Nairobi and Dar es Salaam, and to figure out how they should retaliate against al-Qaeda. A full-scale military campaign against bin Laden and his Taliban allies in Afghanistan was quickly ruled out. The Clinton administration believed that such a drastic move was disproportionate to the scale of the terrorist attacks, and would be hard to sell to Congress and the American people. Moreover, Clinton was deeply entangled in the growing scandal over his dalliance with the White House intern Monica Lewinsky. His presidency had been significantly crippled as a consequence, stripping him of the public trust and political capital required to launch a war. After considering the few practical options remaining, Clinton's advisers determined that the best course of action would be to conduct a surgical air strike against bin Laden.

On August 17, while the special prosecutor Kenneth Starr was grilling Clinton for five excruciating hours about his sexual liaisons with Lewinsky, the CIA director, George Tenet, provided the president's national security team with a list of potential al-Qaeda targets.

At the top of the list was one of bin Laden's favorite hideouts, a sprawling *jihadi* training complex in eastern Afghanistan's Khost Province known as Zawar Kili, whence bin Laden had issued his February 23 fatwa. That evening—after insisting for eight months, "I did not have sexual relations with that woman"—Clinton appeared on national television to confess, "Indeed I did have a relationship with Ms. Lewinsky that was not appropriate. In fact, it was wrong. It constituted a critical lapse in judgment and a personal failure on my part for which I am solely and completely responsible."

The day's salacious revelations generated a paroxysmal flood of media coverage that eclipsed all other news for days, although Clinton insisted none of it influenced his thinking on how best to strike back against bin Laden. Shortly after his televised mea culpa, the president authorized cruise-missile attacks against two terrorist targets: a pharmaceutical factory in Sudan believed by the CIA to have been used by al-Qaeda to manufacture chemical weapons; and Zawar Kili—where, according to CIA intelligence, a summit would be held on August 20 between bin Laden and the senior al-Qaeda leadership.

Arrayed across a ten-square-mile maze of twisting ravines and rock-studded ridgelines, Zawar Kili consisted of more than a hundred buildings augmented by seventy limestone caves that had been expanded into elaborate underground bunkers, the largest of which extended the better part of a mile into the side of a mountain. Actually a complex of heavily fortified villages, the so-called training camp was located just north of the Pakistan border, fourteen miles south of Khost City, and twenty miles east of the canyon where Pat Tillman would die six years later.

Zawar Kili was well-known to U.S. intelligence analysts. During the Soviet occupation in the 1980s it functioned as an important base for the Americans' mujahideen allies, and numerous CIA officers, diplomats, and Western journalists visited the complex, as had the maverick Texas congressman Charlie Wilson, the man credited with persuading Congress to give billions of dollars in aid to the Afghan mujahideen. Zawar Kili was built by one of the leading recipients of that American munificence, Commander Jalaluddin Haqqani, who had recruited bin Laden to enlarge it for him not long after the latter arrived in Afghanistan. Working together on the Zawar Kili construction initiated a lasting friendship, and Haqqani developed into an important role model for the impressionable Saudi.

Two of the most famous battles between the Soviets and the mujahideen were fought at Zawar Kili. Approximately five hundred hardened Afghan fighters, known as the Zawar Regiment, were permanently based there during the Soviet conflict, and their stronghold was considered a potent symbol of mujahideen invincibility. Eager to deflate this reputation, in September 1985 the Soviets mounted a massive attack on Zawar Kili. The battle lasted for forty-two days, and killed or wounded more than 80 percent of the mujahideen fighters. The survivors held their ground against the infidels, however, and Soviets were eventually forced to concede the battle and withdraw.

In the spring of 1986 the Soviets directed another campaign against Zawar Kili in which jet aircraft fired guided missiles at the entrances to the largest subterranean bunkers. Commander Haqqani and 150 of his fighters were inside one of these caves when a missile made a direct hit on its entrance, trapping the mujahideen behind hundreds of tons of rubble. Other Soviet aircraft carpet bombed the complex soon thereafter, however, and inadvertently blasted away the confining debris, allowing Haqqani and his men to escape unharmed. But after seventeen days of intense fighting, the advanced Soviet weaponry proved to be too much for the mujahideen. With nearly three hundred of their men dead and more than three hundred wounded, they were forced to flee into the surrounding mountains, allowing Soviet and DRA forces to take possession of the complex.

The communists were surprised to find a mosque, bakeries, mechanical shops, a well-stocked library that included CIA bomb-making manuals, and a hotel with comfortable furniture and carpeted floors. There was even a hospital with sophisticated American-made medical equipment. But the Soviets were terrified that a counterattack was imminent, so they held Zawar Kili for only five hours before beating another hasty retreat. Although the Soviets trumpeted their brief occupation as a major victory, Haqqani's fighters immediately reoccupied the legendary redoubt and did not relinquish it again for the remainder of the war.

Undeterred by its indomitable reputation, on August 20, 1998, the U.S. Navy launched sixty-six Tomahawk cruise missiles at Zawar Kili from warships in the Arabian Sea, more than seven hundred miles away. Christened Operation Infinite Reach, the attack destroyed some twenty or thirty buildings but killed only six *jihadis*: three Yemenis, an Uzbek, an Egyptian, and one Saudi. Neither bin Laden, al-Zawahri, Haqqani, nor any other al-Qaeda leader was among the casualties. As it happened, bin Laden had been en route to Zawar Kili just prior to the attack, and probably would have been present at the time the missiles hit if the trip had gone as planned. Upon arriving at a fork in the road midway in the journey, however, he changed his mind on the spur of the moment and asked his driver to take him to Kabul instead of Zawar Kili, a serendipitous turn of events that perhaps saved his life.

More than thirty of the Tomahawks allegedly came to earth well south of the training camp, on the Pakistan side of the border, killing two Pakistani bystanders. According to unconfirmed reports, a number of the eighteen-foot-long missiles landed without exploding, were salvaged by bin Laden, and were then sold to China for at least $10 million. Even more damaging to American interests, bin Laden's stature in the Muslim world was enhanced beyond measure by the failed strike. The president of the world's richest, most technologically advanced nation had taken his best shot at killing bin Laden, and the al-Qaeda leader had survived without a scratch. Like a supervillain in a Marvel comic book, he seemed to be endowed with the ability to absorb the mightiest blows his enemy could deliver, draw energy from them, and become more powerful as a consequence.

Bin Laden gloated in the aftermath of the missile attack, and claimed that it was a ploy by Clinton to divert attention from the Lewinsky scandal. His deputy's reaction was more ominous. "Tell the Americans that we aren't afraid of bombardment, threats, and acts of aggression," al-Zawahri warned in an interview with the BBC. "We suffered and survived the Soviet bombings for ten years in Afghanistan, and we are ready for more sacrifices. The war has only just begun; the Americans should now await the answer."

CHAPTER TWELVE

After Pat was drafted by the Cardinals, he rented an inexpensive one-bedroom apartment in the Phoenix suburb of Chandler, less than a mile from the Cardinals' practice fields and training facility. By late August 1998, around the time of the failed missile strike in Afghanistan, he felt sufficiently confident that he would make the team that he suggested to Marie that she come out to Arizona and move in with him. "I had a hard transition moving out there," she says. "It was definitely a big adjustment for me. The problem wasn't living with Pat; we got along really easily." Her difficulties, she explains, "were more of a typical 'postgraduation freak-out' type of thing. I didn't know anybody. I didn't particularly like living in Phoenix. I didn't know what I wanted to do for work."

About nine months after moving, Marie was hired by the local newspaper the *Arizona Republic* as a designer. "It was a good job," she says, "but in the group of people I worked with, I was the youngest by far. It was my first real work experience. It was fine, but I was a little disillusioned. Like, 'This is it? Why was I in such a hurry to finish college?' "

Pat had no such qualms about his new job in the National Football League. When he was made the starting free safety in the initial game of the 1998 regular season, he became the first rookie to start at that position for the Cardinals in ten years. Arizona lost its first two games, badly, but Pat played well in both of them, making eigh-teen tackles and deflecting a pass. And as the season progressed, the team started to win more games than it lost—something downtrod-den Cardinals fans hadn't experienced in fourteen years.

Learning to play free safety was extremely challenging for Pat, however, primarily because he was frequently required to cover whippet-fast receivers on deep pass plays, something he hadn't had to do much as a linebacker. Although he performed well most of the time, occasionally opposing teams took advantage of his inexperi-ence and relative lack of speed to burn him badly on long passes downfield. By late November, with five games left in the regular sea-son, the Cardinals were 6-5. If they could win three of their remain-ing five games, they would make it to the playoffs for the first time since the strike-shortened year of 1982. Because Pat had made some rookie mistakes, Coach Vince Tobin decided to bench him and start Kwamie Lassiter for the rest of the season instead, hoping the veteran free safety would give the team a better chance of going to the play-offs. When reporters asked Pat how he felt about losing the starter's job, his reply was brief, but his disappointment was clear: "I appre-ciate your concern, but I have nothing to say."

As it happened, the Cardinals lost the next two games, despite re-placing Tillman with Lassiter. But then, with their backs to the wall, the team regained its mojo and won the last three games of the sea-son—two of them via long field goals with no time left on the clock. And, *mirabile dictu,* the resulting 9-7 record was good enough to send the much-maligned Cardinals to the playoffs. A week later, they traveled to Dallas for the NFC wild-card game and stunned the Cow-boys by beating them, 20–7, the first time the Cardinals had won a playoff game since 1947. The dream came to an abrupt end a week after that when they lost to the Minnesota Vikings, but 1998 marked an astonishing turn of fortune for the previously hapless Cardinals, and Pat had contributed much to the success.

He was a good fit with the team, and was comfortable in Arizona, thanks in part to his standing in the local community from his days as a Sun Devil. In April 1999, Pat and Marie bought a house on West Buffalo Street in Chandler. It was nothing lavish: a tidy little faux adobe with sixteen hundred square feet of living space, a tile roof, yuccas and palm trees in the front yard, and a two-car garage. Pat paid $141,400 for it. "Because of the vagaries of the NFL, we didn't know how long we'd be in Phoenix," Marie recalls. "The whole time Pat was with the Cardinals, he was only given one-year contracts. But after his first season we thought we'd be there at least another year, and houses were inexpensive compared to what we were used to in the Bay Area, so Pat bought the house."

Despite Pat's status throughout Arizona as a bona fide celebrity, he and Marie didn't live like most other players in the NFL, and their existence was notably lacking in the customary trappings. When he started playing for the Cardinals, Pat didn't even own a car; he rode his bike to work every day. Eventually he bought a used Jeep Cherokee, and later exchanged that for a secondhand Volvo station wagon, but that's as upscale as he ever got. "The other Cardinals players thought Pat's beat-up old Volvo was hilarious," remembers Benjamin Hill, Pat's childhood friend. "His teammates are all driving blinged-out Escalades, and he has this soccer-mom car."

Although Pat's salary was the minimum allowed under the NFL players' agreement, "it was a lot of money for him coming right out of college," says Marie. "But Pat had always been pretty conservative with money. He was conscious that football wouldn't last forever. Also, he had an appreciation for hard work and people who worked hard to earn a modest salary. Living extravagantly made him kind of uncomfortable."

Pat stood out from his NFL teammates in other ways as well. When it came to pets, for instance, most football players were "dog guys," but not Tillman, who owned two felines during his years with the Cardinals and was an unabashed "cat person." Tillman even went so far as to try to persuade his friend and teammate Zack Walz of "the superiority of cats over all species." During the off-season, Tillman had re-enrolled at ASU to earn a master's degree in history, which also set him apart. "Because of his schedule he couldn't attend classes on campus," Marie recalls, "so Pat would meet independently with a professor from the history department who gave him assignments and worked with him online."

A few of Pat's college friends were still in the Phoenix area—most prominently Jake Plummer, who had signed with the Cardinals a year before Pat did. Both Pat and Marie badly missed their friends and family back in California, though. "The friends he made in high school were his best friends, and they stayed his best friends his whole life. Pat hung out with some of the other Cardinals players, and there was a group of wives I would go out with when the players were out of town. But we never really fit in with the NFL lifestyle. It just wasn't Pat's thing to go to the clubs in Scottsdale on weekends, or play golf during the off-season, which is what most of the other players did for fun."

Pat's taste in recreation ran to more adventurous pursuits that held no appeal for his NFL colleagues, who tended to steer clear of leisure activities that might conceivably result in a career-ending injury or worse—at least in part because their contracts generally forbade them to engage in activities such as skiing or skydiving that endangered life and limb. Pat's contract had such a clause, too, and he was no more eager than his teammates to get hurt or killed. But he relished physical challenges too much to play it safe, contract or no contract.

In the military, when soldiers venture beyond the security of their forward operating bases, which are enclosed by massive blast walls topped with concertina wire, they refer to it as "going outside the wire." The term could just as easily serve as a slogan for how Pat lived much of his life. "I think you've got to get out of your comfort zone," he once explained to a journalist. "If you're kind of comfortable all the time—it's like if you're skiing and you're not falling, you're not trying. I kind of want to push myself. A lot." He believed that to experience personal growth, he had to be willing to take calculated risks. In so doing, he trusted that his strength and athleticism, augmented by good judgment, would keep him from harm. He possessed that trust since before he was even old enough to articulate it.

From the age of three, Pat loved to climb and swing from trees. As he grew older, his fascination with high places led him to scramble on the boulders and crags that bristled from the hills above his home. By high school he and his buddies were amusing themselves by diving off high bridges into rivers and lakes. When he was a homesick seventeen-year-old attending his first Sun Devils training camp in August 1994, he assuaged his loneliness by leaping off a forty-foot cliff he discovered in the hills above the ASU practice fields. Every morning and afternoon the team would assemble for grueling workouts. During the break between training sessions, when most of the players would collapse on their bunks for a couple of hours of rest, Pat would hike alone up to this outcrop and dive repeatedly from its lip into the cool waters of the creek that flowed beneath it.

Not long after classes started at ASU that fall, Pat began to make weekly ascents of a light tower that rose two hundred feet above Sun Devil Stadium—not in search of a cheap thrill, but rather for the tranquility he found up there. Far above the din and bustle of the city, he enjoyed collecting his thoughts and taking in the expansive view. The world below was put into perspective. The lofty vantage calmed his mind.

Hanging on the wall of Benjamin Hill's office is a photograph of him standing with Pat and Jeff Hechtle on a granite ledge in California's Sierra Nevada, forty feet above the surface of Lake Tahoe. Every summer from 1996 until Pat and Kevin joined the Army in 2002, Hill and his future wife, Jamie; Hechtle and his future wife, Cindy; Pat, Marie, and Kevin Tillman; Hill's younger brother, Brandon; and an assortment of their closest friends would vacation together at Tahoe for five or six days. During these cherished gatherings, they would go water-skiing and play endless rounds of Trivial Pursuit, drink a lot of beer, talk all night, decompress. They also engaged in a great deal of cliff diving.

The photo in his office, Hill says, was taken just before he and Hechtle made their first leap from the ledge where they nervously perched. "Pat had just done a jump off the top," Hill remembers. "Jeff and I were trying to get our courage up to do it. There's a bulge in the cliff you need to clear, and you have to get a good jump off the side or you'll hit the rock face on the way down." Marie was waiting in a boat below. After they'd been standing on the ledge for about twenty minutes contemplating all that could go wrong, she yelled, "Jump, you pussies!" These gentle words of encouragement finally shamed them into leaping.

"That particular jump wasn't a big deal," says Brandon Hill. "It's not life-or-death. It's a mental thing. You just have to make up your mind to do it." Pat once even did a backflip off this outcrop. The Hill brothers make clear, however, that Pat also made a number of leaps from other high places where the margin for error was nonexistent. One such leap near Sedona, Arizona, a hundred miles north of Phoenix, was "the craziest thing I've ever seen in my life," Brandon recalls. "I still think about it. If I hadn't witnessed it with my own eyes, I wouldn't have believed it."

The landscape around Sedona is a phantasmagoria of red sandstone spires and forested ravines offering many ways to recreate. Pat couldn't get enough of the place and frequently sojourned there during the seven and a half years he lived in Arizona. One afternoon during Pat's tenure as a Cardinal, he and Kevin went hiking along the rim of Oak Creek Canyon, six miles north of Sedona near Slide Rock State Park. Their route followed the edge of a sheer cliff overlooking the creek. As they walked along the brow of the precipice, they passed a ponderosa pine growing from a jumble of jagged boulders on the bottom of the canyon about ten or twelve feet away from the vertical cliff face. The ledge on which they stood was level with the upper branches of the pine, and Pat decided it would be an interesting challenge to jump from the ledge to the treetop.

Pat pondered the leap for a while, stepped up to the brink, walked away, stepped up to the lip again, and then walked away once more to contemplate the jump for a while longer. After several long minutes, he approached the edge yet again and then launched himself into the void with all the power he could generate. So much adrenaline was surging through his bloodstream that he jumped harder than necessary, causing him to slam into the tree with excessive force. He held on, but it wasn't pretty.

Two weeks later, Pat repeated the hike along the rim of Oak Creek Canyon with Kevin, Brandon Hill, and two other friends. When they arrived at the place where Pat had made the death-defying jump, he decided to do it again. He wanted to see if he could execute the maneuver with less effort this time and stick the landing more gracefully.

When Brandon looked at what Pat intended to do, he thought it was insane. The world record for the standing long jump is twelve feet two inches—only slightly farther than the distance from the canyon rim to the top of the pine. If Pat failed to make it all the way across the gap, or did manage to leap that far but didn't get a solid grip on the tree, he would plummet into the boulders at the bottom, almost certainly killing himself.

Pat, however, was sure that he would avoid these outcomes. He took a moment to eyeball the distance to a strong-looking horizontal branch, and to calculate his trajectory. Then, says Brandon, "he walked up to the edge of the cliff, perfectly composed. His posture was like a gymnast or a diver, only more stable. Most people doing something like that would waver a little. Not Pat. He looked totally in command. In one smooth motion he crouched down, swung his arms, and leapt. Just like that. No hesitation. Didn't think about it at all. It was unbelievable."

Pat judged the leap perfectly. After flying across the gap, Brandon recalls, "he clamped his big old paws around this eight-inch-thick branch he'd been aiming for. His body swung pretty hard from the momentum, but he didn't have any trouble holding on. Then he threw a leg up onto the branch and just shinnied down the trunk to the ground like the jump was no big deal. Sometimes I still lie awake at night thinking about it."

As startling as this leap was, it was run-of-the-mill for Pat. Throughout his life he was constantly devising new challenges for himself, many of which were extremely dangerous. "He didn't do these kinds of things to impress people," says Brandon. "You'd never hear Pat talking about the unbelievable things he pulled off. Any stuff that he did, the only way you'd know about it is if you were right there with him to witness it. He did these things for himself. Most of the time there was nobody even around to see him do it."

Benjamin Hill admits that occasionally when he saw Pat testing himself in some crazy fashion, he couldn't resist admonishing his friend: "Especially during the years he was playing for ASU and the Cardinals, sometimes I'd ask him, 'Why are you putting yourself into these situations where you could so easily get hurt, when you know how good things are going for you right now, and how much is at stake? What's the point?' " The point, Pat would explain to Hill, was that "he felt like he needed to continually challenge himself, physically and mentally, to stay sharp. He'd been doing it his whole life, and believed it's what had gotten him to where he was. If he stopped seeking out challenges because he was afraid of hurting himself, he felt like he'd lose his edge."

Amazingly, considering all the incautious things he'd done over the years both on and off the football field, Pat had suffered very few injuries. Almost everyone who knew him began to take it for granted that he was virtually indestructible.

CHAPTER THIRTEEN

Given the Cardinals' unanticipated success in 1998, Arizonans expected great things of their NFL team in 1999. Alas, they were sorely disappointed: the franchise won only six of its sixteen games. For his part, Tillman was relegated to playing on special teams and occasionally coming off the bench as a second-string safety—although he did start the last game of the season after the first-string safety, Tommy Bennett, went down with a serious knee injury.

Despite his backup role and lower profile, the 1999 season was a positive experience for Pat, in large part because the coaches switched him from the free-safety position to strong safety, a move that suited his talents. As a strong safety he had to worry less about covering superfast wide receivers going deep, and could concentrate more on stopping short passes and running plays, which favored the reflexes he'd honed as a linebacker. Stung by his demotion to second string, he trained harder than ever. He also benefited tremendously from having a year in the NFL under his belt. One of his problems as a rookie had been his overeagerness—his tendency to try to be part of every play and make every tackle. As a consequence he would sometimes be too quick to react and get fooled by misdirection plays. During his second year he learned to rely more on his intelligence instead of raw intensity, which reaped huge dividends. After the final game of the season—a lopsided loss to Green Bay on January 2,

2000—Pat was already looking forward to playing again in the fall, and was determined to hang on to the starter's job he'd won at the end of 1999 by default.

The 2000 off-season, like all off-seasons, "wasn't easy for Pat," says Marie. "He would get restless sometimes. He wasn't the type to golf or hang around the house. He liked to be productive with his time off. I think that's part of why he entered the marathon. It gave him something to work toward and accomplish in the off-season."

Pat had registered to enter the Avenue of the Giants Marathon, held the first week of May in Humboldt Redwoods State Park, just south of Eureka on the far north coast of California. Never having run a race of that distance, he asked for advice from Perry Edinger, who had been the head athletic trainer at ASU when Pat played football for the Sun Devils. Edinger put together a detailed training schedule for him, tailored to fit a five-week vacation through western Europe Pat and Marie had planned to begin on March 6.

Pat had never been across the Atlantic, and a journal he kept throughout the trip reveals his fascination and unjaded delight upon experiencing even the most mundane aspects of European culture. Despite the rigors of travel, he managed to go for a run almost every morning. When he set out for his predawn workout in Paris on the third day of the journey, the doors leading out of the hotel were locked, he wrote, "so I was forced to escape through the second story window to be on my way. . . . My route took me along the Seine River all the way to the Eiffel Tower and back. It was quite the experience to be soaking up that much of Paris so early in the morning. When I returned, the Frenchy at the hotel was giving me a hard time about the window deal. I pretty much just blew him off and returned to my room to get ready for the day. There was no need to bounce Frenchy off the walls after such a fine jog."

As Pat and Marie rambled through Germany, he made it his mission to sample every variety of local beer and sausage he came across, and then offered an assessment of each in his journal. In Munich, he raved about the spicy *Bratwurst* and reacted favorably to a *Schweinwurst,* but upon having his first taste of an almost raw *Weisswurst,* he observed, "The texture was soft and taste not particularly noteworthy. . . . Before I even left the table my stomach was screaming. Marie had to carry my ass back to our room." Pat's dedication to evaluating the local food and drink was such that he even felt compelled to critique the offerings of a McDonald's they patronized in the Berner Oberland region of Switzerland. After seeing a baffling item called a McFu Burger on the menu, he wrote, "I had to have it." It turned out to be "just your standard quarter-pounder-type burger, minus the cheese, plus oriental sauce with lettuce and crazy carrot pieces and what have you. It was delicious. My hat is off to the McFu."

A day later, in Interlaken, he was out on his daily run when he encountered a trail posted with signs warning that the route was closed and access was forbidden—which proved to be an irresistible draw. "Downed trees were all over the path," he wrote, "forcing me to do some nice maneuvers to get through. This of course only enhanced the enjoyment of the run and soon I was off the trail and along the brilliant turquoise river."

Pat loved turning encounters with natural obstacles—boulders, rivers, fallen logs—into makeshift sport. "Out of the blue, he would always come up with creative ways to challenge himself," says his friend Alex Garwood, who is married to Marie's older sister, Christine. Garwood remembers once going on a hike with Pat near Sedona when Pat suggested they abandon the trail and instead make their way down the middle of Oak Creek by jumping from rock to rock:

Pat wanted to see how far he could go without getting his feet wet. We went at least a couple of miles that way. My feet got very wet, very soon. I slipped and fell in repeatedly. He didn't get his feet wet at all. And it was so fun to watch. He not only demonstrated exceptional athletic ability, but brains to match. It was almost like a chess game to him: thinking it through, planning his moves in advance, jumping from rock to rock, rock to bank, bank to tree branch to log to rock. Making these incredibly long, incredibly graceful jumps. And having the trust that he could do it. He had amazing balance—there was a way he'd move his hands to keep his balance that was distinctively Pat.

After Switzerland, Pat and Marie made stops in Venice, Florence, and Rome. On the coast of northern Italy they visited Cinque Terre, where Pat scrambled up the sea cliffs in Monterosso. "Because I hadn't climbed in a while," he admitted, "I felt a bit nervous on some of the rocks." They paused for a couple of days on the French Riviera, which he thought was overrated. In Monaco, he wrote, one could sense the proximity of "big money but you also feel like the party is hidden somewhere. . . . Maybe my blue-collarness is getting the better of me here." Of Cannes, he remarked, "Perhaps I was expecting a bit too much. . . . Was it wrong to expect spectacular beaches? . . . Was it wrong to expect hotties everywhere, or at least every now and again?"

By March 25, Pat and Marie had returned to Paris to rendezvous with Christine and Alex Garwood, who had flown over from California to accompany them for the final two weeks of the trip. After worrying about how pricey the city was, Pat wrote, "Expensive or not, Marie and I should enjoy Paris with the company of Alex and Chris. Marie and I have done a pretty good job of staying off each other's throats but the extra travelers should give Marie a much needed break from me. . . . Naturally, the trip has a way of bringing us very close together while also getting us ultra pissed-off at one another. Needless to say I have truly enjoyed Marie's company and conversation. Hopefully she feels the same. . . . Hopefully."

The next journal entry begins:

It wasn't my fault! Blame Alex. . . . Blame Paris. . . . Oh Lord!! I got fucking hammered last night. Beyond hammered . . . Because we were in Paris, the ladies wanted a nice dinner. Little did they know what they were in for. . . . The restaurant was small and quaint. Jazz played in the background and the help was real cool. A cheese dish and mushroom concoction made up our appetizers . . . the mushroom deal was unbelievable. Unfortunately, with the appetizers came the vino.

For dinner I had lamb, which kicked ass. All of our food was excellent with great sauces. . . . Our conversation was humming, and as the wine was poured it got louder and louder. For dessert the ladies had crème brûlée and Alex a brownie. I opted for more wine.

Now things start to get hazy. Alex and I are getting obnoxious as we get drunk. Like usual, I am swearing up a storm and as Marie tells it, the people around us are not pleased. We are not kicked out, but were politely cut off and went on our way. They were really cool and didn't get pissed but were happy to see us leave.

Remembering that night, Christine Garwood issues a bemused sigh and then elaborates: "A girlfriend of Marie's had been to Paris, and she said we should go to this restaurant. It was a tiny place. When we first got there, nobody was there but us. The waitress was from New Zealand, I think, or Australia. At one point she said something like, 'Oh yeah, the last Americans who were here drank two carafes of wine per person.' So of course Alex and Pat took that as a challenge, and the wine started to flow.

"We were there for several hours. We had some good banter going back and forth with the waitress. The chef came out to chat with us. It was really fun, and the wine kept coming. Pat and Alex had had enough to drink and they started to get loud, and by that time the place had filled up." Two French couples at the table next to them made it clear that the Americans' increasingly raucous behavior had ceased to be amusing. "The waitress and the host were really nice about it," says Christine, "but finally they indicated that Pat and Alex were getting a little crazy and it might be time for Marie and I to get the guys out of there. They were so cool to us. They were like, 'Okay, you had a great dinner, why don't you go take a walk now.' "

As they were strolling back to their hotel, Pat, goofing around, grabbed the iron grate covering the entrance to a closed storefront and started yanking on it, hard, making a racket that attracted the attention of a passerby, a Frenchman who glowered at the Americans to communicate his disapproval. Pat stared right back and drunkenly declaimed, "Don't forget that if it wasn't for us, you'd all be speaking German now." With his view of American boorishness thus confirmed, the satisfied Frenchman departed without further incident, and Marie managed to get Pat moving again in the direction of their accommodations, a tiny room in an inexpensive pension.

When they arrived, Pat immediately passed out next to Marie in one of the two twin beds. Not long after he retired, however, his head started to spin, and he was overcome with the sudden urge to expel the contents of his stomach. Fortunately, he managed to lean his head over the side of the mattress before vomiting; unfortunately, Marie's open rucksack was resting on the floor beside the head of the bed. "He threw up into her backpack," says Christine, "and his puke was *red*. There was nothing in his stomach but wine. Then he rolled over and went back to sleep. Marie cleaned it up. She was not happy about it. She had only brought a few T-shirts and a couple of pairs of pants for the whole trip. And now everything she had was stained red. Actually, it was sort of funny. We laughed about it.

"Pat was a handful," Christine continues. "That's the word my sister used to describe him. She totally loved Pat—we all loved Pat—but he was definitely a handful. During the off-season he'd have people over to their house in Arizona—Kevin, my cousin Frank, friends visiting from Almaden—and they'd stay up until all hours. They'd be extremely loud, even though she'd be sleeping in the next room and would have to get up and go to work the next day. She'd scream and yell a little, then eventually give up: 'Okay, whatever.' She realized that Pat's rambunctiousness was an essential part of who he was, and there wasn't a lot she could do about it, even if sometimes she wanted to."

Although Pat acknowledged in his journal that he overindulged during their *grande soirée Parisienne,* he expressed no regrets about the evening. "We top the night off with Alex passed out on the bed and me puking all over the room," he wrote. "Well, I had a great time, and so did Alex. The girls perhaps could have done without the puke and obnoxiousness, but they'll get over it and I know they had a good time for most of it. The good outweighed the bad. For me however, there was no bad . . . until morning rolled around."

One of the sacred tenets of Pat's moral code was that it's unacceptable to let a hangover interfere with one's duties and commitments. According to Pat's training regimen, such commitments included a short but early run. "Because of last night's antics," Pat wrote of the run, "this morning was rougher than it had to be. Alex and I had an hour run planned and we didn't want to miss it. Because of my puking I was actually fine. Alex, on the other hand, was a mess, getting through the run purely on guts, his body worthless. Fortunately we finished it and got the day off to a good start. It would have set a bad precedent letting the drinking get the better of us."

———

Hammered, trashed, shit faced, plastered, buzzed, polluted, pickled. Regardless of the terminology, Tillman loved to get intoxicated with good friends. He enjoyed almost everything about getting drunk, in fact: the sound of the Guinness going *blub-blub-blub* into the glass; the shedding of cares; the heightened sense of interpersonal connection; the swelling euphoria; the way it caused the music to bore a hole through one's skull; the giddy, fleeting glimpse it seemed to provide into the deepest mysteries of the cosmos. When Pat was lit, recalls Alex, "he'd throw his head back, his eyes would turn into these little slits, and he'd let loose with this booming laugh. Then his arms would shoot out wide, knocking beers over, and he'd act like it was the funniest thing he'd ever seen. But his laugh was so infectious you'd be laughing too. And if you were in a restaurant and the people at the next table were not happy about the noise, he'd look over at them and be, like, 'I have no idea why you aren't laughing, too, because this is really funny.'

"Being with Pat was the best," Alex continues, his voice turning wistful. "The drinking was better, the conversation was better, the laughter was better—everything in life was just better when he was part of it."

Although imbibing was certainly one of Tillman's great pleasures, his favorite beverage wasn't alcoholic. It was coffee, which ran through his life like the Ganges runs through India, lending commonality to disparate experiences and far-flung points of the compass. And although Pat delighted in the rituals associated with coffee—grinding the beans, mashing down the plunger on a French press, perusing the menu at espresso stands—the coffee itself was really just a lubricant, a catalyst, a means to a particular end, which was stimulating conversation.

Marie agrees. "He loved to have people around," she remembers. "He loved conversation. When we'd get together with our good friends—the friends we've had since Almaden—by the end of the night Pat was often the last guy talking. Or if he was tired, he would, like, lay down on the floor, but he would insist that everyone else keep talking, keep the conversation going. Then he would just lie there, listening to his friends' voices."

CHAPTER FOURTEEN

A month after Pat and Marie returned from Europe, Pat drove from Arizona to northern California to compete in the Avenue of the Giants Marathon, and on May 7 ran 26.2 miles through Humboldt County's majestic, dripping redwoods, finishing in three hours, forty-eight minutes, and forty-eight seconds, good enough for 170th place in a field of 666. He was the only player in the NFL to complete a marathon that year.

Training for long-distance running, as it happens, doesn't help a great deal with the maximum intensity, start-and-stop, largely anaerobic demands of playing professional football. But Pat had been working hard in the weight room as well as on running trails. When he arrived in Flagstaff on July 21 for the start of the Cardinals' training camp, he was stronger than he'd ever been, and weighed less than he had since high school, having resolved to raise his play to the highest possible level.

Writing the first entry in the journal he'd decided to keep throughout the 2000 football season, Pat pronounced, "This year is a huge year. This year will decide whether I am a starter, contributing the way I want, or be stuck in a special teams/nickel/backup role for the remainder of my career. The opportunity has been given to me, I'm prepared both physically and mentally, it is all up to me. Huge fucking year, man." Explaining his reasons for journaling (something he had never done during previous football seasons), he added, "1) This is a pivotal year for me and by taking the time to put down my thoughts I might just help myself. 2) I think in the future it will be a good thing to have, both to learn from and laugh at. 3) After keeping my journal in Europe, I learned to enjoy it. I realize it's no good but it's still fun to put your thoughts together. . . . Practice starts tomorrow."

Playing the safety position, Pat confided in his journal, "is still kind of new to me" and is "more mental" than playing linebacker. "For me, it has taken some time to believe I can cover receivers (don't get me wrong; it will never be my strong suit). At linebacker I never doubted my speed or coverage because I had no reason to. At safety I have had to learn how to do it. It's an ongoing process but I feel much more comfortable than the last two years. I really believe I can be a top safety in this league. . . . To get to where I want to be I need to constantly prove myself. I cannot give the coaches any reason to think someone else should be playing. . . . Every day, every play, just fucking concentrate."

As he almost always did, Pat accomplished what he set out to do, impressed the coaches at training camp, and by the final game of the 2000 preseason—in San Diego on August 25—Pat had secured the starting strong-safety job. Like most of the starters, he didn't play much in that last exhibition match before the regular season. "The best part of the game," he wrote, "was the time I got to spend with Ma, Nub, Pooh,"* and the dozen or so other supporters who'd driven down from the Bay Area to watch him play. "It was nice to see everyone after the game, even if it was for a short while. My sources tell me there was high drama going on in the stands: Puking, fighting, yelling, etc. My friends and family clearly brought the thunder I was hoping for. . . .

"The season is now ready to begin. This week I plan on spending a shitload of time watching film and preparing for Sunday," when the

---

* Kevin was born in 1978, when Pat was fourteen months old. Because he couldn't pronounce "Kevin" at the time, Pat called his little brother "Nubbin" or "Nub," and the moniker stuck. As did "Pooh," Pat and Kevin's nickname for their younger brother, Richard, born in 1981, who reminded the boys of the rotund protagonist of the Winnie-the-Pooh stories read to them by their mother.

Cardinals would play the Giants in New York. "Hopefully we'll force the Giants to throw the ball so I can come down with [an interception]. . . . One thing I will concentrate on is putting my face on people. The last couple of games I've not made the plays I should. Sunday I'm going off. . . . I am really fucking excited to get this season going. It's incredibly important I start off with a bang."

As it happened, the official 2000 football season did begin dramatically for Tillman, but not in the way he'd envisioned. The Giants, who would finish that season with a 14-5 record and go all the way to the Super Bowl, were one of the best teams in the NFL. The Cardinals were among the most awful. The game, to put it charitably, was a mismatch. The worst moment for Tillman came in the second quarter. With the Giants back on their twenty-two-yard line, New York's running back Tiki Barber took the handoff from quarterback Kerry Collins, darted through a hole on the right side of the line, and accelerated into the open field. Tillman, positioned perfectly to stop him, dove to make the tackle. Barber danced out of the way, however, causing Tillman to fall on his face, and then galloped seventy-eight yards for a Giants touchdown, the longest run of his career. New York ended up beating the Cardinals, 21–16.

The day after the game Pat wrote in his journal, "I fucking suck. I missed a tackle that resulted in a 78-yard touchdown. Boo. Not quite the jump out of the blocks I was shooting for. Fuck it. I'll do better this week."

There are no further journal entries until September 9, the Saturday before the Cardinals' next game, against the Dallas Cowboys. "What a fucking nightmare," the entry begins.

Since Sunday my athletic career has taken a serious turn for the terrible. I've been swimming in this missed tackle for days, which has made me a bit introverted and quiet. I'm not brooding as much as just focusing on getting better. Practices have been serious for me as I concentrate on no mistakes and making plays. However, because I've been quiet I've given the impression I'm down, and folks have asked if I'm OK. Well, Thursday at practice everything is going fine. I'm playing well, no mistakes, broke up a pass, and feeling good after 7-on-7 [a pass coverage drill] as we go into blitz period [a pass rushing drill]. I ran a great blitz on the first play and on the second I had a sack, but the running back hit me later than I thought he should. Not hard, just enough. I grabbed his facemask, really not wanting to fight, but he grabbed mine (obviously, to be expected) and I just said, "fuck it." I started kneeing him in the gut, then tossed his ass to the ground before I was eventually pried off.

After this fracas Pat wrote in his journal:

Coach [Vince Tobin] kicked my ass out of practice and added insult to injury by making me do the scout stuff. Later on I had to go in and speak to Mr. Tobin, where he said he was "incredibly disappointed" in my play Sunday; I'm "out of control"; and he doesn't think I'm a starter in this league. Pretty much everything I have been working to overcome. This episode really put the cherry atop a fucked-up week.

What is the most disappointing is how well my camp had gone, pre-season, even last week's practice, only to be pissed on by a sub-par opening game. From here I've basically realized they will start Tommy [Bennett, the strong safety who was injured near the end of 1999] as soon as he's healthy. In order to prevent this I'm going to have to pull something crazy off this weekend against Dallas. Oh well, could be worse. All I can do is keep working.

One day after Pat wrote this grim wrap-up of his week, the Cardinals played what would turn out to be their best game of the year, against the Cowboys. Late in the fourth quarter Arizona was backed up to their own fifteen-yard line, trailing the Cowboys by five points, when quarterback Jake Plummer threw the ball to David Boston for a sixty-three-yard gain. Three plays later, with just under two minutes remaining in the game, Plummer passed to Frank Sanders in the end zone for a touchdown. Although the Cowboys only needed a field goal to win the game, Pat and the defense dug in and stopped them cold. When time ran out, Arizona had upset Dallas, 32–31. And Tillman had played brilliantly, including some critical tackles of the superstar running back Emmitt Smith.

"Sunday was a great day," Pat recorded in his journal.

Not only did we beat the Cowboys by one point, but I played, in my estimation, a hell of a game: 7 tackles, 1 quarterback hit, and 3 pass

breakups (one of which should have been a pick). . . . I am overly excited about the game. The whole week I was a fucking mess. Worrying about the future, my ability to play, stuff I never worry about. At
least now if they decide to replace me I have a solid reason for saying they're wrong. Most importantly, though, I'm proud of how I
came back and played well despite last week's shitty game, the coach
telling me I suck, and swimming in my frustration. As Nub so wisely
wrote, I showed "the fortitude and savvy of a champion." As for
shamelessly throwing these compliments about myself in here, I
stand by them. After last week's abortion I need all I can get. My
modesty will return when I'm comfortably holding a starting position. This next week is a bye and I'm hoping to use the time off to
relax. Perhaps take Marie to Sedona or something. Normally I'd go
home but the week crept up quick and we forgot to buy plane tick-
ets that I'd rather not drop $400 for now.

The Dallas game turned around Pat's season. Not only did he
hold on to his starter's job, but he kept getting better and better with
each successive week. During a tough 20–27 loss to the San Francisco
49ers on October 1, Pat made eight tackles and knocked the ball
loose for a fumble. After the game, he wrote, "Jerry Rice even came
up to me and said I played well." A week later against the Cleveland
Browns, he made thirteen tackles and broke up a pass on the last play
of the game to give Arizona their second win of the year.

———

On the morning of October 12, 2000, four days after Tillman helped
the Cardinals defeat the Browns, the USS *Cole*—a billion-dollar,
505-foot-long guided-missile destroyer—arrived in the Yemeni port
of Aden on the southern tip of the Arabian Peninsula to top off its
fuel tanks at an offshore buoy. Two years earlier, some of the cruise
missiles launched against the Zawar Kili training camp in Khost,
Afghanistan, during the unsuccessful attempt to kill Osama bin
Laden had been fired from the *Cole*. One of the most heavily ar-
mored and technologically sophisticated vessels in the U.S. Navy, its
AEGIS radar system was capable of defending it against hundreds of
enemy missiles or fighter jets simultaneously bearing down within a

two-hundred-mile radius. The ship had been designed to be nearly invincible against the most advanced weapons systems the Pentagon had been able to imagine.

At 11:18 a.m., by which time the *Cole* had finished taking on fuel and was getting ready to cast off, two men in a twenty-foot-long fishing boat powered by an outboard motor—an open fiberglass skiff called an *houri* that was ubiquitous in Yemeni waters—pulled alongside the immense destroyer and came to a stop, in the manner of a minnow swimming up to a whale. The two Arabs on board the *houri* smiled and waved at American sailors standing above them at the rail of the *Cole*. The sailors assumed the little boat had been summoned by an officer on the bridge to haul away the destroyer's garbage. A moment later one of the smiling Arabs detonated a bomb made from hundreds of pounds of C-4 plastic explosive packed into a welded steel casing shaped to concentrate the force of the blast. The explosion, accompanied by a tremendous fireball, punched a jagged, thirty-five-foot-by-thirty-six-foot hole through the thick steel hull of the ship, killing seventeen sailors and injuring thirty-nine others, many of whom lost limbs and/or were horribly burned.

The suicide bombers turned out to be members of al-Qaeda. According to *The 9/11 Commission Report,* the operation had been "supervised directly by bin Ladin. He chose the target and location of the attack, selected the suicide operatives, and provided the money needed to purchase explosives and equipment." Analysis by the CIA determined that the blast had very nearly sunk the *Cole,* and could easily have killed as many as three hundred sailors. Like the rented van packed with explosives that had been detonated beneath the World Trade Center in 1993, which had come very close to bringing down the Twin Towers, the attack on the *Cole* had fallen just shy of destroying its target. But the *jihadis* who had directed both attacks were learning from their mistakes and continually refining their stratagems accordingly.

For his part, bin Laden had hoped the attack would provoke the United States into invading Afghanistan. Expecting to be targeted, he fled the compound where he had been staying near Kandahar and hid first at a compound outside of Kabul, then at a compound in Khost Province. The Americans considered a retaliatory missile attack against the al-Qaeda leader, similar to the strike on Zawar Kili in 1998, but eventually scrapped the plan because they weren't sure where he was and they didn't want to be embarrassed by another failure. Annoyed by the Americans' refusal to take the bait, bin Laden resolved to keep attacking prominent symbols of American hegemony until the United States would finally have no choice but to invade Afghanistan and become mired in an unwinnable war, just as the Soviets had. As cited in *The 9/11 Commission Report,* a covert CIA source stated that bin Laden had "complained frequently that the United States had not yet attacked. According to the source, bin Ladin wanted the United States to attack, and if it did not he would launch something bigger."

———

Three days after the attack on the USS *Cole,* Tillman made nineteen tackles in a 14–33 loss to the Philadelphia Eagles. The following Sunday, October 22, the Cardinals were routed by Dallas. Two days after the game Pat wrote, "You thought we got beat last week. . . . You should have seen Sunday: 48–7. The worst part is the score was better than it actually was. [The Cowboys] absolutely ran through us. Our front line is unable to even slow the runners down, let alone tackle them." Pat took some small satisfaction from the fact that when these opposing runners got into the backfield, they usually couldn't get past him. He made sixteen tackles on that day, prompting him to note, "At the very least I can cling to that."

Two weeks later, Pat played his best game of his professional career, making an amazing twenty-one tackles against the Washington Redskins. At one point he sprinted from the far side of the field and threw himself into the legs of the Washington ballcarrier Stephen Davis, who had gained thirty-two yards on the play and would have continued running all the way into the end zone for a touchdown if Tillman hadn't torpedoed him. Pat's tackle preserved a rare Cardinals victory—their third, and last, of the season.

CHAPTER FIFTEEN

On November 7, two days after the Cardinals' win over the Redskins, Americans went to the polls to elect a new president. Although Al Gore received 543,816 more votes than George W. Bush (51,003,926 to 50,460,110), the popular vote was immaterial. The office would go to the candidate who garnered a majority of the electoral votes, and the electoral vote count remained uncertain for more than a month after the election. By the morning of November 8, it was clear that Gore had won at least 255 electoral votes and Bush had won at least 246. But 270 such votes were required to win the presidency, and it was far from certain who rightfully deserved to receive Florida's 25 electoral votes because it was impossible to say who had won the popular vote in that state, owing to widespread voting irregularities.

When Florida's ballots were initially counted, Bush led Gore by 1,784 votes (out of some 6 million votes cast), prompting an automatic recount. On November 10, after that recount, the margin of victory was reduced to 327 votes, at which point Gore exercised his right under Florida law to demand that the ballots be carefully recounted again, this time by hand, in four counties that had a preponderance of Democratic voters. The upshot was a series of bitterly disputed recounts that dragged on for weeks, sparking a corresponding flurry of lawsuits and much gnashing of teeth.

More than a little of the postelection anguish (on the part of Democrats, at any rate) derived from the fact that 97,421 Floridians had voted for the third-party candidate Ralph Nader. Throughout his campaign, Nader had labeled Bush and Gore "Tweedledum and Tweedledee," insisting there was no real distinction between their positions. At a press conference in September 2000 Nader had proclaimed, "It doesn't matter who is in the White House, Gore or Bush." Now it appeared that enough voters had believed him to skew the outcome of the election. Exit polls indicated that had he not been in the race, 38 percent of his voters would have voted for Gore, 25 percent would have voted for Bush, and the remaining 37 percent wouldn't have bothered to vote at all. In other words, without Nader on the ballot, Gore would have beaten Bush by nearly thirteen thousand votes and become president of the United States by a comfortable margin.

But Nader of course *was* on the ballot, and on November 8 the Florida vote was therefore too close to call. When November gave way to December, it remained that way, despite the ongoing recounts. The waters were muddied by several contradictory rulings from various Florida courts, some of which favored Gore, others of which favored Bush. Complicating matters even further, federal law stipulated that in order to preclude a possible congressional challenge to the legitimacy of the representatives Florida appointed to the electoral college, the state's vote count had to be completed and certified by midnight on December 12. Missing this deadline, as it turned out, would not have invalidated the Florida election results: more than a third of the fifty states failed to meet the December 12 target without incident. The crucial deadline for certifying Florida's vote count didn't actually fall until January 6, 2001. But if the December 12 deadline wasn't particularly important, it was widely perceived to be, and therefore infused the ongoing drama with an added measure of tension.

On December 8, Gore appeared to have prevailed in the legal arena when he won a key ruling by the Florida Supreme Court, which ordered yet another manual recount of some forty-five thousand disputed ballots throughout the state. As this recount got under way, Bush's lead rapidly diminished. On December 9, however, before the tally could be completed, the U.S. Supreme Court voted 5–4 to issue an injunction that halted the recount in response to an emergency plea filed by Bush's attorneys. At the time this stay was granted, Bush's lead had dwindled to 154 votes and appeared to be fast on its way to vanishing altogether.

The December 9 injunction provoked furious protests from Democrats and was derided by legal scholars as a transparently partisan attempt by the Rehnquist Court to hand the election to Bush. Unmoved by the firestorm of criticism, the Supreme Court justices issued their momentous decision in *Bush v. Gore* three days later, at 10:00 p.m. on December 12. Again by a vote of 5–4, the Court ruled that the December 12 deadline for certifying the vote count would in fact be binding, and because completing a constitutionally valid recount would be impossible within the two hours that remained before the clock struck midnight, there would be no further reckoning of Florida's disputed votes.

Incensed Gore supporters quickly pointed out that just six paragraphs earlier in the text of the same ruling the Court had declared, "The press of time does not diminish the constitutional concern. A desire for speed is not a general excuse for ignoring equal protection guarantees." Furthermore, the Gore camp argued, the only reason a recount couldn't be completed by the court-mandated deadline was that the same five-justice majority had stopped the recount three days previously with their December 9 injunction, predetermining the outcome of their December 12 ruling.

Critics found numerous other reasons to cry foul over the Court's hastily rendered decision. Among the most compelling were allegations that two of the five justices who voted with the majority in favor of Bush—Antonin Scalia and Sandra Day O'Connor—unequivocally violated the federal judicial conflict-of-interest statute by participating in *Bush v. Gore*. In the instance of Scalia, two of his sons were affiliated with law firms that happened to be representing Bush at the time. Regarding O'Connor, who was seventy years old and in poor health, she had stated on several occasions that she was very eager to retire from the Court and did not want a Democrat to nominate her successor. Had Scalia and O'Connor recused themselves, as the statute clearly required, the vote would have been 4–3 in favor of Gore.

It wasn't simply Gore supporters who were outraged by the Court's decision. In a dissenting opinion that was uncharacteristically harsh in tone, Justice John Paul Stevens (a Republican appointed by President Gerald Ford) lamented that the outcome of *Bush v. Gore* "can only lend credence to the most cynical appraisal of the work of judges throughout the land. . . . Although we may never know with complete certainty the identity of the winner of this year's presidential election, the identity of the loser is perfectly clear. It is the Nation's confidence in the judge as an impartial guardian of the rule of law."

Be that as it may, the highest court in the land handed down its decision, which allowed Florida's secretary of state, Katherine Harris, to certify the vote with Bush's minuscule lead still intact, which in turn gave Florida's twenty-five electoral votes to the Republican candidate. Twenty-four hours after the Supreme Court issued its decisive ruling, Gore addressed the nation, declaring, "Let there be no doubt: While I strongly disagree with the Court's decision, I accept it. I accept the finality of this outcome which will be ratified next Monday in the Electoral College. . . . While we yet hold and do not yield our opposing beliefs, there is a higher duty than the one we owe to political party. This is America and we put country before party. We will stand together behind our new president." And thus did Bush become the forty-third president of the United States, a turn of events that would have no small impact on the life of Pat Tillman.

On April 27, 2008, four years after Tillman's death, Justice Scalia was interviewed by CBS correspondent Lesley Stahl on the television show *60 Minutes*. "It has been reported that he [Scalia] played a pivotal role in urging the other justices to end the Florida recount, thereby handing the 2000 election to George Bush," Stahl observed, and then confronted Scalia face-to-face: "People say that that decision was not based on judicial philosophy but on politics."

"I say nonsense," he replied, deflecting the accusation with an imperious smirk. When Stahl wouldn't drop the issue, he snapped, "Get over it. It's so old by now."

Twelve days after the Supreme Court ruling that would put Bush in the White House, Tillman and the Cardinals were back in the nation's capital to play their final game of the year, which they lost to the Redskins in a blowout. Tillman performed well, nevertheless, capping a season of stellar play. Pat was credited with 224 tackles, setting a new Cardinals record. Had he made that many tackles on a better team, he almost certainly would have won enough votes to play in the Pro Bowl, the NFL all-star game, but because Arizona went 3-13 for the season he was ignored in the balloting process.

However, Tillman wasn't overlooked by Paul Zimmerman, the esteemed football writer known to his readers as "Dr. Z," who publishes a list of the NFL's best players in *Sports Illustrated* at the conclusion of each season. After meticulously analyzing every play Tillman made all year, Zimmerman declared Pat to be the most accomplished strong safety in the league in 2000. Players who made his list at other positions included such luminaries as Donovan McNabb, Marshall Faulk, Randy Moss, Ray Lewis, and Warren Sapp. In a column titled "My All-Pro Team," Zimmerman acknowledged that his elevation of Tillman to this elite circle would surprise many readers. Football aficionados, he wrote, were likely to "glance at my all-pro list and sneer, 'Pat Tillman! Who the hell is that? Dr. Z's going loony on us.' "

But Zimmerman explained why he held Tillman in such high regard. He began his evaluation of Pat with a three-day review of his play throughout the 2000 season, during which, Zimmerman wrote, he had a "dim awareness" that Tillman had a number of good games and should be analyzed further. "And then," he continued,

> stringing together all his numbers, I discover, hello, that he has defeated the competition. . . . I couldn't believe the margin by which he outscored everybody on my board, so I started making calls to personnel people whose opinions I respect. . . . You want to laugh at me, go ahead. But I'll show you, for instance, my chart of Tillman's performance against New Orleans, when he was knocking down anything with a heartbeat and the Cardinals had the NFC West champs on the ropes for a while, or my documentation of his work in the September victory over the Cowboys, when I got him for six great pass defense plays and 10 stops near the line of scrimmage, both high numbers for a strong safety this season.

After his piece was published, Zimmerman later acknowledged, some sports announcers from the major television networks ridiculed his selection of Tillman as an All-Pro player, pointing out that he was "not the greatest in coverage, etc. But what I had seen was a wild and punishing tackling machine, a guy who lifted the performance of everyone around him. You could see the fire in the whole defensive unit when he led the charge to the ball." In the final analysis, one came away believing that Dr. Z was absolutely right: at the end of the 2000 season, Tillman deserved to be considered one of the best players in professional football.

––––––––

Zimmerman's article was posted on the Internet on January 3, 2001. In the nation's capital that day, Richard Clarke—the Clinton administration's national coordinator for security, infrastructure protection, and counterterrorism—briefed the incoming Bush administration's new national security adviser, Condoleezza Rice, on the dire threat the United States faced from Osama bin Laden and al-Qaeda. Clarke writes in his book *Against All Enemies: Inside America's War on Terror,* "My message was stark: al-Qaeda is at war with us, it is a highly capable organization, probably with sleeper cells in the U.S., and it is clearly planning a major series of attacks against us; we must act decisively and quickly, deciding on the issues prepared after the attack on the *Cole,* going on the offensive."

On January 25, Clarke alerted Rice that six recent intelligence reports uncovered statements from al-Qaeda operatives boasting of an upcoming attack. Over the following weeks, he repeatedly implored her to persuade President Bush to give much higher priority to terrorism in general and bin Laden in particular, but his e-mails and memos were met with apathy and annoyance.

––––––––

The Cardinals had paid Tillman a salary of $361,500 for his services in 2000, and had given him a contract that lasted only a single year. Based on his performance in the just-completed season, the St. Louis Rams—a terrific team that had won the Super Bowl a year earlier—believed Tillman was worth considerably more than that. On April

13, 2001, the Rams' management offered him a five-year deal for $9.6 million, $2.6 million of which would be paid up front, upon signing. Frank Bauer, Tillman's agent, immediately called him with the good news. "I get Patty on the phone," Bauer remembers, "and tell him, 'Listen to me. The Rams really want you, and I don't see Arizona matching their offer. I'm going to fax the Rams' offer sheet to you. You have to sign it.' "

Bauer assumed Pat would leap at the deal, as almost any player would. Instead, Tillman told him, "I need to think about this."

"Patty!" Bauer replied. "What are you doing to me here! You're killing me!" Tillman said he'd let Bauer know his decision in a day or two. "So Pat calls back," according to Bauer, "and he tells me, 'Look, Frank, the Cardinals drafted me in the seventh round. They believed in me. I love the coaches here. I can't bring myself to take the offer from the Rams.' I said, 'Patty, are you nuts? Are you fuckin' crazy? The Rams want to pay you $9.6 million! If you stay with the Cardinals, it doesn't take a rocket scientist to figure out that you're gonna be playing for $512,000.' Pat says, 'I've made my decision, Frank. I'm going to stay with the Cardinals.'

"In twenty-seven years," Bauer continues, "I've never had a player turn down that big of a package in the National Football League. I've had players take twenty grand less per year to stay at clubs they really wanted to play for, but turning down nine and a half million? That's unheard of. You just don't see loyalty like that in sports today. Pat Tillman was special. He was a man of principle. He was a once-in-a-lifetime kid."

After he declined the Rams' offer, the Cardinals offered Tillman another one-year deal for the 2001 season that would pay him the league minimum for a fourth-year player, $512,000, just as Bauer predicted. Pat signed the contract, provoking expressions of astonishment from players, coaches, and fans around the league. For his part, however, Tillman had no regrets.

He was one of those rare individuals who simply can't be bought at any price. Although he had no qualms about making a boatload of money if it happened to mesh with his master plan, Pat was impervious to greed. His belief that other things in life took priority over amassing wealth never faltered. But if Tillman was uncommonly resistant to the temptations of the baser human appetites, and was thereby well defended against attempts by others to manipulate him into doing their bidding with such enticements, he found it nearly impossible to resist appeals to his sense of decency and justice. Paradoxically, this latter trait would ultimately prove to be his downfall.

CHAPTER SIXTEEN

Although Pat spoke self-deprecatingly about his intelligence, and claimed that his academic success in college came from hard work rather than brainpower, his intellectual curiosity was boundless, and he was a compulsive reader who never went anywhere without a book. Pat Murphy, the celebrated Arizona State University baseball coach, remembers seeing Pat in the bleachers during most of the Sun Devils' baseball games when Kevin was on the team. "He always had a book with him," says Murphy. "Between innings, or anytime there was a lull, he'd have it open and he'd be reading something."

Because he loved engaging in informed debate, Pat made an effort to study history, economic theory, and world events from a variety of perspectives. Toward that end he read the Bible, the Book of Mormon, the Quran, and the works of writers ranging from Adolf Hitler to Henry David Thoreau. Although Tillman held strong opinions on many subjects, he was bracingly open-minded and quick to admit he was wrong when confronted with facts and a persuasive argument.

With his shoulder-length hair and outspoken views, Tillman had been considered a maverick ever since his arrival in Tempe to attend ASU, and he'd done many things in the ensuing years that confirmed his unconventional reputation in the minds of Arizonans. He was an ardent advocate for the rights of homosexuals, for instance, and once demanded of Lyle Setencich, an ASU football coach for whom he had great respect, "Could you coach gays?" When Setencich answered not only yes he could, but that he already had, Tillman's esteem for the coach grew even higher.

Curiously, however, nothing seemed to enhance his nonconformist reputation more than his decision to enter a triathlon in the summer of 2001. Two months after turning down the Rams' offer and re-signing with the Cardinals, Pat flew to Cambridge, Maryland, to compete against sixteen hundred people in the Blackwater Eagle-Man Triathlon. When a reporter for ESPN asked Tillman what had motivated him to enter his first triathlon (after suggesting he must be a "pathological, clinically calibrated masochist"), Pat replied, "We've got a long-ass off-season. Doing stuff like this gives me something to focus on. I feel like a bum not doing anything in the off-season. It forces you to stay on a schedule, keeps you from going out and drinking each night, doing something stupid."

But there was more to his decision than he shared with ESPN. Pat was agnostic, perhaps even an atheist, but the Tillman family creed nevertheless imparted to him an overarching sense of values that included a belief in the transcendent importance of continually striving to better oneself—intellectually, morally, and physically. Endurance events like marathons and triathlons, which favor bony ectomorphs, were not Tillman's strong suit—hence their appeal to him: they were especially challenging to a guy with the hulking physique of a professional football player.

Pat didn't expect to beat many expert triathletes, but he wanted to demonstrate to himself that he could finish the event's 1.2-mile swim, 56-mile bike ride, and 13.1-mile run. Being competitive by nature, he also looked forward to competing against himself—he was eager to see just how good a triathlete he could become in the limited time he had to prepare for the race. He took pleasure, during his twice-daily runs, rides, and swimming sessions, in forcing himself to ignore the lactic acid burning in his arms and legs, push through the pain, and cover whatever distance he'd set for himself that day a few seconds faster than he had the week before. It made him physically stronger, needless to say, but more important, he believed, it developed something that might be termed character.

On June 3, after undergoing three months of rigorous training,

Pat completed the seventy-mile EagleMan event in six hours, ten minutes, and eight seconds. This was almost two hours slower than the winner, and placed him 956th among the 1,278 finishers, but the race—and the training that preceded it—were immensely satisfying to him. In many ways Tillman had approached this triathlon the same way he approached football—he just happened to have genes that made him really, really good at the latter and not the former.

———

On June 30, 2001, the CIA issued a top secret report known as the Senior Executive Intelligence Brief that included an article titled "Bin Laden Threats Are Real." By late July "the system was blinking red," according to the CIA director, George Tenet, and could not "get any worse." Yet the highest-ranking members of the Bush administration—including National Security Adviser Condoleezza Rice, Secretary of Defense Donald Rumsfeld, Deputy Secretary of Defense Paul Wolfowitz, Vice President Dick Cheney, and President Bush himself—continued to express doubts about the seriousness of the threat posed by bin Laden. Two senior officials in the CIA's Counterterrorist Center were so dismayed by the failure of the White House to heed their impassioned warnings that they considered resigning and taking their concerns to the media.

On July 27, the day Tillman and his teammates arrived in Flagstaff for the start of the Cardinals' 2001 preseason training camp, the counterterrorism czar Richard Clarke informed Rice that the danger of an imminent attack from al-Qaeda had most likely passed. He warned, however, that new intelligence indicated the attack had merely been postponed for a few months and "will still happen."

Ten days later, on Monday, August 6, George W. Bush received a confidential document known as the President's Daily Brief while vacationing at his ranch in Crawford, Texas. The memo, a summary of important intelligence assembled by the CIA, included a two-page assessment of the current threat posed by terrorists. At the top of this report was a headline in boldfaced type that read, "Bin Ladin Determined To Strike in US." In its concluding paragraphs, the report warned that information gathered by the FBI indicates patterns of suspicious activity in this country consistent with preparations for hijackings or other types of attacks, including recent surveillance of federal buildings in New York.

The FBI is conducting approximately 70 full field investigations throughout the US that it considers Bin-Ladin-related. CIA and the FBI are investigating a call to our embassy in the [United Arab Emirates] in May saying that a group of Bin Ladin supporters was in the US planning attacks with explosives.

This memo was the thirty-sixth occasion during the preceding eight months that the CIA had alerted the White House to the threat posed by al-Qaeda or bin Laden. After a CIA officer finished briefing President Bush on the memo, according to Ron Suskind's book *The One Percent Doctrine,* the commander in chief was openly disdainful of the warning it contained. "All right," Bush told the officer in a sarcastic tone of voice, "you've covered your ass," and then dismissed him. (Three years later, after the confidential memo was declassified and released to the public, the president's national security adviser, Condoleezza Rice, would insist that the confidential memo contained nothing more than "historical information based on old reporting. There was no new threat information.")

Growing increasingly desperate to convince Rice, Rumsfeld, Cheney, and Bush of the need to take decisive action to prevent the major attack that he believed bin Laden was about to launch within the borders of the United States, Richard Clarke sent Rice a scathing e-mail that challenged her to imagine how she and her White House colleagues would feel "when in the very near future al-Qaeda had killed hundreds of Americans: 'What will you wish then that you had already done?' " Clarke issued this urgent call to action at the beginning of September 2001, exactly one week before the attacks of 9/11.

————

By the conclusion of the Cardinals' training camp at the end of August, Pat was feeling secure about his job as a starter, and was looking forward to the team's first game of the season. Most teams in the NFL played their initial game on September 9, but due to the vagaries of the league schedule Arizona wasn't slated to play until the following Sunday, September 16.

On the Tuesday before that first game for the Cardinals, the players were given the day off, as they usually were on Tuesdays. Pat was intending to sleep late that morning, but shortly after 7:00 a.m. mountain standard time he was jarred awake by a ringing phone. It was his brother Kevin, sounding frantic, yelling at him, "Get your ass up and turn the TV on!"

When Pat raced into his living room and switched on his television, the first thing he saw was a film clip of a Boeing 767 crashing into the World Trade Center at 590 miles per hour, sending a fluorescent blossom of fire bursting through the upper floors of the south tower. A newscaster was explaining that the footage showed United Airlines Flight 175 striking the tower an hour earlier, at 9:03 a.m. eastern daylight time, and that the entire building had just collapsed with thousands of people still inside. Another Boeing 767, American Airlines Flight 11, according to the reporter, had flown into the north tower at 8:46 EDT, and that building was now burning out of control. Twenty minutes later Pat was still staring at the screen, transfixed, when the north tower plummeted to the ground before his eyes. "I left to go in to work," says Marie, "but he sat there watching all morning, and it had a big impact on him."

Shortly after the first tower had been struck from the north, eyewitnesses reported that the jet had been attempting to swerve away from the building before crashing into it, prompting many people to assume the collision was a terrible accident. But when the second jet flew into the south tower from the opposite direction, there was no mistaking that a sophisticated attack on New York was under way. Like most Americans, Pat found it very difficult to get his mind around this. It seemed beyond belief.

With Marie at work, eventually he left the house and went to the Cardinals' training facility, where he resumed his vigil in front of a television among his teammates. Footage of tiny figures leaping from the upper floors of the burning towers and tumbling through space left an indelible impression on him. Pat was especially affected by images of people jumping from the buildings holding hands.

Several days later, at the request of the Cardinals' public relations department, Pat submitted to an interview that was videotaped for distribution to the news media. When asked to speak about how the national tragedy had affected him, Pat reflected, "You don't realize how great a life we have over here. . . . Times like this you stop and think about just how—not only how good we have it, but what kind of a system we live under. What freedoms we're allowed. And that wasn't built overnight. And the flag's a symbol of all that. A symbol of— My great-grandfather was at Pearl Harbor. And a lot of my family has . . . gone and fought in wars. And I really haven't done a damn thing as far as laying myself on the line like that. So I have a great deal of respect for those who have. And what the flag stands for."

The league canceled all the games that had been scheduled for the Sunday and Monday following September 11, but had announced the season would resume on the twenty-third, when the Cardinals would play the Denver Broncos. With the tape rolling, the interviewer tried to elicit a statement from Pat to the effect that he and the other players were eager to resume playing football, in spite of the attacks that had killed nearly three thousand people. Tillman did his best to stick to this upbeat script. "I want to play now," he started to mumble, looking uncomfortable, "if for no other reason—just because this thing has already done enough damage. Let's move on. Let's move on, let's go out there, sit out there for the national anthem." It was becoming painfully obvious, however, that these words weren't coming from his heart. "I don't know," he stammered, attempting to continue. Then he sighed, collected his thoughts, and declared, "It's hard because . . . I play a goddamn— We play football, you know? It just seems so goddamn . . . It is so unimportant compared to everything that's taken place."

At the time, nobody who saw this interview assigned great portent to this statement, or to the depth of emotion with which it was delivered. Looking back at it again in light of subsequent events, however, it seems obvious that Tillman had already begun to think seriously about making changes in his life—changes that, in the context of the al-Qaeda strikes on New York and Washington, would entail doing something he considered to be of greater consequence than playing football.

CHAPTER SEVENTEEN

Because the league suspended play following the attacks on September 11, when the Denver Broncos came to Tempe on the twenty-third, the Cardinals hadn't played a game since their final exhibition game on August 30, more than three weeks earlier. Pat and his teammates were understandably rusty, although it wasn't apparent initially. Jake Plummer completed his first five passes for 109 yards, and Arizona scored a field goal and a touchdown early in the game to take a 10–0 lead. But then the Cardinals squandered their momentum by making three turnovers, and the Broncos' offense, reenergized, steamrolled the Cardinals' defense. Denver won, 38–17.

Pat played poorly. His lowest moment occurred with 6:05 remaining in the third quarter. The Broncos had the ball on the Cardinals' thirty-six-yard line when Denver quarterback Brian Griese threw a pass toward the receiver Eddie Kennison, who was being covered by Tillman. Kennison had gotten away from Pat, however, and was open in the end zone, so Pat grabbed him illegally to prevent him from catching the football. Although the pass was incomplete, a referee saw the infraction and charged Pat with a pass interference penalty, which gave Denver a first down on the Cardinals' one-yard line. On the next play, Griese threw the ball to the fullback Patrick Hape for an easy touchdown, putting the Broncos ahead, 31–10.

Pat was furious at himself for the rest of the day, but by the time he went to bed that night he had already regained his perspective,

and was looking forward to using the episode as a learning experience to improve his performance in the future. "For the most part,"
Marie explains, "Pat put football in its proper place. If he had a bad
game, he would take it hard. It was his job, and he took it seriously.
But there were only a handful of instances that I can remember when
he was really, really upset about it."

The following Sunday, September 30, the Cardinals lost at home
again, this time to the Atlanta Falcons, 34–14. Only 23,790 specta-
tors had shown up to witness the defeat, Arizona's smallest home
crowd in many years. The Sunday after that, the Cardinals flew to
Philadelphia to play Donovan McNabb and the red-hot Eagles in
Veterans Stadium. Sixty-six thousand three hundred and sixty fans
were there, a sellout, to cheer their beloved Eagles. The start of the
game was delayed nine minutes, however, so that a speech from the
president of the United States could be broadcast live to the crowd.
At 1:00 p.m., as the players from both teams stood on the field before the opening kickoff, a surreal image of George W. Bush materialized above them on the stadium's JumboTron.

Dressed in a dark suit with a red tie, sitting in the White House
Treaty Room with an American flag behind his right shoulder, the
president pronounced, "Good afternoon."

> On my orders, the United States military has begun strikes against
> al-Qaeda terrorist training camps and military installations of the
> Taliban regime in Afghanistan. These carefully targeted actions are
> designed to disrupt the use of Afghanistan as a terrorist base of
> operations, and to attack the military capability of the Taliban
> regime. . . .
>
> More than two weeks ago, I gave Taliban leaders a series of clear
> and specific demands: Close terrorist training camps; hand over lead-
> ers of the al-Qaeda network; and return all foreign nationals, in-
> cluding American citizens, unjustly detained in your country. None
> of these demands were met. And now the Taliban will pay a price. By
> destroying camps and disrupting communications, we will make it
> more difficult for the terror network to train new recruits and coor-
> dinate their evil plans.
>
> Initially, the terrorists may burrow deeper into caves and other

entrenched hiding places. Our military action is also designed to clear the way for sustained, comprehensive and relentless operations to drive them out and bring them to justice. . . .

We did not ask for this mission, but we will fulfill it. The name of today's military operation is Enduring Freedom. We defend not only our precious freedoms, but also the freedom of people everywhere to live and raise their children free from fear. . . .

In the months ahead, our patience will be one of our strengths—patience with the long waits that will result from tighter security; patience and understanding that it will take time to achieve our goals; patience in all the sacrifices that may come.

Today, those sacrifices are being made by members of our Armed Forces who now defend us so far from home, and by their proud and worried families. A Commander-in-Chief sends America's sons and daughters into a battle in a foreign land only after the greatest care and a lot of prayer. We ask a lot of those who wear our uniform. We ask them to leave their loved ones, to travel great distances, to risk injury, even to be prepared to make the ultimate sacrifice of their lives. They are dedicated, they are honorable; they represent the best of our country. And we are grateful.

To all the men and women in our military—every sailor, every soldier, every airman, every coastguardsman, every Marine—I say this: Your mission is defined; your objectives are clear; your goal is just. You have my full confidence, and you will have every tool you need to carry out your duty.

I recently received a touching letter that says a lot about the state of America in these difficult times—a letter from a 4th-grade girl, with a father in the military: "As much as I don't want my Dad to fight," she wrote, "I'm willing to give him to you."

This is a precious gift, the greatest she could give. This young girl knows what America is all about. Since September 11, an entire generation of young Americans has gained new understanding of the value of freedom, and its cost in duty and in sacrifice.

The battle is now joined on many fronts. We will not waver; we will not tire; we will not falter; and we will not fail. Peace and freedom will prevail.

Thank you. May God continue to bless America.

Tillman stared up at the towering video screen alongside his team-mates and pondered the president's words. The strikes against bin Laden, al-Qaeda, and the Taliban of which Bush had spoken had commenced exactly two hours earlier when four American ships, an American submarine, and a British submarine launched a synchro-nized barrage of cruise missiles toward Afghanistan. The first of these fifty missiles had exploded into their targets just thirty-three minutes before Bush had begun his address to the nation. When images of the military action were shown on the JumboTron, the crowd filling the stadium let out a thunderous, cathartic roar. The attacks of 9/11 were being avenged. The United States was now at war.

The game between the Cardinals and the Eagles began immedi-ately after the president's speech. Arizona won it, 21–20, when Jake Plummer threw a thirty-five-yard touchdown pass to MarTay Jenk-ins on fourth down with only nine seconds left on the clock. Tillman had to leave the game in the first quarter, however, with a severe sprain to his right ankle after he received an illegal cut block from the Eagles' Jon Runyan, a six-foot seven-inch, 330-pound offensive tackle. Although Pat hopped off the field on one leg without assis-tance, the injury turned out to be serious. Other than the broken tibia he suffered when he was twelve years old, it was the only debilitat-ing injury Pat ever received on a football field, despite the fact that he was one of the hardest-hitting and most aggressive players in the league.

Immediately after returning to Arizona, ignoring the pain, Pat be-gan working out so he wouldn't lose too much strength or speed as the ankle slowly healed. While his teammates practiced, Pat ran end-less laps around the field with an inflatable cast on his foot. And as he continued to rehabilitate the injury over the weeks that followed, he closely followed the war in Afghanistan.

On October 19, the first American ground troops—a small con-tingent of Army Rangers—landed eighty miles south of Kandahar. For the first months of the war, though, the Bush administration was extremely reluctant to involve more than a handful of Special Oper-ations Forces in the conflict, relying instead on air strikes and ex-mujahideen militias whose services were purchased with duffel bags full of hundred-dollar bills. Most of these mercenary fighters (who received some $70 million all told) were Tajiks, Uzbeks, Turkmen, and Hazaras affiliated with the so-called Northern Alliance, which had been battling the Taliban for control of Afghanistan for the better part of a decade.

Despite the severity of Pat's injury, he missed only four games before returning to the lineup against the Giants on November 11, a game the Cardinals lost, 17–10. Two days later, Northern Alliance fighters, supported by American bombers, took control of Kabul, forcing the Taliban to scatter into the surrounding mountains. The Taliban had been vanquished from the Afghan capital with surprising ease, and without the death of even a single American soldier. The Bush administration, ecstatic over the painless victory that seemed at hand in Afghanistan, accelerated a secret plan it had been formulating to invade Iraq, although it would be many months before the president's intent to launch a second war would be revealed to the American public.

On November 25, a CIA officer named Johnny Michael Spann was gunned down by the Taliban during a prison uprising that occurred outside the northern city of Mazar-i-Sharif while Spann was interrogating prisoners of war—the first American to die in combat during Operation Enduring Freedom. Ten days after that, three U.S. Green Berets were killed and five others were gravely wounded on the outskirts of Kandahar when a U.S. Air Force B-52 bomber struck them with a two-thousand-pound, satellite-guided "smart" bomb that had been calibrated "for maximum blast effect."

The latter accident occurred during a desperate firefight between the Taliban and American Special Forces. An inexperienced Air Force tactical air controller had just calculated the coordinates of an enemy fighting position and was about to call in an air strike when the batteries died in his precision GPS device, causing its display screen to go dark. Frantically, the air controller put new batteries into the GPS, the numbers flashed back on the screen a moment later, and he directed the B-52 flying overhead to drop its lethal payload on these coordinates. The air controller was unaware, however, that after a battery replacement his GPS automatically defaulted to display the coordinates of its own position. He mistakenly called in these coordinates instead of the Taliban's position, and the upshot was the first three members of the American military to die in the Afghanistan war were victims of fratricide.*

Among those wounded and nearly killed by that errant bomb was Hamid Karzai, who, at the behest of the United States, had just been appointed the interim leader of Afghanistan. Born in Kandahar to a prominent Pashtun family, Karzai had fought against the Soviets in the 1980s, and his leadership skills were duly noted by the CIA. Like Haqqani, he became one of the CIA's most trusted mujahideen commanders. By the end of the Soviet-Afghan War, Karzai had established close personal ties with CIA director William Casey and President George Herbert Walker Bush.

Impressed by the stability the Taliban brought to Afghanistan when they appeared on the scene in 1994, Karzai initially endorsed their rise to power with great enthusiasm. His support of Mullah Omar continued until 1999, when Taliban fanatics murdered his father, at which time Karzai joined forces with the Northern Alliance against the Taliban and vowed to avenge this murder, in keeping with the tenets of *Pashtunwali*.

At the time he was wounded by the misdirected U.S. bomb on December 5, 2001, Karzai was leading eight hundred Pashtun militiamen in a battle against the Taliban outside of Kandahar. Fighting alongside twenty-four American Green Berets, Karzai and his forces had been skirmishing with the Taliban for two days when several hundred of Omar's fighters mounted a surprise assault, prompting the Green Berets to call in the air strike that killed the three Americans and almost killed the newly installed Afghan leader.

As this incident was unfolding, bin Laden was three hundred miles away, hiding with a large number of defiant al-Qaeda fighters in a network of covered trenches, caves, and underground bunkers, most of which had been constructed by bin Laden during the Soviet war with assistance from the CIA. This complex of caves occupied just a few square miles of rugged, sparsely forested terrain on the

---

* Those victims, all members of the Army Special Forces, were Master Sergeant Jefferson Davis, Sergeant First Class Daniel Petithory, and Staff Sergeant Brian Prosser. Although Johnny Michael Spann was killed ten days earlier, he was employed by the CIA, not the Armed Forces.

slopes of a fourteen-thousand-foot massif called Tora Bora. Believing that bin Laden was within their grasp, six CIA operatives directed an intensive air attack on Tora Bora's frigid heights, carpet bombing al-Qaeda positions with wave after wave of fifteen-thousand-pound "daisy cutters," five-thousand-pound thermobaric "bunker busters," and other instruments of overwhelming devastation. The air assault was bolstered by operations on the ground conducted by approximately seventy American Special Operations troops (some fifty of whom were Delta Force operators, the nonpareil of the U.S. military), a dozen British commandos, a handful of German commandos, and two thousand Afghan mercenaries commanded by a hodgepodge of local warlords who, in return for multimillion-dollar payments from the CIA, had momentarily put aside their hostilities to form an ad hoc coalition dubbed the Eastern Alliance.

Before the heaviest bombing began, according to a tape-recorded message from bin Laden broadcast on Al Jazeera two years later, he had directed his fighters to dig "one hundred trenches, spread across an area no more than one square mile—one trench for every three brothers—so as to avoid heavy human casualties from the bombing. . . . The bombing continued around the clock—not a second went by without warplanes flying over our heads, day and night. The American defense ministry command room, with all its allies, put everything they had into blowing up and destroying this small area. They tried to eradicate it altogether."

It appeared as though the onslaught from the sky had succeeded when, during the evening of December 11, the al-Qaeda fighters contacted one of the Eastern Alliance commanders and begged for a truce in order, they said, to negotiate the terms of their surrender. Despite vehement objections by the Americans, the Afghans agreed to the truce on the morning of the twelfth. Believing that bin Laden had no intention of capitulating, and that the cease-fire was merely a gambit to allow al-Qaeda forces to regroup, early that morning twenty-five American Delta operators and British Special Boat Service commandos attempted to climb toward bin Laden's redoubt in order to continue their attack when eighty Eastern Alliance fighters on the American payroll leveled their weapons at the Western commandos and forced them to turn back.

At 5:00 that evening, by which time no enemy had come forward to surrender, the Americans declared the truce to be invalid, ignored the protests of the Eastern Alliance, and resumed their assault on bin Laden's caves with even greater fury than before.

Giant orange fireballs again flared across the slopes of Tora Bora as B-52s, F-18s, and B-1 stealth bombers released their payloads over al-Qaeda positions. As the exploding ordnance shook the earth around him, bin Laden concluded that his forces were about to be eradicated and his own death was imminent. Wounded in the left shoulder, disillusioned and resentful, he put pen to paper and composed his last will and testament from a cramped subterranean bunker eighty-two hundred feet above sea level. "If every Muslim asks himself why has our nation reached this state of humiliation and defeat," he wrote, "then his obvious answer is because it rushed madly for the comforts of life and discarded the Book of Allah behind its back. . . . The Jews and Christians have tempted us with the comforts of life and its cheap pleasures and invaded us with their materialistic values before invading us with their armies, while we stood like women doing nothing because the love of death in the cause of Allah has deserted the hearts."

Confirmation that the al-Qaeda leader had given up and was preparing to die seemed to come on December 14, when the CIA intercepted a radio transmission from bin Laden in which he thanked his "most loyal fighters" for their sacrifices, asked their forgiveness for losing the battle of Tora Bora, and then promised that the battle against the infidels and crusaders would continue on other fronts. After the radio transmission, bin Laden's forces continued to fight for three more days until the battle came to a gruesome end. Although scores of enemy surrendered, the last al-Qaeda fighters holding out on the mountain killed themselves with hand grenades rather than surrender. On December 17, when the bombs stopped falling, the shooting ceased, and smoke from the battle finally drifted from the flanks of Tora Bora, American and British commandos immediately entered the warren of tunnels and bunkers, within which they were sure they would find the remains of bin Laden. A thorough search, however, turned up no trace of him.

The truce on December 11–12, it became apparent, had been a ruse to allow the al-Qaeda leader to make a deal with an Eastern Alliance commander who subsequently helped bin Laden escape for a purported payment of $6 million. The CIA had assumed the sheik's radio message on the fourteenth was a final farewell to his followers issued shortly before dying in one of the caves. Belatedly, the Americans came to understand that it was merely a send-off to his rear guard before he lit out for Pakistan.

This revelation infuriated the CIA and Delta Force operators who participated in battle. Eliminating Osama bin Laden was the primary objective of the entire post-9/11 campaign. In late November, when they realized that they had bin Laden cornered, the man who ran the CIA's operations in Afghanistan, Hank Crumpton, went to the Oval Office to warn President Bush and Vice President Cheney that they didn't have nearly enough American troops on the ground to seal off Tora Bora. According to Ron Suskind's book *The One Percent Doctrine,* Crumpton told Bush and Cheney, "We're going to lose our prey if we're not careful."

A week earlier, twelve hundred Marines had arrived in Kandahar. Crumpton implored General Tommy Franks to immediately transfer most of these Marines north to where bin Laden was dug in, but Crumpton's request was ignored. As an alternative, the CIA leader on the ground at Tora Bora requested that a more modest contingent of Rangers be dispatched to block escape routes into Pakistan, but this plan was rejected by Major General Dell Dailey, the head of the Joint Special Operations Command. The American presence at Tora Bora would thus remain limited to the eighty or so Special Ops Forces and CIA personnel who were already in place there. A request by the Delta Force squadron commander to at least seed bin Laden's potential routes of egress with hundreds of CBU-89 antipersonnel mines, dropped from the air, was also denied.

Responsibility for blocking the avenues of escape from Tora Bora thus fell almost entirely to Afghan militia fighters from the Eastern Alliance—a motley assortment of mutually hostile former mujahideen commanders and sub-commanders who were deeply suspicious of American ambitions in Afghanistan, but whose loyalty had nevertheless been expensively rented by the CIA. In retrospect, the decision to rely on these untrustworthy warlords for such an utterly crucial task probably doomed the mission from the outset.

Bin Laden had close personal ties going back more than fifteen years to several of the commanders who had been paid to block his retreat. Instead of killing "the world's most wanted man," one or more of the warlords who'd taken the CIA's cash opened their arms to bin Laden and ushered him safely through the cordon—probably first to Jalalabad, then north on horseback into the snow-choked canyons of Konar Province, and from there across the mountains into Pakistan. According to the journalist Peter Bergen, Jalaluddin Haqqani played a key role in bin Laden's escape. "Lutfullah Mashal, of the Afghan Interior Ministry, told me that it was Haqqani who saved bin Laden after the fall of the Taliban," Bergen wrote in the October 2004 issue of the *Atlantic,* "affording him refuge in Khost not long after the terrorist leader had slipped out of Tora Bora."

Bin Laden later gloated about eluding the CIA's clutches:

Despite the unprecedented scale of [the Tora Bora] bombardment and the terrible propaganda all focusing on one small, besieged spot, as well as the hypocrites' forces, which they got to fight against us for over two weeks, non-stop, and whose daily attacks we resisted by the will of God Almighty, we pushed them back in defeat. . . . Despite all this, the American forces dared not storm our positions. What clearer evidence could there be of their cowardice, of their fear and lies, of the myths about their alleged power? The battle culminated with the resounding, devastating failure of the global alliance of evil, with all its supposed power, to overcome a small group of *mujahideen,* numbering no more than three hundred, in their trenches within one square mile, at temperatures as low as ten degrees below zero Celsius. We suffered only six per cent casualties in the battle, and we ask God to accept them as martyrs. As for those in the trenches, we lost only about two per cent, thank God. If all the forces of global evil could not even achieve their objective over one square mile against a small number of *mujahideen* with such modest capabilities, how could they expect to triumph over the entire Islamic world?

By the first days of 2002, American forces and their allies had killed hundreds of Taliban and al-Qaeda fighters throughout Afghanistan, and most of the rest had dispersed into the countryside or fled over the border into the tribal regions of Pakistan. The insurgents were far from defeated, however, and the three enemy leaders who had been marked for elimination at the top of a hit list assembled by the American military brass—Osama bin Laden, Mullah Mohammed Omar, and Jalaluddin Haqqani (whom Omar had recently promoted to commander in chief of the Taliban forces)—were still emphatically at large.

Back in November, a series of air strikes by U.S. bombers, attack helicopters, and an unmanned Predator drone armed with Hellfire missiles had been carried out specifically to assassinate Haqqani. Although thirty-eight people were killed in this campaign, including several Haqqani relatives and bodyguards, Haqqani was unscathed. In January of the new year, after helping bin Laden escape from Tora Bora, Haqqani started reorganizing his network of fighters from a base in the Pakistani city of Miram Shah, just ten miles from the highly permeable border with Afghanistan's Khost Province, whence he would direct Taliban strikes on U.S. and NATO targets with impunity over the years that followed.

PART TWO

War is always about betrayal, betrayal of the young by the old, of idealists by cynics and of troops by politicians.

—Chris Hedges, "A Culture of Atrocity"

CHAPTER EIGHTEEN

Tillman and the Cardinals played their final game of the NFL season in Washington, D.C., against the Redskins, on January 6, 2002—the makeup for what was supposed to have been their first game of the season, which had been canceled in the aftermath of 9/11. At half-time Arizona led 17–6, and by the end of the game Pat had recorded a team-leading eighteen tackles, but his brilliant performance was for naught: Arizona lost, 20–17, leaving them with a disappointing 7-9 record. Nobody suspected that it was the last football game Pat would ever play.

Throughout the autumn of 2001 many NFL players expressed outrage over the attacks on New York and Washington, declared their support for the war in Afghanistan, and made a lot of noise about wanting to kill bin Laden with their bare hands. But none of them took any meaningful action. They continued playing football and leading comfortable lives, with no discernible sacrifice. This didn't sit well with Pat. Given the enormity of what happened on 9/11, he felt he should do more than issue empty pronouncements.

Near the end of the football season Kevin Tillman had come to Phoenix for one of Pat's home games, and afterward, Marie recalls, "Pat started talking to Kevin about joining the Army. They were hanging out in the backyard after the game. All the talk at that point was strictly hypothetical. But that night Pat came in to bed and just mentioned out of nowhere, 'What if I joined the Army?' He said it in a sort of nonserious way, but there was a part of me that knew he was serious. I understood him well enough to know why he would feel he needed to do something like that. It wasn't really a surprise."

In the weeks that followed, says Marie, Pat continued to "just run the idea through his head. Then, as he got more and more serious about enlisting, Pat and I started having conversations about it. But it was a long process."

Jeff Hechtle's parents had a friend who'd enlisted in the Marines and joined one of the Force Recon units, a Special Operations detachment roughly analogous to the Army's Green Berets. In February 2002, Pat and Marie drove up to Provo, Utah, where the ex-Marine lived, to ask him what being in the military was really like. Over the next couple of days Pat and the ex-Marine went climbing on frozen waterfalls that hung from the walls of Provo Canyon like ghostly blue curtains, and on the belay ledges they did a lot of talking. "Pat was trying to figure things out," Marie says: " 'Should I go in as an enlisted man? Or should I go in as an officer?' I wasn't really part of those conversations. But we of course talked about it all the way home in the car. He needed to work through everything in his head.

"It wasn't like 9/11 happened and Pat immediately said, 'I'm joining the Army.' He did a lot of research first. He weighed all the pros and cons. What was it going to be like for him? What was it going to be like for me? He considered things from every possible angle. He didn't even bring Kevin into it until he'd already made his decision. First he wanted to figure it out on his own, to be sure it was the right thing."

Pat and Marie continued to discuss the matter intently. "I was definitely concerned," she explains. "How could I not be? But mostly I was concerned for his safety. He was always trying to reassure me that nothing was going to happen to him. 'Statistically, I'm more likely to die in a car wreck,' he would say."

Exactly five years after the September 11 attacks, staring out a window at throngs of New Yorkers scurrying through lower Manhattan, Marie muses, "I never explicitly asked him, 'Why are you doing this?' Because I understood Pat well enough to already know. . . . If it was the right thing for people to go off and fight a war, he believed he should be part of it.

"He saw his life in a much bigger way than simply, 'I am a professional football player, and if I walk away from this, my life is over.' Football was part of who he was, but it wasn't the be-all/end-all. He was looking in other directions even prior to 9/11. I always knew he would stop playing football before they had to kick him off the field. It was just a matter of time. . . . I mean, Pat could have played for years, retired, then golfed for the rest of his life. But I knew he was never going to do that."

After carefully weighing all the factors, Pat sat down at his computer and typed a document titled "Decision," dated April 8, 2002:

Many decisions are made in our lifetime, most relatively insignificant while others life altering. Tonight's topic . . . the latter. It must be said that my mind, for the most part, is made up. More to the point, I know what decision I must make. It seems that more often than not we know the right decision long before it's actually made. Somewhere inside, we hear a *voice*, and intuitively know the answer to any problem or situation we encounter. Our voice leads us in the direction of the person we wish to become, but it is up to us whether or not to follow. More times than not we are pointed in a predictable, straightforward, and seemingly positive direction. However, occasionally we are directed down a different path entirely. Not necessarily a bad path, but a more difficult one. In my case, a path that many will disagree with, and more significantly, one that may cause a great deal of inconvenience to those I love.

My life at this point is relatively easy. It is my belief that I could continue to play football for the next seven or eight years and create a very comfortable lifestyle for not only Marie and myself, but be afforded the luxury of helping out family and friends should a need ever arise. The coaches and players I work with treat me well and the environment has become familiar and pleasing. My job is challenging, enjoyable, and strokes my vanity enough to fool me into thinking it's important. This all aside from the fact that I only work six months a year, the rest of the time is mine. For more reasons than I care to list, my job is remarkable.

On a personal note, Marie and I are getting married a month from today. We have friends and family we care a great deal about

and the time and means to see them regularly. In the last couple of
months we've been skiing in Tahoe, ice climbing in Utah, perusing
through Santa Fe, visiting in California, and will be sipping Mai Tais
in Bora Bora in a little over a month. We are both able to pursue any
interests that strike our fancy and down the road, any vocation or
calling. We even have two cats that make our house feel like a home.
In short, we have a great life with nothing to look forward to but
more of the same.

However, it is not enough. For much of my life I've tried to follow a path I believed important. Sports embodied many of the qualities I deem meaningful: courage, toughness, strength, etc., while at
the same time, the attention I received reinforced its seeming importance. In the pursuit of athletics I have picked up a college degree,
learned invaluable lessons, met incredible people, and made my journey much more valuable than any destination. However, these last
few years, and especially after recent events, I've come to appreciate
just how shallow and insignificant my role is. I'm no longer satisfied
with the path I've been following . . . it's no longer important.

I'm not sure where this new direction will take my life though I
am positive it will include its share of sacrifice and difficulty, most of
which falling squarely on Marie's shoulders. Despite this, however, I
am equally positive that this new direction will, in the end, make our
lives fuller, richer, and more meaningful. My voice is calling me in a
different direction. It is up to me whether or not to listen.

"Pat decided that going into the military was what he needed to
do," Marie explains. "After he made his decision, he called Kevin
and said, 'This is what I'm doing.' He never said, 'Come with me'—
but he didn't have to. . . . I remember talking to Pat about it and saying, 'It's not fair to Kevin in some ways. Because you know he's going
to come with you.' "

On his own, Kevin had actually been toying with the idea of joining some branch of the Special Operations Forces for years, since
well before 9/11, although nothing had ever come of it. Upon graduating from college in June 2001 with a bachelor's degree in philosophy, Kevin signed a contract to play professional baseball for the
Cleveland Indians, and in early 2002 was employed as an infielder on

one of the Indians' minor-league teams. While playing baseball in college, however, he'd suffered a nagging rotator cuff injury from which he'd never fully recovered, and increasingly he'd been entertaining thoughts of leaving baseball and going down a different road. When Pat told Kevin that he was thinking about enlisting in the military, Kevin decided to enlist along with him, as Marie had predicted.

"When they were growing up in New Almaden," Marie explains, "Pat and Kevin were always together. There was never any competition or resentment. Even though they were so close in age, Kevin wasn't bothered by all the attention Pat got. Kevin and Richard were each very talented in their own right, and their parents were careful never to single out Pat, but there's no getting around the fact that Pat was the one who was usually in the limelight—which for a lot of people would be tough to take. But not for Kevin and Richard. All three brothers just loved each other to death."

———

Pat and Marie announced to their families and friends that they would be getting married in San Jose on May 4, 2002. Kevin was then living in North Carolina, playing second base for the Burlington Indians, and he asked his team manager for time off to attend the wedding. When the manager refused, citing club policy, Kevin asked to be released from his contract, the Indians granted his request, and he showed up at Pat and Marie's home in Chandler in mid-April, free from professional obligations.

By now both Pat and Kevin were certain they were going to join the military, but they decided not to break the news to anyone until after the wedding, so as not to distract from the festivities. They were leaning toward joining one of the branches of the Special Operations Forces. Shortly after arriving in Arizona, Kevin visited an Army recruiting office in a strip mall off Chandler Boulevard, a few miles east of Pat and Marie's home, to gather some basic information. Soon after this initial visit, Kevin, Pat, and Marie visited the same recruiting office together.

"Kevin and I pretended that we were a married couple," Marie says, "and we sat down at a table across from this recruiter to ask him detailed questions. Pat just kind of stayed in the background with his hat pulled down over his eyes, because he didn't want any-one to know who he was." One of the things Pat and Kevin had been undecided about was whether to become officers or go in as enlisted men—ordinary grunts. This meeting with the recruiter convinced them to forgo the officer track. They didn't want to remain back at headquarters sending other soldiers into harm's way. If they were go-ing to join the military, they wanted to be part of an elite combat force—to be in the thick of the action, share the risk and hardship, and have a direct impact.

The recruiter explained to them that the minimum commitment for Rangers was three years. "Before going in there," says Marie, "they thought they were going to have to join for four years. When we heard they could be Rangers and only have to be in for three years, I was like, 'Okay! That's *much* better than four years.' So I was pretty happy about that. I was also happy that we could have some control over where we lived. If they had gone into the regular Army, they could have stationed us who knows where. With the Rangers, there were three possible places we could have been stationed: Fort Lewis, near Seattle; or one of two bases in Georgia—Fort Benning and Fort Stewart. At that time you could actually pick where you wanted to be."

When they left the recruiting office after about an hour, Marie re-members, "I was thinking, 'We can live near Seattle! We'll be done in three years instead of four!' Also, we learned that Rangers deploy overseas for relatively short periods; they're usually gone for only three months at a time, compared to troops in the regular Army, who would go overseas for twelve months at a time. And by becoming Rangers, they would be with elite soldiers who knew what they were doing, so I assumed that would make things safer for Pat and Kevin. I came out of there feeling that it didn't sound that bad, all things considered—if I could put out of my mind the fact that they would be in combat situations."

Pat, Marie, and Kevin traveled to San Jose at the beginning of May for the wedding and then returned briefly to Arizona before Pat and Marie departed for their honeymoon in Bora-Bora on May 10. In the interim, Pat and Kevin returned to the Army recruiting office, where they signed contracts committing them to three years of mili-tary service, beginning in July. Because he'd been such a big football star for both the Sun Devils and the Cardinals, Pat was a celebrity throughout Arizona, and he and Kevin were recognized while they were signing documents, prompting fears that their enlistment would be leaked to the news media. Although they had intended to tell their family of their plans in person after Pat returned from Bora-Bora, Pat and Kevin decided they should notify them right away over the phone instead, lest Richard or their parents learn of their impending enlistment from the evening news.

When the Tillman brothers made these calls on May 8 and 9, the announcement was not well received by their loved ones. Knowing Pat and Kevin as well as they did, nobody doubted that once they were in the Army, they would insist on being sent to the front lines. This prospect was especially upsetting to Dannie and Richard.

While Pat and Marie were honeymooning in the South Pacific, Uncle Mike Spalding—Dannie's brother—flew out to Arizona and tried to convince Kevin that joining the Army was a terrible idea and they should call the whole thing off, but to no avail. Marie's parents called Pat's agent, Frank Bauer, and asked him to talk Pat out of it as well, but Bauer had no more success than Uncle Mike did. So Pat and Kevin's parents, in conjunction with Marie's parents, decided to attempt an intervention.

It took place at the Tillmans' cottage in New Almaden, soon after the newlyweds returned from Bora-Bora. In attendance were Pat, Kevin, and the Tillman parents; Marie and her parents; Marie's sister, Christine Garwood; and her husband, Alex Garwood. "It wasn't a real intervention," says Marie, "because Pat and Kevin knew what was coming. But Pat believed that everybody had a right to tell him what they thought, and to try and talk him out of it. By that point, though, there was no talking him out of it. It was a done deal. So the intervention turned into a disaster. It was very upsetting."

"I think Pat opened the discussion," recalls Christine. "He was like, 'Okay! Tell me whatever you want to tell me! Throw it out there, and I'll respond as best I can. Bring it on!' It started out with orderly give-and-take, but Dannie was very emotional. Her big concern was that they could be hurt or killed. Pat kept insisting, 'That's not gonna happen.' And that's exactly how we all felt—that it wasn't even a possibility. But Dannie wasn't convinced."

Pretty soon it became clear that no argument or entreaty would be sufficient to convince Pat and Kevin to abandon their plans. So in desperation the petitioners directed their pleas to Marie. "They thought that it was my job to stop it," she says. "I felt like a lot of people were pointing fingers at me, saying, 'You're the only one who can do anything; why don't you put your foot down and tell Pat not to go?' But I didn't feel like I needed to answer to anyone, not even our families. It was between Pat and me. I understood why he was doing it, and I supported him. Our conversations about how this decision came about were really nobody's business. So I was a little upset by that. By all of it.

"Pat cared a lot about the people around him," Marie continues. "He didn't hurt people on purpose. It killed him that it hurt his mom or hurt me. That was very, very difficult for him to handle. But he had to do what he thought was right."

Marie and Christine's father, Paul Ugenti, tried to sway Pat with an economic rationale. "Obviously, my dad loved Marie and he loved Pat," says Christine. "And knowing the way Pat's mind worked, he tried to appeal to his logic. He pointed out that Pat would be leaving football at the peak of his career, and the peak of his market value as a player, and might not be able to return to the NFL." Pat countered that he would be away from football for only three years, and would probably have no trouble playing again. Mr. Ugenti then responded by reiterating how much money Pat was giving up—that joining the Army would potentially cost him and Marie many millions of dollars in the long run.

The emphasis on the financial downside pushed Pat's mother over the edge. "Why are you talking about *money*?!" she exclaimed. "This isn't about money! Pat and Kevin could get killed!" She began to sob, imploring her two eldest sons, "Life hands out plenty of trouble without even asking. Why do you want to go out looking for it?" She reminded them that the current commander in chief of the nation's Armed Forces was not a man who inspired trust or confidence. Then, as her emotions got the better of her, she asked everyone to leave.

CHAPTER NINETEEN

In April, the Cardinals had offered Pat a three-year contract that would pay him $3.6 million to keep playing football for Arizona. Upon returning to Chandler after the intervention in May, Pat informed the Cardinals' head coach, Dave McGinnis,* that he was declining the offer in order to join the Army. McGinnis was taken aback, but he said he understood Pat's reasons for enlisting. When he tried to discuss strategies for announcing Pat's decision, and asked how Pat was going to handle the overwhelming interest from the news media that would inevitably follow, Pat simply replied, "I'm not." He explained that his decision to enlist spoke for itself, and he would be doing no media interviews of any kind. And from that day forward he did none.

In early June 2002, Pat and Kevin appeared at the Military Entrance Processing Station in downtown Phoenix, across the street from the arena where the Phoenix Suns, the professional basketball team, play their home games. The Department of Defense operates sixty-five such offices across the nation; each MEPS screens new recruits for all four branches of the military—Army, Navy, Air Force, and Marines—to determine if they are qualified. The daylong process

---

* McGinnis had succeeded Vince Tobin as head coach after Tobin was fired in the middle of the 2000 NFL season.

includes an aptitude test, medical exam, and background check, and concludes with the recruits swearing an oath of enlistment.

The first indication that it might prove difficult for Pat to adapt to the Army's hidebound ways occurred when Pat, Kevin, and several other recruits lined up before an especially abrasive master sergeant who began shouting contradictory orders at them before they'd signed any documents committing them to enlist. Pat felt compelled to point out to the master sergeant, "Hey, you're confusing everybody. Besides, you're treating us like assholes, and we haven't even signed up to be treated like assholes yet."

As soon as the sergeant recovered from his shock that a recruit would dare to address him in this fashion, he jumped down Pat's throat. Unintimidated, Pat yelled right back at him, and the two men came close to exchanging blows before some other recruits interceded. Despite this inauspicious episode, at the end of the day Pat and Kevin signed away their freedom, recited the oath of enlistment, and received orders to appear at Fort Benning, Georgia, on July 8, 2002. For three years thereafter, their lives would be under the nearly absolute control of the U.S. Army. Pat was twenty-five years old, and Kevin was twenty-four. Each would be starting at a base salary of $1,290 per month.

As Pat and Kevin departed Phoenix on the appointed day, Pat pulled a journal bound in brown leather from his backpack and began documenting his impressions of the long stint stretching ahead of him. The first entry, dated July 8, begins, "It will be interesting to see how this little adventure pans out. At the moment I care little about the 'moral stance' that got this fiasco started. . . . As I taxi down the runway on my way to Georgia, all I can think about is how nice it was to sit with Marie, sipping hot chocolate and watching *Gosford Park* last night. Or how comfy my big bed is with Marie's naked body pressed against me. I hope Marie is happy at home. . . . I hope Ma's OK. . . . I hope Pooh's OK. . . . I hope Kevin doesn't get hurt. . . . I know what I'm doing is right, but at times it is very difficult to see it that way."

After landing in Atlanta, the Tillmans boarded a bus for the two-hour ride to the Thirtieth Adjutant General Reception Station at Fort Benning, known as Thirtieth AG, where they arrived shortly after midnight on July 9. They would spend the next nine days "in-processing" here, bunking in a fifty-foot-by-fifty-foot concrete "bay" with 110 other new recruits in a nightmarish state of purgatory before moving on to the bona fide hell of basic training.

Both Pat and Kevin were astonished, and appalled, by the immaturity of many of the eighteen- and nineteen-year-olds among whom they found themselves at Thirtieth AG. These were not the kinds of men they'd envisioned themselves fighting alongside and entrusting their lives to. To be sure, not all of their fellow recruits were suspect. Some were intelligent and motivated, and would go on to become excellent noncommissioned officers of the sort who have formed the crucial backbone of the world's armies since Alexander the Great battled the forebears of today's Afghan insurgents in 330 B.C. But a disturbing number of the recruits in their bay struck the Tillman brothers as indolent whiners and losers who had enlisted not out of any sense of duty, or even adventure, but rather because their parents had booted them out of the nest and they lacked the qualifications to land a minimum-wage job.

Twenty-four hours after the Tillmans arrived at Thirtieth AG, a fresh recruit named Túlio Tourinho showed up in the middle of the night and immediately crawled into his bunk. He was a Brazilian national whose family came to the United States when he was five years old in order for his father to get a doctorate degree, and then five years later returned to Brazil, where Túlio dreamed of one day making a life for himself in the States. He eventually achieved this goal by winning a scholarship to attend his final year of high school in Uniontown, Pennsylvania, after which he remained in the United States on a student visa and obtained a bachelor's degree from Morehead State University in eastern Kentucky.

On September 11, 2001, Túlio was happily employed as a high-school teacher in Winchester, Kentucky. The attacks on New York and Washington affected him so profoundly, however, that at the end of that academic year he enlisted in the Army, even though he wasn't a U.S. citizen. His American-born wife, pregnant with their first child, "wasn't very pleased," Túlio admits, "but she supported me."

When he arrived at Thirtieth AG after midnight, he says, "I was dead tired. I'd just received a whole bunch of shots that were making me completely ill. I was trying to overcome this roller-coaster ride of emotions that was tearing my insides out. And all around me were these immature kids who were talking and yelling and making silly, obnoxious noises throughout the night." He felt as if he were at a sleepover with a hundred fourteen-year-old boys who had attention deficit disorder. After he tried in vain to get some rest, the racket finally became so intolerable that Túlio yelled at the top of his lungs, in a voice well practiced in the art of disciplining unruly students, "Shut the fuck up! I am thirty years old, I quit my job to serve my country, left a wife pregnant with our first child at home, whom I love and miss dearly, and I will be goddamned if I'm gonna let some fucking immature juvenile punks prevent me from getting a good night's sleep! Now, shut the fuck up right now or I'm going to beat you back to your fucking mommies!

"All of a sudden the entire bay got quiet," Túlio remembers. And it stayed that way for the remainder of the night, which made an impression on another older recruit who had been trying to sleep nearby. In the morning this guy approached Túlio, introduced himself as Pat Tillman, and thanked him for bringing order to the bay.

"We were wondering when somebody was going to speak up," Pat said to the Brazilian, "because these kids are just relentless. They don't let anybody rest."

A conversation between the two men followed, during which, Túlio recalls, "Pat told me briefly what was going on and what I needed to do to get into the game. He offered to help me out. Immediately I noticed his appearance. He was quite a large-size man. But it was his vocabulary I noticed most, and his demeanor, and his poise." It was the start of an enduring friendship between Túlio, Pat, and Kevin.

"I had no idea who Pat was at the time," Túlio says. "Neither he nor Kevin ever mentioned that he was a professional football player. I found out later from the chatter that he was famous. We ended up going through all of basic training together, and I depended on Pat and Kevin for intelligent conversation. I guess they did the same with me. We counted on each other for support. We had college degrees, which set us apart from almost all the other recruits in our cycle. And Pat and I were both married. We just hit it off."

Six days after the Tillmans arrived at Thirtieth AG, some high-ranking officers showed up at their bay for an inspection, and Pat wrote that encountering them was "awkward. Getting used to the idea of saluting to officers constantly . . . is odd. Of course I understand and appreciate the point of showing respect to superiors but the caste separation between officers and enlisted men is foreign." This, alas, was only the first of many aspects of military culture that struck Pat as archaic, bizarre, and counterproductive.

On July 17, Pat happily noted in his journal:

We are leaving this place tomorrow and going down to start boot-camp. . . . It's about time. . . . I've written a few letters to Marie. . . . I miss her more and more and hope she is well. One thing that I found horrible in college was that I got used to her not being around. I never again want to get used to that. It's much better to be sad than calloused. I look forward to the time when both of us have the lifestyle we used to enjoy. . . . Not only will these next 3 years make me a stronger person, mentally and physically, I know it will also free up my conscience to enjoy what I have. My hope is that I will feel satisfied with my accomplishment . . . enough to relax for a while and just be. Be, with Marie.

Three days later Pat wrote, "Well, we are now in Basic and I'm starting to get more comfortable. Yesterday was a complete disaster." Things started to go badly when he forgot to lock his locker, prompting one of the drill sergeants to hurl its contents across the floor. And "to add insult," Pat mused, "if that wasn't enough, I was written up for it. I fucked up my cadence calls, lost shit, got yelled and screamed at. . . . I was a mess. Oh well, just keep working and we'll see what happens. . . . Our drill sergeants are tough but quality people and I believe they will teach us a lot. Still missing my love."

A day after this—thirteen days after arriving at Fort Benning—Pat wrote:

As always, Marie is on my mind. I have been unable to speak with her . . . since we've been here, and I miss the sound of her voice. . . .

Often it bothers me that I am not by her side. Sometimes I feel like I've left her all by her lonesome to fend against the world. I suppose there is a reason for my feeling that way: My actions could be interpreted as such. I just hope to hell she doesn't feel that way. I love her to death and know that eventually this will be good for us both. Hopefully, she will one day see it that way. In the meantime I struggle with the guilt of what I've done. Naturally I'm a confident person and know all will be well and in a few years we'll be right back in the driver's seat kicking life's ass. But I'm also aware that there is the possibility I'm wrong. If Marie's, Ma's, Kevin's and Pooh's, and Dad's life was somehow hurt on account of me, I couldn't forgive myself.

I console myself in the knowledge that I did this with noble intention. Sometimes one must purposefully convince himself that he is right as doubt creeps in. Fortunately the doubt is a small voice and I can control it.

My wife and family mean the world to me, as do my friends; I cannot allow this to bring pain to them.

Pat's entry for July 25 begins:

Yesterday was a combination of bittersweet for me. The bitter taste came from the fact that Nub & I did awful in our land navigation. . . . The sweet of the day was the fact we went on two long marches with our stuff on. It was nice to move on out of here for a while and meander about. It will probably take me a while to get used to lugging around a sack all day but I only have to look around me to stop feeling sorry for myself. . . .

One thing I find myself despising is the sight of all these guns in the hands of children. Of course we all understand the necessity of defense. . . . It doesn't dismiss the fact that a young man I would not trust with my canteen is walking about armed. . . .

My moods at this point, with the exception of the constant loneliness & guilt associated with my separation from Marie, vary depending on how I'm doing at my tasks. Blow the land navigation, feel bad for a few hours; do something to help someone or get my marching calls correctly, feel good for a few hours. . . .

On the whole, in spite of any worries or fluctuating moods, Nub and I are standing fast and moving right along. How important it has been to have Nub around has been covered but must be reiterated.

When Pat left home for the Army, he carried with him a laminated photograph of Marie taken on their wedding day. Unabashedly sentimental, he wrote that this "picture of Marie, outside of my ring, is my most prized possession. It's amazing how beautiful she is in her wedding dress. . . . What a fantastic day that was." Gazing at the little photo in the barracks, he contemplated his marriage and other major milestones. "It is amazing the turns one's life can take," he reflected, then listed a few: Spending time in jail for assaulting Darin Rosas, he wrote, "was huge, drastically changing my mindset and priorities. That experience aged me about ten years and I credit it for my success with academics and football in college."

On the next page of his journal he pondered what impact his enlistment would have on his life. Having completed just three weeks of his military commitment, with 153 weeks remaining, he wrote:

Everything about my life has completely shifted. Everything. I planned on having kids, continuing my football, and enjoying life as always. Now I'm sitting in a fucking barracks with 53 kids. This path needs to hurry itself up and brighten. . . . I do my best to control it, but sometimes I get so incredibly frustrated around here my fucking jaw muscles want to collapse my teeth on themselves. Today Marie's letters came and I needed so badly to be with her, hold her, make love to her. . . . I can see her writing. Picture her next to the cats, searching for the words to put on paper. I flatter myself and imagine a tear rolling down her cheek, her giant eyes glowing and full of feeling. . . . How the hell I have been able to keep her after all these years is a goddamn miracle. Why does she put up with it? Who does this? Who takes a perfectly perfect life and ruins it? A perfectly happy wife and marriage and jeopardizes it? AHHH! If I do not strangle someone while I'm here I was touched by an angel.

A day later, on July 29, he was able to speak with Marie on the phone for the first time in more than two weeks. "It wasn't for long," he wrote, "but how nice it was. . . . I was a mess. Just like in the clink: fine when I'm there but give me a person I love and I can hardly pull the lump out of my throat. She had to talk the whole damn time while I got a hold of myself. . . . Her voice was so soothing, I'll be able to survive off that for weeks to come."

For the next two months of basic training, Pat struggled to keep his emotions on an even keel. His celebrity didn't make things any easier for him. Although he'd declined all of the numerous requests for media interviews and tried to keep a low profile, his fame followed him to boot camp. Even without Pat's cooperation, the Bush administration turned his enlistment into a marketing bonanza for the so-called Global War on Terror. On June 25, Secretary of Defense Donald Rumsfeld sent a memo to Secretary of the Army (and former Enron executive) Tom White, with a newspaper article about Tillman attached; the memo said, "Here is an article on a fellow who is apparently joining the Rangers. He sounds like he is world-class. We might want to keep an eye on him."* On June 28, Rumsfeld wrote a personal note directly to Pat declaring, "It is a proud and patriotic thing you are doing." A month later, Pat received a flattering letter from Major General John Vines, the commander of the Army's Eighty-second Airborne Division, urging Kevin and him to forgo their plans to become Rangers and join the Eighty-second Airborne instead. The Army, the Department of Defense, and the White House were paying close attention to everything Pat did.

"It definitely made things more difficult for him," recalls Túlio Tourinho:

The drill sergeants bent over backwards not to show favoritism toward him. Through it all, Pat just tried to be the best soldier he could. Whenever he was told to do something, he executed it. When there was a job to be done, he always did more than his share. . . . If there is one thing certain about stress, and about despair, it's that it will inevitably show who you really are. And the amazing thing

---

* According to Rumsfeld's senior military assistant at the time, Lieutenant General Bantz Craddock, this was the only time he could remember Rumsfeld ever writing a personal note commending the enlistment of an individual soldier.

about Pat is that the despair and stress never revealed anything ugly about him. That astounded me, because when things got hard and the kids were being utterly disrespectful, I would become an ugly individual at times. I would lose it and tell them they were being spoiled brats. But Pat was restrained. He had fortitude.

Pat's enlistment made waves throughout the Army, from four-star generals at the Pentagon to buck privates at boot camp. "Officers and other soldiers didn't really know how to react or what to do with him," says Marie.

They weren't quite sure who he was—they were like, "Why is he here? He's not so great just because he played professional football." Pat anticipated that reaction to a certain extent. But it was definitely hard for him. I think it was maybe a little easier for Kevin because he wasn't so much under the magnifying glass. Pat felt more pressure. He was being looked at more closely. And he was feeling responsible for how everything might affect all the rest of us. His parents are worried. Richard is worried. He's worried about me. He's wondering, "Did I ruin Marie's life and Kevin's life by doing this?" With his family, he always assumed that type of responsibility, for as long as I've known him.

Pat had been introspective since childhood, but the Army seemed to make him even more so. "What kind of man will I become?" he wondered in his journal on August 7. "Will people see me as an honest man, hard working man, family man, a good man? Can I become the man I envision? Is vision and follow-through enough? How important is talent & blind luck? . . . There are no true answers, just shades of grey, coincidence, and circumstance."

CHAPTER TWENTY

During the first week of September, Pat, Kevin, and their fellow recruits were taught how to shoot several types of machine guns. "Of course this is fun," Pat noted on September 5, "but I do not get too fired up about guns no matter what they are." The first weapon they shot was the M249 Squad Automatic Weapon, commonly referred to as the SAW, which Pat would later be assigned to carry in Iraq and Afghanistan. Just before it was Kevin's turn to fire it, a recruit opened the weapon's feed tray while a round was still in the chamber, inadvertently released the bolt, and the cartridge exploded. The blast peppered his face, neck, and chest with brass shrapnel, and burned him badly. He could easily have been killed. Chastened by the accident, Pat observed, "You forget, or don't think about, just how incredibly dangerous these weapons are until something like this takes place."

A day later the platoon went into the field for an overnight bivouac, during which they engaged in simulated combat with laser-tag gear. After Pat was selected to be one of the team leaders for these exercises, his team of five was ambushed by two snipers as he led them down a hill. During the mock firefight, he wrote, "We were coordinated and the communication was clear," enabling his team to repel the attackers and survive the faux ambush. During a second exercise, however, communication between members of his team broke down, they acted as panicked individuals rather than as a unified team, and in the resulting chaos all the men under his command were "killed" by the snipers. Sobered, Pat remarked that it was a "great learning experience."

The worst part of the day, however, had nothing to do with the simulated massacre during the ambush. That evening after returning to the barracks, he confessed to his diary, "Sometimes I'm overwhelmed with an injection of intense sorrow that is difficult to control. An intense need to be close to Marie, surrounded by her touch, smell, sound, beauty, and ease. It's as though one week of pain is condensed into 5–7 minutes. . . . What have I done?"

A day later Pat revisited his roiling feelings:

Just when I think my emotions have flat-lined they rear their ugly head. Yesterday, from out of nowhere, I got so fucking mad/upset/sad that I was having trouble maintaining my cool. It only lasted a short while but it was strong and surprised me. All I wanted was to squeeze Marie, tell her how much I care, give her back all that I've taken. . . . In a way it is refreshing in that this place has yet to callous or numb me. Somehow I enjoyed letting myself long for my wife and the life I left behind. It makes me *feel* and *appreciate* and *love*. It makes me feel very alive, and aware of my struggle. I do not intend to get dramatic, but life is about feeling and emotion. . . . Love, laughter, and joy, as well as pain, longing and sorrow, are all part of the ride. Without the latter you cannot truly appreciate the former, cannot come to understand just how much you truly care. . . . I'm experiencing and growing, and with this comes some suffering, but it's part of the deal. I feel I'm headed in the right direction. . . .

Passion is what makes life interesting, what ignites our soul, drives our curiosity, fuels our love and carries our friendships, stimulates our intellect, and pushes our limits. . . . A passion for life is contagious and uplifting. Passion cuts both ways. . . . Those that make you feel on top of the world are equally able to turn it upside down. . . . In my life I want to create passion in my own life and with those I care for. I want to feel, experience, and live every emotion. I will suffer through the bad for the heights of the good.

On September 11, Pat wrote a letter to Marie that began, "Who would have guessed that a year ago today would do such a number on our life in Eden. . . . Well, you take life as it comes. This separation craziness will end soon enough, and when it does we will once again be back in our Eden." As agonizing as it was for him to be apart from Marie, it reminded him how intensely he loved her, and how much she enriched his life.

"These last few weeks," he continued,

> have given me such an appreciation for everything we have in our life that were I to get hurt tomorrow and all my plans were dashed, it would all have been worth it. . . . These next few weeks and most of the next three years we will be pushed and tried as a couple just as hard as Nub & I will be individually. When we come out of this intact, spirits unbroken, we'll be stronger, closer, and happier than we could ever have been otherwise. Anything else will seem trivial to what we've weathered.

> I'm already pleased at the strides we've made despite our distance. Even after all that's taken place and the miles between us, I still feel as close, if not closer, than we've ever been. The tighter we get, the more incredible a person I see, and the more proud I am to know I'll be sharing the rest of my life with you. Of course I do not expect these feelings to be reciprocated, especially not while I've left you all alone; for now it's enough that I feel it.

> A year ago completely changed our life. It taught me what truly matters. . . . It clarified the direction I need to head and it reinforced that you're the best thing that has happened, or ever will happen, to me. . . . I love you.

On Friday, September 20, Pat and Kevin completed basic training. When they learned that the Tillman brothers would be getting a thirty-hour pass to mark their graduation, Marie and Jeff Hechtle, Pat's high-school amigo, booked a flight to Georgia in order to spend the brief holiday with them. "In the days leading up to it everybody was walking on eggshells," Túlio remembers. "The Army hung the idea of the mid-cycle pass over our heads like a guillotine. If you do anything wrong, so much as breathe incorrectly or stand with an improper posture, they threaten to take it away from you."

At 1:00 p.m. on Saturday, when the pass was due to commence, Pat, Kevin, and Túlio gathered with the rest of the recruits in the main assembly area for inspection, attired in their new Class-A dress uniforms and spit-shined boots. Because they would be required to report back at the base at 7:00 p.m. on Sunday, they were desperate not to waste a single minute of freedom. "We had a plan of action how to get out of there as quickly as possible," says Túlio. "As soon as we were dismissed, Kevin ran upstairs to grab our stuff, and I ran to a phone booth to call a cab for the three of us." Kevin, Pat, and Marie had booked rooms at a Days Inn near the gate to the base, and Túlio had reserved a room to meet his wife at a motel right across the street.

When the cab pulled up to the Days Inn, Marie was standing in front of the motel waiting for them. "As soon as the cab stops," Túlio remembers, "Pat leaps out the door. Marie runs up and jumps on him, knocking him off balance, and they both fall to the ground. They just lay there, kissing each other and staring at each other—him caressing her face, caressing her hair, telling her how much he missed her, how much he loves her. They stayed there on the ground like that for what seemed like ten minutes, although I'm sure it couldn't have been that long. It was an amazing moment. A demonstration of absolute love. It affected me very strongly."

Shortly after returning to his barracks after the visit was over, Pat wrote,

What a glorious weekend. . . . What an absolutely glorious weekend. All the build-up and expectation, all the yearning and planning, for a mere 30 hours. For just one night of freedom . . . Seeing Marie and spending time with the woman I love was incredible. We said things we longed to say for months, held one another the way we've longed to for months, and enjoyed the company we've been missing for so long. . . . The hours the four of us spent were not in a whirlwind of action, drinking, or traveling. We simply drank loads of coffee, ate numerous coffeehouse treats, had a marvelous dinner, and talked for hours on end. Three hours at one coffee shop, three at another, three in the hotel or car—all we did was yak & yak & yak. Every subject was fair game: home, Arizona, Pooh, friends, future, business, our present situations, etc., etc., etc. We just ran for hours without a break, or a dip in its quality. . . .

> The fact that Hechtle took the time and expense to come out . . .
> Acts like that are never forgotten and sure to be reciprocated. He is
> an amazing friend and my whole family is fortunate to have him in
> our life. What a gesture. . . .

Jeff Hechtle's willingness to fly all the way across the country just to
spend a few hours with him was especially meaningful to Pat because
he felt like some of his most valuable friendships had suffered since his
enlistment, and he confided in his journal at length about this sense of
abandonment. In one entry he wrote, "Because of the lengths I've
gone to, and the importance on which I place my relationships, I'm
somewhat put off by the lack of letters from my friends at home. . . .
No question I am overly sensitive, but . . . It's funny, these last 6–7
years I've noticed some of my close friends putting governors on our
relationship. In most cases it is I who calls, I who sets up dinner, I who
makes the effort. Why this is the case is not exactly clear. . . . I care
about my friends openly and unselfishly and—though realizing I
sound like a woman—am bothered by their apparent lack of interest."

"I think most of his friends didn't necessarily understand how
difficult the Army was for him and Kevin," Marie says. "While they
were going through all this crap at boot camp, it seemed to Pat that
everyone else was just going about their lives, and had kind of forgotten about them. That's why when Hechtle flew out to Georgia,
Pat appreciated it so much."

Pat, of course, appreciated Marie's visit even more. She was his
crucial source of emotional comfort—a calm, steady force that anchored his life and brought him tremendous joy. "It was so nice to
see Marie," Pat wrote, "so incredibly nice. . . . Simply put, the visit
allowed me to express to Marie those things that have been burning
in my gut. I'm sure she still hates me for everything, but at least she
will know how her hate holds nothing to my own self-loathing. This
comes across as down, but I assure you the visit was nothing but positive. Around here one is allowed a little self-loathing."

By 7:00 on Sunday evening Pat and Kevin had said their good-
byes to Marie and Hechtle, and were back in their barracks. When
Pat sat down to write in his journal twenty-four hours later, he was
still soaring from the visit. "It's funny how quickly things can be put

into perspective," he reflected. "A few hours with Marie & Hechtle, coffee & muffins, and of course Nub has reminded me just how petty all the annoyances and frustrations that I experience are. As we sat around discussing our tribulations we, and our visitors, could not help but laugh at ourselves for ever letting any of this place under our skin. Once again (and we'll see for how long) I feel centered and focused on what's important."

As it happened, it didn't take long for Pat's reveries to be brought to a screeching halt by the routine insults of Army life. Although he and Kevin had completed basic training, they remained in Georgia to begin five weeks of what the Army calls advanced individual training, or AIT, which is scarcely distinguishable from basic. On September 24, just two days after Marie's departure, Pat wrote, "My mind is everywhere but here: Marie, home, future, past, Pooh, Ma, friends, etc.—but not Fort Benning; left, right, left, right; or 'Front lean & rest position! Move!' Especially now that we will spend the next two and a half weeks rehashing old stuff, my interest will fall further. We are bored to tears and fed up with this place. We need to move on."

Later that week, with even less cheer, he wrote, "You know what we did today? We fucking sat in our platoon area all day. For four hours we cleaned weapons, for another three or so we sat with our rucksacks taking inventory and collecting our linens. It may have been the most unproductive day of my life. This place is fucking tired. . . . For whatever reason, I'm hesitant to write too negatively about how I feel or what I'm going through. I feel obligated to take the high road in my journal. I feel that I should express my consummate belief that ultimately people are good and all will be well, yet this is not how I always feel."

Referring to his barracks as "this house of gnats," Pat vented,

Often I am so disgusted with the people I'm surrounded with that my heart fills with hate. I've been exposed to an element of people that can be worse than any I've encountered, including in Juvenile Hall. They're resentful, ungrateful, lazy, weak, and unvirtuous, as often as not. They bicker, complain, lie, tell tall tales, mope, and grumble incessantly. . . .

Perhaps I keep this out of my journal because I'm disappointed in myself. When Nub and I embarked on this journey I just kind of assumed these kids would fall in line. . . . Many times I struggle to maintain my cool through their chaos. Kevin and I are forced to yell and swear as opposed to recommend and suggest. . . . Perhaps I'm not as good a leader as I think.

Ultimately I believe in a general goodwill, and I've not become bitter, however I've not maintained as high a road as I'd hoped. I suppose when you wrestle with pigs, you're going to get dirty. . . . I continue to learn.

As Marie elucidates, "The thing about Pat that was so great was that he was an idealist who believed in the good in humanity. He always wanted to see the good in people. Unfortunately, that's not the case all the time, and it was upsetting for him when he was confronted with that. He treated people in a certain manner and expected to be treated in kind, but in the Army it didn't always work that way. He was twenty-five, and a much more mature twenty-five than other twenty-five-year-olds. Most of the other guys were eighteen-year-old kids who were immature for eighteen. He had a hard time with that."

On September 29, looking forward to the next phase of their training—airborne school, due to begin at the end of October, which would put them in the company of more elite soldiers, and would teach them how to parachute out of airplanes—Pat wrote, "All I can think of is getting the hell out of here. Away from mediocrity, ineptitude, whining, and boredom. My hope is that Airborne will expose us to a more motivated group of people and give Nub and me the freedom to be ourselves."

The next day their company practiced "ground fighting"—a variety of Brazilian Jiu-Jitsu, recently adopted by the Army, that emphasizes submission techniques such as joint locks and choke holds. Near the end of the session, recruits were allowed to challenge anyone to fight in front of the entire 110-man company. A swaggering young recruit who had been a high-school wrestling champion stood up, glowered at Pat, and announced, "I want Tillman!"

Kevin, according to Pat's journal, was "disgusted with the fact they even allowed us to fight these yahoos," and jumped to his feet to accept the guy's challenge so Pat wouldn't have to. Whereupon "this joke of a kid" had the temerity to insult Kevin by saying, " 'Not you, your older brother.' Kevin simply embarrassed the kid. He stared him down, called him out, tossed his ass around, choked him out repeatedly.* . . . After the first choke the guy realized he had made a mistake and was completely intimidated—he could not even look at Kevin." Kevin fought three matches with the recruit in quick succession, effortlessly defeating him on each occasion in front of the drill sergeants and all the other recruits. "This young man was trying to make a name for himself and use us as a vehicle for it," Pat noted. "I'm very proud and honored at the way Kevin jumped to defend what he believed was an insult. He carried himself like a man and spoke with action not words."

They completed the final trial of boot camp on October 17, a seven-day ordeal known as the field training exercise, or FTX. "Ahh," Pat wrote, "to be back from our week of rain, muck, & marching. . . . Were it not for the drizzle I doubt very much the ex- perience would have been a difficult one. However, that curveball was no joke. Normal tasks . . . become a bitch and marches that are otherwise simple turn rough. . . . We slept outside in the cold with nothing but our clothes and a poncho. All I could do to keep warm was spoon with old Nub." A thirty-two-mile march carrying heavy rucksacks, Pat confessed in his journal, "broke our asses off. Feet still fucking killing me . . . Despite what I expected from this basic train- ing, Nub and I were pushed a little. No kidding, it was not an easy deal. . . . Tougher than expected at the end, a worthy task. Solid way to finish up . . . These kids have reason to be proud. They weathered the storm. . . . I'll give it to this place, it was a good finale, now get me the fuck out."

On October 21, the Fort Benning Public Affairs Office leaned on Pat and Kevin to do a media interview. Although they met with the officer sent to talk them into it, Pat wrote, he and Kevin simply re-

---

* In Brazilian Jiu-Jitsu, "choking someone out" is a common, safe, and officially sanctioned maneuver, the equivalent of pinning an opponent during a wrestling match.

peated "what we've said from the beginning: 'We're not talking.' Anyhow, the meeting was uneventful, but our free time afterwards was priceless." For an hour and a half following the meeting the Tillman brothers sat around chatting with each other, drinking coffee, and listening to National Public Radio, which led off that afternoon with a report about President Bush's efforts to inveigle the UN Security Council to authorize the use of force in Iraq. When a drill sergeant came around to escort them back to the barracks and found his famous recruits "assed out" listening to liberal commentary on NPR, he laughed at them but let it slide.

A "Turning Blue" ceremony—wherein the recruits would receive light blue cords to wear on their Class-A dress uniforms, designating them as infantrymen—was scheduled for October 25. Marie, Richard, and both Tillman parents would be flying to Georgia to attend. Pat was very excited about seeing everyone. "I'm tired of our surroundings," he wrote,

> and need the positive *chi* of those I love to recharge my batteries. . . .
> It's been almost a month since I've spoken with Marie. If she hasn't
> run off with anyone, she surely hates my guts. Once again those
> strong feelings of guilt and pain for all I'm putting her through sur-
> face. My hope is that during the weekend she visits, I can pull off
> some miracle and express just how much I miss her and give her
> something to sustain another six weeks of our separation. The poor
> girl is such a superhero—actually at this point a Greek tragedy hero-
> ine. I need to hurry and put an American (happy) ending to this
> story. . . .
>
> I cannot speak for Kevin, but I feel no sense of accomplishment
> from finishing this place. I've learned no ultimate lessons and im-
> proved my character in no way. The only positive things this place
> has presented are a cast of solid characters, namely our drill ser-
> geants, Tulio Tourinho, and a few others. . . . It will probably take a
> while for me to get perspective on everything that's happened and,
> who knows, maybe eventually I'll feel it was a positive. Right now, it
> was not. Kevin and I have gained only a pessimistic view of human
> nature. All our altruistic goals coming into this place have been ig-
> nored and trampled on. Fortunately we believe that this awful envi-

ronment will not follow us. As we move along we expect to meet more people who are here [to accomplish] good, as opposed to, "because they have to be here." . . . I am not a negative man, I do not want to report bad, I want to rise above and bring everyone along with me. However, this place fucking blows . . . period.

CHAPTER TWENTY-ONE

Airborne school and the Ranger Indoctrination Program turned out to be both instructive and demanding, and Pat's outlook brightened considerably during the six weeks it took for him and Kevin to complete the two courses. Learning to jump out of airplanes was thrilling, and RIP involved enough suffering to hold Pat's attention. The latter has a notoriously challenging curriculum designed to impart tactical skills Rangers need for Special Operations warfare, while simultaneously pushing recruits past their physical and mental limits in order to cull the weak and insufficiently motivated. Upon graduating from RIP shortly before Christmas, Pat and Kevin received the tan berets the Army awards to the elite forces of the Seventy-fifth Ranger Regiment, after which they were assigned to a unit called the "Black Sheep": Second Platoon, Alpha Company, Second Ranger Battalion, based at Fort Lewis, Washington.

Russell Baer was a twenty-two-year-old private when the Tillmans arrived at Fort Lewis. "There had been a lot of buzz about them coming," Baer says.

All the tabs—the veteran Rangers—were talking smack about how they were gonna smoke the NFL dude. The first time I laid eyes on Pat and Kevin they were standing with their duffels next to the other new guys, who were nervous and sweating. Pat and Kevin didn't look scared at all. They acted confident, like they had done this every day of their lives. . . . I imagined they would be egotistical jocks. But during those first days, as I watched them interacting with the other noogs,* I knew I would get along with them. Pat didn't go around beating his chest. He would talk to these goofy, scrawny-looking privates and treat them as equals.

The Seventy-fifth Ranger Regiment is the Army's premier infantry unit. As with the Army's Green Berets and Delta Forces, Navy SEAL teams, Air Force Special Operations Wings, and Marine Special Operations Battalions, the Ranger Regiment functions under the auspices of the U.S. Special Operations Command. Rangers consider themselves to be superior warriors, members of a lofty tribe that has little in common with the "regular Army"; derogatorily, they refer to soldiers from the regular Army as "Legs." To set itself apart from other Army units, the Ranger Regiment maintains unique customs and merciless rituals. When newly minted Rangers arrive at Second Battalion fresh out of RIP, it is de rigueur for the old hands to put the noogs through the grinder, lest they fail to appreciate their place in the pecking order. The Ranger who assumed primary responsibility for edifying Pat in this regard was a corporal from Mountain Home, Arkansas, name of Jason Parsons.

"We heard that this Tillman guy was coming in," Parsons recalls.

I was like, "Oh boy, that's just what we need, a prima-donna football star. . . ." I was a little pessimistic about it. . . . I figured he was gonna be a huge problem. So when he gets there, I go up to where he was standing at parade rest with his brother. First thing I noticed was "That dude has a thick neck." I was expecting a little bit bigger guy. But he still had a pretty thick neck. Looking at him I thought, "Yeah, he's strong." And then I did what any good NCO would do: I messed with him a little bit.** Not full-on smoking him, just messing with him a little bit. I took the opportunity to give him some shit, just to

* Army slang for "new guys."

** NCO is the acronym for noncommissioned officer, that is, a corporal or sergeant of any grade.

kind of see how he would react. You get a lot of feedback in the first thirty minutes of someone being there: what their character is, how they relate to people, how they think about themselves. I thought he came across as arrogant. A little bit of cockiness is a good thing in a Ranger, definitely, if you can back it up. And football players are used to working their asses off, so I figured he had a work ethic.

At first Pat conducted himself very well. He had been disciplined. I was happy about that. But then I noticed he was being treated differently from the rest of the recruits by one of the other NCOs.

The sergeant in question, according to Parsons, "was doing the whole 'You want to be my buddy?' thing. In Ranger Regiment, NCOs aren't supposed to be buddy-buddy with the new guys. That's not the way it works. You don't treat them as equals. You need to let the noogs know that they are in a subordinate position, to get things rolling in the right direction.

"So starting off, me and Tillman had a lot of friction. I was probably the first guy who let him know he wasn't special. . . . Throughout his life he was used to being the guy in charge, but in my life I was also used to being in charge, and I had the rank, so that's the way it went. He had a few issues with that, but we straightened them out pretty early on."

According to Marie, it was a struggle for Pat when NCOs like Parsons went out of their way to "stuff him up," just to show him who was boss. "Pat was used to a certain level of control in his life," she explains,

which completely disappeared as soon as he joined the Army. I think he knew in theory how hard it would be, but until you actually experience it, you can't appreciate what it's really like. In his sports career he was always rewarded for how well he performed. In the military it doesn't work that way. It's all based on how long you've been in, and what your rank is. It doesn't matter how capable you are. I think that was a little shocking for both Pat and Kevin. Dealing with that was really difficult, but Pat had such a strong sense of who he was that it didn't change him. He learned how to function within the system, how to deal with it, but he never let them break his spirit. The Army never changed him at all.

Pat's ability to weather his initiation into the Ranger fraternity was enhanced considerably by the fact that Marie was back in his life again, and they were living away from the base. Two months before Pat and Kevin reported to Fort Lewis, while they were still at boot camp in Georgia, Marie had flown to Seattle and spent several days looking for a house for them to rent. "When they first joined the Army," she says, "I was like, 'Maybe we should just live on base. It might be easier.' But Pat said, 'Absolutely not! We're not living on base!' So I went out there to see what kind of place I could find, because the Army didn't really give you much money for housing if you wanted to live off base."

In his journal, Pat had expressed the hope that she would find "a quaint little cottage somewhere with personality and charm," along the lines of his childhood home in New Almaden. As it turned out, the first house she looked at, ten miles from Fort Lewis, fit this description almost precisely: a cute two-bedroom brick bungalow with wood floors and a fireplace, perched on a gentle slope above Puget Sound, surrounded by azaleas and rhododendrons and wintercreeper, with a big madrone tree in the side yard, a weeping cherry by the front steps, and a porch looking out across the water toward Fox Island and—when the clouds parted—the immense, mysterious peaks of the Olympic Mountains. The air was saturated with the scent of salt water and cedar forests. Seabirds wheeled overhead. There was even a view of the Tacoma Narrows Bridge, which arched through the mist over the eponymous strait like an image from a dimly remembered dream.

Marie signed a lease for the cottage and then returned in November to clean, paint, and move all their belongings up from Arizona while Pat and Kevin went through jump school and RIP. By the time they'd graduated, their new home was all ready for the brothers' arrival. "Pat and I loved that house," Marie says wistfully. "And Kevin did, too. Even today, Kevin and I still have this special feeling about living there, like it was some sort of utopia. Which is so funny, considering what they were going through in the Army.

"They would go to work and do this god-awful stuff, but we lived in this little fantasy bubble away from all that. They would come home, and it was like a separate world. Pat wanted that and needed that. He didn't want our life to be a military life. And it wasn't, in a lot of ways. Pat never came home in uniform. They would come and go in regular clothes. When they were home, they would get up in the morning and leave for work, almost like they had normal jobs." Eventually Marie landed a good job of her own in downtown Seattle, forty miles to the north on Interstate 5, and when she returned in the evening after work, she says, "They would be home waiting for me. There were chunks of time when they were gone to Ranger School or overseas or whatever, but then they would come home, and it was like they had never left. The three of us were away from everything and everybody, and for Kevin and me both, we had all that we needed, which was for Pat to be there."

The already strong bond between the three of them grew even stronger. When Pat and Kevin weren't on the base, they were usually with Marie; they didn't socialize much with others, and Pat drank very little alcohol. He regarded being a Ranger as one of the most serious challenges he'd ever undertaken, and he didn't want to do anything that might dull his focus on the task at hand.

———

When they enlisted, the Tillman brothers assumed they would be deployed to Afghanistan to fight Osama bin Laden, al-Qaeda, and the Taliban—a war that seemed vital to protecting national security. During the 2000 presidential campaign, Bush had repeatedly promised that if he was elected, his administration would promote a "humble" foreign policy. "I'm going to be judicious as to how to use the military," he pledged during his second debate with Al Gore. "It needs to be in our vital interest, the mission needs to be clear, and the exit strategy obvious. . . . I think the United States must be . . . humble in how we treat nations that are figuring out how to chart their own course." The Tillmans, like most Americans, therefore had no reason to suspect that in November 2001, President Bush and Vice President Cheney had instructed Secretary of Defense Donald Rumsfeld to secretly create a detailed plan for the invasion of Iraq.

Scarcely two months after the 9/11 attacks, even though bin Laden was still at large in Afghanistan, the president and his most influential advisers regarded the Afghan campaign as a mere sideshow, almost a diversion. Truth be told, the primary focus of the Bush administration had always been taking down Saddam Hussein. On February 5, 2003, Secretary of State Colin Powell went before the United Nations to make the president's argument for invading Iraq, presenting satellite photos and other evidence in a PowerPoint presentation that persuasively—but erroneously—indicated Saddam possessed weapons of mass destruction and had conspired with al-Qaeda to carry out terrorist attacks against Americans. When Powell finished his spiel, it was plain to the world that the United States would be invading Iraq in the immediate future.

Pat was very disturbed. By the time it became clear that war with Iraq was imminent, Pat and Kevin had been training at Fort Lewis for just over a month. Seventeen days after Powell addressed the United Nations, Pat wrote in his journal,

> It may be very soon that Nub & I will be called upon to take part in something I see no clear purpose for. . . . Were our case for war even somewhat justifiable, no doubt many of our traditional allies . . . would be praising our initiative. . . . However, every leader in the world, with a few exceptions, is crying foul, as is the voice of much of the people. This . . . leads me to believe that we have little or no justification other than our imperial whim. Of course Nub & I have . . . willingly allowed ourselves to be pawns in this game and will do our job whether we agree with it or not. All we ask is that it is duly noted that we harbor no illusions of virtue.

At the beginning of March, Pat, Kevin, and the other Rangers of Alpha Company were flown to a small airfield in the desert outside of Ar'ar, Saudi Arabia. "Curious how quickly this whole endeavor has come along," Pat wrote. "Two months out of RIP and Kevin and I are 50 miles off the Iraqi border. . . . The last couple of days have been spent putting up a tent city, stringing concertina wire, and staying up all night with guard duties. We are one of the first to arrive so the task of setting up the place falls on our shoulders."

Contemplating the uncertainty of what lay ahead, he beseeched, "Let Kevin & I come out of this well." Were either of them to be seriously hurt or killed, he acknowledged, "I cannot begin to imagine what it would do to our family." He was particularly concerned

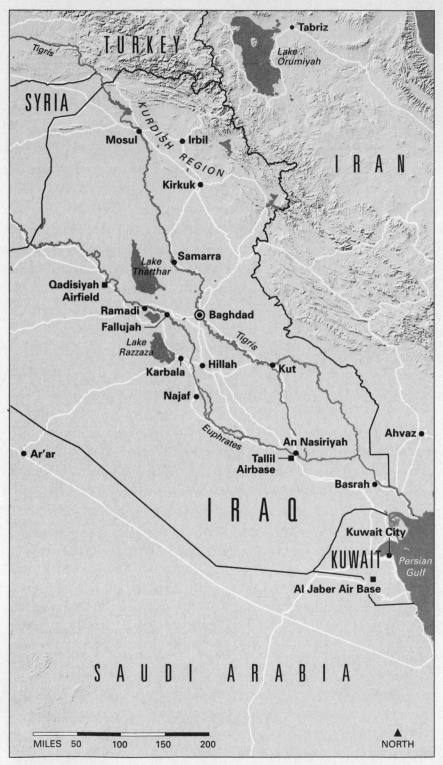

IRAQ.

about Marie: "Needless to say I miss her incredibly and cannot get the picture of her face, before we left, out of my mind. She was so genuinely upset/worried/disappointed that it etched a hole in my mind. . . . I can't wait to start a family with Marie, absolutely can't wait."

"Having kids was definitely something we both wanted," Marie confirms. "It was part of why we decided to get married, to start a family. We were pretty young, but with Pat playing football, we felt settled and could afford to do it. But then when he decided to join the Army, it didn't seem like the right time. Pat was more inclined to still have a baby, but I wanted to hold off until he would be around more. So we decided to wait until after he got out. It didn't seem like that big a deal to wait. We were still really young."

On March 14, the Tillmans' platoon was assigned to act as a QRF—a quick reaction force. They would remain on perpetual standby, prepared to board helicopters and be in the air within ninety minutes to come to the aid of other units that might require rescue or additional firepower. With combat perhaps imminent, the Rangers practiced donning gas masks and heavy charcoal-lined suits called MOPPs (for Mission Oriented Protective Postures) that were intended to safeguard them in the event of an attack with chemical or biological weapons. After trying on his hot, clammy, indescribably uncomfortable MOPP gear, Pat reflected:

> It sounds like we will wear this garb wherever we go. The idea of being shot at is not a warm one, although it's infinitely less frightening than chemical or biological threats. . . .
>
> If Kevin and I are part of a situation where we must fight, every bit of my soul knows we will fight as hard as anyone ever has. We will not question the reasons for our being here or allow any personal beliefs to interfere with our job. My hope is that decisions are being made with the same good faith that Kevin and I aim to display. . . . I hope [this war is about] more than oil, money, & power. . . . I doubt that it is. . . . If anything were to happen to Kevin I would never forgive myself. If anything happens to Kevin, and my fears of our intent in this country prove true, I will never forgive this world.

Sitting in his tent, Pat pulled out an anthology of essays that included Ralph Waldo Emerson's intricately wrought, twenty-page tour de force, "Self-Reliance"—a disquisition on the importance of following one's conscience rather than conforming to the dictates of society:

> God will not have his work made manifest by cowards. . . .
>
> Whoso would be a man, must be a nonconformist. He who would gather immortal palms must not be hindered by the name of goodness. . . . Nothing is at last sacred but the integrity of your own mind. . . .
>
> What I must do is all that concerns me, not what the people think. This rule, equally arduous in actual and in intellectual life, may serve for the whole distinction between greatness and meanness. It is the harder because you will always find those who think they know what is your duty better than you know it. It is easy in the world to live after the world's opinion; it is easy in solitude to live after our own; but the great man is he who in the midst of the crowd keeps with perfect sweetness the independence of solitude. . . .
>
> I suppose no man can violate his nature. . . . A character is like an acrostic or Alexandrian stanza;—read it forward, backward, or across, it still spells the same thing. . . . We pass for what we are. . . . Men imagine that they communicate their virtue or vice only by overt actions, and do not see that virtue or vice emit a breath every moment. . . .
>
> Life only avails, not the having lived. Power ceases in the instant of repose; it resides in the moment of transition from a past to a new state, in the shooting of the gulf, in the darting to an aim.

Pat absorbed the essay over several days. By the time he reached its final lines, he was exhilarated:

> So use all that is called Fortune. Most men gamble with her, and gain all, and lose all, as her wheel rolls. . . . A political victory, a rise of rents, the recovery of your sick or the return of your absent friend, or some other favorable event raises your spirits, and you think good days are preparing for you. Do not believe it. Nothing can bring you

peace but yourself. Nothing can bring you peace but the triumph of principles.

"Let me applaud the hero who is Ralph W. E.," Pat exclaimed in his journal. " 'Self-Reliance' touched my soul. . . . Brilliant, truly brilliant."

On March 19, the night before the invasion of Iraq, Emerson's ideas were still reverberating inside Pat's head, unleashing a torrent of thoughts and feelings. "I want to set the world on fire and make it right," he wrote, but he worried about the pain he brought to those he loved by adhering to his principles:

> My honor will not allow me to create a life of beauty and peace but sends me off to order and conformity. My life becomes everything I'm not. I love my wife more than myself yet drag her through the same puddle. Who do I love? Where is my passion directed? Best I can tell, it's to those who could care less: the general masses. I follow some philosophy I barely understand. . . . My direction is selfish, my *telos* destructive. . . . Sometimes my need to love hurts—myself, my family, my cause. Is there a cure? Of course. But I refuse. Refuse to stop loving, to stop caring. To avoid those tears, that pain . . . To err on the side of passion is human and right and the only way I'll live.

At 5:30 a.m. local time on March 20, some three dozen Tomahawk cruise missiles thundered from their launching bays on warships in the Persian Gulf and Red Sea, and steered toward Iraq to deliver a surfeit of shock, awe, and death to targets throughout Baghdad. "Well the war has certainly begun," Pat wrote from his tent in the desert, thirty-five miles outside of Iraq. "My heart goes out to those who will suffer. Whatever your politics, whatever you believe is right or wrong, the fact is most of those who will feel the wrath of this ordeal want nothing more than to live peacefully."

Pat's platoon was informed they would be parachuting down to a site within Iraq to join the fight. "Our first jump since Airborne school may be combat, how about them apples?" he mused. A day later, however, the mission was delayed indefinitely. And on the night of March 27, when the platoon finally climbed into helicopters and flew off with the Navy's SEAL Team Six to engage the enemy at a place called Qadisiyah Airbase, Pat and Kevin weren't among them.

"Pat was left in the tent," Jason Parsons explains. "That's pretty much all there was to it. He was a new guy without much training under his belt. They wanted to send out the more seasoned soldiers. The noogs tend to be more of a liability than an asset."

Pat was furious. "I knew it was coming," he wrote, "but still I can't help my anger. . . . I'm not out for blood or in any hurry to kill people, however I did not throw my life to shit in order to fill sandbags and guard Hummers. This is a fucking insult that boils my blood. All I want to do is rip out the throat of one of these loudmouth fucks who's going as opposed to me." The fact that Pat believed the Iraq War to be illegal and unjust did not prevent him from wanting desperately to get into the fight, to face enemy fire alongside his comrades, to prove himself in combat. Being left in the tent was also a rude slap to his ego. "I feel like the last kid picked," he complained to his journal, "losing my job my rookie year, not making varsity as a freshman. I want to fucking hurt something. I threw away or postponed a great deal to come here, broke the rules in a way. Here, nothing is based on merit. Everything has to do with time in battalion, time of rank—no comment on ability, aptitude, or skill. . . . I bring up 'rule break' only because I want someone to do this for us. Realize we are not normal privates, break the fucking rules, and put us in a position to add value. Fuck this place."

At the last minute, Private Jade Lane had been chosen for the Qadisiyah mission instead of Pat, Lane says, because he had an M203 grenade launcher attached to his M4 carbine, Pat didn't, "and they wanted more firepower." Lane, for his part, would have been happy to let Pat go in his place. "The first thing I saw when they kicked the helicopter doors open," Lane remembers, "was two huge murals of Saddam on the airfield. You could see all these muzzle flashes lighting up the night, and helicopters with mini-guns were just opening up on enemy targets on the ground—to look out and see that, it was like, 'Holy shit. This is real. This is actually happening.'" As the chopper came in under heavy enemy fire, a twenty-one-year-old Ranger named Manuel Avila was shot twice in the chest, and a crewman on another helicopter was shot in the head.

WHERE MEN WIN GLORY 173

Avila's injuries appeared to be life threatening. Pat, monitoring the mission over the radio back at the base in Ar'ar, was chastened. Avila was part of his four-man fire team, and he was fond of him. "Very quiet, hard working, good man," Pat wrote of his wounded teammate when news of the casualties arrived. "He was actually born in Mexico and came north with his family as a boy. Not exactly the story some folks think of when they bitch about all those 'foreigners' coming over. Bravo, Manuel, you not only do your family, friends, & fellow soldiers proud, you symbolize the men this country was built by. . . . I wait to see how they will all return. What exactly is the look of a man after an encounter with fire, an encounter with a comrade shot, an encounter with death?"

Avila had been the SAW gunner on Tillman's team. When Avila was shot, Pat became the new SAW gunner. Weighing twenty-two pounds (including a two-hundred-round drum of .223-caliber ammunition, the same bullets fired by the M4 and M16), the M249 Squad Automatic Weapon is a belt-fed machine gun designed to lay down high volumes of suppressive fire. Not only did the gun itself weigh a lot, but a SAW gunner was required to carry at least six hundred to eight hundred rounds of ammunition, because the weapon could fire a thousand rounds per minute and tended to use up a lot of bullets in a hurry once the shooting started. "Truth be told," Pat confessed to his journal, "I'd rather stick with the lighter M4, but being that I have no choice, I will learn this new weapon and get proficient at it. This is a heavy casualty-producing weapon, which will change my role a bit. Oh well—improvise, adapt, and overcome."

CHAPTER TWENTY-TWO

Pat and Kevin were finally sent out on their first mission on March 31, as part of an immense contingent of Marines, Rangers, Green Berets, Delta Force operators, SEALs, and Air Force Pararescue Jumpers dispatched to rescue a nineteen-year-old soldier reportedly being held prisoner by Iraqi fighters at a hospital in a city called An Nasiriyah. The prisoner's name was Jessica Dawn Lynch.

Her capture eight days earlier, and the rescue that eventually followed, were about to become the most publicized episodes of the entire Iraq War. The saga of Jessica Lynch would also turn out to have a momentous impact on Pat Tillman—although the wallop wouldn't be delivered until more than a year after she became a household name, and the connection between Lynch and Tillman has not previously been disclosed. On March 23, 2003, Private Lynch had been traveling north on Highway 8, a major freeway leading to Baghdad, as one of thirty-three soldiers in an eighteen-vehicle convoy of the Army's 507th Maintenance Company, which was heading up-country to support a Patriot antimissile battery. The soldiers were for the most part mechanics, supply clerks, and cooks, poorly trained for combat, who did not expect to find themselves anywhere near the front lines. At 1:00 in the morning, the sleep-deprived officer leading the convoy, Captain Troy King, missed a crucial turn onto his assigned route, a six-lane expressway that would have kept him ten miles outside of An

Nasiriyah, a congested city. Approximately five hours later, at a major intersection adorned with a statue memorializing the Iran-Iraq War, King missed another critical turn.

The convoy—a few Humvees escorting an assortment of heavy trucks towing trailers—had unwittingly exited Highway 8, which also would have diverted it around Nasiriyah, and was now headed directly into the city on a four-lane boulevard. The board-flat, barren desert they'd been driving through since leaving Kuwait abruptly gave way to palm groves and lush green shrubbery. About a mile after leaving Highway 8, the convoy motored past several Iraqi T-55 tanks positioned beside the road, but failed to notice them in the dark, and thus continued driving blithely on.

Half a mile farther, the convoy crossed a low, gently arching bridge, longer than two football fields, spanning the greasy, ash-colored flow of the Euphrates River. When they reached the far shore, they were in the heart of Nasiriyah. A military town, it was roughly the Iraqi equivalent of Colorado Springs or Tacoma or El Paso. Its 500,000 residents included three regiments of the Iraqi Army (about 5,000 soldiers) as well as an estimated 800 Fedayeen militia fighters. Lynch's convoy of cafeteria workers and desk jockeys were the first Americans to enter this exceedingly hostile environment since the start of the war three days earlier.

The heavily armed citizens of Nasiriyah had been nervously expecting the Americans to invade their city. Tanks, artillery, and squads of fighters were positioned in strategic locations around the metropolitan area to repel the coming attack. But none of the anxious locals anticipated that the invading force would be a lightly armed convoy of transport trucks, driven by men and women who appeared to be utterly unaware of the Iraqi forces amassed around them. The Iraqis were so astonished by the Americans' cluelessness that they held their fire and merely stared in disbelief.

A few blocks after crossing the Euphrates River, as the convoy entered the urban core of Nasiriyah, it passed an Iraqi military checkpoint manned by armed soldiers who smiled and waved at the Americans as they drove by, and Lynch's convoy continued to roll north through the middle of the city, unmolested, for another three miles.

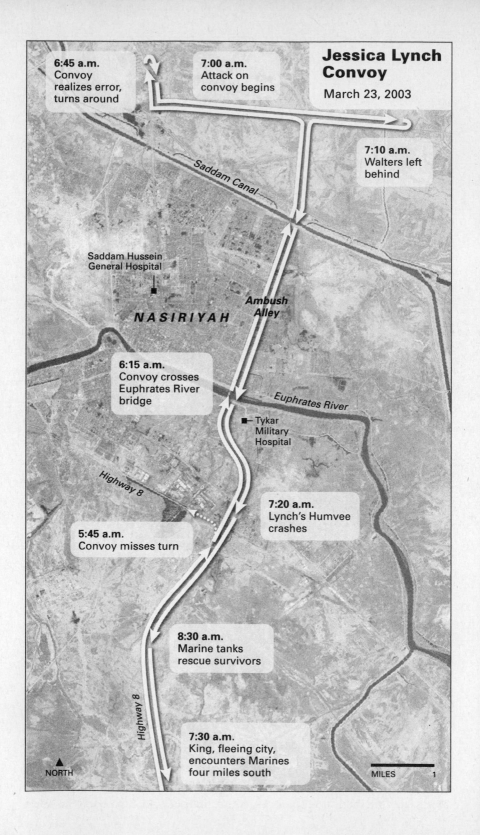

Jessica Lynch Convoy

March 23, 2003

6:45 a.m.
Convoy realizes error, turns around

7:00 a.m.
Attack on convoy begins

7:10 a.m.
Walters left behind

Saddam Canal

Saddam Hussein General Hospital

NASIRIYAH

Ambush Alley

6:15 a.m.
Convoy crosses Euphrates River bridge

Euphrates River

Tykar Military Hospital

Highway 8

7:20 a.m.
Lynch's Humvee crashes

5:45 a.m.
Convoy misses turn

8:30 a.m.
Marine tanks rescue survivors

Highway 8

7:30 a.m.
King, fleeing city, encounters Marines four miles south

NORTH

MILES   1

After crossing a bridge over a waterway called the Saddam Canal and then driving a mile past Nasiriyah's northern edge, Captain King, the convoy commander, stopped to consult his GPS, whereupon he belatedly realized they'd made a seriously wrong turn an hour earlier. Determining that the convoy would need to retrace its route in order to return to the intersection where he'd led them astray, King ordered his troops to lock and load their weapons, turn around, and begin driving back the way they'd just come.

Soon after the Americans reversed course, the Iraqis overcame the paralysis of their initial shock and began shooting at the convoy. Some of the American soldiers panicked, and most of their dust-clogged, improperly maintained weapons jammed. In short order, Captain King lost his bearings in the maze of unfamiliar streets, one truck was disabled by enemy fire, and two other rigs got stuck in soft sand. Sergeant Donald R. Walters, who had been riding in the disabled truck, was inadvertently left behind, taken prisoner by the Fedayeen, and subsequently killed.

As word traveled rapidly through the city that a befuddled, lightly armed American convoy had blundered into their midst, Fedayeen fighters were drawn to the scene like hyenas to a flock of defenseless sheep, and the attack intensified. The convoy splintered, and its vehicles soon became widely separated in the confusion and billowing dust. An American soldier was shot, and then another.

Jessica Lynch and four other soldiers were in a Humvee towing a trailer near the rear of what remained of the convoy. Directly in front of Lynch's Humvee was a five-ton truck driven by Specialist Edgar Hernandez, towing a flatbed trailer. The two vehicles accelerated south through Nasiriyah down a street that the Marines would christen "Ambush Alley," desperately trying to flee the city as Fedayeen on rooftops shot at them with AK-47s, heavy machine guns, and rocket-propelled grenades. Around 7:20, they sped back across the long bridge over the Euphrates River and were nearly out of the kill zone when Hernandez's tractor trailer came upon an Iraqi dump truck that had been positioned across the road to block the Americans' passage. Hernandez swerved onto the right shoulder to avoid hitting the truck, his trailer jackknifed, and a moment later Lynch's Humvee smashed into the back of the flatbed at fifty miles per hour.

Lynch, who was in one of the rear seats, and her best friend, Private Lori Piestewa, who was driving, survived the crash but were gravely injured and taken prisoner by the Fedayeen. The other three occupants of the Humvee perished on impact or shortly thereafter. All told, eleven soldiers from the Maintenance Company lost their lives in the attack on the convoy, and seven were captured.

Lynch and Piestewa, both unconscious, were brought to nearby Tykar Military Hospital, where Piestewa soon succumbed to her injuries. A few hours later, an Iraqi military ambulance transported Lynch to Saddam Hussein General Hospital, a civilian facility two miles across town. Within a few days American forces learned from multiple Iraqi sources, including the husband of an Iraqi nurse who was caring for Lynch, that she was being held at Saddam Hospital. The nurse's husband, a lawyer named Mohammed Odeh al-Rehaief, told some Marines manning a checkpoint outside of the city that he had spoken with Lynch at her bedside. When the Marines asked al-Rehaief to return to the hospital to gather more information, he went back twice and provided the Americans with detailed maps indicating the layout of the six-story building and Lynch's precise location. He also told the Marines that the American girl had been shot in both legs, her head was bandaged, and one arm was in a sling.

Relying on the intelligence provided by al-Rehaief, the operation to rescue her was set into motion on March 31. At dawn, Pat, Kevin, and their fellow Rangers were flown to Tallil, a sprawling, bombed-out Iraqi airfield twelve miles southwest of Nasiriyah that the Americans had captured ten days earlier. After sitting in the sun all day waiting for something to happen, they were informed the mission had been postponed for twenty-four hours. The next morning they again prepared for battle and waited throughout the day. That evening when darkness fell, explosions flashed in the nearby city as a Marine artillery battery began shelling an enemy command post to divert enemy forces away from Saddam Hospital. At midnight, a Special Ops team stormed the hospital, snatched Lynch from her bed, hustled her out on a stretcher to a waiting Black Hawk helicopter, and flew her to safety.

During the rescue operation, the Tillmans remained just outside the city as part of a quick reaction force ready to storm the hospital in the event of trouble. Their role in the rescue "was marginal," Pat admitted in his journal. Throughout the night of April 1–2, "We sat on the airfield freezing our balls off waiting to be called in." But, he reported happily, "the girl, Jessica, was saved, no one was hurt, over-all the mission was a total success."

The definitive account of Lynch's ordeal was published on the front page of the *Washington Post* on April 3. "She Was Fighting to the Death," the headline announced above the story's breathless opening sentence:

> Pfc. Jessica Lynch, rescued Tuesday from an Iraqi hospital, fought fiercely and shot several enemy soldiers after Iraqi forces ambushed the Army's 507th Ordnance Maintenance Company, firing her weapon until she ran out of ammunition, U.S. officials said yesterday.
>
> Lynch . . . continued firing at the Iraqis even after she sustained multiple gunshot wounds and watched several other soldiers in her unit die around her in fighting March 23, one official said. . . . "She was fighting to the death," the official said. "She did not want to be taken alive."
>
> Lynch was also stabbed when Iraqi forces closed in on her position, the official said, noting that initial intelligence reports said she had been stabbed to death. . . .
>
> Lynch's rescue at midnight local time Tuesday was a classic Special Operations raid, with U.S. commandos in Black Hawk helicopters engaging Iraqi forces on their way in and out of the medical compound, defense officials said.
>
> Acting on information from CIA operatives, they said, a Special Operations force of Navy SEALs, Army Rangers and Air Force combat controllers touched down in blacked-out conditions. . . .
>
> "There was shooting going in, there was some shooting going out," said one military officer briefed on the operation. "It was not intensive. There was no shooting in the building, but it was hairy, because no one knew what to expect. . . ."
>
> The officer said that Special Operations forces found what looked like a "prototype" Iraqi torture chamber in the hospital's basement, with batteries and metal prods. . . .

Thanks largely to details first revealed in this article, as well as dramatic video of the rescue distributed to the media by the Army, Jessica
Lynch dominated the news for weeks. The details of the incident provided by military public affairs officers made for an absolutely riveting story that television, radio, and print journalists found irresistible:
a petite blond supply clerk from a flea-speck burg in West Virginia
is ambushed in Iraq and fearlessly mows down masked Fedayeen
terrorists with her M16 until she runs out of ammo, whereupon she
is shot, stabbed, captured, tortured, and raped before finally being
snatched from her barbaric Iraqi captors during a daring raid by
American commandos.

The story was so gripping that little heed was paid to a paragraph
near the beginning of the aforementioned *Washington Post* article,
which stated,

> Several officials cautioned that the precise sequence of events is still
> being determined, and that further information will emerge as Lynch
> is debriefed. Reports thus far are based on battlefield intelligence,
> they said, which comes from monitored communications and from
> Iraqi sources in Nasiriyah whose reliability has yet to be assessed.
> Pentagon officials said they had heard "rumors" of Lynch's heroics
> but had no confirmation.

Over the following weeks, months, and years, subsequent reporting by investigative journalists revealed that most of the details of
Lynch's ordeal were extravagantly embellished, and much of the rest
was invented from whole cloth. Because her rifle had jammed, she
hadn't fired a single round. Although her injuries had indeed been life
threatening, they were exclusively the result of her Humvee smashing
into Hernandez's tractor trailer; she was never shot, stabbed, tortured, or raped. After she had been transferred to Saddam Hussein
General Hospital, her captors treated her with kindness and special
care. And when the American commandos arrived at the hospital to
rescue Lynch, they met no significant resistance.

The spurious particulars did not come from Private Lynch. The
bogus story was based on information fed to gullible reporters by
anonymous military sources. The government official who arranged

for reporters to interview these sources—the guy who deserves top billing for creating the myth of Jessica Lynch, in other words—was a White House apparatchik named Jim Wilkinson. Although his official job description was director of strategic communications for General Tommy Franks (the commander of all U.S. forces in Iraq and Afghanistan), actually Wilkinson served as the Bush administration's top "perception manager" for the Iraq War. As Ben Smith noted in an article published in the *New York Observer* in October 2003,

> Wilkinson has gone from politics to war and back since he worked for George W. Bush in Florida during the 2000 election, and his journey is a mark of the administration's utilitarian approach to marketing war, politics and the presidency. . . . He's also got as pure a Republican pedigree as you can wish, and an edge honed in the bitter partisan wars between Bill Clinton and the Republican House leadership.
>
> Mr. Wilkinson grew up in East Texas and attended high school in Tenaha, population 1,046, then gave up plans to become an undertaker to go to work for Republican Congressman Dick Armey in 1992. Mr. Armey soon became House majority leader; his communications director, Mr. Wilkinson's mentor, was Ed Gillespie, now chairman of the Republican National Committee.
>
> Mr. Wilkinson first left his mark on the 2000 presidential race in March 1999, when he helped package and promote the notion that Al Gore claimed to have "invented the Internet." Then the Texan popped up in Miami to defend Republican protesters shutting down a recount. . . .
>
> For his troubles, Mr. Wilkinson was made deputy director of communications for planning in the Bush White House, and was among the aides who set up the Sept. 14, 2001, visit to Ground Zero that redefined George W. Bush's presidency.

When the invasion of Iraq commenced on March 20, Wilkinson was the president's man on the ground at U.S. Central Command headquarters in Qatar, controlling and carefully shaping information about the war disseminated to the international press. In this capacity, he adroitly stage-managed both the rescue of Jessica Lynch and the subsequent media coverage of her ordeal. It was Wilkinson who arranged to give the *Washington Post* exclusive access to classified intelligence that was the basis for the now-discredited "She Was Fighting to the Death" story that ran on the front page of that newspaper.

In much the same way that sources at the highest levels of the Bush-Cheney administration manipulated the *New York Times* reporter Judith Miller into writing articles seeming to confirm that Saddam possessed weapons of mass destruction, Wilkinson duped reporters and editors at the *Washington Post, USA Today,* and other media outlets into running wildly hyperbolic stories about Lynch. Wilkinson simply sowed a little misinformation where it would have the most impact, sat back, and watched his fabulation go viral, propagated by the media frenzy that he knew would ensue.

The true saga of Jessica Lynch and the subsequent battle of Nasiriyah were actually much more compelling than the tall tale so dexterously engineered by Wilkinson, but they painted a rather more disturbing picture of how the war was unfolding. On March 16, just a week before Lynch was captured, Vice President Cheney had declared on national television, "My belief is we will, in fact, be greeted as liberators," and then predicted, "I think it will go relatively quickly, . . . [in] weeks rather than months." As Michael R. Gordon and Bernard E. Trainor reported in their book *Cobra II,* "The CIA was so sure that American soldiers would be greeted warmly when they pushed into Southern Iraq that a CIA operative suggested sneaking hundreds of small American flags into the country for grateful Iraqis to wave at their liberators." But a cascade of disastrous events that began with the attack on Lynch's convoy threatened to contradict the assurances made by Bush, Cheney, Rumsfeld, and others that Americans would be "greeted with sweets and flowers" and victory would be achieved quickly.

This tragic cascade started with an innocent error, when Lynch's convoy took a wrong fork in the road. By the end of that day, thanks in no small part to this mistake, twenty-nine American servicemen and servicewomen were dead. It was Wilkinson's job to divert attention from this alarming setback lest it undermine the homeland's overwhelming support for Operation Iraqi Freedom. Several days later, after even more bad news further threatened to erode public support for the war, Wilkinson learned that Jessica Lynch was lying in a hospital bed, guarded haphazardly if at all, just a few miles from an American military outpost. Right away, he knew exactly how to make the most of the opportunity.

CHAPTER TWENTY-THREE

In the predawn hours of March 23, 2003, as Jessica Lynch's convoy rolled across the Euphrates River and entered An Nasiriyah, Pat Tillman was asleep on his cot in Ar'ar, Saudi Arabia, having stayed up late the previous evening reading *The Odyssey*, Homer's epic poem about the Greek hero Odysseus and his ten-year effort to make his way home to his wife, Penelope, after the Trojan War. Pat had no knowledge of the tragedy beginning to unfold in Nasiriyah, nor could he have imagined that its aftershocks would one day be a source of unceasing torment to the people he loved.

As the sun crested the horizon that morning in southern Iraq, hundreds of Marines were maneuvering into position to invade Nasiriyah and capture the very bridge that Lynch and the Army's 507th Maintenance Company had just driven heedlessly across, which was deemed crucial to the rapid push of American troops to Baghdad. When the First Battalion of the Second Marine Regiment drew to within several miles of this bridge, Iraqi forces responded with fire from small arms, machine guns, mortars, and artillery. Around 7:30 a.m., in the midst of this skirmish, a Humvee came racing toward the Marines from the direction of Nasiriyah and screeched to a stop, riddled with bullet holes and with its tires on fire. An extremely agitated American Army captain named Troy King jumped out in a state of near hysteria, yelling that a convoy he had been leading had suffered catastrophic losses after coming under attack back in the city.

This made no sense to Major Bill Peebles, the commander of the tank column leading the Marines' advance into the city. No Army units, or those of any other military branch, were supposed to have preceded the Marines into Nasiriyah. When King, struggling to speak coherently, informed Peebles that most of his company of soldiers remained behind—some already dead, others pinned down by the enemy in different areas of the city—Peebles led his tanks off to look for survivors. In short order the tanks spotted several U.S. Army trucks that had been shot full of holes and were in flames. Hiding in a ditch behind the ravaged vehicles, still taking heavy fire, were ten soldiers from the 507th Maintenance Company, four of whom were wounded. The Marines gathered up the survivors, spun their tanks around, and hurried away from Nasiriyah to deliver the wounded to a secure location where they could receive medical aid.

After the tanks departed, Bravo Company—comprising approximately two hundred Marines riding in three Humvees and a dozen amphibious assault vehicles known as AAVs, amtracs, or tracs—moved north toward the bridge over the Euphrates River. Crossing it without encountering resistance, they continued toward their next objective: a second bridge, on the northern edge of the city, spanning the Saddam Canal. The most direct route to this bridge was the road on which Lynch's convoy had been attacked, Ambush Alley. Understandably, they elected to approach the Saddam Canal Bridge by a less hazardous route that swung around to the east. Shortly after crossing the Euphrates, therefore, they turned right, abandoned the pavement, and started rolling across a salt flat that would take them to their objective via this roundabout path.

Unbeknownst to Bravo Company, however, the salt flat was actually a swamp where the city's sewage accumulated beneath a carapace of sunbaked mud. Two tanks attached to the company suddenly broke through the crust and plunged four feet into smelly quicksand. The more they spun their treads trying to crawl free, the deeper the immense vehicles wallowed. A moment later one of the amphibious assault vehicles broke through the crust and became stuck as well, and then another. Within minutes, three tanks, three Humvees, and three tracs were sucked down into the bog.

One of the hopelessly mired tracs served as the mobile command post for Lieutenant Colonel Rick Grabowski, the First Battalion

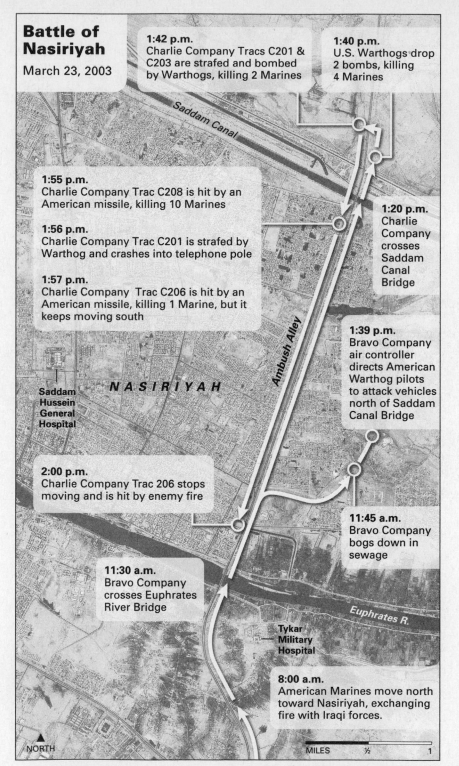

Battle of Nasiriyah

March 23, 2003

1:42 p.m.
Charlie Company Tracs C201 &
C203 are strafed and bombed
by Warthogs, killing 2 Marines

1:40 p.m.
U.S. Warthogs drop
2 bombs, killing
4 Marines

Saddam Canal

1:55 p.m.
Charlie Company Trac C208 is hit by an
American missile, killing 10 Marines

1:56 p.m.
Charlie Company Trac C201 is strafed by
Warthog and crashes into telephone pole

1:57 p.m.
Charlie Company Trac C206 is hit by an
American missile, killing 1 Marine, but it
keeps moving south

1:20 p.m.
Charlie
Company
crosses
Saddam
Canal
Bridge

Ambush Alley

1:39 p.m.
Bravo Company
air controller
directs American
Warthog pilots
to attack vehicles
north of Saddam
Canal Bridge

**Saddam
Hussein
General
Hospital**

NASIRIYAH

2:00 p.m.
Charlie Company Trac 206 stops
moving and is hit by enemy fire

11:45 a.m.
Bravo Company
bogs down in
sewage

11:30 a.m.
Bravo Company
crosses Euphrates
River Bridge

Euphrates R.

**Tykar
Military
Hospital**

8:00 a.m.
American Marines move north
toward Nasiriyah, exchanging
fire with Iraqi forces.

NORTH

MILES   ½   1

commander, who was directing the mission. Containing all of Grabowski's communications equipment, the trac had become trapped near the edge of the salt flat beneath an overhead power line, which seemed to interfere with radio transmissions, making it nearly impossible for the commander to communicate with either headquarters or his other units, Alpha and Charlie companies.

Upon seeing that the American vehicles were immobilized, swarms of Iraqi fighters materialized and began shooting at them from nearby rooftops as scores of local residents simultaneously emerged from their homes and hurried out of the city, fleeing the battle that they knew would soon commence in earnest. Grabowski ordered his men to dismount from their tracs and form a defensive perimeter. Most of them were young recruits who had never seen combat. As they exited the vehicles, many of the Marines appeared scared and confused. Barely under way, the mission was already "Charlie Foxtrot"—a total clusterfuck.

Even before Bravo Company had blundered into the sewage, Grabowski had been feeling a lot of heat from his boss, the Marine brigadier general Rich Natonski. Three hours earlier, shortly after the rescue of the survivors from Jessica Lynch's convoy, Grabowski's men were moving north through the outskirts of Nasiriyah, clearing buildings and skirmishing with the enemy, when the general had helicoptered in from his command post specifically to admonish Grabowski for the sluggish pace of his advance. Donald Rumsfeld's strategy for the entire invasion—for the entire war—was predicated on speed, and officers on the ground were under unrelenting pressure to keep pushing rapidly toward Baghdad, no matter what. Natonski took Grabowski aside, got in his face, and told him, "I need you to fucking get up there and seize the bridges." Adding to the sense of urgency, Natonski explained, twelve Army soldiers from Lynch's convoy were still missing somewhere in the city, and Grabowski's Marines should "be looking for those individuals" as they moved toward the bridges.

Not long past noon, while Grabowski and Bravo Company were struggling to extricate themselves from the reeking bog on the eastern edge of Nasiriyah, Charlie Company moved north across the Euphrates River Bridge, expecting to rendezvous with Bravo Company and then follow them to the Saddam Canal Bridge. Seeing no sign of Bravo Company, and unable to raise them on the radio, Captain Dan Wittnam, the commander of Charlie Company, assumed that Bravo Company must have already gone on ahead. So Wittnam, on his own initiative, ordered his men to proceed directly up Ambush Alley to the Saddam Canal Bridge.

Sergeant William Schaefer, commanding Charlie Company's lead trac, was incredulous. "Say again," he radioed back, requesting confirmation of the orders. Schaefer was concerned because a platoon of tanks was supposed to precede Charlie Company wherever they went, but the tanks assigned to be their escorts were diverted to rescue the survivors of the Jessica Lynch convoy, and hadn't yet reappeared. Emphatic orders had been sent down the chain of command, however, that taking the bridge was to take priority over all else, so Schaefer swallowed his reservations, ordered his driver to put trac C201 in gear, and led the convoy into Ambush Alley. Like all Marines, he had been indoctrinated: "First, accomplish the mission." Compared with the other branches of the Armed Forces, the Marine Corps was relatively frank about where troop safety ranked in the big picture—and more than a few grunts actually took perverse pride in the Marines' reputation for getting the job done at any cost.

With trac C201 out in front, Charlie Company's eleven tracs and three Humvees headed for the Saddam Canal Bridge. Watertight, tublike contraptions that can deploy propellers in order to cross open water, tracs were designed to ferry troops from ships to beachheads. Twenty-six feet long with a gun turret on the roof, a trac is intended to carry twenty men and is impelled by belted treads, like tanks, rather than wheels. Because a trac's light aluminum "armor" is easily penetrated by rocket-propelled grenades (RPGs) and heavy weapons, Major Peebles's platoon of M1A1 Abrams tanks was supposed to lead Charlie Company into the fray. After being diverted to rescue the Maintenance Company soldiers, however, the tanks had burned up so much gas that they'd had to run far to the rear to refuel. When Peebles arrived at the so-called rapid-refueling point, he discovered that its pumps had broken down and it would take forty minutes to refill each of his enormous machines using a siphon. With the tanks thus temporarily hors de combat, Charlie Company's vulnerable tracs clattered toward the northern bridge on their own, without an escort.

As the tracs rolled up Ambush Alley, enemy fighters began to shoot at them from adjacent rooftops, and within minutes the sporadic fire became a furious attack coming from all points of the compass. Somehow none of the Americans running the show—not Natonski nor Grabowski nor the CIA nor any of the generals at Central Command—had any idea that Nasiriyah was a major military hub overflowing with enemy forces. The Marines on the ground had been assured that taking the bridges would be "a cakewalk"—that the residents of the city were Shiite Muslims who despised Saddam and his Sunni minions, and would welcome the Americans as liberators. As Grabowski later explained to a colonel investigating the incident, "Our indications were . . . that the bridges were not going to be defended, that we're going to go in there and just seize them. . . . No one expected that level of a fight in An Nasiriyah. No one." As it turned out, the sectarian dynamics in Nasiriyah, as in the rest of Iraq, were much more convoluted than the neoconservative brain trust at the White House and the Pentagon assumed.

On February 15, 1991, during the first Gulf War, the Voice of America had broadcast a rousing speech by President George H. W. Bush imploring Shia throughout the country to rise up against Saddam. Nine days later, the CIA broadcast a similar message over a radio station called the Voice of Free Iraq, suggesting that the United States would support such an uprising. During the first week of March the Shiite residents of Nasiriyah responded by overthrowing the city's ruling Baathist regime, only to discover that the Americans had no intention of getting involved. Even worse, after routing the Iraqi Army, the U.S.-led coalition signed a peace agreement that explicitly allowed Saddam's government to retain its fleet of helicopter gunships. Having defeated Saddam, the first president Bush and his secretary of defense, Dick Cheney, no longer had any use for the Shia. The Americans feared the uprising they'd fomented would give control of Iraq to the Shia, whose close religious ties with Iran discomfited them even more than Saddam did.

As the Shiite rebellion gained momentum, Saddam's Republican Guard swooped in and savagely crushed the insurgents throughout southern Iraq, including Nasiriyah, summarily executing tens of thousands of Shia while U.S. forces stood by and did nothing to intervene. Bodies of the dead were dumped in mass graves around the city. The embittered survivors understandably felt betrayed by the Americans, and a dozen years later when the second president Bush invaded Iraq, the Shia were not about to be played for fools again.

Instead of being welcomed as saviors by the citizens of Nasiriyah, the Marines who entered the city in 2003 were attacked. While gusts of Iraqi bullets ripped into the American vehicles, local women and children deliberately ran out onto the streets to deter the Marines from shooting back. According to Grabowski, they were "smiling and waving and they knew what they were doing."

Initially the Marines held their fire. As the Iraqi attack intensified, however, self-preservation superseded concerns about civilian casualties. Accelerating to thirty miles per hour, the grunts began shooting frantically with every weapon available as they careened down Ambush Alley trying to escape the kill zone. The twenty-one-year-old lance corporal Edward Castleberry, the driver of trac C201—the column's lead vehicle—used one hand to squeeze off bursts with his M16 as he steered with the other, while the trac's commander, Sergeant Schaefer, eviscerated Fedayeen fighters with a .50-caliber machine gun mounted in the vehicle's turret. "Pieces of people were all over the street," Castleberry later told the *Los Angeles Times*. When an Iraqi ran into the middle of the road and began spraying AK-47 rounds directly into the front of his trac, Castleberry drove over the man in self-defense, crushing him beneath the machine's treads.

Shortly before Charlie Company arrived at Saddam Canal Bridge, trac C211, positioned near the rear of the column and driven by the thirty-one-year-old sergeant Michael Bitz, was hit with two RPGs, critically injuring five Marines and setting the vehicle on fire. Aware that if the trac came to a stop, the two dozen men inside the burning machine would probably be overrun and massacred, the vehicle's commander, Second Lieutenant Michael Seely, pounded on Bitz's helmet and screamed at him, "Go! Go! Go!" They managed to keep the machine rolling north with the rest of the column, spewing oily black smoke, until it had crossed the bridge and traveled approximately a hundred yards beyond, when the engine quit turning and it shuddered to a stop.

Very soon it became apparent that the Marines had driven into a deadly cul-de-sac. Several hundred Fedayeen guerrillas and Iraqi Army regulars were dug into well-defended positions all around the Americans, energetically targeting them with an assortment of light and heavy weapons. The fourteen tracs came to a halt, and the men of Charlie Company scurried from their flimsy vehicles into the surrounding terrain, which offered scant cover. Bitz, Schaefer, and other Marines rushed to pull the moaning, blood-drenched men from Bitz's flaming trac, C211, before the stores of ammunition inside exploded, and loaded them into the designated "medevac" trac, C212. At the same time, mortar squads hurriedly set up three 60-millimeter mortars and began lobbing rounds toward the enemy at such a rapid rate that the tubes began to glow from the heat.

First Sergeant José Henao was in charge of gathering and evacuating the wounded Marines. Although few of Charlie Company's radios were functioning, Henao managed to get a call out to the battalion command post with an urgent request for a medevac helicopter, but the landing zone was receiving way too much fire for any aircraft to come in. Immediately after finishing the call, trac C212 was hit with an RPG, so Henao and another noncommissioned officer unloaded the wounded men inside and laid them down on the east side of the road. The volley of RPGs continued for several minutes, but luckily, Henao testified, "a lot of the RPGs, they weren't detonating. They were just landing, and going by us. I saw one coming straight to our trac. It hit the back, bounced off, and landed about 40 yards away and never exploded."

For the first three days of the war, U.S. forces had raced north from Kuwait without encountering any noteworthy enemy resistance. The greatest impediment to their advance was having to deal with hundreds of Iraqis who rushed forward to surrender as the Americans drew near. The ferocity of the Iraqi counterassault in Nasiriyah thus caught the Marines completely off guard.

Before the invasion, most of the residents of Nasiriyah were in fact terrified of the American military's overwhelming superiority, and assumed they would be obliterated. But when the invaders were led into Nasiriyah by the timid, poorly armed 507th Maintenance

Company, the Iraqis adjusted their opinion of their adversary's purported invincibility. According to the executive officer of the Iraqi Twenty-third Brigade, who was later captured and interrogated by the Marines, the Iraqi forces adopted an entirely different frame of mind when the Americans in Jessica Lynch's convoy "didn't fight when they got engaged," and instead fled the city. All the Iraqi soldiers were "emboldened," the executive officer explained: "It emboldened even the tribal leaders to fight the Americans, because if this is the best you've got, then why not be on the winning side." When the Marines showed up on the same streets where the 507th Maintenance Company had just been routed, the Iraqis assumed that the Marines would also turn tail and run if confronted with a show of force, so they fought with great determination.

Thus did Charlie Company wind up in a desperate fight for their lives. Although they battled the Iraqis courageously, the Marines were surrounded, outnumbered, and outgunned and had no place to hide. The Abrams tanks that had been sent to rescue the Lynch convoy would have shifted the odds decisively in the Americans' favor, but they had still not appeared. Nor was Charlie Company receiving any help from the air. Sending in a couple of Cobra attack helicopters to take out enemy positions from above would also have made a crucial difference for the Marines north of the Saddam Canal Bridge, but the Marine Corps had given Charlie Company neither a forward air controller to call in such air support nor a UHF radio—both of which were required to contact aircraft and tell them where to shoot. So the grunts were left to their own devices. Their only option was to try to keep the enemy at bay until reinforcements arrived.

José Henao went over to one of the mortar crews to see how they were holding up, and kneeled down next to Staff Sergeant Phillip Jordan. Pumping out shells as fast as they could be dropped into his red-hot mortar tube, Jordan calmly remarked to Henao, "We're in a shit sandwich."

"Yes we are," Henao replied, and then hurried off to tend to the wounded men from trac C211, who were calling out for him about seventy yards away.

When Henao had covered about half that distance, there was an enormous explosion back where he had just been talking to Jordan.

RPGs and enemy mortar rounds had been detonating around the Marines for fifteen or twenty minutes, but this explosion was notably larger. It killed Jordan instantly. Slumped near Jordan with the front portion of his head blown off, gurgling and twitching in the throes of death, was Lance Corporal Brian Buesing. Second Lieutenant Fred Pokorney lay dead in the middle of the road several feet away. Three other Marines were gravely injured by the blast.

A moment later, a second tremendous explosion occurred, killing Corporal Kemaphoom Chanawongse, a Thai immigrant, as he was bringing ammunition to resupply Jordan's mortar squad, and wounding another Marine. Hundreds of bullets then began to impact the earth at a fantastic rate, followed many seconds later by a weird screeching noise like a "badass blender," as one grunt described it; another Marine said the sound reminded him of a "buzz saw." Blindingly bright pyrophoric decoy flares drifted down from the sky in the wake of the bullets, fizzing and sputtering like Fourth of July fireworks. "It looked like little sparklers going off about twenty feet in the air," recalled a witness who survived the attack. The Marines' sense of alarm was heightened by their complete bafflement. Only one of the men on the ground seemed to have any idea what was assaulting them.

"I knew exactly what it was," said that man, Second Lieutenant Michael Seely, who had been awarded the Bronze Star and a Purple Heart in 1991 during the first war with Iraq, and was the company's most seasoned officer. "I'd been strafed eight times during Operation Desert Storm by an A-10. I know exactly what they sound like." The A-10 "Warthog" is an American jet aircraft designed to destroy tanks. The Marines of Charlie Company, Seely immediately understood, had been mistaken for the enemy and were being attacked by the U.S. Air Force.

CHAPTER TWENTY-FOUR

Three companies from the First Battalion, Second Marine Regiment were involved in the battle for Nasiriyah on March 23: Alpha, Bravo, and Charlie. A few miles south of where Charlie Company was getting shot to pieces, the Marines in Alpha and Bravo companies were also fighting for their lives. Scattered around the Euphrates River Bridge and to the east of Ambush Alley, they were much too preoccupied with their own problems to give any thought to Charlie Company's predicament. Neither Alpha nor Bravo Company even knew where Charlie Company was, let alone that it was in serious trouble, because radio communications had completely broken down. Some radios had simply gone on the fritz, but the main source of the problem was that most of the Marines in Nasiriyah had never been in combat, and when bullets started cutting the air, almost everybody with a radio began frantically trying to talk at the same time. Several overexcited grunts inadvertently thumbed the "talk" buttons on their microphones even when they weren't speaking—a phenomenon known as "hot miking" that instantly jammed the entire network, creating radio gridlock that persisted for hours.

Many of Bravo Company's vehicles, including the trac that served as Grabowski's mobile command post, remained stuck in the mud several blocks east of Ambush Alley. Grabowski had moved slightly farther north with a handful of tracs and Humvees that managed to avoid the quagmire, but the battalion air officer, Captain A. J. Greene, stayed behind in the now-immobile command post, which was receiving RPG and AK-47 fire from Iraqis on the surrounding rooftops. It was Greene's job to supervise the battalion's three forward air controllers, who were in turn responsible for using their special UHF radios to request air support from any helicopters or jets that might be in the vicinity, and then telling those aircraft what targets to hit with their guns, bombs, and missiles. Greene's radios, however, were working only intermittently.

The forward air controller assigned to direct aircraft in support of Bravo Company was Captain Dennis Santare, who was inside a trac a couple of hundred yards north of Greene's mired vehicle. At approximately 1:20 p.m., Greene managed to get a brief call through to Santare, whose call sign was "Mouth." "Mouth, I need you to get on guard and get any air support you can," Greene said, and then his radio went dead for the rest of the day. The "guard" frequency to which Greene referred was a seldom-used channel set aside for emergencies; the fact that Greene had instructed Santare to use it to request air support suggested to Santare that Bravo Company's situation had turned dire.

Santare immediately got on his UHF radio, switched to the guard frequency, and transmitted, "On guard, on guard, on guard, this is Mouth in the vicinity of An Nasiriyah. We have troops in contact and need immediate air support." He received a callback from a pair of A-10 Warthogs that were passing overhead en route from Kuwait's Al Jaber Air Base to Baghdad on a bombing run; the Warthogs immediately aborted their scheduled mission and began to circle above Nasiriyah, awaiting instructions from Santare regarding the enemy targets he wanted them to take out.

Santare was a skilled, conscientious air controller, but because he was unable to communicate with either Greene or Grabowski, he was forced to make some critical decisions on his own. Santare believed, correctly, that most of the enemy forces were positioned north of the Saddam Canal Bridge, and he worried that the Iraqis were sending down reinforcements from this area to attack Bravo Company. So he told the Warthogs to scan the area north of the canal and "tell me what you see."

The call signs of the Warthog pilots were "Gyrate 73" and "Gyrate 74." Gyrate 73 reported that he had spotted eight or nine enemy trucks massing directly north of the Saddam Canal Bridge, validating Santare's fears about an imminent attack on Bravo Company. While they were observing these vehicles through binoculars from an altitude of fifteen thousand feet, the Warthog pilots saw two Marine Cobra attack helicopters fly near the area, after which one of the enemy trucks appeared to burst into flames, creating an immense plume of black smoke, leading the Warthog pilots to conclude that the vehicle had been hit by one of the Cobras.

Unbeknownst to the Warthog pilots or Santare, the burning "Iraqi truck" was actually Charlie Company's trac C211, which had just come to a stop north of the bridge after being hit with Iraqi RPGs. To the Warthog pilots, who believed the vehicle had been hit by American Cobras, the fact that it was burning seemed to confirm that it was Iraqi, and they used the column of smoke rising from C211 as a point of reference for attacking their targets. Before they fired a single shot or dropped any bombs, however, the Warthogs wanted to be absolutely sure that the vehicles they saw north of the Saddam Canal Bridge were enemy forces, rather than American, so for the next fifteen minutes they conferred with Santare about the exact locations of the Marine positions.

According to the original battle plan, formulated before their vehicles had become bogged down in sewage, Bravo Company was supposed to lead the assault on the Saddam Canal Bridge, which caused Santare to mistakenly assume that Charlie Company was still behind Bravo Company, far to the south, probably mired in sludge somewhere as well. Santare checked with the Bravo Company commander, Captain Tim Newland, who confirmed that Bravo Company was "the lead trace" and that no Marines had advanced north of the Saddam Canal. Santare therefore assured the Warthogs, repeatedly, that there were no American forces north of that easily recognizable waterway. "No one is north of the 3-8 grid," he told Gyrate 73. "There are no friendlies north of the canal." When the pilots then requested clearance to fire on the "Iraqi" vehicles, Santare told them they had permission to light up their targets. The time was approximately 1:40 p.m.

A few minutes before Santare cleared the Warthogs to attack the vehicles by the Saddam Canal Bridge, Charlie Company's commander, Captain Dan Wittnam, managed to get a brief, garbled call through to Grabowski, the commander of First Battalion, during which he said, "Charlie Company has seized the northern bridge . . . and we are halting." He also told Grabowski that one of his tracs had been hit and that he had casualties. Overjoyed that the 176 men in Wittnam's company had taken the Saddam Canal Bridge and moved north of it so quickly, Grabowski slammed his fist down onto the hood of his Humvee in celebration and then radioed headquarters to tell his superiors the good news.

At the time Grabowski learned that Charlie Company was north of the Saddam Canal, Santare was talking to the Warthog pilots from the hatch of a trac that was within a stone's throw of the battalion commander's Humvee. Because of the ongoing radio gridlock, however, Santare never received the news about Charlie Company's position, nor did he call Grabowski to let him know that Air Force jets were circling above the battlefield, about to commence their attack.

In order to communicate with the Warthogs, Santare had to stand in the hatch of his trac, exposed to enemy fire, and balance his bulky UHF radio on the vehicle's roof. Two miles south of the Saddam Canal Bridge, he could catch occasional glimpses of the Warthogs, but couldn't see their targets, so he'd given the pilots permission to attack targets according to their own discretion within a well-defined geographic area—conditions designated Type 3 close air support, or Type 3 CAS.

Two weeks earlier, however, before the start of the war, Grabowski had issued a written order stating that forward air controllers could give aircraft clearance to attack *only* if the controller was able to see both the aircraft and the target *with his own eyes,* conditions known as Type 1 CAS. "We will not authorize Type 3 CAS," Grabowski decreed in the order, "unless approved by the Battalion Commander"—that is, by Grabowski himself. He issued the order specifically to prevent friendly-fire mishaps.

When he gave the Warthogs a green light to attack without first getting authorization from Grabowski, Santare was therefore in violation of the battalion commander's orders, and he knew it. As he later explained to the Friendly Fire Investigation Board convened to examine the incident, "Marines were in *extremis* and I made a time-critical decision. . . . I . . . did not think there was time to find a clear channel to the Battalion Commander to explain the situation, then ask for approval for the fires. . . . Based on the information I had at the time, I believed my company was minutes away from the anvil of a mechanized ambush. I felt that if I did not act, Marines would die."

———

Upon getting clearance from Santare to engage, Gyrate 74 rolled in hot on his first target, a pair of American tracs on the east side of the road just north of the column of smoke, and dropped two five-hundred-pound MK82 bombs on them. As soon as he let the bombs go, Gyrate 74 pulled off, allowing Gyrate 73 to sweep into position and drop a third bomb on some other tracs south of the smoke plume.

At the time, few, if any, of the Marines on the ground knew the Warthogs were overhead. According to a memorandum later issued by the Friendly Fire Investigation Board, "The board believes that Charlie Company Marines mistook the first 3 MK82LD bombs dropped by Gyrate flight as artillery fire." Although the evidence is not conclusive, a careful reading of the board's full report, augmented by independently published interviews with Charlie Company personnel, leaves little doubt that these first three bombs killed Chanawongse, Buesing, Jordan, and Pokorney and wounded four other Marines.

Over the next twenty or thirty minutes each Warthog made five passes over the American vehicles, targeting them with a total of eight five-hundred-pound bombs and three Maverick missiles, as well as repeatedly strafing them with huge Gatling guns mounted in the nose of each airplane. Although the missiles ended up killing a greater number of Marines, it was these GAU-8/A Avenger cannons that induced the most panic and terror among the grunts. The Avenger is the largest, most powerful aircraft cannon in the American arsenal, and it fires bullets the size of Red Bull cans from seven spinning barrels. Milled from depleted uranium, the bullets are designed to pierce the steel armor on tanks, and are shot from the Warthogs' cannons at a rate of sixty-five rounds per *second*. When the Warthogs aimed their guns at Charlie Company, the rounds tore through the tracs' aluminum armor as if they were made of paper. Many seconds after the bullets arrived came the screech of the furiously whirling barrels that delivered them.

It was the distinctive, terrifying noise of the Warthogs' spinning cannons that first alerted the Marines on the ground that they were being attacked by "friendlies," leaving them incredulous. That American aviators could mistake their ugly, utterly unique amtracs for Iraqi vehicles seemed impossible. In desperation the Marines shot off numerous red and green star-cluster flares. William Schaefer even pulled out a three-foot-by-five-foot American flag mounted on an aluminum pole and jammed it into a smoke launcher on the turret of trac C201 to make the Air Force pilots realize they were massacring fellow Americans, but all these efforts were in vain.

After the Warthogs made approximately eight strafing and bombing runs on the Marines north of the Saddam Canal Bridge, Santare, parked two miles to the south, came on the radio to congratulate the pilots for the effectiveness of their attack: "Hey, you're putting smiles on the guys' faces down here." And then he sent the Warthogs about a mile north to check out a suspected enemy compound.

By now the jets' five-hundred-pound bombs and uranium bullets had killed two more Marines: Private First Class David Fribley and Corporal Randal Rosacker. But Gyrate 73 and Gyrate 74 hadn't finished. Finding nothing of interest on their flight north, the Warthogs returned, at which time they saw five tracs moving rapidly south toward the Saddam Canal Bridge. Believing that the machines were Iraqi trucks bound for Ambush Alley to attack Bravo Company, Gyrate 73 got on the radio and informed Santare, "Hey, you've got vehicles from the northern target sector . . . progressing into the city."

"Those vehicles must not get into the city," Santare replied. The five vehicles heading toward the bridge weren't Iraqi, however. They were American tracs packed with wounded Marines making a desperate run south to escape the kill zone and evacuate the injured before they bled to death. The first vehicle across the bridge was trac C208, commanded by Corporal Nick Elliott and driven by Lance Corporal Noel Trevino. In the rear troop compartment were boxes of mortar rounds and ten Marines, several of whom were badly wounded.

C208 was followed by C201 and then C206. As the tracs sped across the bridge at forty miles per hour, Gyrate 74 strafed them with his cannon, hitting all three but failing to stop them. He therefore flew back around and fired a Maverick missile at the lead vehicle, but it overshot C208 and detonated harmlessly beyond.

Although most of the men of Charlie Company understood by now they had been strafed by one or more American A-10 jets, they still didn't realize that the Warthogs were also targeting them with five-hundred-pound bombs and Maverick antitank missiles. After Gyrate 74's missile just missed C208, Gyrate 73 rolled into attack position, got a lock on the same trac, and let his first Maverick go. When C208 was about 150 yards past the bridge, the missile struck the left side of the trac's troop compartment and detonated.

Trac C201, driven by Edward Castleberry, was fifty feet behind C208 when the missile hit. "I saw a white flash and the trac flew a foot and a half off the ground," he testified to the investigating board. "The side blew out. Everyone in the back blew out of it." Blood spattered Castleberry's windscreen. Body parts were hurled in all directions. Castleberry swerved right to avoid hitting the flaming shell of C208, then swerved back left to try to keep the trac on the road, but the steering wouldn't respond. During Gyrate 74's strafing run, the vehicle's transmission oil cooler had been hit with a 30-millimeter uranium round and the hydraulic fluid leaked out, causing the trac to crash into a telephone pole in front of a two-story cinder-block home. As the Marines scrambled out of the wrecked vehicle and ran inside the building for cover, Iraqis started shooting at them from across the street.

When Castleberry had driven past the burning wreckage of C208, he was certain all twelve men inside must be dead. Ten of them were.* But there was an aluminum bulkhead between the troop com-

* The missile killed Lance Corporal Thomas A. Blair, Private First Class Tamario D. Burkett, Lance Corporal Donald J. Cline Jr., Corporal Jose A. Garibay, Private Jonathan L. Gifford, Corporal Jorge A. Gonzalez, Private Nolen R. Hutchings, Lance Corporal Patrick R. Nixon, Sergeant Brendon Reiss, and Lance Corporal Michael J. Williams.

partment and the front part of the trac where Elliott and Trevino had been sitting, and it shielded them from the worst of the missile's blast. Trevino had been temporarily blinded. Elliott's lungs had been seared, his face was badly burned, and shrapnel had torn a large chunk from his right leg. Both men were still alive, however. They crawled out of the flaming vehicle as boxes of ammunition inside it began detonating from the intense heat, got to their feet, and helped each other stagger seventy yards down Ambush Alley to the house where the Marines from C201 had taken refuge.

Gyrate 74, meanwhile, had wheeled around for another run at the vehicles and targeted trac C206, which had followed C201 across the bridge and was now 250 yards south of Saddam Canal, speeding down Ambush Alley. Bearing down from the northwest, the pilot locked his remaining missile on C206. "Fired the Maverick on that one," Gyrate 74 testified, "and it hit and destroyed the vehicle."

The missile detonated as it clipped the back of the trac, blowing open its six-foot-by-five-foot rear ramp and causing a section of the roof to drop into the troop compartment where two wounded Marines were slumped, Sergeant Michael Bitz and Lance Corporal Thomas Slocum. The explosion set the trac on fire and killed at least one of these men, but didn't actually destroy the vehicle, or even stop it. As a C206 crewman later testified, "We got hit with something hard which killed Sergeant Bitz. The trac kept moving and stopped right before the south bridge."

With its rear ramp dragging on the pavement throwing off sparks, and black smoke billowing from its wide-open back end, C206 kept limping forward until it was at the southern end of Ambush Alley, where it finally sputtered to a halt not far from where the Marines of Alpha Company were engaged in an intense firefight of their own just north of the Euphrates River. As soon as the trac stopped moving, Iraqi fighters targeted it with RPGs and machine gun fire. Ignoring the incoming rounds, grunts from Alpha Company rushed to the destroyed vehicle and frantically began pulling dazed survivors from the wreckage, saving six men, but they were too late to do anything for Bitz and Slocum.

After seeing their missiles hit C208 and C206, both Warthogs continued to circle north of Saddam Canal, searching for more targets. Spying an undamaged vehicle parked on the east side of the road, Gyrate 73 locked onto C204 and was within moments of firing his last Maverick when he heard Santare shout into the radio, "Check fire!"

The pilot aborted his attack, pulled up, and asked, "What's going on?"

Santare replied, "Hey, we think we might have had a Blue on Blue, some guys up by the river, but we're not sure. No one really knows."

Lieutenant Michael Seely, it turned out, had finally gotten a radio call through to Grabowski. When Seely, the veteran Marine who'd survived being strafed by an Air Force Warthog twelve years earlier, realized the same nightmare was recurring, he hurried to find a functioning radio, punched in the battalion commander's frequency, and started calling, "Check fire! Check fire! Check fire!" According to Seely, "Soon after that, within a couple of minutes I'm sure—seemed like forever—the friendly fire did cease."

Not long after the Warthogs halted their attack and departed for their base in Kuwait, two of the Abrams tanks that had been diverted to rescue the survivors of the Lynch convoy finally showed up, quickly tipping the advantage to Charlie Company. By sunset the firefight was over, and the Marines held both of the Nasiriyah bridges they'd been told to seize—but at a cost of eighteen dead Marines, at least seventeen of whom were killed by friendly fire. Another seventeen Marines from Charlie Company were wounded, some gravely.

The tragedy was caused by a classic snafu—which is a particularly apt acronym. Originally coined by soldiers in the 1940s, it stands for "situation normal: all fucked-up." Chaos is indeed the normal state of affairs on the battleground, and no army has figured out a way to plan effectively for, let alone alleviate, the so-called fog of war. When the military is confronted with the fratricidal carnage that predictably results, denial and dissembling are its time-honored responses of first resort.

CHAPTER TWENTY-FIVE

On March 28, 2003, General Tommy Franks ordered an inquiry into what caused the casualties in Nasiriyah, as was required by Department of Defense regulations for all incidents of friendly fire. By doing so, Franks enabled the Army's information managers to reply to questions from reporters with their standard gambit: earnest assurances that a thorough investigation was under way, and until it was completed, it would be irresponsible to speculate or comment further.

The investigation, headed by the Air Force general William F. Hodgkins, was completed exactly one year after it was convened. Like most friendly-fire investigations, it was done more or less according to regulations, but with no enthusiasm for determining what really happened, or who should be held accountable. Important eyewitnesses were never interviewed. Video shot from the cockpits of the A-10 Warthogs recorded every second of the attack, but the videotapes went missing soon after the incident.

The pilots known as Gyrate 73 and Gyrate 74 each held the rank of major in the Twenty-third Air Expeditionary Wing, Pennsylvania Air National Guard. Both men had watched the tapes with intelligence officers after returning to their base. Gyrate 73 then turned his tape over to the officer who debriefed him, and the tape vanished, never to be seen again. After watching his tape, Gyrate 74 explained, "I asked Intel, 'Can I keep this and turn it in later? I'd like to look at this tape later on.' " He was allowed to take it, whereupon he "mistakenly" inserted the tape into the cockpit video camera and recorded over it, erasing it. The two most crucial pieces of evidence were thereby destroyed. Nobody ever made any real effort to determine what actually happened to the tapes, and no one was disciplined in any way for the loss of this key evidence.

Despite the destruction of the cockpit tapes and other shortcomings of the investigation, the available facts clearly indicate that at least seventeen of the deaths were the result of fratricide. When General Hodgkins's investigating board released its report, however, it refused to acknowledge that any of the deaths were attributable to friendly fire. On March 29, 2004, in a press release announcing the completion of the investigation, U.S. Central Command summarized the board's conclusions thus:

> A total of 18 Marines were killed and 17 were wounded. Eight of the deaths were verified as the result of enemy fire; of the remaining 10 Marines killed, investigators were unable to determine the cause of death as the Marines were also engaged in heavy fighting with the enemy at the time of the incident.
>
> Of the 17 wounded, only one was conclusively determined to have been hit by friendly fire. Three Marines were wounded while inside vehicles that received both friendly and hostile fire, and the exact sequence and source of their injuries could not be determined.

The brazenness of the board's dishonesty was breathtaking. But mendacity of this sort, it turns out, is common in such inquiries. When the military convenes a friendly-fire investigation board, the organization responsible for the incident is called upon to investigate itself, so there are powerful incentives, both institutional and personal, to assign minimal blame. Although the investigating body typically goes elaborately through the motions of unearthing the facts, seldom is the truth pursued with the zeal demonstrated by, say, the National Transportation Safety Board when it investigates commercial aviation disasters. Military investigations of friendly-fire incidents have a well-documented history of obscuring the truth more often than revealing it.

If fratricide is an untoward but inevitable aspect of warfare, so, too, is the tendency by military commanders to sweep such tragedies under the rug. It's part of a larger pattern: the temptation among generals and politicians to control how the press portrays their military campaigns, which all too often leads them to misrepresent the truth in order to bolster public support for the war of the moment. The fact that the United States has used misinformation to promote the wars in Iraq and Afghanistan is not terribly surprising, therefore. What is alarming is the scale and sophistication of these recent propaganda efforts, and the unabashedness of their executors. The Bush administration took the ruthless stratagems developed by Karl Rove to impugn its political opponents—stratagems that relied heavily on managing public perception by means of deceit—and used them to promote the Global War on Terror, a name that was itself deliberately intended to help sell the wars in Iraq and Afghanistan.

In October 2001, the Department of Defense established the clandestine Office of Strategic Influence specifically to dupe international news organizations into running false stories that would build support for war. When the *New York Times* revealed the existence of this program in February 2002, public clamor forced Donald Rumsfeld to officially kill it. But in November of that year he admitted during a press briefing, without apology, that he had killed it in name only:

> And then there was the Office of Strategic Influence. You may recall that. And "Oh my goodness gracious isn't that terrible, Henny Penny the sky is going to fall." I went down that next day and said, "Fine. If you want to savage this thing, fine: I'll give you the corpse. There's the name. You can have the name, but I'm gonna keep doing every single thing that needs to be done." And I have.

It is now widely understood that the administration presented fraudulent evidence as fact in order to create public support for invading Iraq in advance of the war. Much less attention has been paid to the administration's use of misinformation on an even grander scale to promote the war in the years following the invasion. In January 2003, the White House created the Office of Global Communications, a $200 million program to manipulate public opinion about the coming war, and installed Jim Wilkinson to oversee its operations in the Persian Gulf. According to an article by James Bamford in the November 17, 2005, issue of *Rolling Stone,*

> As the war in Iraq has spiraled out of control, the Bush administration's covert propaganda campaign has intensified. According to a secret Pentagon report personally approved by Rumsfeld in October 2003 and obtained by *Rolling Stone,* the Strategic Command is authorized to engage in "military deception"—defined as "presenting false information, images, or statements."

"Never before in history," Bamford observed, "had such an extensive secret network been established to shape the entire world's perception of a war."

———

March 23, 2003, the fourth day of the Iraq War, had not been propitious for the "Coalition of the Willing"—the disingenuous slogan advanced by the White House to suggest that the invasion had broad international support. Between the Marine casualties and the eleven Army soldiers from Jessica Lynch's convoy who were lost, twenty-nine members of the American military died in Nasiriyah. Another six, including Lynch, were taken captive. Before the day was out, Baghdad television began broadcasting footage of a smiling Iraqi displaying the bodies of four soldiers from Lynch's convoy, twisting the face of one American grotesquely toward the camera in order to show off the wound where the victim had been shot between the eyes.

U.S. Central Command (CENTCOM) endeavored to squelch as much of the bad news as it could, and to a remarkable degree it succeeded. Initially the news media made no mention of deaths from friendly fire in Nasiriyah. The scant information about the battle that was released, moreover, was so distorted that it bore little relation to reality. During CENTCOM's daily news briefing on the evening of March 23, Brigadier General Vincent Brooks blamed the stunning losses suffered by the Marines on the perfidy of Iraqis: "As coalition forces continued their attack north of An Nasiriyah, they encountered forces showing every sign of surrender. As our forces moved to receive this surrender in an honorable way, they were attacked and sustained casualties."

Although this statement was a deliberate fabrication, on the following day a number of American media outlets presented it as fact, as Jim Wilkinson had no doubt intended. On March 24, for example, the Associated Press and Fox News reported,

> Marines [in Nasiriyah] encountered Iraqi troops who appeared to be surrendering. Instead, they attacked. The Americans triumphed, knocking out eight tanks, some anti-aircraft batteries, some artillery and infantry, [General John] Abizaid said. But victory came at a cost: as many as nine dead and an undisclosed number of wounded.

A Hartford, Connecticut, television station, NBC 30, broadcast an interview with Amanda Jordan, the widow of Staff Sergeant Phillip Jordan, who was killed by a bomb dropped from an American Warthog. Having been led to believe that her husband was dead because the enemy had feigned surrender, she lashed out at the Iraqis. "There are rules of war," Mrs. Jordan said angrily, "and those rules were broken. . . . They're saying he was killed in action, but for me it's really murder." A calamitous fiasco that might have undercut the public's enthusiasm for the war was thus transformed into an opportunity to fan the flames of hatred against Saddam and his forces.

In his opening remarks at a Pentagon press briefing on March 25, Rumsfeld continued to pitch the fraudulent story about Iraqis pretending to surrender:

> In recent days, the world has witnessed further evidence of their brutality and their disregard for the laws of war. . . . The regime has committed acts of treachery on the battlefield, dressing their forces as liberated civilians and sending soldiers out waving white flags and feigning surrender, with the goal of drawing coalition forces into the ambushes.

By offering such propaganda to credulous reporters, Wilkinson's Office of Global Communications succeeded in forestalling news re-

ports about friendly fire and other disturbing aspects of the battle for
Nasiriyah, but the city remained beyond the control of American
forces. Thousands of enemy fighters were still moving freely through
the streets, and Fedayeen guerrillas continued to skirmish with
Marines who were securing the two bridges they had captured at
such great cost. As the week dragged on, the Coalition of the Willing
suffered further discouraging setbacks, and the bad news became
harder and harder to contain.

Reports came to light that in the early hours of March 23, a Royal
Air Force Tornado GR4 jet bomber had been shot down by a Patriot
missile fired in error by the U.S. Army, killing the airplane's British
pilot and his navigator.

On the night of March 24, an Abrams tank plunged off a bridge
into the Euphrates River on the west side of Nasiriyah, drowning
Staff Sergeant Donald May, Lance Corporal Patrick O'Day, and Private First Class Francisco Martinez-Flores.

On March 26, a firefight broke out at the intersection where
Lynch's convoy had made its fateful wrong turn three days earlier. In
the ensuing confusion, one Marine unit attacked another Marine
unit, wounding thirty-seven Americans, some critically, and two of
their Kuwaiti interpreters.

On March 27, a U.S. Air Force Warthog mistakenly attacked a
British convoy of Scimitar light tanks outside Basra, seventy-five
miles southeast of Nasiriyah, even though one of the tanks was displaying a Union Jack and all of the vehicles were marked with fluorescent orange panels intended to identify them as coalition forces.
During the American jet's two strafing runs, uranium rounds fired
from its nose cannon pierced the armor on two of the tanks, and they
exploded into flames. One soldier was killed, and three were seriously injured. In this instance, because the wounded soldiers were
British, Wilkinson wasn't able to muzzle them. Quoted in the British
press, one of the furious victims accused the American pilot of being
a "cowboy" who'd "gone out on a jolly" and showed "no regard for
human life."

By the end of the week, the White House was desperate for some
good news to feed to the swarm of journalists who gathered for daily
press briefings at CENTCOM's media headquarters in Doha, Qatar.

And then Jessica Lynch turned up, as if in answer to Wilkinson's prayers.

———

Several Iraqis, including Mohammed Odeh al-Rehaief, had contacted American military personnel to report that Lynch was being held at Saddam Hussein General Hospital. Iraqi Army and Fedayeen fighters were still operating out of the hospital, but as American forces gained control throughout Nasiriyah, the Iraqi military presence at the facility rapidly diminished. By the end of March, the last of the Iraqi combatants had vanished from the hospital and fled the city.

The Iraqi staff at the hospital treated Lynch well, according to doctors and nurses interviewed by the British newspaper the *Guardian*. Dr. Harith al-Houssona, one of the physicians who supervised her care, said that hospital personnel even donated two pints of their own blood to give her. On March 30, al-Houssona actually put Lynch in an ambulance and instructed the driver to drop her off at a nearby American military checkpoint, but Marines shot at the ambulance as it approached, forcing it to turn around and take Lynch back to the Iraqi hospital.

By that time preparations to rescue Lynch were already under way. Approximately a thousand troops had been mobilized, including a contingent from Task Force 20, the most elite Special Operations commandos in the world, and infantrymen from the Second Ranger Battalion. As Pat and Kevin Tillman got ready for the mission, its massive scale—unlike anything they'd seen since arriving in the Persian Gulf—puzzled them. "We leave tomorrow," Pat wrote in his journal on March 30. "This mission will be a P.O.W. rescue, a woman named Jessica Lynch. As awful as I feel for the fear she must face, and admire the courage I'm sure she is showing, I do believe this to be a big Public Relations stunt. Do not mistake me, I wish everyone in trouble to be rescued, but sending this many folks in for a [single low-ranking soldier] screams of media blitz. In any case, I'm glad to be able to do my part and I hope we bring her home safe."

CENTCOM can't be faulted for committing so many troops to the operation. Information provided by the CIA and military intelligence had been extremely unreliable. A week earlier the Marines had been assured that taking the Nasiriyah bridges would be no big deal, only to find themselves in a desperate battle with a large number of very motivated enemy fighters. But Pat's suspicions about the Lynch rescue were well-founded. The resources devoted to the mission were astonishing by any measure, and had been put in place primarily to ensure that it would be a public relations jackpot for those promoting the war. At least seven other American servicemen and servicewomen were also being held captive in Iraq at that time, including five soldiers from Lynch's convoy; yet almost nothing at all was being done to find and rescue these less marketable prisoners of war.

After the Rangers were initially told that the mission to rescue Lynch would take place on March 31, it was pushed back twenty-four hours. Congressman Henry Waxman later alleged that Wilkinson delayed the mission to allow a Special Operations video crew to shoot the rescue for the news media. Although these allegations have not been substantiated, there is no question that Wilkinson was intimately involved with planning the mission, or that it was expertly documented by a combat camera crew from the Fourth Psychological Operations Group included solely for that purpose.

When it finally got under way, the rescue was flawlessly executed. Although the rescue team was targeted with small-arms fire as they approached the hospital in six helicopters, the shooting was light and no aircraft were hit. Ten minutes after the Special Operations team landed, they'd retrieved Lynch, carried her out of the hospital, and loaded her into a waiting Black Hawk. As soon as the helicopter was safely in the air, the first person to be notified was Wilkinson, followed immediately thereafter by CENTCOM media wrangler General Vincent Brooks, President Bush, Vice President Cheney, and Defense Secretary Rumsfeld. Within three hours, a five-minute video of the rescue, carefully edited for dramatic effect, was made available to television correspondents and print reporters in Qatar, who were summoned to the Doha media center in the wee hours of the morning to receive the good news.

Having provided reporters with spurious intelligence reports to hype the story and ensure that Lynch's saga would blow the socks off the folks back home, Wilkinson was eager to get his product into the hands of consumers at the earliest opportunity. The sooner "Saving

Private Lynch" was on the front page of newspapers, the cover of magazines, and the evening news, the sooner the recent spate of depressing events would be relegated to the shadows.

Over the weeks and months that followed, the scheme played out just as Wilkinson hoped it would. More than six hundred stories about Lynch appeared in all manner of media, including a rushed-into-print book that debuted at number one on the *New York Times* nonfiction best-seller list and a made-for-television movie, *Saving Jessica Lynch,* scheduled to attract the largest possible audience during an important network sweeps month. Eventually Wilkinson's rendering of Lynch's ordeal was exposed as propaganda, but by then it had already accomplished what it was meant to accomplish: covering up the truth in order to maintain support for the president's policies. To this day, very few Americans have any inkling that seventeen U.S. Marines were killed by U.S. Air Force jets on the fourth day of the Iraq War.

The Jessica Lynch hoax worked so well, in fact, that the White House would recycle the same tactic thirteen months later, almost move for move, when it was confronted with another series of potentially disastrous revelations. Just as before, a fictitious story about a valiant American soldier would be fed to the media in order to divert attention from a rash of disquieting news. On this occasion, however, the soldier cast as the hero of the fable would be a professional football player whose sense of duty had inspired him to enlist in the Rangers after 9/11.

CHAPTER TWENTY-SIX

On April 9, 2003, seven days after Jessica Lynch was flown to safety, Pat and Kevin Tillman were helicoptered to Baghdad International Airport with their Ranger cohort, where they took up residence in a cavernous aircraft hangar. As they arrived, Marines were attaching a cable to a forty-foot statue of Saddam Hussein in Al-Firdos Square, twelve miles away in the center of Baghdad, preparing to pull it down for a gaggle of photographers and television crews who had flocked to the scene to record the symbolic moment for posterity. A few hours earlier, the capital had officially fallen to American forces. A few hours later, an orgy of unrestrained looting would commence throughout the city and continue for many days.

The Tillmans remained in Baghdad for the next five weeks. Despite the turmoil erupting all around them, their stay was relatively uneventful. Pat fired his weapon only once, on April 21. "Don't get too excited or upset," he wrote in his journal, "they were only warning shots to keep a couple of cars from getting closer and no harm was done."

Their duties allowed plenty of time for conversation. "Pat and Kevin were always talking," recalls Russell Baer, a young Ranger who grew up in Livermore, California, thirty-five miles north of New Almaden. "They spent as much time together as they possibly could. They seemed to have an incredibly rare bond." The Tillman brothers welcomed anyone to join their conversations, however. "Pat was nonjudgmental," Baer emphasizes. "He was interested even in the most idiotic person in the group. He genuinely wanted to find out what they were about. He would challenge them to explain themselves, and some of them would maintain their idiocy and bring nothing to the table, but Pat would always start out by giving them the benefit of the doubt.

"I was friends with Kevin before I was friends with Pat," says Baer, a well-read autodidact with eclectic taste. "I was reading Noam Chomsky's *Propaganda and the Public Mind* and Plato's *Republic.* Kevin had read stuff by both these writers—he'd been a philosophy major in college. So we got into a discussion about literature, which led to further conversations that included Pat. It was great. I finally had people I could talk to.

"Pat was a serious listener. He was one of the first people who really challenged my ideas: 'Do you really believe that? Why? Don't accept everything you read. You should question it all, take what makes sense, and throw away the rest.' He was constantly asking, 'Did you ever consider this? What about that?' He changed the way I thought."

During his stint in the Army, Pat had no trouble establishing meaningful friendships with individuals who didn't share his opinions about politics or religion—which was fortunate, because this described most of the people he encountered while in uniform. An important friend he met during Operation Iraqi Freedom was a Navy SEAL named Steve White whose political orientation was much further to the right than Pat's. But White was bright, mature, and fearless, and he had reached the pinnacle of a demanding, consequential profession; in the world of Special Ops, White was the equivalent of an All-Pro cornerback in the NFL. Pat was drawn to him immediately, and the attraction was mutual.

The first time White invited Pat and Kevin to the SEALs' quarters for coffee, Pat noted in his journal, "For about an hour and a half we bullshat with ten or so of the baddest men on earth. . . . Absolute fucking champions." A couple of days later he wrote, "Last night we again hit the SEALs' tent for coffee and conversation. . . . Steve and I yakked for hours on home, Tahoe, our wives, good eating, all the things I think about constantly. I can't tell you how nice it's been to have these guys around. . . . [They] make all the shit we've gone through worthwhile. They are exactly the type of guys we looked forward to meeting when we decided to join." Thereafter, Pat and Kevin sought out the SEALs for conversation (and, once or twice, an illicit shot of rum) whenever circumstances allowed.

When Pat and Kevin went out on patrols from their base at the airport, both of them found the city to be fascinating and exotic. But after a few weeks of kicking down doors, arresting ordinary Iraqis for questioning, and searching for nonexistent WMD,* the pointlessness and boredom began to grind them down, especially Pat. Then, on the night of April 29–30, four Delta Force operators were shot while on a mission to capture a "high-value target," and Pat helped carry one of the wounded soldiers in from the medevac helicopter to receive treatment. "The man I was carrying had been shot in the abdomen," he wrote. "At this point in the game I was quite surprised to see anyone shot. . . . The danger seemed minimal. It goes to show you never know."

A day later, from the deck of an aircraft carrier off the coast of San Diego, beneath a giant banner proclaiming "Mission Accomplished," President Bush announced "the end of major combat operations in Iraq."

Pat's journal entries expressed growing frustration. He admitted to bouts of depression, as well as disillusionment with some of his superiors: "We've had leaders telling guys to shoot innocent people only to be ignored by privates with cooler heads. . . . It seems their battlefield sense is less than ideal. Given the stress of a situation, I ab-

---

* As Steve Coll wrote in *The New Yorker* in April 2006, Saddam could not bring himself to admit that there were no weapons of mass destruction, "because he feared a loss of prestige and, in particular, that Iran might take advantage of his weakness—a conclusion also sketched earlier by the C.I.A.-supervised Iraq Survey Group. He did not tell even his most senior generals that he had no W.M.D. until just before the invasion. They were appalled, and some thought he might be lying, because, they later told their interrogators, the American government insisted that Iraq did have such weapons. Saddam 'found it impossible to abandon the illusion of having W.M.D.,' the study says. The Bush war cabinet, of course, clung to the same illusion, and a kind of mutually reinforcing trance took hold between the two leaderships as the invasion neared."

solutely will listen to my instincts before diving headfirst into any half-baked scheme of theirs. Perhaps this is not the 'military right,' however these past couple of months have suggested it's necessary."

During their free time, Pat, Kevin, Russell Baer, and Jade Lane, the platoon radio operator, sometimes discussed the geopolitical ramifications of Operation Iraqi Freedom, which increasingly struck them as an imperial folly that was doing long-term damage to U.S. interests. For soldiers to openly criticize the war was exceedingly rare at the time. A Gallup poll conducted in May 2003 indicated that 79 percent of Americans believed the Iraq war was "justified"; among members of the military, support for the war probably exceeded 95 percent. For the Tillman brothers to denounce the war while on active duty in Iraq would no doubt have struck many Americans as treasonous. But Pat and Kevin had been raised to speak their minds, so speak they did.

The Tillman brothers lamented how easy it had been for Bush, Cheney, and Rumsfeld to bully Secretary of State Colin Powell, both houses of Congress, and the vast majority of the American people into endorsing the invasion of Iraq. But Pat and Kevin were not particularly surprised. Their paternal grandfather and two of his brothers were serving in the Navy at Pearl Harbor during the devastating Japanese attack of 1941. Their maternal grandfather had experienced combat as a Marine in the Korean War. One of their uncles had enlisted in the Marines upon graduating from high school and had been stationed in Okinawa during the war in Vietnam. Dannie Tillman had been a history major in college, and when her sons were growing up, family discussions often turned to military history.

Pat and Kevin were familiar with the words of Hermann Göring, Hitler's *Reichsmarschall,* who in 1946, shortly before he was sentenced to death for crimes against humanity, notoriously observed:

Naturally, the common people don't want war; neither in Russia nor in England nor in America, nor for that matter in Germany. That is understood. But after all, it's the leaders of the country who determine the policy, and it's always a simple matter to drag the people along whether it's a democracy, a fascist dictatorship, or a parliament, or a communist dictatorship. . . . Voice or no voice, the people can always be brought to the bidding of the leaders. That is easy. All you have to do is tell them they are being attacked, and denounce the pacifists for lack of patriotism and exposing the country to greater danger. It works the same way in any country.

If anything, Pat was probably even less pleased than Kevin to find himself participating in the invasion of Iraq. Although both brothers were opposed to the war, Kevin was single and not yet on a career path when they enlisted, while Pat had walked away from both a devoted wife and an uncommonly satisfying job in order to help defeat those responsible for 9/11. He ached constantly for Marie. A homebody at heart who was half the world away from the home she had made for him, he felt the distance between them acutely. It's apparent from his journal that Pat was extremely unhappy to be serving in Iraq, and that throughout his tour of duty there he relied on Kevin for emotional support in a way that he never had before.

Pat hadn't sacrificed so much in order to sit on the sidelines of a misguided war that he believed was abetting the enemies of the United States. Paradoxically, though, it's obvious from his diary that some portion of his unhappiness derived from the fact that he hadn't experienced combat yet, and concluded that he probably wouldn't before leaving Baghdad. Part of his rationale for becoming a Ranger was to join the fight. In addition to feeling a responsibility to help with the dirty work, he wanted to know firsthand what it was like to have people trying their best to kill him, and perhaps be required to kill in turn. His feelings about war in general, and this war in particular, were shaped by complicated, emotionally charged, sometimes contradictory notions of duty, honor, justice, patriotism, and masculine pride. He was therefore more than a little ambivalent about going home without a CIB: the Combat Infantryman Badge—a miniature silver rifle mounted on a two-inch rectangle of blue enamel framed with a silver oak wreath, awarded to infantrymen who'd engaged in combat.

Despite the dark frame of mind evident in a number of his Baghdad journal entries, on May 2 Pat wrote, "You know, I have to admit, some of these kids are getting to me. I find myself thinking of things I can do to help their future. As pissed off as I can be with this place, there are some very good people, especially some of these kids. Whether I like it or not, I have a soft spot for some of these little brats."

Pat observed May 4, his first wedding anniversary, by writing a message to his wife:

Happy Anniversary my love!!! A year ago today Marie made me the luckiest man alive, and what have I done in return? Schemed up the most absurd way to drastically shit-can our, until recently, perfect existence. Here I sit in a tent, at Baghdad International Airport, surrounded by kids, half the earth away from where I belong on our anniversary. Unbelievable. This last year has been shit, no doubt, Marie. However in this last year I've grown to love & admire you to a point that only trial and suffering can bring about. This madness has brought out such amazing strength and character in you. Of course this was always there, but this last year has given me the opportunity to see just how amazing, how tough you really are.

For weeks the Rangers had been hearing rumors that they would be packing up and heading home "any day now." Finally it appeared as though their departure from Iraq might actually be at hand. On May 12, Pat wrote, "Lots of good news. . . . Should (of course with the usually skepticism) head home the 15th. Already the wheels are in motion, packing has begun, and excitement is in the air. . . . A bunch of EPWs (Enemy Prisoners of War) escaped from across the street today. Twenty escaped while four have already been caught. Nub and I are rooting for the other sixteen. Sometimes it's hard not to cheer for the underdog. (P.S.—These are not military POWs, but civilians they're holding for info.)"

Pat's journal entry for May 15 consisted of two short lines: "We are leaving at 0300 tomorrow. Thank fucking god." Three days later he and Kevin were sitting in the USO lounge at Frankfurt Airport, waiting to board a flight for the United States. Pat reflected:

All in all I suppose this was a solid experience, if for no other reason than we're coming home safe. . . . We did not fight, or find ourselves in any life altering situations. . . . Perhaps in time this whole experience will seem larger than it does now, more exciting. I admit it was not what I expected of "going to war," but who knows what to expect. I remember my rookie year [in the NFL], a reporter asking about my feelings on going to the playoffs. He mentioned that many players will spend a whole career without being fortunate enough to go. For me, in my first year, I guess I just expected to go every year, though it turned out not to be the case. Perhaps this will ring true here. . . . This could possibly be our first and only taste of combat (limited as it was). But then again, with that "cowboy" at the helm, I wouldn't bet on it.

———

Pat's stint in Iraq wasn't only difficult for Pat; it was hard on Marie as well. "They were gone for two and a half months," she says, "and for most of that time there was no communication between us at all. He wasn't able to call me until the very end, right before they came home, so I had no idea what was going on. We had just moved to Washington State, and I hadn't started working yet. I knew no one. I just sat inside and watched the media coverage of the war on TV all day long. They'd report that another helicopter had been shot down, and I'd wonder if that was Pat and Kevin. I don't even really remember how I got through that period. It was awful."

For Pat to be reunited with Marie on May 19 was an enormous relief. Life was good again. In July, when the Army granted Pat and Kevin a two-week leave, the three of them went to Lake Tahoe and kicked back with their high-school friends from Almaden, just like they had done so many times before the Tillman brothers enlisted.

Upon their return to Fort Lewis, Pat and Kevin began preparing for the rigors of Ranger School, a punishing sixty-one-day trial that every noog must endure in order to earn his "tab": a small cloth patch embroidered with the word "Ranger," which is affixed to the upper left shoulder of his uniform. Until a Ranger is "tabbed," he is not considered a full-fledged member of the brotherhood, cannot be promoted beyond the rank of private first class, and will be routinely subjected to degrading work assignments at the whim of tabbed superiors just to remind him that he is a pissant, unworthy of respect.

"Tabbed guys go out of their way to fuck with the new guys," explains Sergeant Mel Ward, who would become one of the Rangers Pat considered a friend. "They order them to clean toilets, do push-ups. You hear stories of noogs locked in their lockers over the week-end with nothing but a two-quart canteen. When a tabbed Ranger would smoke Pat, he would do what he was supposed to, but you could tell it was really burning him up. Because it was pointless and unnecessary."

"You have to put up with a lot of asinine stuff in the Army," Jade Lane agrees. "And Pat didn't like it. Some twenty-year-old would tell him to do something stupid, like shine your boots, then scuff them up, and then shine them again. That kind of crap he was not into. And he would let them know. Like, he'd say, 'Look, I'll shine my boots, but I'm not gonna scuff 'em up and shine 'em again, because that's just retarded.' And people in the Army don't like being talked to like that. You're supposed to do what you're told. So he would get in trouble sometimes. They'd bring him into the office, write him up for counseling."

In order to escape this abuse, Pat had to graduate from Ranger School, but to be admitted, he first had to achieve at least the nineti-eth percentile in a standard Army Physical Fitness Test, or APFT: sixty-six push-ups in two minutes, seventy-three sit-ups in two min-utes, and a two-mile run in less than thirteen minutes fifty-four sec-onds. One afternoon in July, Pat was notified that he had been chosen for the next opening in Ranger School, assuming he passed an APFT to be administered the following morning. Although Pat had just completed an especially exhausting workout, he figured scoring high enough on the APFT would be no big deal even with sore muscles: throughout basic training, both Pat and Kevin had excelled on each of the several occasions they had taken the APFT; the last time Pat had been tested, he'd done eighty-four push-ups, eighty-one sit-ups, and run two miles in twelve minutes twenty-one seconds.

When Pat took the test the next morning, he easily did enough push-ups and had no trouble running two miles faster than the re-quired time, but he didn't do seventy-three sit-ups in less than two minutes. Actually, he did more than the required number of sit-ups; however, the sergeant judging his performance disqualified several of them on a technicality, so Pat failed the test. It's possible the sergeant didn't count the sit-ups in question because he was in an ornery mood and wanted to show Pat that although he was a famous football player in civilian life, in the Second Ranger Battalion he was just a lowly private. Or perhaps the sergeant had a legitimate reason for disqualifying the sit-ups. In any case, Pat failed the APFT and was therefore denied admission to Ranger School.

He was enraged about not passing the test, as angry as he'd ever been about any mistake he'd made as a football player, but his fury wasn't directed at the NCO who failed him. Not one to make excuses, he blamed only himself, believing that he should have been able to pass the test no matter how many sit-ups the sergeant decided not to count. Making matters infinitely worse, he wouldn't be able to take the test again for at least three weeks.

After stewing for the better part of a month, Pat passed the APFT test at the next opportunity. Because Kevin took it at the same time and also passed, on September 29, 2003, they entered Ranger School together at Fort Benning, Georgia. The nine weeks that followed were punishing. Their class of 253 soldiers was kept awake and on the move twenty hours a day, every day, with the exception of one eight-hour break every three weeks. They slept two or three hours a night, if they were lucky, and subsisted on a daily allowance of twenty-four hundred calories, despite the fact that on most days they burned more than five thousand calories—some days a lot more. They humped ninety-pound loads up and down the Tennessee Valley Divide, crawled through thickets of poison oak, bivouacked in freezing rain with nothing but the clothes on their backs, and were perpetually hungry and exhausted. Some of the soldiers lost more than thirty pounds of body weight. Half of the members of their class failed or dropped out, most of them during the first week.

Pat and Kevin found the experience to be a satisfying challenge. Both of them graduated handily, received their Ranger tabs on November 28, and were promoted to the rank of specialist. Two years after Pat's death, an Army captain named Aaron Swain recalled coaching Pat through the three-week "mountain phase" of the course, during which the soldiers were taught rock-climbing skills on Mount Yonah, in the Chattahoochee National Forest. "Tillman was a stud," Swain attests. "He was the real deal."

By the autumn of 2003, as Swain was testing the Tillmans' mettle in the backwoods of Georgia, it was becoming apparent that the war in Iraq was not turning out as predicted. Increasingly, critics of the administration were comparing it to Vietnam. In mid-October, a videotape was broadcast on Al Jazeera in which Osama bin Laden looked coldly into the camera and exulted, "I am rejoicing in the fact that America has become embroiled in the quagmires of the Tigris and Euphrates. Bush thought that Iraq and its oil would be easy prey, and now here he is, stuck in dire straits, by the grace of God Almighty. Here is America today, screaming at the top of its voice as it falls apart in front of the world."

Bin Laden regarded the invasion of Iraq as a tremendous gift from President Bush—a "rare and essentially valuable" opportunity to spread jihad, as the exiled sheik put it. Not only had the United States eliminated Saddam Hussein, whom bin Laden reviled as "a thief and an apostate," but the American occupation was fueling Muslim rage even more than the invasion of Afghanistan had, inspiring throngs of Arab men to join the ranks of al-Qaeda.

––––––––

The contract the Tillmans had signed upon enlisting committed them to remain in uniform until July 2005. There was a strong possibility that they would be deployed to Iraq again before this date, and find themselves in the middle of the worsening violence there. Soon after graduating from Ranger School, however, Pat was presented with an opportunity to avoid this fate: he was offered a ticket out of the Army.

In December 2003, Tillman's agent, Frank Bauer, was contacted by Bob Ferguson, who, as general manager of the Arizona Cardinals, had played a key role in bringing Pat to the Cardinals and launching his professional football career. Ferguson, who had moved on to become general manager of the Seattle Seahawks, told Bauer that Seattle was very eager to have Tillman on the Seahawks' roster when the football season got under way in the fall of 2004. According to Bauer, when he explained that Pat wasn't due to be released from the Army until the summer of 2005, Ferguson assured him, "We've checked into it. He's already served in a war. He can get out of the service. Just file his discharge papers. We'd love to have him here in the Seattle locker room."

As it turned out, other teams were also interested in signing Tillman for the 2004 season, including the Cardinals, the St. Louis Rams, the New England Patriots, and the Dallas Cowboys. So Bauer asked around, and Ferguson was apparently right: under special circumstances, soldiers who completed a tour of duty in a war zone could be granted an honorable discharge well before their contracts were up. If Pat requested such a dispensation, come the following September he stood an excellent chance of exchanging his Ranger body armor for football shoulder pads, especially given Tillman's stature. Army recruitment commercials were a staple of football games televised on Sunday afternoons and Monday nights, and the National Football League had a close working relationship with the Department of Defense. Strings could be pulled on Pat's behalf.

Bauer excitedly relayed the good news to his client: "So I call Patty and I say, 'Listen to me. I got a couple of clubs that are interested in you. Now, you may want to check with the Army before you say anything, but they're telling me they can get you an early discharge, and these teams want you. Seattle wants you badly.' "

Tillman replied that he was flattered by the interest, but he wouldn't consider leaving the Army before his contract was completed. "I enlisted for three years," he explained to Bauer. "I owe them three years. I'm not going to go back on my word. I'm going to stay in the Army." Bauer leaned on him to reconsider, but got nowhere.

"There were offers from several NFL teams," Marie confirms. "Pat mentioned the Seahawks' offer, and at that point in time he probably would have loved to have gone back and played football for them. But we never really discussed it because it just wasn't going to happen. There was no way he was going to bail out of the Army halfway through. He said, 'I'm going to serve my three years and then go back and play in the NFL after I've finished. That's what my plan was all along. It's the right thing to do. And I'm going to stick with that.' " As much as Pat hated being in the military and forcing Marie to endure all that his enlistment entailed, breaking the commitment he'd made to the Rangers would have violated principles he considered inviolable. The handful of people who understood what made Pat tick knew that leaving the Army early was something he would never consider. It was absolutely out of the question.

PART THREE

I love him who does not hold back one drop of spirit for himself, but wants to be entirely the spirit of his virtue: thus he strides over the bridge as spirit.

I love him who makes his virtue his addiction and his catastrophe: for his virtue's sake he wants to live on and to live no longer.

—FRIEDRICH NIETZSCHE, *Thus Spoke Zarathustra*

CHAPTER TWENTY-SEVEN

Pat and Kevin were given a two-week leave over Christmas, which they spent in New Almaden visiting their family. Shortly after they returned to Fort Lewis in January 2004, a new batch of recruits arrived at Second Battalion, one of whom was a wiry little private from Indiana named Josey Boatright. "Pat Tillman was one of the first guys I met at Lewis," Boatright recalls. "When you first get there, everything is chaos. People are screaming at you, you're running everywhere, you can't do anything right. Amidst all this chaos, this big dude, a specialist, comes into the barracks from the firing range with his weapon and his full kit on. He walks up to me and says, 'Are you the new guy in Second Platoon? My name is Pat Tillman. Relax, this stuff will pass. It'll be over soon. Nice to meet you.'

"It was a shock," says Boatright: "Somebody being nice, talking to you like a human. And his brother Kevin addressed me the same way when I got to the top of the stairs. It didn't dawn on me at the time who he was. Someone told me soon enough, and I got to know him over the weeks that followed. A lot of the Rangers were cocky and arrogant and muscle-bound. They treated the new guys like shit. Pat was never like that. He was always polite. He was a genuinely nice guy."

Boatright, the Tillman brothers, and the rest of the Rangers in Alpha Company spent the remainder of the winter training intensely at

Fort Lewis. Then, in March, they learned that they would be deploying to Afghanistan in early April. "Pat knew they'd be sent over there again somewhere," says Marie, "and he was glad he was going to Afghanistan and not going back to Iraq. Even though he was more disillusioned with the Army by then, he still believed in the war in Afghanistan. Fighting there was why he had joined in the first place."

There was much less news coming out of Afghanistan than out of Iraq. By 2004, many Americans didn't even realize the country was still fighting a war there. "Most people thought Afghanistan would be safer than Iraq," Marie says. "But I knew a little more about what they were supposed to be doing over there. I knew they were supposed to be patrolling along the Pakistani border and it wouldn't be a very safe situation. I was also a lot less naive about war and the Army by now, too. When they went to Iraq, they were straight out of boot camp, and it all happened so quickly I didn't have as much time to think before they left."

In any case, after Pat and Kevin came home from Baghdad and graduated from Ranger School, Marie remembers, "We felt like they had passed the midpoint. It seemed like they were over the hump. They were supposed to deploy to Afghanistan for something like two months, come home for a month, and then deploy back overseas for maybe another three months, and then that was going to be it. So we felt like we only had to get through the next six months or so, and then we were home free. Pat was already starting to think about life after the Army. He talked about how when he got back from Afghanistan it was going to be time to get back into shape for football again." But returning to the NFL was not the only thing on Pat's agenda after his military service was over. He was also looking forward to having a tête-à-tête with Noam Chomsky, a meeting that Pat had prevailed upon Réka Cseresnyés, his old college study partner from Budapest, to arrange.

After they'd graduated from Arizona State, Tillman and Cseresnyés remained good friends, and Pat, Marie, Cseresnyés, and her husband—another ASU classmate named Jared Schrieber—regularly got together for dinner. When Cseresnyés heard that Pat was joining the Army, she says she and Schrieber "challenged him a little bit: 'Are you sure about this? Are you ready to serve under a president you don't really support?' But he thought he owed it to the country to really do something after 9/11. I think he felt he could stay above the politics, somehow, and just do his duty as a patriot. . . . With Pat, if his conscience told him he should do something, he did it, no excuses. He just made it happen as well as he possibly could."

From the early days of their friendship, Cseresnyés and Tillman would recommend books for each other to read, she says, and "probably around 2000 we started reading Chomsky and debating his ideas. His perspective on things was so different from the mainstream media, and that appealed to Pat." Chomsky was a strident critic of the Bush administration and its Global War on Terror, and although Tillman certainly didn't agree with all of Chomsky's views, he concurred with many of them. For example, when Chomsky opined in a radio interview, "If the American population had the slightest idea of what is being done in their name, they would be utterly appalled," it was perfectly aligned with Tillman's own sense of outrage over what he'd witnessed in Iraq. Pat admired both Chomsky's intellectual courage and his straightforward, unembellished turns of phrase.

In 2003, Cseresnyés and her husband moved to Boston so that Schrieber could pursue a graduate degree at the Massachusetts Institute of Technology, where Chomsky happened to be on the faculty. After hearing Chomsky give a presentation at a conference held on the MIT campus, Cseresnyés called Pat to tell him about it, and he got very excited. "I'd like to talk to Chomsky!" Pat blurted. "Réka, arrange something! He's just down the street; I'd like to talk to him!"

"I was like, 'Why not?' " Cseresnyés says. Out of the blue she sent an e-mail to Chomsky with an article about Tillman attached, explaining that "this brilliant and fascinating man" who recently served as an Army Ranger in Iraq wanted to speak with him.

To Cseresnyés's surprise, within a matter of hours she received a reply from Chomsky indicating that he was open to the idea, and urging Pat to send him an e-mail to set the meeting up, although, Chomsky warned, "My life is so intense that even phone calls are scheduled often weeks in advance."

The ball was now in Tillman's court. In an e-mail Pat sent to Cseresnyés on February 9, 2004, he wrote, "I haven't gotten around to writing Noam . . . but I will." As his deployment approached, however, Pat and Marie's lives grew hectic, and he decided to wait to contact Chomsky until after his return from Afghanistan.

"As far as I know," says Cseresnyés, "Pat never contacted Chomsky. And obviously, the meeting never happened. But I would have loved to have been a fly on the wall for that conversation. Knowing Pat, I imagine he would have asked a lot of questions, challenging whatever Chomsky was saying, as Pat always did, trying to understand his perspective more deeply."

Although on the face of it there would seem to have been little in common between the two men—one a young professional athlete-cum-soldier, the other a middle-aged linguist, writer, and antiwar activist—Cseresnyés thinks otherwise. She believes that one of the reasons Pat was so fascinated by Chomsky was the originality of the latter's thinking. "Chomsky asks questions only few would think to ask," she explains, "which is actually very similar to the way Pat was. I saw an article recently about Chomsky that described him as a good listener. How he asked a lot of questions. How he was so down-to-earth. As I was reading it, I was thinking, 'This sounds so much like Pat!'—not necessarily that they believed the same things, but that their minds operated in the same way."

————

During the first months of 2004, as he contemplated his future beyond the military, Pat seemed more at ease than he had in years. "Kevin and I both noticed it," Marie says. "He was very much at peace with himself. It was like he'd gotten rid of any of his hang-ups. He'd sort of been evolving in this direction ever since he went to juvenile hall after the Round Table fight—resetting his priorities, figuring out what really mattered." Pat confided to Marie that the Army had "been difficult in ways he'd never imagined going into it," but that the experience had caused him to learn a lot about himself. He said the emotional trials he'd endured had made him a better person. He said the Army had humbled him. When Pat's mother came to Puget Sound to visit a week before Pat and Kevin shipped out to Afghanistan, Marie joked to her that Pat had become so sensitive he was starting to grow breasts.

On April 7, Marie drove Pat and Kevin to Fort Lewis to catch their flight to Afghanistan, said good-bye, and returned to face their empty house. Shortly thereafter, however, Pat called to say their flight had been delayed two hours, so Marie jumped back in her car and met them at a Starbucks just outside the post's north gate in order to share a few more moments with Pat over a cup of coffee.

When he and Kevin eventually filed into an Air Force transport jet and took off, Pat took out a new journal with a black leather cover and began to write. "To my left sits Nub," he inscribed on the first page.

> We sit inside a C-17 en route to Afghanistan via Germany to refuel. Staring at me, beside my journal, is the laminated picture of Marie in her wedding dress. . . . Undoubtedly she's grown a thick skin these last couple of years and has proven she can weather anything that comes her way. In spite of this I still worry and wish for her happiness while I'm gone.
>
> Across from me sits Sergeant Jackson, my new squad leader, Sergeant Godec, Lieutenant Uthlaut, and First Sergeant Fuller—my whole chain of command. I'm not sure what this trip holds in store; in all likelihood we'll patrol around the border without finding shit. However, in the event that more than this transpires, I feel very good about the men seated across from me. This goes for many of the others I see as I look around. The last few months have given me a new perspective on this place and I'd even go so far as to say I care about many of the folks here. In any case, if the opportunity does arise, I feel confident in how we'll react and trust those who are leading us. Besides, I have Nub-piece to my left. Of course it will all work out.

CHAPTER TWENTY-EIGHT

Thirty hours after departing Fort Lewis, the C-17 jet carrying Pat, Kevin, and their fellow Rangers landed at Bagram Airfield, twenty-seven miles north of Kabul, the base of operations for the U.S. military in Afghanistan. "The first thing I saw as I walked off the plane," Pat noted in his journal, "was gorgeous, jagged, snow-covered mountain peaks." The mountains that stirred him were some of the lesser summits of the Hindu Kush, which nevertheless rise fifteen thousand feet above sea level from the edge of the Shomali Plain, the barren plateau upon which Bagram's two-mile-long runway was built by the Soviets in 1976. Everywhere Pat looked were signs of the Soviet conflict, including a large steel water tower at the center of the base, the side of which had a gaping hole created by a mujahideen rocket. Demolished tanks were visible just outside the wire. Surrounding the airfield was an expanse of denuded earth that had once been fertile farmland and was now sown with hundreds of thousands of lethal mines.

Despite the ravaged environment, Pat remarked that their lodging at Bagram was relatively upscale: "Our wooden, glorified tents are pretty nice, and the showers and food are hot. . . . We should not be here long but in the mean time the accommodations will be appreciated." Within a few days the Rangers of Alpha Company were supposed to be flown 120 miles south to an outpost in Khost Province

PAT TILLMAN'S CHAIN OF COMMAND, APRIL 22, 2004

- President George W. Bush
  - Vice President Richard Cheney

- Secretary of Defense Donald Rumsfeld
  - Assistant Secretary of Defense Lawrence Di Rita

- General John Abizaid, commander, U.S. Central Command (CENTCOM)
- General Bryan Brown, commander, U.S. Special Operations Command (USSOC)
  - Major General Stanley McChrystal, commander, Joint Special Operations Command (JSOC)

- Lieutenant General Philip Kensinger Jr., commander, U.S. Army Special Operations Command (USASOC)

- Colonel James Nixon, commander, Seventy-fifth Ranger Regiment

- Lieutenant Colonel Ralph Kauzlarich, executive officer, Seventy-fifth Ranger Regiment
  - Command Sergeant Major Alfred Birch

- Lieutenant Colonel Jeffrey Bailey, commander, Second Ranger Battalion

- Major David Hodne, cross-functional team commander, Second Ranger Battalion

- Captain William Saunders, commander, Alpha Company

- Captain Kirby Dennis, executive officer, Alpha Company
  - First Sergeant Thomas Fuller, Alpha Company

- First Lieutenant David Uthlaut, platoon leader, Second Platoon

- Sergeant First Class Eric Godec, platoon sergeant, Second Platoon

- Staff Sergeant Matt Weeks, squad leader, Third Squad
  - Sergeant Mel Ward, senior team leader
  - Sergeant Bradley Shepherd, team leader

- Specialist Pat Tillman, acting team leader

- Private First Class Bryan O'Neal

called Forward Operating Base Salerno, whence they would begin patrolling along the Zero Line (Army jargon for the Afghanistan-Pakistan border) as part of a major new offensive dubbed Operation Mountain Storm.

Although the United States had routed the Taliban in the final months of 2001, driving them into the Afghan countryside and across the frontier into Pakistan, by early 2002 the focus of the U.S. military had been redirected to Iraq, and the situation in Afghanistan significantly deteriorated as a consequence. On May 1, 2003, Donald Rumsfeld held a news conference in Kabul to announce that "major combat activity" in Afghanistan had ended and "the bulk of this country is . . . secure." Contrary to such assurances, however, the Americans' preoccupation with Iraq had enabled the Taliban and al-Qaeda to quietly rebuild their forces and reestablish control throughout Afghanistan's eastern provinces.

On June 24, 2003, an audiotape was delivered to a Pakistani newspaper from the Taliban leader Mullah Mohammed Omar announcing a new campaign "to expedite jihad against occupation forces" under a new military strategy. As part of this campaign, the Taliban accelerated their attacks on American forces from bases of operation just across the Zero Line in Pakistan's Federally Administered Tribal Areas—an isolated region of obdurately independent feudal communities beyond the reach of the government in Islamabad, populated by four million largely illiterate Pashtun tribespeople. One of the most important bases for such attacks was the city of Miram Shah, capital of the North Waziristan tribal agency, twenty-four miles south of FOB Salerno. Miram Shah was the headquarters for the Taliban commander Jalaluddin Haqqani and his thirty-year-old son, Sirajuddin Haqqani, who was starting to assume a prominent role as second-in-command of the Haqqani Network.

Operation Mountain Storm was launched to counter these new and increasingly deadly attacks. The Rangers' job would be to find and eliminate pockets of Taliban support in remote border villages occupied by two rabidly xenophobic Pashtun tribes, the Data Khail and the Zaka Khail. On March 20, 2004, as Operation Mountain Storm was getting under way, an article in the *Asia Times* by the Pakistani journalist Syed Saleem Shahzad observed, "In Afghanistan, U.S.-led forces can expect increasing hit-and-run attacks by local Tal-

iban, who will then melt back into the local population." The corner
of Khost Province in which Tillman's platoon would be operating
was described by Shahzad as "a no-man's land, a place no one would
want to go unless he were as tough as the local tribespeople, a guerrilla fighter taking on the U.S., or, perhaps, Osama bin Laden. [It] is
a deep and dangerous maze. . . . The Data Khail and Zaka Khail
have a long history of defiance and have never capitulated to any in-
truder. . . . These two tribes are now the protectors of the Taliban
and al-Qaeda fighters."

On April 11, while still at Bagram, Pat wrote of their upcoming
mission, "When we leave we'll be working in the mountains, right on
the border of Pakistan. We'll be gone for perhaps a couple of weeks,
sleeping in the woods and basically patrolling. It'll more than likely
be cold and less than comfortable, so I'll enjoy my time here. As for
the actual mission, we are supposed to be hitting a nerve or hot
spot. . . . It's less than likely to be true but you never know, you have
to assume it will be."

Two days later the Black Sheep (the nickname given to the
Rangers of Second Platoon) were told to pack up their gear because
they would be departing for Khost in a few hours. "Tonight we leave
on our first mission," Pat's journal entry for April 13 begins. "It
sounds as though there will be quite a bit of sucking involved, as we
will be hiking some pretty steep terrain. As for how long we'll be out,
that is not clear. . . . As I write, a little black & white furball is
purring and rubbing up against my leg. Now he's sipping on the
water I gave him. I'll be sure to keep this entry out of Han or Mc's
hands as to avoid any jealousy issues.* Quite a pleasant little surprise. Unfortunately I'll be unable to bring my journal along. This
may be my last entry for awhile." In fact, among the journals recovered after Pat's death, it would prove to be the final entry altogether.

———

Shortly after midnight on April 14, six days after arriving in
Afghanistan, Pat and Kevin Tillman boarded a Chinook helicopter

* Han and Mc were the cats Marie adopted in 1998, soon after she moved to Arizona to live with Pat. The "furs," as Pat called them, were keeping Marie company
in the cottage above Tacoma Narrows while Pat was in Afghanistan.

with the rest of the Black Sheep and flew south through the darkness
to FOB Salerno, landing well before dawn. Within a couple of years
Salerno would be transformed into one of the largest and busiest military bases in Afghanistan, a frenetic hub of activity occupied by
thousands of troops, boasting a movie theater, a barbershop, a gym,
and a giant chow hall in which steak and lobster would be served by
KBR contractors on Friday nights. In early 2004, however, the base
was little more than an unpaved airstrip, a field hospital, a small tactical operations center, and a few rows of tents. The Black Sheep
spent only a few hours there, just long enough to organize their gear,
mount their weapons on their Humvees, and load the vehicles with
cartons of meals ready to eat, better known as MREs. Then the
Rangers rolled out of the gate and headed toward Spera District,
forty miles to the southwest, in a convoy of Humvees and Toyota
Hilux pickup trucks.

The first twenty-five miles of the drive followed the only paved
road in Khost Province, but where that highway curved north toward
Kabul, the convoy turned southwest and passed into Spera on a
rough dirt road that had been carved tenuously into a canyon wall
above a fast, cold river. Five miles beyond the end of the pavement
they turned sharply to the south and followed a series of dry
riverbeds and goat tracks that led over a craggy sixty-five-hundred-
foot ridge. Upon dropping down the backside of this escarpment, the
convoy rolled through a series of ramshackle villages: Adzalkhel, Tit,
Katinkhel, Magarah, Kandey Kalay. In late afternoon they halted to
bivouac for the night within three miles of the Pakistan border.

The Rangers began searching villages and conducting foot patrols
in Spera's rough backcountry the following morning, but found nothing of interest. As they were setting up camp to bivouac again, an
undercover CIA operator who introduced himself only as "Steve" arrived from a nearby outpost called Border Crossing Point 5, or
BCP-5, which was manned by Afghan Militia Forces, or AMF, recruited and trained by the CIA and U.S. Special Forces. "The CIA
guy told us they'd gotten some good intelligence that a bunch of Taliban and al-Qaeda had been seen massing together and were gonna
attack the BCP that night," says Brad Jacobson, who at the time was
a twenty-one-year-old sergeant. "So we drove down to the BCP to

help the Afghani guys defend it. We were all jazzed: 'Yeah, it's *on*! We're gonna get to fuckin' kill some bad guys!' We stayed up that whole night in our body armor, with rounds in the chamber and helmets tightened, waiting for those motherfuckers to come creeping up the hill. Of course they never came. It was another dry hole."

BCP-5 was situated on a scrubby knoll eighty-three hundred feet above sea level, surrounded by gnarled junipers and pines wrapped in silver bark that peeled off in large swatches to reveal a pale green pericambium as smooth as glass. The ambience was deceptively tranquil. Over the week that followed, the Rangers came and went from this bucolic outpost to conduct their missions.

The next day the Black Sheep drove a couple of miles east into an unpopulated valley, dismounted their vehicles, and climbed to the summit of a nine-thousand-foot peak that demarcated the international border. "We humped up this huge-ass ridgeline," says Sergeant Bradley Shepherd, one of the fire team leaders. "It was relentless." In the valley to the south was a Pakistani village beside one of the main routes used by the Taliban to infiltrate Afghanistan, so the squad spent the night up on the ridge crest to over-watch.

"We saw a couple of dudes with AKs coming up to attack," remembers Jason Parsons, who had been promoted from corporal to sergeant, "but somebody shot off a flare and they ran back down the hill."

At sunset a squall blew in, the temperature plummeted, and it began to rain. "It poured all night," says Jacobson. "Everyone got soaked to the skin. I was freezing. It was a long, shitty night." Rain continued to fall intermittently for the next six days as the Rangers patrolled the surrounding mountains and valleys, searching tribal settlements for signs of enemy activity. They found a couple of rockets, a few rifles, and quite a bit of marijuana, but not much else.

"None of the villages we searched felt very threatening," says Russell Baer. "It was beautiful country—it reminded me of the Sierra. There were little green-eyed kids running around in colorful garments, playing in the rivers."

"We never felt like we were about to be ambushed or anything," Jacobson agrees. "The people seemed friendly. Most of the villages were just a couple of little shacks scattered across the hillsides. At one

To Kabul
70 miles
north

PAKTIA

Routes driven
by Tillman's
platoon

PAKTIKA

Spera

Mana

Magarah

BCP-5

FOB Tillman

▲
NORTH

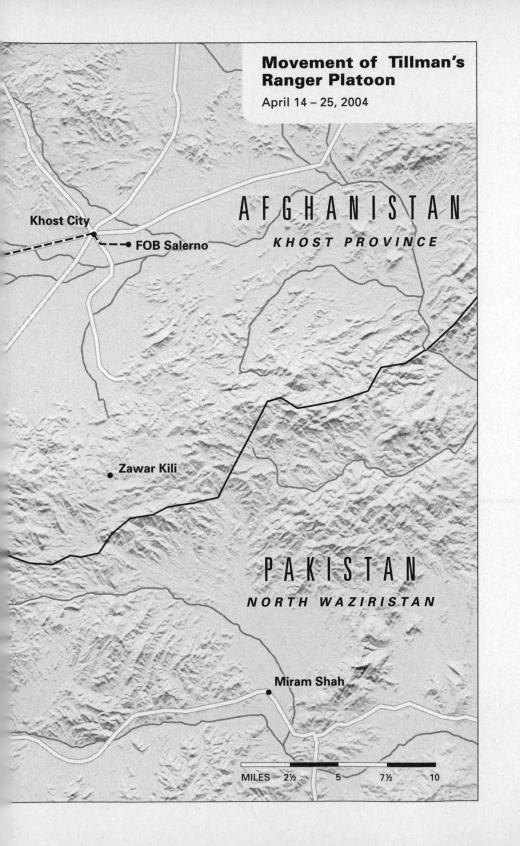

Movement of Tillman's Ranger Platoon
April 14 – 25, 2004

Khost City

FOB Salerno

AFGHANISTAN
KHOST PROVINCE

Zawar Kili

PAKISTAN
NORTH WAZIRISTAN

Miram Shah

MILES   2½   5   7½   10

house there was a camel. I'd never seen a camel out there before. The guy who owned it came outside and offered us tea and sugar candy." The apparent absence of Taliban was both a relief and a disappointment. "We began to think headquarters was giving all the good missions to Bravo Company," says Jacobson, "and sticking us with the leftovers. We got nothing but dry holes."

The majority of the Rangers in Tillman's platoon hadn't joined the Special Operations Forces in order to go camping in exotic lands; they'd enlisted to be part of a rarefied warrior culture. Engaging in mortal combat was not an aspect of their service they sought to avoid. To the contrary, they'd aspired to it since they were small boys. They were itching to confront the enemy firsthand and prove themselves under fire. Approximately half the platoon had never been in a firefight. Most of the untried Rangers yearned to experience the atavistic rush of having to kill or be killed—a desire more common among the male population than is usually acknowledged in polite company.

The unit had been in Afghanistan for nearly three weeks without encountering a single bad guy, and their daily hunt for enemy fighters increasingly had the feel of a wild-goose chase. More than a few of the Rangers who had never been in combat were growing frustrated, and had begun to contemplate the shameful possibility that their tour might end before they earned a Combat Infantryman Badge. There were probably at least ten or fifteen Rangers in the platoon who did not yet have a CIB, and were impatient for something to go down.

On April 20, one of Second Platoon's Humvees conked out and wouldn't start again. The mechanic, Specialist Brandon Farmer, spent the entire day trying to get it running, without success. On the twenty-first, while he continued to work on the unresponsive truck at BCP-5, the rest of the Black Sheep spent the day relaxing at the AMF outpost. By now they'd eaten all their MREs, and were starting to get hungry. Pat began to crave food so intensely that he went down to the garbage pile where the Rangers had been tossing their trash and began sifting through rat-fucked MREs. "Pat was digging around in there for a long time," says Josey Boatright. "Eventually he found a brownie someone had thrown out, and he held it up over his head for everyone to see like he'd discovered buried treasure. We were all laughing at him. But yeah, people were starting to feel run-down by that point. We got so hungry we bought a goat from the locals. Tasted good at first, but then a little later it just ripped my insides out."

In the afternoon, while Pat was off by himself writing in a small spiral notebook in lieu of the leather-bound journal he'd left behind at Bagram, the Afghan soldiers—the AMF—suggested to their American counterparts that they engage in some friendly athletic competition. The Rangers thought this was an excellent idea. The agreed-upon events would be wrestling and rock throwing. The Afghans produced a large chunk of limestone for the official rock, and the contest was on. "So we started taking turns throwing this rock for distance," says Shepherd, "and I'm thinking, 'We have a professional football player in our platoon.' So I went down to where Pat was sitting under this tree, just chilling and writing in his notebook. I was like, 'Hey, Pat. You mind coming up and throwing a rock for us in this contest?' He said, 'Yeah, just give me a minute, let me finish up here.' And then he came up and started throwing rocks with the Afghanis."*

"Pat got along great with the AMF," says Will Aker, an earnest, self-assured nineteen-year-old from western Colorado. "They were so surprised at how big he was—they hadn't seen many guys that muscular. Pat outthrew everyone in the contest. The rock tossed by the closest Afghani wasn't within ten or fifteen feet of Pat's rock, and he was the biggest guy the AMF could come up with. They were real impressed with Pat."

While most of the platoon was socializing with the AMF, Brandon Farmer was leaning into the engine compartment of the problematic Humvee, yet by the end of the day he was still unable to fix it. The source of the trouble was a faulty solenoid, but he didn't know that at the time, and mistakenly assumed it was a bad fuel pump. He requested a new pump from Salerno, which was flown in after dark

---

* Although the inhabitants of Afghanistan are correctly termed "Afghans," members of the American military commonly refer to them as "Afghanis" or "hajjis." The "afghani" is actually the Afghan unit of currency, analogous to the U.S. dollar.

with a load of MREs. The installation of the new part failed to fix the problem, however. So in the morning Farmer hooked the broken vehicle to the rear of a functional Humvee with a thick nylon tow strap, and at 7:00 the platoon started driving north to clear a village called Mana—the last mission the Black Sheep needed to complete before returning to FOB Salerno. The AMF commander stationed at BCP-5 ordered seven of his Afghan fighters to accompany the platoon and guide them to their destination.

———

It was well past sunrise on April 22 by the time the convoy finally rolled out of BCP-5 with the inoperable Humvee in tow. Although it was Ranger policy not to travel during daylight hours in order to reduce the danger from remotely detonated roadside bombs (generally called improvised explosive devices, or IEDs), headquarters insisted that Second Platoon clear Mana immediately in order to stay on a predetermined schedule. This bothered more than a few of the soldiers in the platoon, especially Sergeant Jacobson, who had witnessed the fatal incident that had inspired the edict against driving by day.

Five months earlier, while the Tillman brothers were attending Ranger School in Georgia, most of the other Rangers in Alpha Company were in Afghanistan, where the commander of the Second Ranger Battalion, Lieutenant Colonel Jeffrey Bailey, had deployed them on a one-month "surge." According to Jacobson, "We ended up getting sent on a convoy from Bagram all the way to Asadabad," the capital of Konar Province, 150 miles northeast of BCP-5. On November 14, 2003, as they continued northwest from Asadabad on a narrow dirt road known as IED Alley, Jacobson remembers, "The truck I was riding in blew a hose, so we stop, the mechanic jumps out and fixes the hose, and we start driving again." While Jacobson's truck was stopped, the Humvee that had been behind them pulled around and took the lead. A short while later, as they were rounding a curve above the Pech River, Jacobson says, "There is the loudest explosion I've ever heard. It was the vehicle in front of us, which had just switched places with us." An enemy fighter had detonated a gigantic IED under the Humvee as it rolled by.

"The Humvee was just demolished," says Jacobson.

I've never seen a Humvee so destroyed. One of our good buddies, Jay Blessing, had been driving it. He had been blown completely out of the jeep, down onto a flat area next to the river. One of his legs was all the way across the water on the far shore. A bunch of EMTs ran down to him as fast as they could, but there was nothing they could do. It was horrible. He suffered. That was the first time I'd seen someone die. Jay was a really good guy, super-dedicated to the unit. He'd just reenlisted the year before. He had the opportunity to get out and make a lot more money as a civilian contractor, but he decided to stay in and keep doing his part.

Sergeant Blessing, from Tacoma, Washington, was twenty-three years old.

The population along the Pech River and in the nearby Korengal valley was known to be extremely hostile to Americans, and that stretch of road had been the site of several previous IED attacks. "When Jay was killed," says Jacobson, "I understood this was the kind of risk we'd signed up for. But I was really pissed off that we had been ordered to drive during the day. It was a really stupid call. Ninety-nine point nine percent of IED attacks happen during the day." Thanks to infrared lasers on their weapons that were invisible to the enemy, and sophisticated night-vision optics that turned darkness into an eerie green twilight, American forces owned the Afghanistan night. Taliban and al-Qaeda fighters understood this, and usually tried to even the odds by staging their attacks during daylight hours.

"The enemy knew we were coming even before we left the base," Jacobson continues. "They sat there watching us and then blew the IED by remote control from up on the hill just when Jay drove over it. So why the fuck were we moving during the day? I believe Lieutenant Colonel Bailey made the call; he was the one pushing the pins back in the TOC [Tactical Operations Center]. It really made me question authority. I talked to my platoon sergeant about it; I talked to my first sergeant about it. Nobody would come right out and blame Bailey. That's insubordination. In the military you get fired for that kind of shit. But a lot of us talked about it among ourselves."

Following Blessing's death, Bailey instituted a policy forbidding

Ranger convoys to travel during daylight hours. But this rule was ignored so routinely thereafter by Ranger commanders, including Bailey himself, that for all intents and purposes the edict didn't exist.

Thus did the Black Sheep depart BCP-5 in broad daylight, bound
for Mana under the command of Lieutenant David Uthlaut, towing
an inoperable three-ton Humvee on the morning of April 22, 2004.
The route followed the bed of a river down a pinched, serpentine
canyon that descended fifteen hundred feet in three miles. It had
rained the night before, making the track muddy and slick. Because
the vehicles had to maneuver between tight boulders and over jagged
rocks, the convoy managed to move no faster than walking speed. As
it was dragged along behind a Humvee driven by Sergeant Parsons,
the derelict vehicle took such a savage beating that it eventually
foundered.

After being towed for four hours, during which the platoon managed to travel just five miles, the Humvee's front suspension had disintegrated, its tie-rods had snapped, and the front wheels were
flopping uncontrollably in opposite directions. "At that point it had
no steering whatsoever," says Parsons. Towing the Humvee with any
of the platoon's working vehicles was therefore no longer a possibility, so at 11:17 a.m. the convoy came to a halt where it was, which
happened to be in a village called Magarah. As the Rangers dismounted their trucks and fanned out to create a security perimeter,
Lieutenant Uthlaut conferred with Farmer, the mechanic, and Eric
Godec, the platoon sergeant, to determine what to do next.

Farmer concluded in short order that they lacked the necessary
spare parts to repair the Humvee in Magarah, so Uthlaut got on the
satellite radio and called FOB Salerno to request that they either send
a heavy wrecker to tow the damaged vehicle back to the FOB or dis-
patch a Chinook helicopter to sling load it out.

Major David Hodne, Lieutenant Colonel Bailey's subordinate,
was running the show in the Ranger TOC that morning at Salerno,
but Uthlaut never communicated with him directly. Instead, Uthlaut
talked to the Alpha Company executive officer, Captain Kirby Dennis, who relayed Uthlaut's communiqués to the Alpha Company
commander, Captain William Saunders, who in turn relayed what
was said to Major Hodne. And then Hodne's decisions would filter

back down the chain of command in reverse order to the platoon leader on the ground in Magarah. Uthlaut thereby received word from Dennis via e-mail* at 1:30 p.m. that a wrecker could come only as far as the end of the pavement—fifteen miles from Magarah—because the roads were too rough beyond that point, and that evacuating the Humvee by helicopter was not an option. The unstated reason for the latter was that the war in Afghanistan was the Bush administration's neglected stepchild. When it came to allocating resources, Iraq had been given a much higher priority by Defense Secretary Rumsfeld, resulting in a severe and chronic shortage of helicopters throughout Afghanistan. Due to an insufficient number of operational Chinooks and crews to fly them, a minimum of four days' advance notice was required to airlift a vehicle.

With a sling-load operation ruled out, and because abandoning the fubar Hummer was considered so completely unacceptable to the brass at Bagram that it wasn't even discussed as an option, Uthlaut was told he would have to figure out a way to get the six-thousand-pound albatross to the paved highway, where the wrecker would take it off his hands. Not long thereafter, an Afghan from the village approached one of the platoon's interpreters to say that if the Rangers paid him, he would tow the Humvee to the pavement with his "jinga" truck. (Jingas are five-ton diesel rigs, ubiquitous throughout South Asia, used to transport everything from rice to firewood to opium.) Uthlaut hired the jinga driver, and then, while Farmer and several of the Rangers jacked the front of the Humvee up off the ground and chained it to the back of the jinga truck, the platoon leader engaged in an extended e-mail discussion with Dennis "to figure out what to do about our Mana mission," as Uthlaut put it.

They considered three options: (1) split the platoon, sending one element to accompany the jinga (with Humvee in tow) to meet the wrecker at the paved highway and sending the other element directly to Mana to begin the clearing operation; (2) have the entire platoon escort the jinga/Humvee to the pavement, leave the inoperable vehicle with the wrecker, and then have the entire platoon travel to Mana to

* After the initial radio call from Uthlaut to Dennis, all further communications between them throughout the day were via e-mail.

clear the village; (3) have the entire platoon escort the jinga/Humvee all the way back to FOB Salerno, and cancel the Mana mission altogether.

Uthlaut was strongly opposed to splitting the platoon, which he thought would unnecessarily expose his men to greater danger. All of Uthlaut's noncommissioned officers were vehemently opposed to splitting the platoon. Captain Saunders stated repeatedly that he was opposed to splitting the platoon. By this time it was past 3:00 in the afternoon, however, and Major Hodne was growing increasingly impatient. The problematic Humvee had already delayed the mission for two full days while Farmer had tried to fix it at BCP-5. When Saunders asked Hodne what he should order Uthlaut to do, Hodne angrily replied, "Hey, we can't have an entire platoon brought to a stop for one broken vehicle."

After this exchange with Hodne was over, Saunders testified, "My understanding was that he said to split the platoon."* Against his better judgment, therefore, Saunders told Captain Dennis to order Uthlaut to divide the platoon and proceed immediately with the bifurcated mission.

Uthlaut received this order at 4:00. He sent an e-mail back to Dennis in which he adamantly reiterated his objections to this plan. Uthlaut further explained that it would be nearly dark by the time half the platoon reached Mana, and that it would be dangerous, impractical, and in violation of standard operating procedure to clear a village after dark. Dennis replied that Uthlaut's men weren't being ordered to clear the village that evening; the order was simply for them to arrive at Mana before nightfall, over-watch the village through the night, and then begin the clearing operation in the morning after the other half of the platoon had delivered the Humvee to the pavement and then joined them at Mana.

---

* Major Hodne would later insist that the decision to split the platoon was Saunders's, not his, but the sworn testimony of virtually every other Ranger interrogated about this matter contradicts Hodne. Hodne would also claim that he didn't even know the platoon had been divided at Magarah until the Black Sheep returned to FOB Salerno three days after Tillman's death—which prompted Hodne's commander, Lieutenant Colonel Bailey, to testify, "To the degree that he didn't know it, it would only have been because he wasn't listening."

"After the response from Captain Dennis," Uthlaut testified, "I wanted to ensure I understood the intent, which was that one element would set up an assembly area north of the village, but not start clearing the village. That element was to basically wait for the rest of the platoon to arrive. My point was that we could accomplish the same end state by going with option two: bringing the whole platoon to the hardtop and bringing the whole platoon to assembly area north of the village."

After making his case that the mission could be accomplished just as effectively and just as quickly without splitting the platoon, Uthlaut was baffled by headquarters' stubborn insistence on dividing it. He asked Dennis, "So the only reason that you want me to split my platoon is to have boots on the ground in the sector before dark?"

"Yes," Dennis replied.

Dismayed and frustrated, Uthlaut nevertheless accepted that headquarters had spoken and that he had no choice but to follow orders. A moment later, Uthlaut testified, "I then received a radio call on the same net" requesting detailed information about where the platoon would be splitting, and what route each of the two elements would be traveling, so that A-10 Warthogs could be dispatched from Bagram to provide air support in the event of enemy contact. "I handed the radio off to my Forward Observer," Uthlaut said, "and told him to brief the Air Support on these routes. I then called all of my squad leaders and platoon sergeant to brief them on the plan. I told them who was assigned to each element. . . . I showed my squad leaders and platoon sergeant the routes of both elements. I then informed them that my element had to move out because we had to be set up by nightfall north of Mana."

During an investigation of Tillman's death seven months later, Brigadier General Gary Jones asked Alpha Company first sergeant Thomas Fuller, "I mean, what necessitated in this mission right here that they had to get down there so quickly?"

"I don't think there was anything," Fuller testified under oath. "I think that a lot of times at higher [headquarters]—maybe even, you know, higher than battalion [headquarters]—they may make a timeline, and then we just feel like we have to stick to that timeline. There's no—there's no 'intel' driving it. There's no—you know, there's no events driving it. It's just a timeline, and we feel like we have to stick with it; and that's what drives that kind of stuff." In other words, the sense of urgency attached to the mission came from little more than a bureaucratic fixation on meeting arbitrary deadlines so missions could be checked off a list and tallied as "accomplished." This emphasis on quantification has always been a hallmark of the military, but it was carried to new heights of fatuity during Donald Rumsfeld's tenure at the Pentagon. Rumsfeld was obsessed with achieving positive "metrics" that could be wielded to demonstrate progress in the Global War on Terror, or the illusion thereof.

————

It was now approximately 5:30. The Black Sheep had been in Magarah for more than six hours. "When we first got there," says Jacobson, "the whole village came out to greet us. They were curious. The kids would stick their hands out for gum and candy from the MREs. At first most of them would keep their distance, but as soon as someone is brave enough to come up and make contact, they all get closer, and all of a sudden your jeep is surrounded by guys. You start getting claustrophobic because they're so close, and you're like, 'No! Stop! You need to move back!' They think it's a game to see how close they can get before you chase them off." According to Jacobson, however, "The vibe was pretty chill. There were probably two hundred people out there, all told, and I would say 90 percent of them were friendly. But there were a few guys in their twenties and thirties who were kind of sitting on the hill, scowling at us. They looked shady, and they were taking everything in."

When Uthlaut was negotiating with the jinga driver through an interpreter about towing the Humvee to the paved highway, there had been dozens of locals crowded around them. Many of these villagers overheard exactly where the convoy was headed. This was still at least two hours before the platoon departed Magarah, ample time for word of the Rangers' plans to circulate through the community and for an ambush to be planned.

"Security was pretty lax," says Parsons.

We had a pretty good amount of people who kept coming through our perimeter. Wasn't a whole lot we could do about it. You could be a dick, I guess, and threaten to shoot anyone who approached too close, but you wouldn't win a lot of hearts and minds doing that, and hearts and minds was supposed to be what the whole thing was about. . . . Ended up, one of the kids in the village, about eight years old, he comes up and keeps trying to talk to me. He went away and came back down right before we were getting ready to leave, and handed me a note written in English. All it said was "Come see me." The kid pointed at the note, then pointed up at a house on the hill. I took the note and thought, "This might be important." So I pass it up to Godec [the platoon sergeant], but at that point we was getting ready to move out and he said, "I don't have time for this shit." I argued with him a little bit about it, but the whole rank thing put me at the losing end of the argument. I suppose the note could have been about anything. May have been warning us about the whole ambush situation. May have been about nothing at all.

CHAPTER TWENTY-NINE

As soon as Uthlaut's final request to reconsider the order to divide the platoon was denied, he hurried off to brief Eric Godec and his three squad leaders—Greg Baker, Jeffrey Jackson, and Matt Weeks—none of whom was happy about it. First, however, Uthlaut told his radio operator, Jade Lane, to pack up the satellite radio and grab something to eat because they were about to get moving. So Lane and Pat Tillman sat down together and shared an MRE, Lane says, and as they ate, for some reason the conversation turned to the gender identity of Afghan males. It is common in rural areas of Afghanistan to see men—even battle-scarred fighters—wearing flowers in their hair and thick black eye shadow made from soot. Males of all ages often hold hands with each other. It is not unusual, at remote militia outposts where no women are present, for there to be a young cook-boy in the camp who also serves as a sex slave for the fighters. Pat was fascinated by the apparent acceptance of such behavior in this exceedingly macho, rigidly Islamic society that deems homosexuality to be both a sin and a mortal crime.

According to Lane, Pat pulled a small spiral notebook from the right cargo pocket of his pants "and read me a part of this journal he'd been writing, about how Afghani men acted effeminate, which he thought was because the lack of females in their everyday lives kind of pushed the men into a more feminine state of mind. . . . Anyway, he read me this stuff from his notebook, and then about fifteen or twenty minutes later we rolled out."

Immediately before an Army platoon embarks on a mission, all the soldiers will typically assemble for a "convoy brief" or "mission brief" by the platoon leader; if headquarters issues a "fragmentary order" that subsequently changes the mission, the platoon leader will give his soldiers a "FRAGO brief" before proceeding. In either case, the platoon leader or platoon sergeant will explain exactly where the platoon will be going, precisely what they will be doing, and other pertinent information. During the briefing, all soldiers typically will be reminded what to do if a vehicle is attacked with an IED and what to do if they are ambushed by enemy fighters. In the event of the latter, they will be reminded to respond initially with an intense fusillade of suppressive fire, but then to quickly "control your fires"— that is, to sharply reduce the volume of fire and shoot no more than necessary. They will be reminded to "go where your team leader goes, and shoot where your team leader shoots." They will be reminded to follow the current rules of engagement. If AMF or other Afghan soldiers will be involved in the mission, the U.S. forces will be reminded of that fact as well, and will be admonished not to mistake these friendly Afghan troops for Taliban or al-Qaeda. Above all, the American soldiers will be reminded to "PID your targets"—that is, to positively identify whomever they intend to shoot as an enemy combatant before pulling the trigger.

Because less than an hour of daylight remained, however, and Uthlaut had been ordered to get half his platoon to Mana before nightfall, there was no time to give a FRAGO brief to the entire platoon before moving out of Magarah. In the pointless rush to get under way, none of the standard caveats listed above was mentioned. Beyond Uthlaut, the platoon sergeant, and the three squad leaders, only a few of the Black Sheep understood where they were going or why the platoon had been split.

Uthlaut took command of Serial One, the element headed for Mana. He assigned Godec to take charge of Serial Two, which would escort the jinga truck, with the busted Humvee in tow, to the paved highway. And then, just before driving out of the village, Uthlaut contacted headquarters one last time to ask if they would reassess

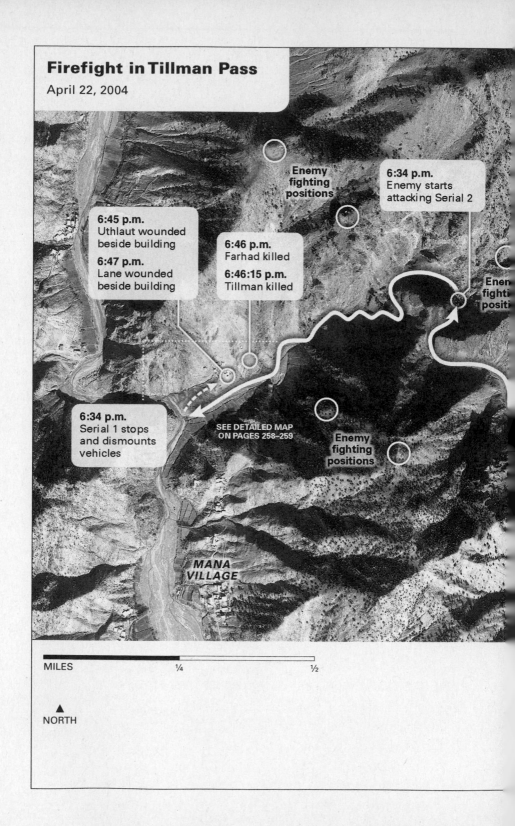

Firefight in Tillman Pass
April 22, 2004

Enemy fighting positions

6:34 p.m.
Enemy starts attacking Serial 2

6:45 p.m.
Uthlaut wounded beside building

6:47 p.m.
Lane wounded beside building

6:46 p.m.
Farhad killed

6:46:15 p.m.
Tillman killed

Enemy fighting positions

6:34 p.m.
Serial 1 stops and dismounts vehicles

SEE DETAILED MAP
ON PAGES 258–259

Enemy fighting positions

MANA VILLAGE

MILES   ¼   ½

▲
NORTH

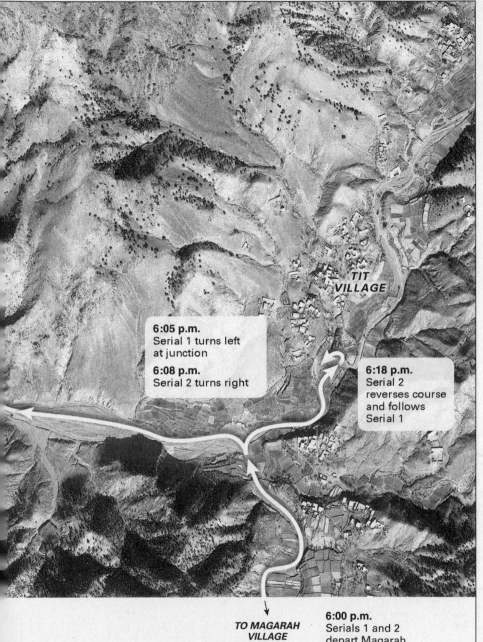

6:05 p.m.
Serial 1 turns left
at junction

6:08 p.m.
Serial 2 turns right

*TIT
VILLAGE*

6:18 p.m.
Serial 2
reverses course
and follows
Serial 1

*TO MAGARAH
VILLAGE*
1.5 km south

6:00 p.m.
Serials 1 and 2
depart Magarah
Village traveling
north along
the river

their decision to divide the platoon. "I made one final coordination with Captain Dennis," Uthlaut testified, "pertaining to the .50-cal machine gun that was on the broken Humvee." Because the fubar vehicle would be going with Serial Two, Uthlaut's element would be heading out without this reassuring heavy weapon. "I emailed Captain Dennis relating that one of our elements would not have a .50-cal," Uthlaut said, "and my question was whether or not that would affect the chosen course of action (splitting the platoon). Captain Dennis replied that the .50-cal did not change the situation and to continue to execute, as discussed."

So the six vehicles in Serial One left Magarah around 6:00, with Uthlaut's Humvee at the head of the convoy. Pat Tillman was in the second vehicle, a Hilux pickup piled high with cartons of rations. "He was in the back of the truck sitting on top of these cardboard boxes, looking like the king of MREs," says Sergeant Mel Ward, who was driving a Humvee immediately behind the Hilux. "It was obvious he was going to get bounced off the first time the truck hit a bump, so somebody told him to get down from there," prompting Pat to climb down and wedge himself into the backseat of the pickup's crew cab.

The last vehicle in Serial One was a Hilux with a machine gun mounted in its bed, occupied by three Afghan soldiers. A few minutes after this AMF truck rolled north out of Magarah, the first vehicle in Serial Two—a Humvee commanded by Staff Sergeant Greg Baker—also departed the village, followed by the remaining five vehicles in the second element. Kevin Tillman was at the very tail end of the parade, manning the gun turret of a Humvee being driven by Jason Parsons, with Eric Godec, the platoon sergeant, in the passenger's seat. Immediately in front of them was the wrecked Humvee being towed by the jinga truck.

As the twelve vehicles of the two elements pitched and heaved slowly down the riverbed that led out of Magarah, the distance between the last vehicle in Serial One and the first vehicle in Serial Two was no more than a couple of hundred yards. A mile and three-quarters north of the village, Uthlaut's Humvee arrived at a fork in the wadi and turned left, followed by the other vehicles in Serial One. A few minutes later when Baker's Humvee arrived at this junction, he turned to the right, as did the next two Humvees in Serial Two, but when the Afghan jinga driver got to the fork, he stopped his battered red truck and refused to follow.

When Uthlaut was ordered to send half his platoon to the paved highway with the broken Humvee, he was led to believe that headquarters meant for him to reverse the route the Black Sheep had driven from FOB Salerno to BCP-5 eight days earlier, which was the most direct way back to the pavement and was the only route he was familiar with. It was a treacherous track, however, which would take his Rangers up and over a sixty-five-hundred-foot escarpment by means of steep, extremely rugged goat trails. When the Black Sheep first traveled this route on April 14, they encountered terrain so precipitous that their vehicles were in danger of rolling over and tumbling hundreds of feet down the mountainside; upon eventually making it to the valley on the other side, the platoon told Captain Saunders that the route was "impassable." According to Saunders, Uthlaut's men insisted "they would not drive it again. They just said it was too dangerous."

Nevertheless, Uthlaut had interpreted his orders to mean that this was the route Serial Two was supposed to take, and during his extended e-mail debate with headquarters about dividing the platoon, nobody told him otherwise. When his many objections to the plan fell on deaf ears, he dutifully split the platoon and ordered Serial Two to escort the jinga over the mountain, even though he and all the men under his command thought doing so was risky and pointless. In the Army, you follow orders.

But then the jinga driver, who was intimately familiar with the local topography, balked at hauling the wrecked Humvee over the mountain. Through an interpreter, he managed to explain to the Americans that if Serial Two simply followed Serial One west to Mana and then turned north just past the slot canyon, they could reach their destination via a much easier route. Although more circuitous, it would actually take them to the paved highway more quickly and with considerably less risk by going around the mountain instead of over it. This made good sense to Sergeant Godec, so he ordered Serial Two to reverse course and go the same way Serial One had gone. When all the Humvees managed to get turned around,

Godec put the jinga truck at the front of the procession, and the convoy began rolling slowly down the rock-strewn floor of the wadi toward the entrance to the narrows, approximately fifteen minutes behind Serial One.

As the vehicles of Serial Two bumped along the riverbed into the maw of the slot, its steep sides and tight confines put many of the Rangers on edge. "The canyon was unbelievably narrow and the walls just shot straight up," says Brad Jacobson, who was driving the second-to-last vehicle in the convoy. "I've never seen anything like it in my life. And the way the sun was setting, the shadows—it was creepy." Just after he entered the narrows, as he steered his Humvee around a sharp bend to the left, there was a loud explosion, and the vehicles ahead of him came to a sudden halt. "Everyone started yelling, 'IED! IED!' " Jacobson remembers. "That was our first instinct—that a vehicle had gotten hit with an IED, and when that happens, you immediately stop and dismount. But about five seconds later there was another explosion, and I realized we were getting hit with mortars."

The first mortar round exploded on the floor of the canyon between the jinga truck, which was in the lead, and Greg Baker's Humvee, which was next in line. The second mortar hit the side of the canyon above the convoy, sending rocks crashing down around the vehicles, and then a third mortar exploded in the same area. A few seconds later the convoy started receiving fire from small arms, prompting Godec to get on the radio. "Go! Go! Go!" he yelled. "It's not IEDs! It's mortars!" When the Rangers got back in their Humvees and tried to drive out of the kill zone, however, they couldn't, because the jinga truck was stopped at the head of the line, blocking the way, and the vehicle's Afghan driver was still outside the vehicle, cowering beneath an overhang at the base of the cliff.

"There was a lot of tunnel vision, a lot of panic," recalls Jason Parsons, who was driving the last vehicle in the convoy. "I seen a silhouette on top of the hill to our north which I believed was a possible forward observer for the enemy, calling in the mortar rounds on us. So I engaged that position, and the rest of my trigger-happy crew engaged that position as well." Pedro Arreola targeted the northern ridgeline with his 240 Bravo machine gun, and Kyle Jones shot twenty rounds from his M4 toward the same area.

Kevin Tillman, up in the turret of Parsons's Humvee, thought about shooting his Mark 19 grenade launcher, a machine gun that vomits forth egg-size, high-explosive bomblets at the rate of one per second. But he was worried about firing it in such a narrow canyon, lest the grenades strike the vertical rock walls above the convoy and bounce back down. According to Kevin's testimony, "My immediate reaction was, 'If I shoot this weapon, it's going to land right back on my head or someone else's head.' . . . So I didn't fire." He did, however, attempt to lock and load the Mark 19 to be prepared to shoot, but when he pulled back the charging handle to feed a round onto the bolt face, the gun jammed, and he was unable to fire a single grenade during the entire firefight.

Baker, meanwhile, ran ahead to where the jinga driver was hiding and shouted, "Hey! We have to get this vehicle out of here!" Baker forced the Afghan to get back in the driver's seat, hopped into the cab beside him, and got him to start moving forward so the convoy could escape the ambush. Baker's Humvee, driven by Sergeant Kellett Sayre, followed close behind the jinga as the Rangers riding in it blasted the ridge to the north with a .50-caliber machine gun, a 240 Bravo machine gun, two or three M4s, and a M203 grenade launcher.

The convoy drove as fast as possible down the eastern portion of the canyon, but they were seldom able to move more rapidly than five miles per hour due to the rough terrain; enemy fighters continued to shoot at them all the while from the ridge far above. Baker, in the passenger's seat of the jinga, impulsively smashed out the window with the butt of his M4 and returned fire. When he broke the window, Baker testified, the jinga driver got "all pissed at me. I thought that was kind of weird at the time."

As Parsons's Humvee bounced down the wadi, the canyon was so narrow, he says, that "we lost the 240 [machine gun] mounted on Arreola's side because he didn't pull it in; the gun hit a rock and got yanked off." Parsons had to stop while Arreola jumped off and retrieved the weapon, which had its buttstock sheared off in the collision.

The third vehicle in the convoy, rolling just behind Baker's Humvee, was a Humvee commanded by Sergeant First Class Steven Walter, who saw another mortar round explode high on the canyon wall above them, after which the nervous and confused jinga driver stopped yet again, bringing the whole convoy to a halt behind him, because the canyon remained much too narrow for anyone to drive around the big truck. At this second stop, most of the Rangers once more dismounted their Humvees. Looking up at the high ground to their north, Walter said that he "observed four enemy personnel on the northern ridgeline," running west along the high ground, wearing "gray man-dresses." Walter shot at them with his M4, and Brad Jacobson quickly set up a mortar tube and fired a 60-millimeter mortar toward the ridge crest as well.

Within a couple of minutes Baker convinced the jinga driver to start moving again, and the convoy proceeded through the confines of the limestone slot, by which time most, if not all, of the enemy fire had ceased, although the Rangers in Baker's Humvee continued shooting hundreds of rounds as they drove. Approximately three-quarters of a mile beyond the place where they were first attacked, the jinga lurched out of the western end of the narrows, the valley abruptly opened up, and the truck came to a halt again, as did Baker's Humvee just behind it. As the vehicles rolled to a stop, they came into view of Bryan O'Neal and Pat Tillman, who were kneeling behind a pair of low boulders on the hillside above, looking down from only ninety yards away.

CHAPTER THIRTY

When the first mortar exploded near Serial Two at the eastern end of the canyon, Serial One had just exited the western end of the narrows. Upon hearing the explosions and ensuing gunfire, twelve of the twenty Rangers in Serial One, including Tillman, scrambled out of their vehicles and, under the command of Staff Sergeant Matt Weeks, hurried toward high ground overlooking the mouth of the narrows to provide covering fire for Serial Two. Uthlaut and his radio operator, Jade Lane, stayed behind to establish satellite radio communications with headquarters from Uthlaut's Humvee in order to call in tactical air support, after which they intended to move up to the high ground themselves.

The route upward was steep and strenuous, prompting Tillman to ask Weeks for permission to shed his body armor, which weighed twenty-five pounds, in order to be able "to maneuver faster," a request that was in keeping with his approach to athletic challenges. Throughout his football career Tillman had elected to wear fewer and smaller pads than many of the other players, believing the resulting increase in speed and maneuverability made him less likely to receive an injurious hit. The Army did things differently from the NFL, though. Ever since the invasion of Iraq, body armor (or, more specifically, the unavailability of effective body armor for some soldiers) had been a sensitive issue. As a result of political fallout, a decree had come down from the highest levels of Central Command

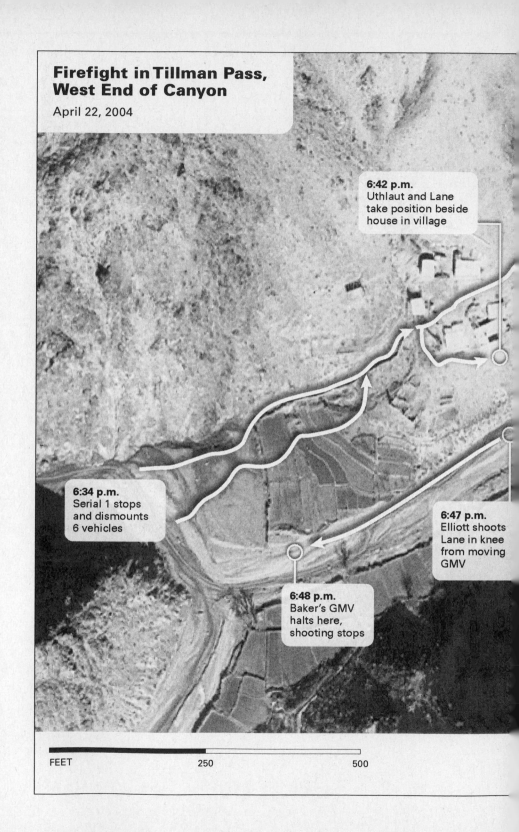

Firefight in Tillman Pass, West End of Canyon

April 22, 2004

6:42 p.m.
Uthlaut and Lane take position beside house in village

6:34 p.m.
Serial 1 stops and dismounts 6 vehicles

6:47 p.m.
Elliott shoots Lane in knee from moving GMV

6:48 p.m.
Baker's GMV halts here, shooting stops

FEET   250   500

6:39 p.m.
Weeks's squad takes positions along spur

6:39 p.m.
Tillman, O'Neal, and Farhad take positions at boulders

6:44 p.m.
Baker's GMV stops behind jinga truck

6:45 p.m.
Johnson shoots 40-mm grenade that wounds Uthlaut

6:44 p.m.
Jinga truck stops

6:46 p.m.
GMV turns corner of terraced field, Baker shoots Farhad

6:46:15 p.m.
Alders shoots Tillman from moving GMV

▲
NORTH

that regulation body armor absolutely must be worn whenever contact with the enemy was likely. Weeks thus told Tillman that "no, he couldn't" drop his armor.

After five minutes, the squad reached a grubby settlement. As they moved warily between the crumbling adobe buildings, struggling to catch their breath, they constantly scanned for anyone or anything that appeared threatening. They saw only one male beyond the age of puberty—a crippled old man. There were some forty other people present as well, but all of them were women or very young children. The conspicuous lack of adult males in the settlement during the evening mealtime, when at least one man is typically present in every household, suggested the Pashtun villagers were allied with the Taliban and that the absent men were somewhere up on the adjacent ridges, participating in the ambush on Serial Two.

Beyond the village the squad labored upward through low clumps of snakeweed to the crest of a bald spur, where everyone halted except Tillman, O'Neal, and Sayed Farhad,* the Afghan militia fighter, who continued over the top and dropped sixty yards down the far side of the spur to a pair of large rocks overlooking the canyon floor where they, too, came to a stop. When an enemy fighter began shooting at them from the opposite side of the canyon, across the wadi, Tillman directed O'Neal and Farhad to fire at the enemy position. Then Tillman sprinted back up the slope, under fire, to let Weeks know what they were up to.

When he arrived atop the spur, Tillman explained to Weeks that he'd found cover for his team behind some boulders, and that they were engaging bad guys located across the valley. Weeks rose up on one knee, peered over at the rocks where Tillman's team was positioned, and expressed his approval of Pat's plan of action. After which Tillman ran back down the slope to rejoin O'Neal and Farhad. One of seven Afghan Militia Forces who had rolled out of Magarah as part of Serial One, Farhad had been awed by Tillman's physical prowess and charmed by his congenial manner during the previous day's rock-tossing contest. Perhaps this explains why, when Farhad saw Tillman

---

* For more than a year after Tillman's death, the Army reported that the identity of this Afghan soldier was unknown and then announced that his name was Thani. This is incorrect. He was named Sayed Farhad.

and O'Neal rush up the hill independently from the other Rangers in Weeks's squad, he spontaneously decided to follow them, even though the rest of the AMF remained with their trucks in the wadi. And thus did Farhad wind up beside Tillman and O'Neal at the boulders.

Back up on the crest of the spur, the radio on Weeks's chest began to spit and crackle: it was a broken transmission between the vehicles of Serial Two. Although Weeks immediately tried to reach them, he later testified, "every time I'd make a transmission . . . it would be stepped on by somebody"—he would be interrupted by soldiers attempting to transmit on several radios at the same time. Weeks could hear Rangers from Serial Two frantically calling other Rangers in Serial Two, but in the chaos of the firefight they didn't seem to be able to hear one another's transmissions, nor did they seem to hear his transmissions. Despite several attempts, Weeks never raised anyone from Serial Two.

The last person to join Weeks atop the spur was Russell Baer, who arrived drenched in sweat. "I was dragging ass," he admits. "I was pissed at myself for being so smoked." As he was struggling up the slope to catch up to his squad, Baer began hearing strange buzzing and cracking noises, almost like static electricity. "I remember thinking, 'What the fuck is that sound?' " he says. "It wasn't like anything I'd ever heard. I didn't realize until later that it was the sound of rounds whizzing past."

Specialist Jean-Claude Suhl was positioned not far from Baer. He immediately understood that they were being shot at. "You'd hear the snap of the rounds" cutting the air, he recalled. But neither Suhl nor anyone else in Serial One could tell where the shooting was coming from.

The forward observer assigned to Serial One, Specialist Donald Lee, heard an airplane flying overhead, and wondered if the A-10 Warthogs he'd requested for close air support had arrived on the scene. Warthogs have jet engines that emit a deafening, high-pitched scream, however, and the aircraft Lee was hearing sounded more like a lawn mower. "As I listened closer I knew it was a Predator drone," he testified. Several other Rangers also said they heard the drone. A small, unmanned, prop-driven airplane powered by a snowmobile engine, it was being flown by a pilot sitting in a trailer in the Nevada desert by means of a joystick and video screen. Predator drones are equipped with hi-tech cameras that function in daylight or darkness; some carry missiles as well. Cloudy conditions at Bagram, it turned out, had kept the Warthogs from ever taking off, but headquarters later confirmed that a Predator was overhead during the firefight, and a civilian contractor at Bagram said that he remembered seeing the Predator's video feed. During the numerous investigations that would be undertaken over the next three years, the Army and the CIA nevertheless asserted that no such video existed.

As Lee listened to the Predator circling overhead, a 40-millimeter grenade exploded thirty feet from Russell Baer, who was lying prone on the spur above Weeks. "It was really fucking close," Baer recalls, shaking his head. "I saw a puff of dirt rise up, then BOOM! It blew my eardrum out, ruptured it." He believes the explosion "wasn't big enough to be a mortar round. If it was, I'd be dead. I think it was a 203 round"—a 40-millimeter grenade fired from an M203 grenade launcher, which is a tubelike attachment that snaps into place beneath the barrel of an M4 carbine. Neither Taliban nor al-Qaeda forces possessed M203 grenade launchers.

Another 40-millimeter grenade exploded just fifteen feet from Bradley Shepherd, showering him with gravel. Not long after that, says Josey Boatright, "I remember hearing a hard whistle, then this distinct screaming noise. I had no idea where it was coming from." Unbeknownst to Boatright, the latter was the sound of an AT4—a one-shot disposable bazooka that shoots a powerful rocket designed to penetrate fortified bunkers or steel armor. It had been fired by a Ranger in Serial Two named Chad Johnson, who was standing just out of sight beyond a low rise. The grenades that had nearly nailed Baer and Shepherd a moment earlier had probably been lobbed from Johnson's M203 grenade launcher.

Unaware that they were being shot at by fellow Rangers, Sergeant Mel Ward figured their position was being bracketed by enemy mortars, so he yelled to their squad leader, "Sarn't Weeks! We're taking indirect!"*

---

* Rounds lobbed from mortars, howitzers, grenade launchers, and other varieties of artillery are known as indirect fire. Bullets shot from rifles and machine guns are called direct fire.

Catching a glimpse of some movement on a distant ridge that he thought was the shooter, Jean-Claude Suhl let loose with a burst from his 240 Bravo machine gun, prompting the Rangers beside him to start frantically squeezing off rounds with their smaller-caliber M4 carbines, ratcheting up the tension and chaos, until Weeks shouted, "Cease fire! Everybody cease fire!" All they were doing, he later explained, "was kicking up dirt on the hilltops. . . . They weren't able to see what they were shooting at, and furthermore . . . the distance was about 800 meters from where we were to where they were shooting, and you know, with M4s that's kind of futile." He commanded his men to control their emotions and refrain from shooting unless they could positively identify what they were shooting at.

"Weeks only fired one round during the entire firefight," says Boatright. "He stayed real calm. Beforehand, when we were back in the rear, he was more on edge, more hyper. But it was eerie how calm he got once the shooting started. After that I always called him 'My God of War.' He'd been there before. He stayed cool and took control because he knew that's what he had to do."

Although they couldn't identify the enemy shooters, incoming rounds continued to pepper the earth around the Rangers hunkered along on the spur. Because the shots seemed to be coming primarily from the east, Weeks and his men dropped just below the crest to the west, the opposite side of the spur from the pair of boulders where Tillman's fire team was positioned.

These boulders rested on a steep slope, about three feet apart, with one slightly uphill and to the east of the other. Tillman was kneeling next to the higher rock, O'Neal was kneeling behind the lower rock, and Farhad was standing on the exposed hillside fifteen or twenty feet downhill and to the west of O'Neal. Although the boulders were approximately six feet long, they protruded barely twelve inches above the ground on their uphill sides. As Tillman and O'Neal kneeled behind them, the rocks rose no higher than the soldiers' thighs.

The rocks nevertheless provided a clear view of the mouth of the canyon. Not long after Tillman rejoined O'Neal and Farhad at the boulders after speaking with Weeks atop the spur, the lead vehicle in Serial Two, the jinga truck, came rumbling out of the narrows and halted next to the stone retaining wall of a terraced opium field that jutted into the riverbed. A moment later a Humvee sped out of the canyon as well and came to an abrupt stop behind the jinga. Several American soldiers then hopped out of the Humvee and started shooting up the slope toward Tillman's fire team.

———

Staff Sergeant Greg Baker, a highly regarded squad leader, had arrived in the jinga truck. Six Rangers and an Afghan interpreter under Baker's command arrived in the vehicle now parked behind the jinga. A version of Humvee favored by Special Operations Forces called a GMV (for ground mobility vehicle), it had no armor, roof, doors, or windows except the front windshield, in order to give soldiers unimpeded sectors of fire from every seat.

The Rangers riding in this GMV had started firing their weapons when the first mortar shell had exploded near Serial Two at the eastern entrance to the canyon, and they'd continued shooting at real and imagined enemy positions on the cliffs above them as they drove through the gorge. The shooting stopped for a little while when the GMV exited the western end of the canyon and came to a halt behind the jinga, but it resumed again after several Rangers climbed out of the vehicle.

Although Tillman, O'Neal, and Farhad could see Baker's men shooting up at them, initially the fire was intermittent, and they weren't terribly concerned. It was only "maybe a couple bursts from an M4," O'Neal later testified. "We did a lot of waving up top, like, 'Hey, we're friendly,' because it wasn't—it wasn't real serious. Like, they weren't really seriously shooting at us to where we thought we really, really had to get down. And I figured, you know, it was just a mistake anyway, like they shot a couple times and they were like, 'Oh, they're friendly up there, so stop shooting.' " After Tillman and O'Neal waved and shouted "Cease fire!" a few times, the shooting petered out, O'Neal recalled, "So we figured we were fine."

When they had first arrived at the boulders overlooking the wadi a few minutes earlier, Tillman had seen an enemy fighter firing at them from atop a lightly forested promontory high on the other side of the canyon; the mortar that had shot the opening salvos was probably located here as well. Although O'Neal could see muzzle flashes emanating from the enemy's weapons on the other side of the valley some four hundred yards away, he couldn't make out the actual shooters. So Tillman fired a burst from his SAW at this enemy gun emplacement to indicate where he wanted his team to lay down suppressive fire, after which, says O'Neal, "Me and the AMF soldier then began to engage the position that Pat was directing us to fire on." When Baker's Humvee drove out of the narrows, O'Neal and Farhad were still shooting at the enemy position across the canyon.

Down on the valley floor, after approximately a minute the Rangers firing at Tillman's position climbed back into their Humvee, which started moving again, then drove around the parked jinga truck and turned the corner where the wadi bent sharply to the right past the corner of the opium field. Kellett Sayre was driving. Greg Baker, who had gotten out of the jinga during the stop, was now back in the front passenger's seat of the Humvee. Immediately behind them, up in the turret, Stephen Ashpole manned the heavy .50-caliber machine gun. In the waist seat to his right was Chad Johnson, a rifleman and grenadier. To Ashpole's left was Trevor Alders, a SAW gunner. Steve Elliott was standing at the right rear of the Humvee, where his 240 Bravo machine gun was mounted on a swing arm. In the rear seat were James Roberts, a young rifleman and grenadier, and an Afghan interpreter known as Wallid.

Having just blasted their way out of the ambush kill zone, Baker and his men were amped and jumpy. Several of them had never previously been in a firefight. Their weapons were charged, and they remained hyperalert, primed to shoot anything or anyone who seemed to pose a threat.

Although some soldiers in the platoon said Baker could be vain and arrogant on occasion, even his critics conceded that he was an exceptional soldier and a superb squad leader. In Iraq, before being promoted to the leader of First Squad, Baker had been Kevin Tillman's team leader, and both Tillman brothers had remarked on more than one occasion that Baker was "shit hot" and "totally squared away"—among the highest compliments one Ranger can pay another. Pat and Kevin were so impressed with him that they'd even expressed the desire to be in Baker's squad.

As the Humvee rounded the corner delineated by the stone wall of the opium field, Baker "noticed AK-47 muzzle flash to my right side" in the gloaming. The flash was from a Kalashnikov automatic rifle belonging to a small dark-skinned man with a black beard. The beard and the AK-47 caused Baker to deduce, correctly, that the shooter was an Afghan. But this Afghan was wearing BDUs—a version of the American battle dress uniform printed with the same three-color desert camouflage pattern as the Rangers were wearing—which should have alerted Baker that he was AMF, not Taliban. The uniform of the enemy was the *shalwar kameez*—what the Rangers referred to as a "man dress" or "man jammies": the tunic-and-baggy-pants ensemble worn by virtually every male Pashtun in Khost who wasn't a member of the AMF or Afghan National Police.

Baker testified that he noticed the Afghan was wearing BDUs, even in the fading twilight. But Baker also saw that the Afghan's weapon was pointed in his direction with flames spitting from its muzzle. Baker believed that the Afghan was trying to kill him, and his reflexes took over: he put his eye to the scope of his M4, centered its red electronic dot on the Afghan's chest, thumbed the selector lever from "SAFE" to "SEMI," and then squeezed the trigger six times in rapid succession. No more than three seconds elapsed from the time he first noticed the Afghan until he completed firing the six rounds.

Although Baker was shooting from the front seat of a Humvee bouncing over a rocky riverbed, his target was less than sixty-five yards away. "We trained a lot, and he was an excellent marksman," Jade Lane, the platoon's radio operator, reflects. "For him to shoot the guy from a moving vehicle at that range would not be an amazing feat." Two of the .223-caliber bullets from Baker's carbine hit the Afghan in the chest, his legs crumpled beneath him, and he flopped to the ground in a twisted heap.

The dead Afghan was not an enemy fighter. He was Sayed Farhad, the twenty-seven-year-old AMF soldier who'd attached himself to Tillman and O'Neal. And he hadn't been shooting his AK-47 at Baker; actually, he'd been trying to protect Baker and his men by providing covering fire, shooting at the enemy position far above the wadi on the south side of the canyon in order to deter the bad guys from firing down at the American vehicle as it rolled past.

As Kellett Sayre steered the Humvee around the corner of the opium field, he saw the six vehicles of Serial One parked three hundred yards straight ahead. Glancing up the slope to his right, he identified four Rangers high on the spur, frantically waving their arms to signal that they were fellow Americans. Sayre barked, "Friendlies on top!" hoping to prevent his colleagues in the Humvee from doing anything stupid, but he was a split second too late. The other soldiers in the truck had already started to shoot, after which Sayre's frantic screams of "Cease fire! Cease fire!" were lost beneath the din of gunfire. In the ensuing fusillade, hundreds of bullets were directed at the boulders where Tillman and O'Neal had taken cover.

Kneeling behind his boulder, believing the Rangers in Baker's Humvee had recognized him and Tillman as American soldiers, O'Neal was dumbstruck by the enormous volume of fire suddenly aimed at his position. Large-caliber rounds slammed into the earth all around him. Dozens of bullets struck the rocks behind which he and Tillman now hid, blasting shards of limestone from the boulders like shrapnel. According to O'Neal's testimony to Brigadier General Gary Jones during a subsequent investigation, the Rangers in the Humvee "fired for a good forty-five seconds to a minute. It felt like forever, so maybe it could have been like a minute, minute and thirty seconds, but it felt like a couple of hours, sir, you know what I mean, sir?"

When asked if he recognized the faces of any of the shooters, O'Neal replied, "I could just see persons, sir. There wasn't enough light to recognize faces, but I could tell that they were my buddies, you know? I could tell that they were friendlies, guys that I worked with and I just—I mean, I didn't know who was who. I just knew that they were my friends."

Eventually, O'Neal testified, he tossed his rifle aside "because I thought maybe if I threw my weapon down they would stop firing at us." But the shooting didn't stop, so he flung himself onto the ground and curled into a fetal position. "I began to pray out loud," he said. "I was sure I was going to die. . . . Pat then asked me why I was praying, he asked me what it could do for me."

As Baker's Humvee kept driving down the wadi, the shooters continued to spew bullets with reckless disregard, raking the entire hillside. Sayre, in desperation, reached back and grabbed the left leg of Stephen Ashpole, who was standing just behind him in the gun turret; although Sayre repeatedly yanked on the machine gunner's trousers with one hand while steering with the other, frantically trying to get him to stop shooting, Ashpole was so focused on firing his weapon that he failed to notice.

Up on the spur above Tillman, Weeks's squad was spread across the open slope, completely vulnerable to the fusillade. Private Will Aker looked down at the Humvee and saw Steve Elliott spray bullets from his 240 Bravo machine gun across the spur and into the buildings of the village. "He looked real panicked," Aker recalls. "He was shooting everywhere. One of his bullets hit, like, this far from my foot." He holds his hands twelve inches apart to demonstrate how close it was.

"You could see rounds impacting all around us," remembers Russell Baer, a SAW gunner. "The air was filled with weird noises as bullets whizzed by. They just wouldn't stop shooting. I came so close to shooting back at those guys. I knew I would be able to kill everyone of them with my SAW. It didn't seem like anything else was gonna stop them. I'm glad I didn't do it, but it definitely crossed my mind."

CHAPTER THIRTY-ONE

At the beginning of the ambush, when Sergeant Weeks had led his squad up through the village and onto the crest of the spur overlooking the mouth of the canyon, the platoon leader, David Uthlaut, and his nineteen-year-old radio operator, Jade Lane, had remained behind at the vehicles in order to call headquarters and sound the alert that Serial Two had been ambushed. After completing their radio communications, they moved up to the village and positioned themselves beside a two-story mud home above the wadi, where they began shooting at enemy fighting positions across the canyon with their M4 carbines. "We were right next to the building," says Lane. "The PL [platoon leader] and me were using the wall as cover. I remember the PL was standing up and I was on a knee. Suddenly there was an explosion that blew me to the ground. It fucked up the PL's face really bad. He was bleeding all over the place, bleeding out of his mouth. He was really messed up and didn't even realize it. It wasn't until I told him—I was like, 'Hey, sir, you're pretty fucked-up.' He said, 'I am?' Then he touched his face and saw that his Nomex* was just soaked in blood." Ten or fifteen seconds later a bullet demolished Lane's left knee. As he crawled away trying to find cover

---

* All the Rangers wore fire-resistant Nomex gloves.

from the incoming fire, another bullet hit him in the chest, ricocheted off his body armor, and grazed his right shoulder, searing his flesh.

Lane assumed he had been shot by a Talib wielding an AK-47, and that Uthlaut had been wounded by an enemy mortar. In truth, the bullets that hit Lane had been fired by a machine gunner on Greg Baker's Humvee, and the blast that nailed the platoon leader had come from a 40-millimeter high-explosive round most likely fired from Chad Johnson's M203 grenade launcher.

When he lobbed the grenade that probably shredded Uthlaut's face with shrapnel, Johnson was standing near Baker's Humvee beneath Tillman's position, just out of sight around the last bend in the wadi. Less than a minute after Uthlaut was wounded, the Humvee roared around the corner and came into view. "As soon as it rounded the corner," Lane remembers,

> the guns on it just opened up and you could see a massive amount of rounds coming in. Even before I saw the vehicle, I could see rounds hitting next to where Tillman and O'Neal were, impacting on the ground, but at that point I didn't know it was coming from Baker's Humvee. I thought they were still under some serious fire from the enemy. I even got on the radio and was screaming at the ETAC,* "We need help! We need fire support right now!" I didn't know that what we really needed was for our own guys to stop shooting at us. Once they came around the corner, I knew instantly that those rounds were not coming from the enemy. As they got closer, I could see where the 240 Bravo was aiming. I couldn't, like, recognize Elliott's face, but I knew that whoever was on the 240 was shooting at our position.

When Stephen Ashpole, the .50-caliber machine gunner, was later asked by investigators why he and the other Rangers on Baker's vehicle didn't positively identify their targets before firing, he explained:

> You are drilled into as a private, shoot where your team leader shoots. . . . We came around a curve. . . . Sergeant Baker then called

---

* "ETAC" stands for "enlisted terminal attack controller"—an airman who's responsible for calling in air strikes in support of Army units on the ground.

fire and I transitioned my weapon and saw some quick shapes and fired where Sergeant Baker and the other guys were firing. . . . I know there is a conflicting issue about PID-ing your target, but Sergeant Baker was one of those great soldiers. So if he was to call fire somewhere, you would trust him. Part of your job is following that. I fired where he called fire. . . . I do not fault Sergeant Baker for doing what he did, when he saw an Afghani firing in our direction. It was one of those split-second decisions that unfortunately turned out disastrous.

Other members of the platoon were less magnanimous about the failure of Baker and his men to control their fire. Sergeant First Class Steven Walter, who was in a Humvee fifty yards directly behind Baker's Humvee, testified, "I had a clear view of his vehicle." As Walter rounded the last bend in the wadi, he witnessed Ashpole shooting his .50-caliber machine gun into the village, he said, and could "see the injured A.M.F. soldier on the side of the spur, he was wearing a tiger-striped uniform, and I could see four Rangers further up the spur on top, which I later found out was Staff Sergeant Weeks' squad. . . . I could clearly see the uniforms and helmets at this time of the Rangers on top of the spur. . . . When I identified the friendly locations, I pointed them out to my vehicle and I also called on the radio to Staff Sergeant Baker's to cease fire. I received nothing back."

The next vehicle to exit the narrows after Walter was a Humvee driven by Brad Jacobson, with Master Sergeant John Horney in its front passenger's seat. Ahead, they could see Baker's Humvee shooting up the hillside. "As soon as we got around the corner," Jacobson remembers, "Sarn't Horney was, like, 'Those are friendlies up there! Those are friendlies!' His voice was real upset. I have tunnel vision because I'm driving, just trying to haul ass without hitting rocks, but I look up and see dudes waving on the high ground. You could see the whole fucking platoon right there. And I'm sorry, but they were pretty obvious. It was dark, yeah, but it wasn't *that* dark. . . . Nobody was being shot at by any Taliban at that point. Those guys in Baker's truck who fucking went to town on the dudes up on the hill? They were just trigger-happy."

According to Walter's testimony, "I was dumbfounded at the fact that the .50-cal gunner was lighting up, so I was trying to get a hold of that [redacted] and see what he was doing. He was just wasting ammo." At this point, Walter said, the vehicles of Serial One were parked just ahead, clearly visible. As Baker's Humvee drove past the two-story building where Uthlaut and Lane were positioned, Elliott continued to target it with his 240 Bravo machine gun, even as the Humvee rolled to a stop behind Serial One. "His tracers were actually going towards the rest of the convoy, which was just making the bend," Walter testified. "So I was trying to call him and tell his 240-Bravo gunner to stop shooting back towards . . . with the way those tracers looked they were flying right over this little knoll. Right at the rest of the convoy." Elliott had such poor awareness of what he was shooting at, in other words, that he almost hit the Humvees in Serial Two that were following behind him.

From the time Baker killed Sayed Farhad until the shooting finally ended, not much more than a minute elapsed, perhaps two at the very most. Near the beginning of this brief span, as bullets were striking the hillside around Pat Tillman and Bryan O'Neal, Tillman tried to calm the young private by saying, "Hey, don't worry, I've got something that can help us." Tillman then raised himself off the ground high enough to huck a smoke grenade toward the wadi, hoping to signal to Baker and his men that they were shooting at American soldiers.

O'Neal said he "heard a hissing sound, it was a purple smoke grenade that Pat had set off. The fire then stopped, and Pat and I got up. . . . We both thought everything was good at the time." It was, however, just a momentary pause in the onslaught. Within moments the Rangers in Baker's truck resumed shooting.

Ten or fifteen seconds later, O'Neal noticed that Tillman's voice took on a distinctly different tone—Pat had "a cry in his call" is how O'Neal described it—and O'Neal assumed Tillman had been hit. Tillman, it turned out, had taken one or more shots to the chest plate of his body armor—sharp blows that would have felt like a jackhammer striking his sternum. Astounded that his fellow Rangers would act so recklessly, he began to holler at the top of his lungs, "What are you shooting at?! I'm Pat Tillman! I'm Pat fucking *TILLMAN!*" His an-

gry, disbelieving cries, however, had no discernible effect on the gunfire emanating from Ashpole, Elliott, and Trevor Alders as they drove
by, all of whom fired at Tillman from less than 120 feet at their closest point—the distance from home plate to second base on a baseball
diamond.

Alders, who had never been in a serious firefight, was the SAW
gunner on Baker's Humvee, positioned on the left side of the vehicle,
responsible for the "nine o'clock" sector of fire—which happened
to be oriented away from where the Rangers perceived most of the
enemy to be during the ambush. As Ashpole, Elliott, and Johnson
blasted at targets on the right-hand side of the vehicle, Alders—a
small guy, just five feet five inches tall, and prone to mask his insecurities with displays of bravado, according to some platoon mates—
felt frustrated to be missing out on most of the action. Whenever the
opportunity arose, he testified, he turned to the "three o'clock"—the
right side of the vehicle, facing the hillside where Tillman was—and
"got my gun into the fight." The SAW is a formidable weapon that
can fire sixteen rounds per second and has an effective range of more
than half a mile. As Alders seldom hesitated to point out, he was an
expert SAW gunner.

Under oath, over a period of two years, Alders provided five separate accounts of the firefight to various investigators. According to
a written statement he submitted in June 2004 in defense of his actions, when the Humvee turned the corner of the terraced poppy field
(where Baker shot Farhad), Alders "heard shots fired, followed by
'Contact three o'clock.' Everyone echoed the command. I stood up,
reoriented from the nine o'clock to the three o'clock, and looked for
where everyone was shooting. I noticed that it was what appeared to
be a small stone wall with sticks laid against it on both sides. . . . I
fired 20 rounds (two 10 round bursts) at that wall with only a few
seconds between the first and second. I identified two sets of arms
straight up. The arms did not indicate any signs of a cease-fire or any
other hand and arm signal."

Puzzled by the implications of this statement, a special agent from
the Army Criminal Investigation Command later inquired of Alders,
"Why would you fire on two sets of arms if they were straight up in
the air?"

"This was a third world country," Alders replied, "and they don't have hand and arm signals like we do. It was my perception they were trying to signal somebody."

Another baffling aspect of Alders's testimony was his insistence that the raised arms he shot at were behind a stone wall. The only stone walls up on the hillside were a pair of goat corrals, which stood on the crest of the spur some distance above where Sergeant Weeks's squad was located. But no Rangers were ever positioned behind the goat corrals or anywhere near them during the firefight. The only men who were defiladed by rocks of any sort were Tillman and O'Neal, who had taken cover behind a pair of low, long boulders. Perhaps, due to the tunnel-like perspective of his gun scope, Alders mistook these boulders for a stone wall.

In any case, five months after submitting his written account of what happened, Alders described the event again in oral testimony to another Army investigator: "I stand up, I turn around, I see where they're shooting, I really don't see anybody, see a stone wall. OK, that's where they're shooting, it's a fortified position, I put a ten round burst into the stone wall and then that split-second, hands pop up. I think to myself, OK, that's obviously where the enemy's at, I put that same ten-round burst down across the wall, because I couldn't see a solid silhouette of somebody. I was trying to get their hands down."

When the investigator asked if he ever saw any "friendlies" up on the hillside, Alders replied, "No, I didn't see any—a soul or anybody up there, sir. I mean, Sergeant Baker said when he engaged up there he saw the silhouette of what turned out to be the A.M.F. soldier, firing above us, but—I mean, I guess the A.M.F. guy was already down by the time I'd turned around, because I didn't see anybody up there, sir. I mean, all I saw was two sets of arms and I just assumed it was two *hajjis* hitting the dirt and I mean, they were getting hammered on by the whole jeep, sir."

From the numerous divots scarring the boulders around Tillman's final position, investigators determined that he was fired on by a .50-caliber machine gun, an M249 SAW, and possibly one or more M4s. But the autopsy performed on Tillman after his death leaves little doubt that he was killed by the SAW. And the only SAW gunner who fired at the hillside was Trevor Alders.

Some Rangers in the platoon regarded Alders as a chest thumper who talked big but often had to ask others to help carry his load. Pat, however, had always gone out of his way to be nice to him. "Alders was pathetic," says one of his platoon mates. "He was a child. Pat was just about the only guy in the platoon who treated him with respect." The previous September, when they were at Fort Benning preparing to attend Ranger School, Pat and Kevin were granted a four-day pass. Alders happened to be at Benning then as well. When Pat and Kevin were invited to spend their leave at the home of some good friends of their mother's who lived in Buckhead, just outside of Atlanta, Pat encouraged Alders to tag along. He gratefully joined them, and was treated like kin.

Seven months later, as Pat sat behind his boulder above the wadi— wounded, shouting his name, waving his hands over his head to signal that he was an American soldier—it's impossible to know what was going through his mind. His attention, however, would almost certainly have been focused on the open Humvee driving along the gravel riverbed just forty yards below, carrying seven of his Ranger comrades, two or three of whom were shooting in his direction. If Tillman had a football, it would have been pretty easy for him to hit the vehicle with a tight spiral pass.

Gazing down at his brothers in arms, he would have seen Alders, positioned on the far side of the Humvee, turn to face him and then point his weapon up the slope. Although Pat probably couldn't make out Alders's features in the twilight, he would have known who it was from Alders's compact stature and the fact that he was holding a SAW. Shortly after Alders brought the weapon to his shoulder, Pat would have seen a flash from the gun's stubby barrel. Concurrent with the muzzle flash, three .223-caliber bullets pierced the right side of his forehead, just below the rim of his helmet, killing him instantly.

Although the entrance wounds were deceptively small and clean—each was just five-sixteenths of an inch in diameter, and all three were grouped tightly together—when the high-velocity, copper-jacketed bullets collided with the frontal bone of Tillman's skull, they broke apart and began to tumble wildly, with devastating effect. As they careened through his flesh and then exited his body, the bullet fragments obliterated much of the cranium, expelling his brain onto the ground. What remained of Tillman's head was mostly skin and fasciae, and resembled a punctured balloon.

Upon hearing the first burst from Alders's SAW shred the air, Bryan O'Neal threw himself facedown on the ground and tried to press his body into the earth behind the boulder. As he lay there, slightly below and to the west of Tillman, O'Neal testified, "I remember hearing what I thought was running water. I thought that Pat had urinated on himself. I asked Pat if he had urinated on himself, but he did not answer. I looked at the rock next to us, and I remember seeing a stream of blood. I didn't believe what I was seeing. I then saw what appeared to be pieces of blood and tissue. I thought I had been shot at first, I then realized that I was fine. I sat up, took a knee, and looked at Pat. He looked like he was kind of sitting, his back was on the hill, he was laying back. I remember that I started yelling for help."

––––––

Baker's Humvee rolled to a stop behind the parked vehicles of Serial One at 6:48 p.m., and the shooting ended a moment thereafter. From start to finish, the firefight had lasted fourteen minutes.

According to Steve Elliott's testimony, "I eventually heard 'Cease fire.' . . . It seemed like it was coming from everywhere. The vehicle was stopped at that point and I saw an A.M.F. soldier who had come around to the back of the vehicle. The impression I got from him was that he was worked up and he wanted us to stop firing. I don't recall exactly if this A.M.F. soldier was waving his arms and/or calling out 'cease fire.' He was pretty worked up."

Most of the Rangers in both serials were deaf from the gunfire. According to Sergeant Mel Ward, one of Weeks's two team leaders who was up on the spur above Tillman's position, "When I could hear again—which took a little while, because the .50-cal makes a lot of noise—the first thing I noticed was someone screaming, 'Oh my fucking God! Oh my fucking God! Oh my fucking *God*!' I didn't know who it was, but because of the way he was screaming, I assumed he was wounded, probably in pieces." After telling his fire team to stay where they were and pull security in case there were still Taliban lurking, Ward hurried down to where the screaming was coming from.

Ward arrived at the boulders about the same time as Staff Sergeant Weeks. O'Neal "was in a state of hysteria," Weeks testified. He was drenched with Tillman's blood and spattered with splinters of bone and chunks of brain matter. His helmet was off. His gun was lying on the ground.

"It was our guys that did it! They fucking killed him!" O'Neal screamed at Weeks. "We were waving our arms! How did they not know we're here?"

Weeks shouted at O'Neal to put his helmet on, pick up his weapon, and "square himself away." After ordering O'Neal to pull security over a nearby sector to give him something to do, Weeks called Eric Godec, the platoon sergeant, and reported over the radio, "I've got one Eagle KIA, call sign Tango," indicating an American had been killed and his last name started with the letter *T*.

By this time Sergeant Bradley Shepherd, Weeks's other team leader, had also arrived on the scene. "First thing Ward did," says Shepherd, "after he sees Tillman is pretty much decapitated, he falls on his knees and hugs him. Starts crying." Ward—a taciturn, physically imposing, politically conservative Ranger who was two years older than Tillman—does not believe men should cry in public, if at all, and is embarrassed that his peers saw him "being a pussy." Only a couple of hours earlier, however, while the platoon had been cooling its heels in Magarah, Tillman and Ward had pulled security together off and on through much of the long afternoon, during which they had talked about their wives and families and what they intended to do when they got out of the Army. When Ward came upon Pat behind the boulder, he thought about this final conversation and was "taken over by events," as they say in the military.

"I was crying, which surprised me," Ward remembers. "I took a knee by Pat's body and put a hand on his chest." A wary, exceedingly private man, Ward has spoken about what happened only to his wife and Army investigators. "Seeing your friend like that was pretty difficult," he admits. "We had, uh . . . We had just spoken and . . . um . . ." Four years after the event, his voice breaks and his eyes water. "I thought I'd be able to talk about this by now without being a big bitch about it. . . . But, um . . . I mean, he wasn't just lying there like someone who's been shot in a John Wayne movie, where it looks like maybe he's only sleeping."

Ward pauses for the better part of a minute to regain his composure and then continues. "It was getting dark. After all the noise, all of a sudden it was really quiet. I remember just sitting there with Pat for a while. And then it was, like, okay, someone is going to have to take care of this now."

"Aker walked up," says Shepherd, "and when he saw Tillman, he turned white as a ghost. Godec was around by then, and as soon as he saw Aker's reaction, he knew Aker shouldn't be there. So he ordered him, 'Go down and get some ponchos and get 'em right now.' "

As Private Aker started walking down the hill to fetch ponchos and Skedcos* for packaging the bodies, Parsons's Humvee pulled to a stop in the wadi directly below the boulders where Pat was killed. Kevin was up in the Humvee's gun turret. The last vehicle in Serial Two, it had driven out of the canyon a few minutes earlier, after the shooting had already stopped. At the moment Pat had been fatally struck, Kevin was still back in the throat of the narrows, completely unaware of the unfolding tragedy.

Weeks immediately approached the Humvee to ask Parsons if there was a Skedco on it, prompting Kevin to inquire, "Who got hit?"

"Of course I knew," Weeks testified, "but I told him I didn't know at that point in time, because I didn't want to have to deal with that situation."

Soon thereafter, Aker reached the wadi, and he, too, asked Parsons if there was a Skedco and/or ponchos on the vehicle. When Parsons demanded, "What's going on?" Aker took him around to the rear of the Humvee and revealed they had two KIA, one of whom was a Ranger. "When I asked who it was, he whispered real quietly that it was Tillman," says Parsons. "We were down on a knee behind the vehicle. At that point I was like, 'Oh, man.' Because Kevin was right there above us in the turret pulling security."

Parsons said nothing to Kevin. He, Aker, Jacobson, Horney, and a young private named Marc Denton carried ponchos and Skedcos up the hill and helped Ward and Shepherd wrap the bodies of Tillman and Farhad, strap them onto the stretchers, and bring them down the precipitous slope in the dark. Ward picked up Tillman's

---

* A Skedco is a lightweight plastic litter for evacuating casualties.

SAW, MOLLE vest, and the hundreds of rounds of ammo he'd been carrying, and hung this heavy load over his shoulders on top of his own kit. "Then we started working Pat and the AMF guy down to the vehicles," he says. "It wasn't easy. I got pretty smoked."

Just above the riverbed, Shepherd and Denton were lowering one of the Skedcos down a vertical embankment to Parsons and Aker when "Tillman came unpackaged," according to Parsons. Pat's upper body slid out of the poncho and hit Aker in the chest. "Aker had a really bad response to it," Parsons recalls. After they wrapped Pat up and strapped him back into the Skedco, Jacobson dragged the stretcher down the riverbed to a landing zone where a helicopter could evacuate the bodies.

It was about 7:40. Standing guard in the turret, staring up into the darkness through a night-vision device mounted on the brow of his helmet, Kevin watched his colleagues labor to haul a large object down the hillside above him. "They brought down somebody in a Skedco," he testified. "And I asked, 'Who the fuck was that?' "

"It's an A.M.F. soldier," someone in the vehicle replied.

"I'm like, 'What?' " Kevin told the investigator. "That didn't make any sense. . . . So I started to get a little weird feeling, you know, because my brother's a pretty loud-type guy." Kevin hadn't heard Pat's booming laugh or seen any sign of him since arriving at Serial One's location after the firefight. The last time Kevin had talked to Pat was back in Magarah before the platoon was split.

Parsons hopped into the Humvee, drove it 250 yards down the riverbed, and parked behind the rest of the convoy. Kevin resumed pulling security in the turret, but his "weird feeling" persisted. So he asked Parsons, "Where's Pat?"

"He asked me, like, three times," says Parsons. "I just ignored him the first two times. When he asked me again, I decided, 'All right, I'm gonna tell him.' "

Russell Baer was sitting in the back of Parsons's Humvee, he remembers, when "Parsons got up inside the turret with Kevin. He said to him, 'I don't want to be the one to tell you this, but your brother is dead.' Just like that. That's how Kevin found out Pat had been killed. They were right above me. I overheard him. That's how I found out, too. It was fucked."

"I told him straight-out," says Parsons. "Kevin and me went back and forth on that for a minute, because he had the whole disbelief thing going on. But finally it ended up sinking in that his brother was KIA."

"Kevin got completely silent," says Baer. "He looked around for about five seconds and then quietly got off the jeep. Then he started walking around, screaming 'fuck!' over and over. . . . What do you do? I wanted to do something, but I didn't know how to make things better. It was devastating even for me; I can't imagine what it must have been like for Kevin. For him to lose Pat—I mean, they weren't just brothers; they were joined at the hip. I remember the medic— Doc Anderson, an older guy—asking Kevin for his rifle. Kevin was all tensed up. Yelling. Walking aimlessly back and forth. That's when Doc took his weapon." Parsons, worried about how Kevin might react to his brother's death, had asked Anderson to confiscate Kevin's gun.

When Parsons informed Godec and Staff Sergeant Jonathan Owens, who was Kevin's squad leader, that he'd told Kevin that Pat was KIA, "Owens got in my face about it," Parsons recalls. "Said I shouldn't have told him. I ended up snapping back at him, 'Hey, Kevin is a grown man. I'm not gonna treat him like a kid. I'm not gonna lie to him about something like this. It's his brother. If it was your brother or sister out there who died, you'd want to know what happened.' " Parsons still had no idea that Pat had been killed by friendly fire, however, so he didn't reveal that aspect of the tragedy to Kevin, nor was it revealed by any of the numerous Rangers in the platoon who by then knew with absolute certainty how Pat had died.

A pair of Black Hawks appeared out of the darkness and descended amid a hurricane of debris created by their downwash. As the Rangers watched the helos approach through their night-vision devices, the tips of the rotor blades appeared to throw off balls of bright green flames—static electricity generated by the rotors cutting through the blowing sand. Uthlaut and Lane, both seriously wounded, were put on one of the birds, the bodies of Pat and Farhad were loaded onto the other, and at 7:58 the two helicopters lifted off into the night. Nine minutes later they touched down beside the field hospital at FOB Salerno. Approximately an hour after that, a Chinook returned to the wadi and flew Kevin to Salerno as well.

For the rest of the Rangers, says Josey Boatright, "It was a rough night. Everybody was exhausted and pretty freaked. We racked out by the vehicles in the wadi, but nobody slept much. I had Pat's blood all over my leg from where I drug his stuff. That smell—all night my sleeping bag smelled like blood."

In the morning the Black Sheep cleared Mana and the adjacent settlements. While the platoon was searching houses, Brad Jacobson remained outside pulling security. At one point he looked skyward and saw a pair of Army helicopters flying high overhead. Beneath each of the massive Chinooks, swinging from a long nylon sling, was a Humvee being transported to Salerno. "It was a quiet reminder," Jacobson testified in a sworn statement, "that perhaps if our leadership had done their job right in Bagram and had gotten that helicopter to us like we asked, none of this would have happened."

PART FOUR

He who learns must suffer. And even in our sleep
pain that cannot forget, falls drop by drop upon the
heart, and in our own despite, against our will,
comes wisdom to us by the awful grace of God.

—AESCHYLUS, *Agamemnon*

CHAPTER THIRTY-TWO

While Pat and Kevin were deployed in Iraq, Marie had been hired by a company called the Creative Group located in a skyscraper in Seattle's urban core. "I loved working there," Marie says. "I worked with a couple of girls I really liked, and enjoyed being in downtown Seattle during the week. It was nice to get away from the empty house in University Place. At the end of the day I'd maybe have a drink with one of my girlfriends and then drive back home when the traffic wasn't quite so bad."

Just before 5:00 p.m. Pacific standard time on April 22, ten and a half hours after Pat was shot, the office receptionist summoned Marie to a conference room. An Army master sergeant named William Donovan, wearing a formal Class-A uniform and accompanied by an Army chaplain, walked into the room and asked if she was Marie Tillman and then asked if she was married to Specialist Patrick Daniel Tillman. When she replied yes to both questions, Donovan testified, "I told her, her husband was killed in action in Afghanistan today. . . . That's pretty much all I had to say, then I answered the questions, of course."

Marie's first question was to inquire if Kevin was okay, and then she asked how Pat was killed. Donovan told her, "We don't have any of the information right now, but it was from a gunshot wound to the head, and it was during an ambush." According to Donovan,

"She was more concerned about Kevin at that point. Oh, she asked if her—if Pat's family had been notified yet. [They had not.] . . . From there, me and the chaplain had already worked it out how we were going to—you know, we figured we didn't want her driving. So the chaplain drove her in her vehicle, and I drove the [redacted] vehicle with [redacted] back to their place in—I forget where they live."

Before leaving her office, Marie called her parents to tell them of Pat's death. With a preternaturally calm demeanor that hid her true state of mind, she asked them to notify her sister and brother-in-law, Christine and Alex Garwood, both of whom were extremely close to Pat. A few minutes later, Marie learned that someone from the Army was en route to Dannie Tillman's residence in New Almaden to notify her that Pat had been killed. Pat's parents had divorced six years earlier, and Marie realized that Dannie would probably be home alone when the Army messenger arrived at her front door. So Marie hurriedly called Alex and asked him to contact Dannie's brother, Mike Spalding, to request that he attempt to get there first. Alex was unable to reach Uncle Mike, though, so he decided to go to Dannie's house himself.

By this time Pat's mother had a feeling that something wasn't right from the odd messages she found on her answering machine when she got home from her job teaching special education at Bret Harte Middle School. Alex remembers that as he was sitting in his car inside his garage in Los Gatos, preparing to drive to Dannie's, he received a call from Dannie on his cell phone. According to Alex, "She asked, 'Is something wrong with the boys?' I thought, 'It's not my place to tell her.' Maybe that was just cowardice on my part, but I replied, 'You need to call Marie right now.' Then I hung up and drove over to her place as fast as I could, trying to beat the Army over there."

With trepidation, Dannie called Pat and Marie's home above Tacoma Narrows, but when Marie picked up the phone, her voice sounded calm, which eased Dannie's fears somewhat. When she asked Marie what was going on, however, Marie was unable to speak. Dannie repeated the question; and again there was nothing but silence from the other end of the line. Dannie asked yet again, and this time Marie replied, "He's dead."

"Dead! Who's dead?!" Dannie demanded.

"Pat's dead."

Dannie ran out the front door of her house. Her shrieks prompted people in adjacent homes to rush outside to see what was wrong. Alex pulled in to her driveway a moment later. "Dannie's neighbors Peggy and Syd were consoling her," he says. "I went up and gave her a hug. Not long after that, an Army sergeant showed up, a woman, looking flustered. She'd gotten lost. As she got out of her car, she was trying to button the jacket to her uniform, and we were all just standing there waiting for her to get all these buttons buttoned. I remember thinking, 'Look, we know why you're here. Who cares about your uniform?' Then it was just like in the movies: 'On behalf of a grateful nation, your government regrets to inform you that your son Patrick Daniel Tillman was killed in action.' "

As soon as Dannie could collect herself, she asked the sergeant where Kevin was, and if he was all right, and then she called her ex-husband and gave him the terrible news. He immediately drove to the house. "When Mr. Tillman walked in," Alex says, "he and Dannie hugged across the table. He kind of pulled her across into this desperate embrace. The sergeant and I went outside to let them be alone. As we stood out there, we could hear them wailing—these primal kind of screams."

—————

Marie's parents, Paul and Bindy Ugenti, and her sister, Christine Ugenti Garwood, flew to Seattle on April 22 to be with Marie as soon as they learned of Pat's death. "We got up to her house in Washington that evening," says Christine. "The minute I saw her, I gave her this big hug, expecting her to fall apart. But she wasn't crying, which surprised me. While I was struggling not to lose it, Marie was just sitting there; she was strangely calm. I don't know, maybe it was just too huge for her to process, but she was acting completely numb. She seemed preoccupied with making sure that Kevin was okay, that Dannie was okay, that Richard was okay, that Mr. Tillman was okay—she was directing all her energy to helping others, focusing on what needed to be done so she wouldn't have to feel anything, and it freaked me out."

While they stayed with Marie, the Ugenti parents slept in Kevin's bedroom and Christine slept on the couch. "In the mornings," Christine remembers,

> I would get into bed with Marie and talk. There were so many details she had to take care of. I remember getting in bed with her and asking, "What's going on? The military people are coming to your house and asking you all these questions, and you're doing all this stuff, and nobody's even talking about Pat, what a great person he is. . . ." Marie started crying when I said that, and talked about how she was really feeling. She was devastated, obviously, but for some reason she felt like she had to keep it together—there were so many people around the house she felt it was important not to fall apart. I understood. I remember telling her, "You don't have to apologize for the way you're reacting. I'm just worried about you."

———

At 10:00 p.m. on April 22, when Kevin stepped out of a helicopter at Forward Operating Base Salerno after being flown from the canyon where Pat was shot, he was summoned to the TOC—the Tactical Operations Center—to meet with Major David Hodne. "Kevin was obviously distressed about the incident," Hodne testified, "and I attempted to console him. . . . He declined my offer to meet the chaplain that was inbound. He asked me to promise to exact revenge on the ambushers." Hodne assured Kevin that whoever was responsible for Pat's death would pay dearly for their actions. This would turn out to be the first in a long string of broken promises and self-serving lies proffered to the Tillman family by commissioned officers of the U.S. Army.

By this time all phones and Internet terminals available to enlisted men at Salerno had been shut down to prevent soldiers from communicating news about Pat's death to anyone beyond the FOB. There was nothing unusual or nefarious about such a lockdown; it was standard policy at bases in Afghanistan and Iraq whenever there were American casualties, in order to allow next of kin to be notified before word leaked to the media. Setting the wheels in motion to notify the Tillman family, at 11:08 p.m. a functionary in the Salerno TOC sent an e-mail to U.S. Central Command in Tampa, Florida, stating little more than that Specialist Patrick Daniel Tillman had been killed in action during an ambush after suffering a gunshot wound to the head.

The next morning at dawn, back in the canyon where the Black Sheep had been attacked, First Sergeant Tommy Fuller walked up to the rocks where Pat had been shot. He had arrived shortly after the firefight the previous evening with the Alpha Company commander, Captain William Saunders, and Third Platoon, who had rushed to the canyon from Salerno to support the stunned soldiers of Second Platoon. Behind the uppermost boulder, Fuller testified, "Tillman's brain was still on the ground." He put it in a Ziploc bag, which he placed inside an ammo can, and then gave the can to one of his sergeants so it could be returned to Salerno and sent back to the States with Pat's body. This ammo can, and the remains it held, were never shipped to the United States. They simply vanished, and have never been accounted for.

After talking to several of the survivors of the firefight, Fuller realized that Pat had been shot by his comrades, and he shared this conclusion with Captain Saunders. Upon interviewing the men of Second Platoon, Saunders concurred with Fuller's assessment of the cause of death.

Around 8:30 a.m., Lieutenant Colonel Jeffrey Bailey, the commander of the Second Ranger Battalion, arrived on the scene, spoke with soldiers from both serials, talked at length with Fuller and Saunders, and walked the ground. "The three of us got together," Bailey testified. "So I said, 'Alright. I think I agree with you. We need to do an investigation.' So I called Major Hodne [at Salerno] and told him my gut feeling was that Tillman had been killed by friendly fire. . . . There was no doubt about it. It was a case where there were six or seven Rangers that saw the vehicle shooting at them."

Hodne recommended that Bailey select an officer named Captain Richard Scott to conduct an investigation according to Article 15-6 of the Uniform Code of Military Justice. Bailey agreed, and Scott was appointed to head the so-called 15-6 investigation.

Given that he would be probing the death of such a high-profile soldier, Scott was a curious choice for the job. Although a highly regarded officer, Scott was a mere captain, and under the direct command of Hodne, the very man whose order to split Uthlaut's platoon culminated in Tillman's death. As both Hodne and Bailey were aware, Article 15-6 required "the investigating officer to be senior in rank to anyone whose conduct or performance he may investigate," which precluded Scott from probing the actions of Hodne or Bailey. The investigation of Tillman's death thus took an irregular turn right out of the gate. Other irregularities soon followed.

Bailey alerted his boss—Colonel James Nixon, the commander of the entire Ranger Regiment—that Tillman was the victim of fratricide. Nixon then told his boss, Lieutenant General Philip Kensinger Jr., the commander of the U.S. Army Special Operations Command (USASOC), as well as a two-star general named Stanley McChrystal who ran the most covert branch of the U.S. Armed Forces, the Joint Special Operations Command (JSOC). Major General McChrystal was in charge of the high-risk counterterrorism missions undertaken by Navy SEALs, Delta Force operators, and Army Rangers. Exceptionally capable, unafraid to bend rules to get results, he commanded the guys who'd rescued Jessica Lynch, as well as the units that would later capture Saddam Hussein and kill Abu Mussab al-Zarqawi. He was politically shrewd. He worked under the radar. Vice President Cheney and Secretary of Defense Rumsfeld kept in close touch with him and trusted him absolutely.

An hour or two after Kensinger and McChrystal were informed that Tillman was killed by friendly fire, word of the fratricide was sent via back channels to the highest levels of the Pentagon and the White House. The facts of Tillman's death were restricted to a tight cadre.

That afternoon—April 23—Pat's coffin was loaded onto a helicopter, and Kevin accompanied the body from Salerno to Bagram. Before departing, Kevin asked Bailey, Hodne, and virtually every other Ranger he encountered to try to find the small notebook Pat had been using to record his thoughts and observations, so that it could be returned to the Tillman family; Kevin made it clear that recovering this notebook was extremely important to him. Even as his superiors assured Kevin they would leave no stone unturned in their hunt for the notebook, they were taking extraordinary steps to keep him in the dark about how Pat was killed.

Standard operating procedure dictates that when a soldier is killed in action, his or her uniform is left on the body for shipment back to the United States, to be removed during the autopsy and analyzed as forensic evidence. For reasons that have never been explained, Tillman's blood-soaked uniform and body armor were removed at Salerno and placed into a trash bag before the body was flown to Bagram. On the night of April 23, Sergeant James Valdez testified, a captain named Wade Bovard "came to me with an orange plastic bag containing Tillman's clothes. He then related that he wanted me to burn what was in the bag for security purposes. Additionally, Captain Bovard related he wanted me alone to burn what was in the bag to prevent security violations, leaks, and rumors."

Before destroying the items in the bag, Valdez went through the pockets of Tillman's uniform. In the cargo pocket of his pants he found Pat's notebook, after which he started a fire in an empty oil drum and destroyed the notebook, uniform, and body armor. As these items were burning, Valdez stated, "Captain Bovard came out one time to ensure that everything was going all right. . . . Captain Bovard then came back right at the end, when I was finishing."

The Rangers of Second Platoon arrived back at Salerno on the morning of April 25, still reeling from what had happened on the twenty-second. Tommy Fuller had brought back the vest of ammo pouches that Pat had worn over his body armor, sodden with blood and riddled with bullet holes. A fragment from a green-tipped SAW round that had struck a grenade remained in one of the pouches. That afternoon Fuller burned the vest in the same barrel Valdez used to destroy Pat's other belongings two days earlier.

First Platoon showed up back at the FOB not long after the Black Sheep. The previous night, acting on a tip provided by sympathetic villagers in Magarah, they'd captured four men who allegedly participated in the ambush. All were local tribesmen who said they had been paid modest sums by a fifth figure, a notorious Talib, to attack the American platoon. According to the sworn testimony of Major Hodne, "Gul Zaman is the one we assessed to be the trigger man/leader for the ambush. To my knowledge, Zaman was not captured and fled to [redacted]."*

* Apparently, Hodne was unaware that Gul Zaman, a thirty-three-year-old Wazir tribesman raised in a nearby village, was sitting in a prison cell at the Guantánamo Bay detention camp on April 22, 2004, where he'd been held since his arrest on January 21, 2002, for being an "enemy combatant." Zaman was freed from Guantánamo on April 20, 2005, after a military tribunal determined that he was an innocent Afghan who had been wrongly charged.

By now every Ranger in the platoon knew that Pat had been killed by another Ranger, but on Bailey's orders they were admonished in the strongest possible terms not to disclose this knowledge to anyone under any circumstances. Kevin, desperate for information about how Pat met his end, repeatedly called the Salerno TOC from Bagram and asked to talk to Bryan O'Neal, because he knew O'Neal had been nearby when Pat was shot. "I had to call like eight times," Kevin testified. When he finally got Bailey on the phone, Kevin pleaded, "Where's O'Neal? Where's O'Neal? Give me somebody to talk to."

"Kevin was a basket case," Bailey testified. "So I kept putting him off." When Kevin refused to drop the matter, Bailey finally allowed Kevin and O'Neal to speak to each other, but first he sternly reiterated to O'Neal that he was under orders to say nothing about friendly fire.

"And he didn't say anything to me," Kevin recalled. "He just kind of watered the thing down. He talked for like three minutes and told me, 'We were running up the hill and . . . the A.M.F. guy got shot. And then Pat got shot, and we were shooting our asses off. And when I looked down, Pat was shot. And then I don't remember anything after that." Based on what O'Neal had told him, Kevin was certain Pat had been killed by the Taliban.

"I wanted right off the bat to let the family know what had happened," O'Neal stated, "especially Kevin because I worked with him in the platoon. . . . And I was quite appalled that when I was able actually to speak with Kevin, I was ordered not to tell him what happened."

The remains of soldiers killed in Afghanistan and Iraq are received and processed at Dover Air Force Base in Delaware. On April 26, Kevin arrived at Dover with Pat's body. Russell Baer had been sent along to keep Kevin company during the long journey home. Before leaving Salerno, Baer, too, was warned to keep his lips sealed. "Me and Kevin hardly said a word to each other the whole way back," Baer says. Marie Tillman flew in from Seattle to meet their plane when they arrived in Dover.

An autopsy was performed at the base mortuary by Dr. Craig Mallak, the chief of the Armed Forces medical examiners, and Dr. James Caruso, chief deputy medical examiner. Four months earlier, Mallak had disseminated a policy throughout all branches of the military explicitly stating that deceased soldiers were to be sent to Dover with their uniforms, their body armor, and their helmets, which were to be considered crucial forensic evidence. When they saw that Pat had arrived naked, without any of this evidence, Mallak was furious. "We kept asking, 'Where are the clothes?' " he testified. When he learned they had been burned, Mallak said, "I thought, 'Why would you do that?' "

The Army withheld from Mallak its knowledge that Pat had been killed by friendly fire, another serious breach of protocol. Instead, he was told that Pat "was shot by insurgents or Taliban." According to Mallak, he "immediately had concerns about the case" because "the gunshot wounds to the forehead were atypical in nature, and that the initial story we received didn't—the medical evidence did not match up with the scenario as described." He was sufficiently troubled by this discrepancy that he asked the Army Criminal Investigation Division to look into it, but the CID refused. Perturbed, Mallak and Caruso declined to sign their names to the autopsy examination report when it was completed.

On the night of April 28, following the autopsy, Marie, Kevin, and Russell Baer brought Pat home. From the San Francisco airport, a hearse took Marie, Kevin, and Pat's remains to a mortuary in San Jose, where Pat's parents, his brother Richard, and one of his uncles met them shortly before midnight. As sad as the reunion was, everyone was tremendously relieved to see Kevin.

On April 30, Pat was cremated. A public memorial service was scheduled for Monday, May 3, to be held at the San Jose Municipal Rose Garden.

CHAPTER THIRTY-THREE

On the evening that Pat's remains arrived back in San Jose, *60 Minutes II,* the CBS television news program, ran a story about the torture and abuse of Iraqi inmates by U.S. soldiers at a prison outside of Baghdad called Abu Ghraib. The account, accompanied by snapshots taken by the abusers of their sadistic acts, was shocking. As Alberto Gonzales, the White House counsel,* watched the program in the West Wing he muttered darkly, "This is going to kill us."

Two days later, on April 30, an even more disturbing story about Abu Ghraib written by the journalist Seymour Hersh was posted on the Web site of *The New Yorker* magazine. The alleged abuse of Abu Ghraib prisoners included sexual humiliation, sodomy, beating, murder, and the rape of a sixteen-year-old Iraqi girl, provoking outrage around the world. The revelations added significantly to the Bush administration's growing difficulties in Iraq, where the war had recently taken a dramatic turn for the worse.

Donald Rumsfeld and General Richard Myers, the chairman of the Joint Chiefs of Staff, had known since mid-April that the *60 Minutes* exposé was imminent. At their request, broadcast of the Abu Ghraib story was delayed for two weeks so as not to exacerbate the intense battle then raging in the Iraqi city of Fallujah.

---

* Gonzales would be appointed attorney general by President Bush ten months later.

The violence in Fallujah had been precipitated on March 31, when Iraqi insurgents ambushed a convoy being guarded by four paramilitary contractors working for Blackwater USA. After they were killed in a grenade attack, the bodies of the four Americans were set on fire, dragged through the streets of Fallujah by a mob, and then hung from a bridge over the Euphrates River. In response, two thousand American troops launched a massive assault on the city on April 4, initiating ferocious urban combat that continued for the next twenty-seven days. By the time U.S. forces were pulled out of Fallujah on May 1, twenty-seven American troops were dead, and more than ninety had been wounded. The commander of one of the insurgent factions, a previously unheralded figure named Abu Mussab al-Zarqawi, emerged after the battle as a hero to Sunni Iraqis for standing up to the Americans and forcing them to withdraw from the city, transforming him from a nobody into a dangerous foe.

The upshot of these disquieting developments was that the White House was frantic to come up with something to divert attention from the deadly quagmire that Iraq had become, precisely as Osama bin Laden had gleefully forecast. The president was facing an increasingly tough campaign to win a second term in the White House, the election was barely six months away, and his approval ratings were plummeting. When Tillman was killed, White House perception managers saw an opportunity not unlike the one provided by the Jessica Lynch debacle thirteen months earlier.

The administration had tried to make Tillman an inspirational emblem for the Global War on Terror when he was alive, but he had rebuffed them by refusing to do any media interviews. If there had been a way to prevent the White House from exploiting him after his death, Tillman would have done that, too, as he made clear to Jade Lane in Iraq. "When we were in Baghdad, our cots were next to each other," Lane remembers. "Pat and I used to talk at night a lot before we'd rack out. I don't know how the conversation got brought up, but one night he said he was afraid that if something were to happen to him, Bush's people would, like, make a big deal out of his death and parade him through the streets. And those were his exact words: 'I don't want them to parade me through the streets.' It just burned into my brain, him saying that."

Following Tillman's death, there was nothing to prevent the Bush administration from using his celebrity to advance its political agenda. Jim Wilkinson, the master propagandist who had used the Jessica Lynch rescue to cover up the Nasiriyah catastrophe during the invasion of Iraq, had been appointed by Karl Rove as director of communications for the upcoming Republican National Convention, and was therefore no longer available to orchestrate the Tillman spin. But Wilkinson had trained his successors well before departing. They wasted no time in concocting a narrative about Tillman that they hoped would distract the American public in the same way that Wilkinson's fable about Lynch had. The fact that Tillman had been cut down by his Ranger buddies rather than by the Taliban was potentially problematic for the White House, although there were ways to keep that information from entering the public domain for a while, maybe even a long while.

The moment the White House learned of Tillman's death, the president's staff went into overdrive. On April 23, the day after Tillman perished, approximately two hundred e-mails discussing the situation were transmitted or received by White House officials, including staffers from Bush's reelection campaign, who suggested to the president that it would be advantageous for him to respond to Tillman's death as quickly as possible. Jeanie Mamo—Bush's director of media affairs—sent an e-mail to Lawrence Di Rita, Rumsfeld's press secretary, asking for details about the tragedy so she could use them in a White House press release. By 11:40 a.m., a statement about Tillman had been drafted and forwarded to Press Secretary Scott McClellan and Communications Director Dan Bartlett, who immediately approved the statement on behalf of President Bush and then disseminated it to the public, even though doing so violated the Military Family Peace of Mind Act—a policy mandated by Congress and signed into law by the president just five months earlier—which was intended to give families of war casualties twenty-four hours to grieve privately before any public announcement was made about the victim. Because the Tillman family wasn't notified of Pat's death until the evening of April 22, the White House was legally forbidden to issue its press release before the evening of the twenty-third.

Bartlett later explained that he rushed out the statement about Tillman illegally, and with such extraordinary haste, in order to accommodate overwhelming interest from the media, noting that the story "made the American people feel good about our country . . . and our military." Needless to say, the White House statement did not disclose that Tillman had been killed by friendly fire.

While he was alive, Tillman had been the object of tremendous public fascination, and White House officials guessed that selling him as a fallen war hero would send the media into an orgy of adulatory coverage. They were not disappointed. Thousands of tributes to Tillman appeared in all manner of media over the days and weeks that followed. On April 25, just two days after the initial White House press release, a "Weekend Media Assessment" compiled by the Army chief of staff's Office of Public Affairs reported that stories about Tillman had generated the greatest interest in the Army "since the end of active combat last year," adding that the Tillman stories "had been extremely positive in all media." As with the frenzy that followed the Jessica Lynch rescue, neither the White House nor military perception managers had to do much to sustain the media's focus on Tillman's death; indeed, they did little more than monitor the coverage and make copies of all the published articles for their files—although that didn't deter the Army from deciding to ratchet up the media hysteria to an even higher level by awarding Tillman a couple of posthumous medals.

The Second Ranger Battalion initiated work on the medals within hours of Tillman's death, when Lieutenant Colonel Bailey directed Major Hodne to recommend Tillman for a Silver Star, the third-highest military decoration for valor that can be awarded to a member of the U.S. Armed Forces. "I am the person who actually wrote the recommendation for the Silver Star award for Specialist Tillman after his death," Hodne testified. "We began preparing that award either the night of the incident in which he was killed, or the following day." On April 27, Hodne e-mailed a draft of his Silver Star citation, along with a narrative of Tillman's actions and two witness statements justifying the award, up the chain of command so that it could be announced at the memorial ceremony in San Jose on May 3.

The two witness statements for the Silver Star were attributed to Private First Class Bryan O'Neal and Sergeant Mel Ward. O'Neal testified that he was put in front of a computer and told to type out a statement, which he did, but after he wrote it, his words were embellished so egregiously that he never signed it. In Ward's case, he didn't even remember writing such a statement. During the investigation, Ward says, "When they showed me a Silver Star recommendation that I supposedly wrote for Pat, it was unsigned, which is a big red flag for me, because in the Army you can't submit anything without signing it. They would have handed it right back to me and said, 'Hey, stupid, you need to sign this.' Besides, it didn't sound like my words. . . . It sounded really hokey—something I would never have written." Despite these falsified, unsigned statements, the recommendation was expedited by Major General McChrystal, Colonel Nixon, and Lieutenant Colonel Bailey, and on April 29, Tillman's Silver Star commendation was signed by Les Brownlee, acting secretary of the Army.

On April 30, the Army issued a press release announcing that the Silver Star would be awarded to Tillman "for his selfless actions after his Ranger element was ambushed by anti-coalition insurgents." Yet again, nothing was said about fratricide being the cause of Tillman's death. As Brigadier General Howard Yellen later testified, "For the civilian on the street, the interpretation would be that he was killed by enemy fire."

———

Because only a handful of people in Washington were informed that Tillman had actually been killed by friendly fire, in the first days following the tragedy General McChrystal had begun to worry that speechwriters at the White House and the Pentagon might inadvertently script something that, if spoken by President Bush or a high-ranking administration official, would expose them as liars should the truth about Tillman happen to leak out. McChrystal's concerns became more acute on April 28 when an e-mail sent from the White House speechwriter John Currin to Rumsfeld's office indicated that the president would be talking about Tillman on May 1 at the annual White House Correspondents' Association dinner.

To forestall any potential gaffes, on April 29 McChrystal e-mailed a high-priority personal memo (known as a "Personal For" memo, or simply a "P4") to General John Abizaid, the CENTCOM commander; General Bryan Brown, commander of U.S. Special Operations Command (USSOC); and Lieutenant General Kensinger, commander of the U.S. Army Special Operations Command (USASOC).

"Sir, in the aftermath of Corporal* Patrick Tillman's untimely yet heroic death in Afghanistan on 22 April 04," McChrystal stated,

> it is anticipated that a 15-6 investigation nearing completion will find that it is highly possible that Corporal Tillman was killed by friendly fire. This potential finding is exacerbated by the unconfirmed but suspected reports that POTUS [the president of the United States] and the Secretary of the Army might include comments about Corporal Tillman's heroism and his approved Silver Star medal in speeches currently being prepared. . . . I felt that it was essential that you received this information as soon as we detected it in order to preclude any unknowing statements by our country's leaders which might cause public embarrassment if the circumstances of Corporal Tillman's death become public.

As it turned out, Kensinger had learned on April 23 that fratricide was definitely the cause of death, and it's likely that Abizaid and Brown already knew as well. The real intent of McChrystal's P4 was to alert his superiors that someone needed to warn President Bush and Secretary Les Brownlee that the 15-6 would confirm Tillman's death by friendly fire, which increased the likelihood that the truth might eventually be exposed one day. The president and the secretary therefore needed to be especially mindful of what they said about Tillman when making public statements.

In the speech Bush gave at the correspondents' dinner two days later, he lauded Tillman for his courage and sacrifice, but pointedly made no mention of how he died, indicating that McChrystal's memo had been read and heeded by the president and/or his advisers. Later, Abizaid, Kensinger, and the White House would all deny receiving McChrystal's memo or knowing at the time that Tillman's death was a fratricide.

---

* Tillman was posthumously promoted to the rank of corporal.

On Monday, May 3—one day shy of Pat and Marie's second wedding anniversary—two thousand people gathered at the San Jose Municipal Rose Garden for Pat's memorial service. Lieutenant General Kensinger was in attendance, and sought out the family before the ceremony to personally express his condolences. Although he obsequiously assured the Tillmans that he would do everything in his power to help the family through this difficult period, he said nothing to correct their understanding, based on the intentionally misleading details provided by the Army, that Pat had been shot by the Taliban.

The memorial commenced with the keening of bagpipes, after which friends, coaches, teammates, family members, and various luminaries shared their memories of Pat from the stage. ESPN broadcast the entire event live on national television. Maria Shriver spoke, and Senator John McCain. Pat's ex-teammate Jake Plummer described his old pal as fearless, tough, caring, and "one of the most beautiful people to have ever entered my life." Plummer remembered a game in which Pat had received the football after the opposing team kicked it off: "He wasn't supposed to, but he happened to catch the ball. He almost took it to the house." Laughing, Plummer recalled, "When he got tackled he jumped up and looked around like, 'What's the big deal? This ain't that hard.' "

Dave McGinnis, who coached Pat for his entire NFL career, observed, "If you wanted [Pat's] opinion, all you had to do was ask him. And if you didn't want his opinion and didn't ask him, he'd still give it to you."

Larry Marmie, the defensive coordinator for the Arizona Cardinals who had loved Pat like a prodigal son, was visibly crushed by his death. "Pat lived life on his terms," Marmie told the audience with a faltering voice, "he walked away from the comfort and material things that most of us desire, he sought out danger for what he deemed to be a greater good." Marmie described Pat as "fiercely unique," with "a strong dislike for the easy way out. He was caring, he was thoughtful, and he was soft. Pat was soft in the heart. He was humble yet confident, reserved, but he was hard. You wanted this guy on your team, and it didn't have to be a football team. . . . It was fun coaching Pat. It was challenging coaching Pat. It was an honor to coach Pat. I learned a lot from him. Players are usually trying to earn the respect of their coach. I found myself trying to earn Pat's respect."

Many people spoke movingly of Pat, but perhaps the most captivating tribute came from Steve White, the Navy SEAL whom Pat and Kevin had befriended during Operation Iraqi Freedom. On the morning before the service, an Army representative asked White to announce that Pat had been awarded the Silver Star. In order to do that, White felt that first he needed to get the facts straight, so he requested that somebody in the Second Ranger Battalion provide him with details about the fatal firefight. "I called an enlisted person, whose name I cannot recall," White later testified. After this Ranger read the Silver Star citation to White over the phone, White rephrased the official narrative in his own words and then read it back to the Ranger. According to his sworn testimony, White asked this Ranger "if it was an accurate summarization, and he said it was, and that is what I went with in my speech."

White began his encomium to Pat by explaining how they met in Saudi Arabia just before the start of the Iraq War. "Pretty much every night for the next three months if we weren't working," White recalled,

we were out drinking coffee and enjoying each other's company out there, getting to know each other. . . .

I got the news early on Friday morning about Pat's death. I'd been spending the day flying back home, and I watched the news on every layover, waiting for the word to break. Once I saw that it was out, I contemplated at that point calling Marie. I knew that there was going to be a lot going on and I didn't want to add to it. When my wife picked me up at the airport, she asked if I'd called Marie. I gave her my reason, and she looked at me and said, "If the tables were turned right now, would he have called me?" That's the kind of man Pat was. I immediately picked up the phone. . . .

The Silver Star and the Purple Heart that Pat has earned will be given to Marie at a private ceremony. The Silver Star is one of this nation's highest awards; the Purple Heart is rewarded for wounds received in combat. If you're the victim of an ambush, there are very few things that you can do to increase your chances for survival, one of which is to get off that ambush point as fast as you can. One of the vehicles in Pat's convoy could not get off. He made the call; he dismounted his troops, taking the fight to the enemy, uphill, to seize the tactical high ground from the enemy. This gave his brothers in the downed vehicle time to move off that target. He directly saved their lives with that move. Pat sacrificed himself so that his brothers could live.

"I, like everyone in the audience, was greatly affected listening to the young Naval officer speak," wrote Dannie Tillman, recalling White's eulogy in *Boots on the Ground by Dusk*. "He was the first person to give us an account of Pat's death." The details White shared about Pat's final moments brought Dannie a small measure of peace, she said, which had been absent since the family learned of his passing eleven days earlier.

At the conclusion of the ceremony, three Rangers in formal military dress marched up to Marie and Pat's parents and presented each of them with a folded American flag. The soldier who handed a flag to Dannie was Russell Baer. That evening, the Tillmans invited White and Baer to a gathering of their friends at Dannie's cottage in New Almaden. Pat's father asked Baer to share his recollections of the firefight. It was an awkward moment for the young Ranger. He told the Tillmans as much detail as he could without violating the order not to reveal that Pat was shot by his Ranger comrades, which of course led everyone to believe that Pat had been killed by the Taliban.

Afterward, Baer was furious that the Army had forced him to lie to Pat's family and friends. "I had just handed the parents the flags," he said. "I saw the look on their faces. A few days earlier the guys I worked with had killed Pat and another guy, injured two more, and shot at me, and I wasn't allowed to tell anyone." When he was ordered to return to Fort Lewis the next day, he decided to go AWOL instead, and went to stay with his grandparents in Livermore. When Baer failed to report for duty, the sergeant major of the Second Ranger Battalion repeatedly called his cell phone and left threatening messages. "He called me a deserter," says Baer. "He said I was the worst Ranger ever. I sat in my grandparents' house staring at a wall and didn't return the calls."

The day after the memorial service, Captain Richard Scott delivered the final report of his 15-6 investigation of Tillman's death to Lieutenant Colonel Bailey. Scott's 15-6 determined, among other things:

- "Leadership played a critical role and greatly contributed to the fratricide incident that killed SPC Pat Tillman."
- "By the time they were approaching the ridgeline where friendly forces were positioned; [sic] serial two was not receiving enemy fire. In fact, serial two never received effective enemy fire throughout the entire enemy contact. . . . It is clearly evident that the leaders in serial two failed to positively control their weapon systems and their Rangers."
- "Gross negligence" was a factor in Tillman's death, and headquarters should further investigate to determine whether there was criminal intent.

Scott's report went up the chain of command to Colonel Nixon and Lieutenant Colonel Bailey and then disappeared. In response to repeated inquiries about what happened to it, the Army simply replied, "It does not exist." Nixon would later explain to investigators that because he believed the inquiry was "deficient," he didn't consider it a "completed investigation" and never signed Scott's final report. Officially, therefore, the investigation never happened. Nixon opined that in hindsight, "Captain Scott did not have the experience to investigate the matter." On May 8, Nixon appointed Lieutenant Colonel Ralph Kauzlarich—Nixon's second-in-command, the executive officer of the Seventy-fifth Ranger Regiment—to initiate a new 15-6 investigation at the regimental level.

———

Following the memorial service in San Jose, Kevin and Marie returned to their house above Puget Sound. Although they did their best to struggle through each day, neither of them was ready to confront the gaping void left by Pat's absence.

Back in Afghanistan, the Black Sheep of Second Platoon continued to function as a combat unit even though Pat was dead and Uthlaut and Lane were in an Army hospital convalescing from their wounds. "Despite what happened," says Sergeant Bradley Shepherd, "it was still the beginning of our deployment, and we were in enemy territory. The Army needed us to be combat effective. They tried to get us to put everything behind us and focus on the matter at hand."

"They had to go back to trusting each other," Jade Lane elaborates. "It's a necessity over there. There was a war going on. Guys had to watch each other's backs. They had to do their jobs. I think they fell back into that groove pretty quickly and kept moving forward. But for some of us that just wasn't a possibility."

On the evening of May 22, exactly one month after Pat's death, the Black Sheep returned to Fort Lewis from Afghanistan. It was a Saturday night, so Kevin wasn't required to be at the base, but he drove in to greet his comrades when they arrived. "We were happy to be home," says Shepherd. "Guys were laughing and joking and looking forward to getting drunk, and Kevin was just standing there by the CQ desk, right inside the entrance, and I'll never forget the look on his face when we walked in. You could tell he was like, 'Pat is dead. How come everyone is celebrating?' He was hurt, and pissed, and I understand why. It haunts me to this day."

Kevin went home and didn't see any of the Black Sheep again until Monday morning when he reported for duty. He worked out with Ashpole and Elliott, oblivious to their role in Pat's death, and then helped his platoon mates sort out their gear and clean their weapons. Around 11:00 a.m., Sergeant Jeffrey Jackson, Kevin's squad leader, told him that Tommy Fuller, the first sergeant of Alpha Company, wanted to see him in his office.

Upon the Second Ranger Battalion's return to Fort Lewis, Lieutenant Colonel Bailey had realized they had a serious problem. More than a year remained on Kevin's Army contract, and he would be spending those months in close proximity with many soldiers who were privy to the circumstances of Pat's death. Some of those soldiers were upset about being ordered to lie. Guilt, anger, and alcohol were likely to loosen tongues.

According to Bailey's testimony, he called his boss, Colonel

Nixon, and said, "Sir . . . We're back, and I cannot separate these guys. I mean, you've got 600 Rangers. Everybody knows the story. This is going to get out. I'd like to go ahead and do it."

Without exception, every colonel and general officer interrogated by investigators—Bailey included—insisted that from the moment Pat was killed, he wanted to immediately notify the Tillman family that fratricide was the cause of their son's death. But each officer claimed that he felt obligated to wait until a thorough investigation had been completed in order to avoid telling "the family something that was not true," as Nixon phrased it, "and it took a considerable time to get the truth." All of them seemed to be reading from the same patently disingenuous script, reciting a series of self-serving rationalizations intended to justify what was actually a very calculated effort to deceive not just the Tillman family but also the American public—who of course was the real target of the misinformation campaign.

Each of the aforementioned officers testified under oath that there was never any doubt whatsoever that Tillman had been killed by friendly fire. Scott's investigation, which confirmed the fratricide, was completed on May 8 and then expunged, causing it for all intents and purposes to vanish from the face of the earth. Kauzlarich's investigation, which unequivocally determined that "Corporal Tillman's death was the result of fratricide," was completed on May 16, but then kept under extremely tight wraps, treated as if it were a grave threat to national security.

Nixon's sworn testimony notwithstanding, it's difficult to fathom how the obsessive secrecy, falsified documents, and destruction of evidence were intended to protect the family from receiving a false impression of how Pat died. The available evidence indicates the Seventy-fifth Ranger Regiment engaged in an elaborate conspiracy to deliberately mislead the family, and high-ranking officials at the White House and the Pentagon abetted the deception. As Bailey's testimony underscores, the only reason the Army finally decided to come clean was that Kevin was about to learn the truth on his own.

When Bailey recognized that it was no longer possible to keep the secret contained, First Sergeant Fuller was ordered to break the news to Kevin. After being summoned to Fuller's office, Kevin sat down and listened as Alpha Company's highest-ranking noncommissioned officer explained that Pat "may have been killed" by Rangers in his own platoon, but the words didn't register. "It just didn't make any sense," Kevin testified. He had been told that Pat was "running up the hill and he got shot. . . . But I didn't—it just didn't even cross my mind that he got hit by his own guys. . . . I mean, it didn't cross my mind at all. . . . I thought he had been killed by the enemy."

Kevin was reeling when he walked out of Fuller's office. He'd just spent the morning working alongside the soldiers who were responsible for his brother's death, and they had all acted like everything was fine. "I did my PT [physical training] with two of the people that killed Pat," Kevin testified, "and then went to breakfast with the PL [platoon leader] who eventually got fired—telling him, 'Hey, you did a good job out there'—not having a clue what really went on in that first part, so I'm trying to pump the PL up."

Kevin went home and told Marie what had just been revealed to him. A day later Bailey came to their house and officially notified them that fratricide was the cause of Pat's death. Bailey, Kevin, and Marie then made plans to fly to San Jose so that Kevin could inform his parents in person late Friday night, May 28. Bailey assured Kevin and Marie that no information would be released to the media until the rest of the Tillman family had been notified.

Kevin was told of the fratricide by the Alpha Company first sergeant on Monday, May 24. So why did Bailey wait until the night of the twenty-eighth to notify the Tillman parents? The timing is baffling until one learns that the decision by Bailey and Nixon to preemptively let the cat out of the bag caught the Pentagon and the White House by surprise, and generated no small amount of consternation at those institutions. Rumsfeld's office wanted time to come up with a plan for containing the damage before the news was released to the media. Toward that end, it was decided that there would be no public disclosure until Saturday, May 29—the start of the Memorial Day weekend, when few reporters would be at their desks and not many Americans would be paying attention to the news.

On May 28 a video teleconference was held on a secure military network to hash out a game plan for announcing the fratricide. Participating were Bryan Brown, the four-star general in command of

USSOC; Vice Admiral Eric Olson, deputy commander of USSOC; Lieutenant General Kensinger, commander of USASOC; Lieutenant General James Lovelace, representing the secretary of the Army; Major General R. Steven Whitcomb, CENTCOM chief of staff; a smattering of colonels; at least one lawyer; and Lawrence Di Rita, the number-two guy at the Pentagon, who was a close personal friend of Rumsfeld's. Although Di Rita's official title was assistant secretary of defense for public affairs, his responsibilities at the Pentagon were considerably greater than merely serving as Rumsfeld's press secretary. In truth, Di Rita's relationship with Rumsfeld was roughly analogous to Lewis "Scooter" Libby's relationship with Dick Cheney, or Karl Rove's relationship with the president. Di Rita was a major player in the Bush administration.

The ensuing discussion between Di Rita and the military brass was tense. The greatest disagreement concerned the choice of a spokesman to stand before the television cameras and announce that the Army had shot its poster boy. General Brown wanted someone from Rumsfeld's office to do it, but Di Rita immediately quashed that idea. Part of his job was to make sure Rumsfeld's fingerprints were wiped clean from crime scenes like this; he wasn't about to let anyone associated with his boss appear within a hundred miles of this scandal. Instead, Di Rita decreed that a uniformed general would be the bearer of bad tidings. Because Tillman was a Ranger who had been killed by fellow Rangers, and it was the Ranger Regiment that had failed to keep a lid on the fratricide, the job was given to Kensinger, the highest-ranking officer in the Ranger chain of command. "They wanted to keep, sir, the other organizations separate from it," a colonel who was present explained to an investigator. Everyone agreed that under no circumstances should Kensinger take any questions from the media after making the announcement. The press briefing was scheduled for the following morning at Fort Bragg, North Carolina.

Friday afternoon, in advance of the briefing, Dannie Tillman got home from work to find a message on her machine from Billy House, a reporter at the *Arizona Republic,* the Phoenix newspaper, asking her to call him. When she phoned him back, House asked what she thought of the news he'd just received from an Army source that Pat's death may have been from friendly fire. Having been told repeatedly that Pat had been shot by the Taliban, Dannie slammed the phone down, stunned. The news had been leaked to the press before she had been notified.

Later that evening, Kevin called Steve White, the Navy SEAL he and Pat had befriended in Iraq, to tell him that Pat was a victim of fratricide. When White learned that he had been used to deliver propaganda, he testified, "I was shocked." He said he felt let down by "my military. . . . I am the guy that told America how he died, basically, at that memorial, and it was incorrect. That does not sit well with me."

The next morning at 9:15, Kensinger stood stiffly before the assembled news media at Fort Bragg and recited his lines, which had been vetted by Di Rita:

> Good morning. I would like to make a brief statement on the events surrounding the death of Corporal Pat Tillman on 22 April in Afghanistan. I will not be taking questions. A military investigation by U.S. Central Command into the circumstances of the 22 April death of Corporal Patrick Tillman is complete. While there was no one specific finding of fault, the investigation results indicate that Corporal Tillman probably died as a result of friendly fire while his unit was engaged in combat with enemy forces. . . . We regret the loss of life resulting from this tragic accident. Our thoughts and our prayers remain with the Tillman family. Thank you all for being here this morning.

At the insistence of his superiors, the statement Kensinger had been given to read declared that "Tillman *probably* died as a result of friendly fire," even though the official investigation was unequivocal in its determination that fratricide was the cause of death.

Following the press conference, perception managers from the Pentagon congratulated each other for limiting the damage. An Army colonel noted in an e-mail that the "story will run hot today and diminish over the weekend." A CENTCOM public affairs officer replied encouragingly that a recent attack in Saudi Arabia would help "dilute the story somewhat."

Kensinger's brief, insincere announcement on that Saturday morning would turn out to be the only public statement issued by any official from the White House or the Pentagon acknowledging that Tillman had been killed by American soldiers, not enemy insurgents, as the world had been actively encouraged to believe.

CHAPTER THIRTY-FOUR

Over the previous weeks, the Tillman family had been starting to come to terms with Pat's death. Then came the revelation of fratricide, which made them feel like he had been killed all over again. One small consolation was that the family learned an investigation had been completed—Lieutenant Colonel Kauzlarich's 15-6. They were invited to Fort Lewis on June 16, 2004, to receive a briefing on its conclusions from Colonel Nixon and Lieutenant Colonel Bailey, prompting Pat's father to request a copy of the 15-6 report before the briefing, in order to be able to ask informed questions. The Army refused to provide one in advance.

The meeting lasted for three hours. Bailey gave a PowerPoint presentation to explain how the fatal firefight unfolded. When the Tillmans asked if the soldiers responsible for Pat's death would be court-martialed, Bailey replied that he didn't know. Nor did Bailey or Nixon provide satisfactory answers to most of the other questions the family asked. As the meeting ended, the Tillmans were belatedly handed copies of the 15-6 report, which only raised even more disturbing questions.

When the Army announced the disciplinary action that had been taken in response to Pat's death, the Tillmans were stunned. Major David Hodne and Captain William Saunders each received nothing more than a written reprimand for "failing to provide adequate command control of subordinate units." Staff Sergeant Greg Baker was busted in rank and "released for standards"—"RFS'd," in Army lingo—meaning he was expelled from the Rangers and sent to the regular Army. The three machine gunners in Baker's Humvee—Trevor Alders, Steve Elliott, and Stephen Ashpole—were also RFS'd from the Rangers to the regular Army. Lieutenant David Uthlaut, the platoon leader, was RFS'd and received a verbal reprimand from Bailey for "dereliction of duty." For their part, Bailey was promoted from lieutenant colonel to the rank of colonel, and Nixon was made a brigadier general. All of which was regarded by the Tillman family as a despicable affront to Pat.

Some soldiers in Second Platoon took issue with the discipline meted out as well. There was unanimous agreement that Uthlaut was scapegoated. "Everybody thinks Uthlaut got the shaft," says Jade Lane. "They shit-canned the PL for splitting the platoon, even though he didn't want to split it at all. But because he was responsible for the platoon overall, he was booted out of the Rangers. If the Army has to decide whether to punish a lieutenant colonel at headquarters or a lieutenant in the field, you better believe the lieutenant's going to take the hit every time. Shit rolls downhill."

Lane says there was disagreement among his platoon mates about the punishments doled out to Baker and the shooters:

Some guys were like, "It was an accident. It was nobody's fault." Well, I think everybody realized it was an accident. They didn't shoot Pat and the AMF soldier on purpose. But some of us felt like the shooters were responsible for their actions, and the Army should have held them more accountable than they did. I'm not saying they need prison time. But to get nothing more than an RFS—that's a slap on the wrist. You can get RFS'd for accidentally discharging your weapon, or not showing up for formation, or talking back to an officer. You can get RFS'd for getting a traffic ticket. So the Army gives the same punishment for killing two innocent people? The punishment just doesn't fit the crime.

Despite the lenient sanctions given to Greg Baker, Trevor Alders, Stephen Ashpole, and Steve Elliott, all four soldiers objected vehemently when they learned they had been RFS'd, insisting that getting booted out of the Rangers for the fratricides of Tillman and Farhad was draconian. The greatest objections came from Trevor Alders, the SAW gunner who, according to the available evidence, fired the bullets that ended Tillman's life. On June 4, Alders submitted a five-and-a-half-page, single-spaced letter in which he insisted he did nothing wrong and implored the Seventy-fifth Ranger Regiment to reconsider his punishment. "I believe my actions were the right thing at the right time since I was not aware of a friendly force nearby," he wrote.

> I am adamant to state my case before those making the decision on my fate because I do not feel justified in being Released For Standards. . . . One thing that makes this so hard is that someone who does not know the people I work with or me is making this decision regarding my career and my life. . . . I ask why is it that a young Ranger that does everything that is taught to him to do to be successful on the battlefield is being released? . . . I went off the information that was at my disposal at that specific time to make the decision in that firefight. Is it my fault that the area of operation for the other half of my element was not pointed out since we changed our route in the beginning of our movement? . . . I do not think that I should be Released For Standards from the unit that I love, dedicated so much to, and sacrificed so much for. . . . If I am removed from the Regiment for this I do not feel the proper justice will have been done. . . . I am the littlest man in all of this being only 140 pounds soaking wet at 5'5" and if I have to have the largest voice on this then I will because if my [chain of command] won't support what they have trained me to do then who will? I have not pushed myself to keep up and surpass others around me just to be fired without my honor as a warrior. . . . I gave 100% and then some every time I did anything in this unit. . . . Now someone wants to rip the heart out of me. . . . I hope that after reading this you will take into consideration all that I have stated when it comes time to make your decision. I pray to God almighty that justice will be done and my fate to be an honorable one. Rangers Lead The Way!

The thrust of Alders's letter seemed to be that the primary victim of the tragedy was not Pat Tillman or Sayed Farhad but Trevor Alders.

On Sunday, September 19, 2004, during halftime of a football game between the New England Patriots and the Arizona Cardinals played in Tempe, the Cardinals honored Pat with a halftime ceremony, during which Marie, Richard, and Pat's parents walked out onto the field and stood on the fifty-yard line. Marie received heartfelt cheers when she expressed thanks to the crowd for the overwhelming support the Tillman family had received from Arizonans. A huge Cardinals jersey imprinted with the number 40 was unfurled in the bleachers. Up on the JumboTron, President George W. Bush delivered a brief video tribute to Pat, but the crowd greeted the canned speech with a loud chorus of boos, apparently believing the gesture was inspired not by any genuine respect for Tillman, but rather because Bush was trailing in most opinion polls and the presidential election was just forty-four days away.

Because the Army had betrayed Dannie Tillman's trust so completely, and because she had come to the conclusion that it was more interested in burying the truth than in illuminating it, soon after the Cardinals' tribute she compiled a long list of questions that Lieutenant Colonel Kauzlarich's 15-6 investigation had failed to answer to her satisfaction. Then she e-mailed the questions to John McCain, the senator representing Pat's home state of Arizona, along with a formal request that he help her receive the information she sought.

The nature of the anguish felt by the bereaved when a husband, child, or sibling is killed in combat varies from person to person but is almost always devastating. When the cause of that loss is fratricide, the torment is apt to be greater still. It is not unusual for survivors of the deceased to be overwhelmed by their woe, and to sink into a state of despair that renders them passive and numb. It would have been convenient for the Army, the Pentagon, and the White House if the Tillmans had succumbed meekly to their pain in this fashion, allowing the incident to fade unobtrusively into the past, hidden among the war's long tally of other tragedies. If that's what these institutions anticipated, however, they underestimated the tenacity of Dannie Tillman. Channeling her grief into determination, she resolved to take whatever steps were necessary to uncover what really happened to her son, and to discover why the Army lied to her family and the nation, after which she intended to hold the guilty parties accountable.

Thanks to her perseverance, on November 8—six days after George W. Bush was elected to a second term as president—Kensinger appointed Brigadier General Gary Jones, the commander of the Army Special Forces, to conduct still another 15-6 investigation to address new questions raised by the Tillman family. Yet again, however, the Army was being investigated by itself.

As part of General Jones's inquiry, on November 13 he interviewed Kauzlarich. Near the end of this interrogation, Kauzlarich became defensive about a number of deficiencies in his investigation alleged by Dannie Tillman. "Nobody is satisfied with the answers in that family that they've been given," he complained.

"Why do you think that the family is not satisfied?" Jones asked.

Kauzlarich explained that shortly before the Second Ranger Battalion sent Pat's remains home from Afghanistan, he was arranging a repatriation ceremony when a sergeant approached him and said, "Hey, sir. Kevin Tillman doesn't want a chaplain involved in his repatriation ceremony." When Kauzlarich, an evangelical Christian, asked why, the sergeant replied, "Well, evidently he and his brother are atheists. That's the way they were raised."

To which Kauzlarich angrily declaimed, "Well, you can tell Specialist Tillman that his ceremony ain't about him, it is about everybody in the Joint Task Force bidding farewell to his brother, so there will be a chaplain and there will be prayers."

Pat had in fact made his wishes known quite explicitly in this regard, and had clearly stated his views on religion, life, and death on several occasions as well. During his time on earth, he wrote in his journal while serving in Iraq, he wanted "to do good, influence lives, show truth and right." He believed it was important to have "faith in oneself" and to aspire to "a general goodness free of religious pretensions. . . . I've never feared death per se, or really given a shit what happens 'after.' I'll cross that bridge when I come to it. My concerns have to do with the 'now' and becoming the man I envision. . . . I think I understand that religious faith which makes the holy brave and strong; my strength is just somewhere else—it's in myself. . . . I do not fear what may await me, though I'm equally confident that nothing awaits."

Before deploying to Iraq, Pat had filled out a standard Army document noting his preferences for funeral arrangements in the event of his death, in which he unequivocally declared that he did not want either a chaplain or a civilian minister to officiate at any memorial services that might be held, and that all arrangements pertaining to his death or funeral should be made by Marie. On the final line of the document, which asked if he had "any special instructions," Pat scrawled in block letters, "I do not want the military to have any direct involvement with my funeral."

The fact that neither Pat, nor Marie, nor any of the other Tillmans wanted a military chaplain to formally offer prayers at a memorial service for Pat was incomprehensible to Kauzlarich. "Those that are Christians can come to terms with faith and the fact there is an afterlife, heaven, or whatnot," he testified to Jones. "I'm not really sure what they believe or how they can get their head around death. So, in my personal opinion, sir, that is why I don't think they'll ever be satisfied."

Kauzlarich speculated further on the relationship between the Tillmans' religious views and their dissatisfaction with the investigations during a subsequent interview with the journalist Mike Fish, published online at ESPN.com:

KAUZLARICH: There's been numerous unfortunate cases of
        fratricide, and the parents have basically said, OK, it was an
        unfortunate accident. And they let it go. So, this is—I don't
        know, these people have a hard time letting it go. It may be
        because of their religious beliefs. . . . So when you die, I
        mean there is supposedly a better life, right? Well, if you are
        an atheist and you don't believe in anything, if you die what
        is there to go to? Nothing. You're worm dirt. So for their
        son to die for nothing, and now he is no more—that is
        pretty hard to get your head around that. You know? So I
        don't know, I don't know how an atheist thinks. I can only
        imagine that that would be pretty tough.
    FISH: So you suspect that is probably a reason that this thing is
        dragging on?
KAUZLARICH: I think so. . . .
    FISH: OK. What do you think would make the family happy? . . .

KAUZLARICH: You know what, I don't think anything will make
them happy, quite honestly. I don't know, maybe they want
to see somebody's head on a platter. But will that really
make them happy? No, because they can't bring their son
back.

On May 16, 2007, in a letter to Kauzlarich's commanding officer, Major General Carter Ham, and Representatives Henry Waxman (Democrat) and Tom Davis (Republican) of the House Committee on Oversight and Government Reform declared, "We believe these statements were crass, insulting to the Tillman family, and completely inappropriate for an Army officer and an official representative of the U.S. military speaking to the press."

For her part, Dannie Tillman told Waxman that she was "appalled" by Lieutenant Colonel Kauzlarich's comments, which revealed his utter failure to grasp why the Tillman family was angry.

———

In March 2005, the Jones investigation was completed and approved by his superiors. This 15-6 was much more thorough than the one done by Kauzlarich, and if one takes the time to painstakingly study its bewildering, heavily redacted 2,099 pages, one is rewarded with a reasonable understanding of how Tillman was killed, and how the Army's bungled response to the fratricide unfolded. But the evidence buried among the pages of the report did not support the most important conclusions ultimately issued by General Jones, leaving the Tillman family more dissatisfied and distrustful than ever. After relentless prodding from Pat's mother, in August 2005 the Department of Defense inspector general's office announced that it would conduct a "review of the Army's handling of the Tillman incident."

Seventeen months later, on March 26, 2007, portions of this review—which was authored by Thomas F. Gimble, the acting inspector general—were made public. At one point during Gimble's investigation, Dr. Craig Mallak—the pathologist who performed Pat's autopsy, the chief of the Armed Forces medical examiners—was asked, "Would you have any reason to believe that this would be anything other than a friendly fire? For instance, do you think that there would be any criminal intent on somebody's part?"

Without hesitation, Dr. Mallak replied, "Sure. . . . It makes us suspicious because every story, including the most current 15-6, doesn't match the medical evidence." One of the inconsistencies that troubled Mallak was the fact that the three .223-caliber rounds that killed Tillman struck his brow in an exceedingly tight cluster, less than two inches from one another. "I've asked everybody in the office," Mallak testified, "if they thought they could [shoot] a cluster that closely together of three rounds from an M16—a three-round burst from 100 yards, from 50 yards—and everybody said no." Mallak then offered a hypothesis that might explain the exceedingly close proximity of Tillman's wounds: "If somebody said, 'Yeah, I spun around and a three-round burst went off on my M16 and I was about ten yards away,' I would say, 'OK, that makes sense.' "

Based on this testimony, the journalist Martha Mendoza wrote an article for the Associated Press published on July 27, 2007, in which she reported that Mallak "said that the bullet holes were so close together that it appeared [Tillman] was cut down by an M-16 fired from a mere 10 yards or so away." Predictably, Mendoza's article uncorked a torrent of speculation that Tillman had been deliberately assassinated—speculation that still rages among conspiracy theorists today. But Mallak had assumed the bullets that killed Tillman had been fired from an M16 (or an M4, a very similar weapon), because he was unaware that Trevor Alders had been firing a Squad Automatic Weapon—which happens to use the same ammunition as the M16 and M4.

Unbeknownst to Mallak (and Mendoza), in November 2006, Dr. Robert Bux and Dr. Vincent DiMaio—forensic pathologists considered to be among the world's leading authorities on gunshot wounds—had carefully examined Mallak's autopsy report and photographs and concluded, "The pattern of the bullet impacts suggests that the rounds were all part of a single burst from the Squad Automatic Weapon." Several expert SAW gunners, including members of Tillman's platoon, have confirmed that it would not be especially difficult for a competent SAW gunner to place three rounds within a two-inch-diameter target from a distance of forty or fifty yards, even while shooting from a moving vehicle.

An unfortunate aspect of the hysteria ignited by Mendoza's article was that it obscured the fact that Gimble's investigation confirmed most of the failings in Jones's 15-6 asserted by Dannie Tillman. Gimble found, for example, that "Corporal Tillman's chain of command made critical errors in reporting Corporal Tillman's death and . . . bears ultimate responsibility for the inaccuracies, misunderstandings, and perceptions of concealment that led to our review." But Gimble was much too credulous in accepting testimony from high-ranking Army officers that the chain of command had acted in good faith. He saw the problem as little more than "perceptions of concealment" rather than deliberate acts of deception on the part of the Army. Inexplicably, and by his own admission, Gimble also made no effort to investigate the role his boss, Donald Rumsfeld, or the White House may have played in the cover-up.

On April 24, the House of Representatives Committee on Oversight and Government Reform, chaired by Henry Waxman, summoned Gimble to explain the apparent shortcomings of his two-year inquiry at a hearing titled "Misleading Information from the Battlefield." Representative John Sarbanes of Maryland said to Gimble, "You talk about how the first investigation [Captain Scott's 15-6] was deficient. The second investigation [Kauzlarich's 15-6] was deficient. Then there was a third investigation [Jones's 15-6] that was deficient. There was a failure to abide by the protocols that would normally be triggered right away in terms of having a legal investigation into friendly fire death . . . , that the Regimental Commander [Colonel Nixon] failed to notify the Army Safety Center of a suspected friendly fire death as required by Army regulation." Sarbanes was therefore puzzled by Gimble's "strange credulity," pointing out that when Army officers repeatedly violated procedures and protocols, "it makes it hard to believe that after a certain point of time this was accidental—that there wasn't some kind of pressure; maybe not direct, but an atmosphere of indirect pressure being brought to bear." Gimble did not dispute Sarbanes's observation.

In addition to Gimble, Jessica Lynch, Kevin Tillman, Dannie Tillman, Bryan O'Neal, and Steve White testified at the hearing. Lynch recalled how her family's home "was under siege by the media, all repeating the story of the little girl from West Virginia who went down fighting. It was not true. . . . The bottom line is the American people are capable of determining their own ideals for heroes. They don't need to be told elaborate lies. . . . The truth of war is not always easy. The truth is always more heroic than the hype."

When it was Kevin Tillman's turn to testify, he spoke about his older brother at length, and with electrifying conviction:

> Revealing that Pat's death was a fratricide would have been yet another political disaster during a month already swollen with political disasters, and a brutal truth that the American public would undoubtedly find unacceptable. So the facts needed to be suppressed. An alternative narrative needed to be constructed. . . .
>
> Over a month after Pat's death, when it became clear that it would no longer be possible to pull off this deception, a few of the facts were parceled out to the public and to the family. General Kensinger was ordered to tell the American public . . . that Pat died of fratricide, but with a calculated and nefarious twist. He stated, "There was no one specific finding of fault," and that he "probably died of fratricide." But there *was* specific fault, and there was nothing probable about the facts that led to Pat's death. . . .
>
> After the truth of Pat's death was partially revealed, Pat was no longer of use as a sales asset, and became strictly the Army's problem. They were now left with the task of briefing our family and answering our questions. With any luck, our family would sink quietly into our grief, and the whole unsavory episode would be swept under the rug. However, they miscalculated our family's reaction.
>
> Through the amazing strength and perseverance of my mother, the most amazing woman on Earth, our family has managed to have multiple investigations conducted. However, while each investigation gathered more information, the mountain of evidence was never used to arrive at an honest or even sensible conclusion. . . .
>
> The handling of the situation after the firefight was described as a compilation of "missteps, inaccuracies, and errors in judgment which created the perception of concealment." . . . Writing a Silver Star award before a single eyewitness account is taken is not a misstep. Falsifying soldier witness statements for a Silver Star is not a misstep. These are intentional falsehoods that meet the legal definition for fraud.
>
> Delivering false information at a nationally televised memorial

service is not an error in judgment. Discarding an investigation [Scott's 15-6] that does not fit a preordained conclusion is not an error in judgment. These are deliberate acts of deceit. This is not the perception of concealment. This *is* concealment.

Pat is, of course, not the only soldier where battlefield reality has reached the family and the public in the form of a false narrative. . . .

Our family has relentlessly pursued the truth on this matter for three years. We have now concluded that our efforts are being actively thwarted by powers that are more . . . interested in protecting a narrative than getting at the truth or seeing that justice is served.

That is why we ask Congress, as a sovereign representative of the whole people, to exercise its power to investigate the inconsistencies in Pat's death and the aftermath and all the other soldiers that were betrayed by this system.

The one bit of truth that did survive these manipulations is that Pat was, and still is, a great man. . . .

But the fact that the Army, and what appears to be others, attempted to hijack his virtue and his legacy is simply horrific. The least this country can do for him in return is to uncover who is responsible for his death, who lied and who covered it up, and who instigated those lies and benefited from them. Then ensure that justice is meted out to the culpable.

Pat and these other soldiers volunteered to put their lives on the line for this country. Anything less than the truth is a betrayal of those values that all soldiers who have fought for this nation have sought to uphold.

Waxman, the oversight committee chairman, observed,

The Tillman family wants to know how all of this could have happened. . . . One of the things that make the Afghanistan and Iraq wars so different from previous wars is the glaring disparity of sacrifice. For the overwhelming number of Americans, this war has brought no sacrifice and no inconvenience, but for a small number of Americans, the war has demanded incredible and constant sacrifice. Those soldiers and their families pay that price proudly and without complaint. This is what Jessica Lynch and Pat Tillman did, and it is

what their families have done, but our government failed them. . . .
The least we owe to courageous men and women who are fighting
for our freedom is the truth.

At the end of the hearing, Waxman stated in frustration, "What
we have is a very clear, deliberate abuse intentionally done. Why is it
so hard to find out who did it?"

On July 31, 2007, Secretary of the Army Pete Geren held a press
conference at the Pentagon to answer this and other questions about
the alleged cover-up. Brushing aside overwhelming evidence to the
contrary, Geren simply asserted that there was no cover-up. Although
he admitted that there were "errors and failures of leadership," he insisted there was "no intent to deceive" by anyone in the Army: "No
one has found evidence of a conspiracy by the Army to fabricate a
hero, deceive the public or mislead the Tillman family about the circumstances of Corporal Tillman's death." The perception that the
Army vigorously misled both the Tillmans and the public for five
weeks, Geren assured the assembled media, resulted from nothing
more than a "misunderstanding of Army regulations and policy
about secrecy.

"Almost incredibly, but true," he insisted with a straight face, it
was merely a coincidence that Army personnel falsified documents,
withheld information, and violated regulations "up and down the
chain of command. . . . There was no cover-up. There was misin-
formed action on the part of multiple soldiers, and you had a perfect
storm of mistakes by many soldiers."*

This was a new tack. For three years the Army had been insisting it misled the Tillman family in order to avoid telling them
"something that was not true," as Colonel Nixon put it. Perhaps
Geren realized that Nixon's rationale was rather too reminiscent

* Geren nevertheless announced the punishment of one officer: Lieutenant General
Kensinger, who had retired from the Army eighteen months previously, was cen-
sured for lying under oath to investigators. This prompted a reporter to ask Geren,
"You've described a litany of errors and mistakes going more than three years involving a lot of people, yet all the blame falls on General Kensinger. . . . He happens to be retired. Is there a coincidence there?" To which Geren replied, "I believe
the buck stops with General Kensinger."

of the infamous explanation given by an Army major in 1968 in response to questions from journalists about why it was necessary to wipe out the Vietnamese village of Ben Tre during the Tet Offensive. "We had to destroy Ben Tre," explained the officer, "in order to save it."

For whatever reason, Geren jettisoned Colonel Nixon's fatuous rationale, choosing instead to defend the cover-up with a fresh bit of casuistry. Rangers are Special Operations Forces, went Geren's new reasoning, so Tillman's platoon was by definition on a covert mission that had to be kept secret. This, despite the fact that it was supposed to be a routine clearing operation that had been piggybacked onto the platoon's journey back to FOB Salerno: "Hey, let's just . . . turn one last stone and then get out" is how Major Hodne described the mission in his testimony during the Jones 15-6 investigation. As Hodne explained, the only reason the Black Sheep were dispatched to Mana in the first place was to check the village off a list so Alpha Company could proceed to a new area of operations.

In Geren's telling, however, it was an important Spec Ops mission, which meant that it was supposed to be covert. After Tillman was killed, soldiers in the Seventy-fifth Ranger Regiment were therefore under the impression "they were to keep all information close-hold, including keeping it from the family until the investigations were complete and approved by higher authority."

But this fails to explain why, if the Rangers believed it was crucial for "operational security" to keep details of the mission secret, the Army didn't keep details about the Silver Star Tillman had been awarded during the mission "close-hold," or why the Navy SEAL Steve White was given an account of the fatal firefight to read at Tillman's nationally televised memorial service. Such mendacity has damaged the Army's credibility beyond repair in the eyes of the Tillman family.

On August 9, 2007, nine days after Geren addressed the nation, President Bush held a press conference at the White House to trumpet his signing of an unrelated bill titled the "American Competitiveness Initiative." Afterward, while taking questions from the press, the president was asked about Tillman by the CNN correspondent Ed Henry:

HENRY: You speak often about taking care of the troops and
honoring their sacrifice. But the family of Corporal Pat
Tillman believes there was a cover up regarding his death,
and some say perhaps he was even murdered, instead of just
friendly fire. At a hearing last week on Capitol Hill your
former Defense Secretary, Donald Rumsfeld, and other
officials used some version of "I don't recall" 82 times.
When it was his turn to step up, Pat Tillman gave up a
lucrative NFL career, served his country and paid the
ultimate sacrifice. Now you have a chance to pledge to the
family that your government, your administration will
finally get to the bottom of it. Can you make that pledge to
the family today, that you'll finally, after seven
investigations, find out what really happened?

BUSH: Well, first of all, I can understand why Pat Tillman's family,
you know, has got significant emotions, because a man they
loved and respected was killed while he was serving his
country. I always admired the fact that a person who was
relatively comfortable in life would be willing to take off
one uniform and put on another to defend America. And the
best way to honor that commitment of his is to find out the
truth. And I'm confident the Defense Department wants to
find out the truth, too, and we'll lay it out for the Tillman
family to know.

HENRY: But, Mr. President, there have been seven investigations
and the Pentagon has not gotten to the bottom of it. Can
you also tell us when you, personally, found out that it was
not enemy fire, that it was friendly fire?

BUSH: I can't give you the precise moment. But obviously the
minute I heard that the facts that people believed were true
were not true, that I expect there to be a full investigation
and get to the bottom of it.

The president neglected to mention that three months earlier, as
part of the investigation launched by Congress to finally and defini-
tively "get to the bottom of it," Representative Waxman had sent a
letter to the White House formally requesting "all documents re-

ceived or generated by any official in the Executive Office of the President, including the Communications Office and Office of Speechwriting . . . that relate to Corporal Tillman," and sent a similar request to the Department of Defense. The recipients responded by sending Waxman more than thirty thousand pages of material, most of which were nothing more than press clippings about Tillman. E-mails, memos, and other documents that might have shed light on the cover-up were conspicuously withheld. As Emmet T. Flood, special counsel to the president, explained, "We have not produced certain documents responsive to the Committee's request because they implicate Executive Branch confidentiality interests." Despite praising Tillman's patriotism and courage at every opportunity, the White House in fact used every means at its disposal to obstruct the congressional investigation into Tillman's death and its aftermath, President Bush's blithe assurances notwithstanding.

In a report issued in July 2008, Waxman's oversight committee noted, "The White House was intensely interested in the first reports of Tillman's death," sending or receiving some two hundred e-mails concerning Tillman on the day following the tragedy. But after the Army belatedly revealed to the American public that he was the victim of fratricide, "the White House could not produce a single e-mail or document relating to any discussion about Corporal Tillman's death by friendly fire. . . . [T]he intense interest that initially characterized the White House's and Defense Department's reaction to Corporal Tillman's death was followed by a stunning lack of curiosity about emerging reports of fratricide and an incomprehensible carelessness and incompetence in handling this sensitive information."

CHAPTER THIRTY-FIVE

On April 25, 2004, three days after Tillman's passing, the Black Sheep of Second Platoon assembled at FOB Salerno to debrief and decompress. The meeting was led by a chaplain, an Army captain named Jeff Struecker, who was famous in the Ranger Regiment and beyond for surviving the disastrous 1993 firefight in Mogadishu, Somalia, described in the best-selling book *Black Hawk Down,* by Mark Bowden. A number of the Rangers were distraught over Tillman's death, and looked to Struecker for guidance.

"Speaking from his experience in Somalia, Chaplain Struecker said it really helped him to talk about what happened over there, instead of carrying it around inside," says Mel Ward, remembering that meeting. "I'm not religious in any way, but Pat was a personal friend, and to have to package him and handle his body like we did . . . I didn't know what the long-term effects of that would be. You see these old guys on the History Channel talking about being in World War II. A guy will still be bawling over some friend that died sixty years earlier. I don't want to be that guy. So I talked about what happened, my little piece of it. Others did too."

Ward didn't judge any of the other soldiers, even the shooters—not initially. But then he heard that some of them may have gotten together and changed their stories between the first investigation and the second. "I would not ordinarily point fingers at anyone on the ground," he says. "Friendly fire happens. But if someone has lied or changed their story, they can fucking hang. I don't care who they are. If you are going to lie and cover up what happened to someone who gave their life, who believed so firmly in the importance of coming over here that he left his wife without a husband—then you deserve to fucking swing. When I started hearing about the false award recommendations, spinning the facts, changing their stories—I was so pissed. The dishonor the Army is doing to Pat's family by the things that have led to this fucking media frenzy, it's unforgivable."

After Pat's death, Ward decided not to reenlist when his Ranger contract was up. Although being a noncommissioned officer in the Special Operations Forces, he says, "is something I'm naturally good at," the aftermath of the Tillman fratricide left him terminally disillusioned with the Army leadership. "From the moment you first join the Ranger Battalion," Ward explains,

> it's ingrained in you that you will always do the right thing. They're not like, "Please do the right thing." It's "We will fucking crush you if you don't do the right thing." You will adhere to every standard. You will always tell the truth. If you fuck up once, you're out on your ass. Then you see something like what they're doing to Pat—what officers in the Ranger Regiment are doing—and you stop being so naive. The only two times where I personally was in a position to see where the Army had the choice to do the right thing or the wrong thing, both times they chose to do the wrong thing. One of those times was what they did to Pat. It made me realize that the Army does what suits the Army. That's why I won't put that uniform back on. I'm done.
>
> If I had been killed that day, and it had not suited the Army to disclose to my wife the manner in which I died, nobody would ever know what really happened because I'm not famous. I'm not Pat. It wouldn't have been a news story. For the rest of her life, my wife would think I was killed by whatever bullshit story they decided to make up. They'd write up a couple of medals like they did for him, and that would be it.
>
> I think my wife would deserve to know the truth about how her husband died. And I think Pat's wife deserves the same.

The enormity of Dannie Tillman's loss drove her to embark upon what has proven to be a Sisyphean effort to pry truth and justice from the Army and the U.S. government. Pat's death provoked a different kind of reaction in Marie Tillman.

"I didn't feel like I could focus on the investigation and maintain my sanity," Marie explained in September 2006, still trying to cope with Pat's death two and a half years after his passing.

> I would read through the documents, picture Pat being shot, and it haunted me.. I couldn't detach this person that I loved from the horrific details in the documents, and I couldn't function in that state of mind. I had a lot of guilt at first that I wasn't able to focus on fighting the military, but I also realized that if I went down that path, I'm not sure I could have kept it together. When Pat died, I shut down in a lot of ways—I lived in a pretty dark, quiet place for years and struggled. . . .
>
> I have an enormous amount of respect for Dannie and how she has handled everything. Trying to get answers from the military is like banging your head against a wall, and she carried that burden for all of us. I wasn't able to do it, but I'm grateful for her strength, and what she has done to uncover the truth and hold people accountable. To know Pat and know how he lived his life, and then to see how his death was treated by the military and government is heartbreaking—it goes against everything he stood for.

In May 2004, a week after the memorial service for Pat in San Jose, Marie returned to her rented home overlooking Puget Sound. "I got back to town on a Monday or Tuesday," she remembers.

> I wasn't supposed to return to the office until the following week, but I was just sitting around the house. So I went back to work.
>
> Probably for the first couple of months that I was back, I would sit at my desk and look out the window all day. The company I worked for was really understanding. They let me come in and just sit there. I had no idea what I was supposed to do next. The life I'd

had was basically gone. So every morning I would get up at quarter to five, get in the car, go up to Seattle, and look out the window. I'd get home at seven at night, sit on the couch for an hour, talk to Kevin, and go to bed. That was it. And I did that for months and months and months and months.

Kevin decided he was going to stay in the Army and finish his commitment. In some ways that made things easier for me, and I decided to stay there with him. It gave me some time before I needed to make any decisions about where to go.

Kevin fulfilled his contract with the Army in July 2005. "By that time," says Marie, "I knew I needed to leave. I was like, 'If I don't leave now, I'll never leave.' That's what I felt—that I'd just keep doing what I'd been doing. The house was exactly like it was the day Pat left for Afghanistan. Right after he died, it was comforting to be there. And then it got to a point where it made me really sad to be there. There was a layer of dust everywhere, and . . ." She pauses to collect herself. "And it was just really sad. . . . So I packed up everything and came here."

"Here" is New York City, where Marie found a job and a small apartment on Manhattan's Upper East Side. "It was great that Kevin and I had each other for support that first year," she says. "But then I needed to get away. Not from him—I just felt the need to get away from everything. That was part of my reason for moving here. . . . The city can be a good distraction.

"Everybody deals with grief in different ways," Marie points out. "I kind of retreat. I just need my own space. . . . Sometimes it's good to be around the people who cared about him and knew him. But sometimes it's too much. I just knew that I had to deal with things in my own way."

On more than one occasion, people have asked Marie if she harbors any anger toward Pat for enlisting in the military and going off to war. "I was never mad at him for that," she says. "You love someone for who they are; I can't really be angry with him for enlisting, because needing to do that was part of who he was." Furthermore, she explains, "When Pat joined the Army, it made me tougher. Definitely. Had he not joined the Army, of course, he'd still be alive; but it also made me able to deal with his death. Because of the way Pat was, I discovered a lot of things about myself.

"There is something about Pat that affected almost everybody who was close to him. It's made me want to continue living in a way that honors him. I want him to be proud of the way I live my life and handle things. . . . I'll admit it: It's hard. It's hard to keep going, but I know that for me to just give up, that would piss him off."

Marie decided "the best way to honor our relationship and the life Pat and I had together is to not get swallowed in the grief and anger and other negative emotions, which are definitely there, and can take over if you let them." Toward that end, shortly after Pat was killed, Marie, Alex Garwood, Réka Cseresnyés, Benjamin Hill, Kevin Tillman, and Jared Schrieber established the Pat Tillman Foundation,* the aim of which was to carry Pat's legacy forward by motivating young people to better themselves and their communities. Marie agreed to be chairman of the board of directors, a position that has evolved over the ensuing years into a demanding full-time job thanks to the organization's rapid growth.

To achieve its goals, the foundation endowed a two-semester curriculum at Arizona State University's W. P. Cary School of Business. Called the Leadership Through Action program, it is distinguished from leadership programs at other universities, says Marie, "by its focus on action—which of course was what Pat was all about. He didn't just talk; he acted on his beliefs and tried to have a real impact on the things he considered to be important." Between fifteen and twenty "Tillman Scholars" are accepted into the program each year, and currently Marie is spearheading an effort to expand it to other academic institutions around the nation.

To raise funds, the Pat Tillman Foundation holds a pair of 4.2-mile running events each April in Tempe and San Jose; the distance is based on the number Pat wore on his jersey when he played football for ASU: 42. In 2008, some 15,500 runners and walkers participated in Pat's Run Tempe, and 6,000 in Pat's Run San Jose. "The number of people who come out has been growing every year," Marie says. "It's amazing."

* www.pattillmanfoundation.org.

The foundation has received hundreds of letters and e-mails recounting how ordinary folks were inspired by Pat's example to undertake extraordinary challenges. Although such tangible evidence of Pat's impact on the world has been a solace to Marie, she concedes that his death in April 2004 has left a void of such immensity that it's probably impossible for other people to even imagine the pall it still casts. "It left a hole in my life that's huge," she says.

At some point, Marie predicts, "The sadness will run its course." A moment later, with stoic certainty, she adds, "But it's never going to go away."

PART FIVE

"... But you, Achilles,
there's not a man in the world more blest than you—
there never has been, never will be one.
Time was, when you were alive, we Argives
honored you as a god, and now down here, I see,
you lord it over the dead in all your power.
So grieve no more at dying, great Achilles."

I reassured the ghost, but he broke out, protesting,
"No winning words about death to *me*, shining Odysseus!
By god, I'd rather slave on earth for another man—
some dirt-poor tenant farmer who scrapes to keep alive—
than rule down here over all the breathless dead...."

—HOMER, *The Odyssey*

POSTSCRIPT

January 5, 2007. Twelve miles south of the hillside where Pat Tillman lost his life, a dozen sandbag bunkers squat atop an outcrop of naked bedrock wreathed in smoke from smoldering garbage. Patches of dirty, crusted snow scab the ground. The stench of an overflowing latrine hangs in the air. In the distance, badlands corrugate the landscape without apparent end, their slopes dotted with pines and junipers and thorny, stunted oaks.

This bleak outpost, surrounded by tangles of razor wire, is occupied by a platoon of American infantrymen augmented by approximately forty Afghan National Army troops. Designated Observation Post Four—OP4, for short—it's the northernmost of four hilltop encampments established around the perimeter of Forward Operating Base Tillman to prevent the latter from being overrun by enemy forces. Situated half a mile from the Afghanistan-Pakistan border, the so-called Zero Line, OP4 provides a bird's-eye view of a route used by al-Qaeda and the Taliban to infiltrate Afghanistan from havens in North Waziristan—one of Pakistan's Federally Administered Tribal Areas. Although nominally governed by Pakistan, in reality the Tribal Areas function as autonomous states beyond the control of Islamabad. Launching their assaults from North Waziristan, fighters under the command of Jalaluddin Haqqani attack FOB Tillman or its observation posts every three or four days, on average.

The majority of these attacks originate from the vicinity of a Pakistan Army firebase dubbed the Gray Castle by the American troops because of its crenellated concrete walls. Perched atop a butte directly across the border from OP4, the Gray Castle is so close to the American encampment that Pakistani soldiers are visible with the naked eye as they stand guard on the parapets. Last night, OP4 was hit by a barrage of Taliban rockets fired from the vicinity of the Gray Castle, prompting the commanding officer of FOB Tillman to request a meeting with his Pakistani counterpart in order to avert such attacks in the future.

The two officers, each accompanied by a large contingent of subordinates and security forces, grimly face each other across the border on the morning following the incident, buffeted by a frigid breeze. Major Umar, commander of Pakistan's Thirty-ninth Frontier Corps, is a trim, dapper man wearing an immaculately pressed uniform and kid-leather driving gloves. He begins the dialogue by adamantly denying that the rocket attack originated in Pakistan. When the U.S. Army captain Scott Horrigan—dressed in battle-worn camouflage and scuffed combat boots—replies that azimuth analysis of the fresh blast craters at OP4 leaves no doubt that the rockets had been launched from high ground just north of the Gray Castle, Umar grows indignant. "You may claim that the attacks come from Pakistan," he declares in perfect King's English, "but I had ten patrols in the area last night, and they didn't hear anything, didn't see anything. We will look at your claims, but no, I don't think any of these attacks are coming from Pakistan territory. And if I can be so bold to say it, I don't think the enemy, the miscreants, have the courage to use my area to fire upon American or Afghan positions. I will not allow that. . . . If any miscreants dare to come into this area, I will personally deal with them myself."

Despite Umar's assurances, a preponderance of evidence gathered by American intelligence operatives indicates that the Pakistani Frontier Corps has been extensively infiltrated by the Taliban throughout the Tribal Areas, and that Pakistani forces have cooperated both passively and actively in numerous attacks on American and NATO troops—notwithstanding the fact that Pakistan is a putative ally of the United States and that Islamabad has received more than $10 billion from Washington since September 2001 to fight al-Qaeda and the Taliban. Two nights after the powwow between Umar and Horrigan, OP4 is hit with nine more enemy rockets; during the first three weeks of January, the FOB is attacked a total of six times by enemy forces based in Pakistan.

On January 27, the frustrated Americans hold another meeting with Pakistani military officers, on this occasion taking the highly unusual step of inviting them to tour a radar installation at FOB Tillman, during which the Pakistanis are shown classified data gathered from Q-36 anti-battery radar that pinpoints the precise locations within Pakistan from which recent rocket barrages were launched. Afterward, Captain Dennis Knowles expresses doubt that this new evidence will persuade the Pakistanis to do anything to curtail the attacks. "I'll bet you five bucks," he predicts, not bothering to mask his irritation, "that OP4 is hit again tonight."

At 6:15 that evening, an hour after dark, an Afghan soldier sees a light flicker on a hillside across from OP4 and pops off a few AK-47 rounds at the incandescent pinprick, whereupon an estimated fifty to sixty Haqqani fighters immediately return fire from positions to the west, north, and east. For the next fifteen minutes, a squall of bullets, rocket-propelled grenades, mortar rounds, 107-millimeter rockets, and 105-millimeter Howitzer shells shreds the air over OP4 without pause, and the shooting continues at a lesser rate for another hour before the multipronged attack is repelled and the insurgents retreat back to their hideouts in Pakistan. A young private named Harker is shot in the left thigh, requiring a Black Hawk helicopter to swoop down under fire and medevac him to Bagram. By the time the battle sputters to an end, more than thirteen thousand rounds have been fired at the enemy, killing three Taliban and reportedly wounding ten more.

In April 2004, Pat Tillman was deployed to Afghanistan as part of a campaign to subdue the forces of Jalaluddin Haqqani and bring Khost Province under control of the elected government of President Hamid Karzai. During the half a decade since Tillman perished in that effort, neither of those aims has been achieved—the Taliban/

al-Qaeda presence in Khost and adjacent Paktika Province is stronger now than it has been at any time since the first months of the U.S. invasion in 2001–2002. Villagers throughout the area defiantly fly the white flag of the Taliban from their homes. Less than a mile from the eastern end of Tillman Pass (the name U.S. soldiers spontaneously bestowed upon the canyon where Pat was killed), a loudspeaker at a bustling madrassa blares anti-American messages into the surrounding community while young boys are instructed in the principles of jihad within the school's walls.

As these words are being written in early 2009, Spera is classified as "denied territory" by the U.S. Army—meaning it's denied to American and NATO forces, not the enemy's. The district is firmly in the grip of the Haqqani Network, which has maintained close ties to al-Qaeda ever since bin Laden and Haqqani developed a strong personal bond during the Soviet-Afghan War. Haqqani's fighters have adopted increasingly vicious means of achieving their ends, including massive suicide bombings, assassinations of local officials and teachers, and the indiscriminate beheading of villagers. Although Jalaluddin is still the nominal head of the Haqqani organization, leadership of day-to-day operations has been passed to his son, Sirajuddin Haqqani, known as Siraj. According to the Army lieutenant colonel Dave Anders, "Siraj is the one dictating the new parameters of brutality associated with Taliban senior leadership." The Army is offering a five-million-dollar reward for information leading to Siraj's capture or elimination.

The revival of the Taliban/al-Qaeda insurgency isn't limited to Khost and Paktika provinces; the entire nation has spiraled deeper into violence and chaos. Afghanistan presently supplies 95 percent of the opium used in the global heroin trade, and narcotics production accounts for half of the country's gross domestic product. The Taliban takes a significant percentage of this drug money, which is the insurgents' primary source of revenue, and much of the rest flows to high-ranking members of the Karzai administration, further debasing a government that was permeated with corruption even before the Taliban renaissance. Having squandered most of the credibility he once had with the Afghan people, Karzai is presently teetering on the brink, along with his government. On April 27, 2008, a cadre of

Haqqani insurgents carried out an audacious, elaborately planned attempt to assassinate Karzai during the Afghan National Day military parade in the heart of Kabul. Although the president escaped injury, four others were killed, including a member of parliament who was sitting near Karzai in the reviewing stands.

Taliban and al-Qaeda forces now move freely throughout the Pashtun regions on both sides of the Afghanistan-Pakistan frontier, and Osama bin Laden—still on the loose—is believed by most of the U.S. intelligence community to be securely ensconced on Pakistan's side of the Zero Line. Attacks on U.S. and NATO forces in Afghanistan have increased precipitously in each of the past three years. Insurgents have established hundreds of new bases and training camps in Pakistan's Tribal Areas. Seth G. Jones, the author of a highly regarded study for the RAND National Defense Research Institute titled *Counterinsurgency in Afghanistan,* warned in June 2008, "The United States faces a threat from Al Qaeda today that is comparable to what it faced on September 11, 2001."

There is broad agreement across the political spectrum that the alarming expansion of the Afghan insurgency occurred because the Bush administration's preoccupation with Iraq led to a strategy dubbed "economy of force" (a euphemism for "war on the cheap") when it came to Afghanistan. But the mounting troubles on the latter front are attributable to much more than ill-conceived policies. The greatest threats to peace and stability in Afghanistan are now firmly rooted outside its borders, in Pakistan, where the Taliban and al-Qaeda have found safe haven since early 2002. Owing to the convoluted, fractious, and exceedingly volatile nature of Pakistani politics, subduing the insurgent forces running amok within Pakistan presents a quandary of such apparently intractable complexity that it's unclear how American diplomats and military leaders might even begin to grapple with the problem, let alone engineer a remedy.

Chaos, in the meantime, sweeps across both Pakistan and Afghanistan, and the blood-dimmed tide is loosed. On July 7, 2008, during morning rush hour in Kabul, the Afghan capital, a *jihadi* detonated a powerful car bomb outside the Indian embassy, killing more than fifty people, including the Indian defense attaché, although most of the victims were ordinary Afghan citizens who'd been standing in line to apply for visas for travel to India. American intelligence agencies determined that the suicide bomber who carried out the attack was a Haqqani operative.

Additionally, the *New York Times* reported that the ISI—Pakistan's powerful national spy service—had played an active role in planning the embassy bombing, and that "the highest levels of Pakistan's security apparatus"—including the leader of Pakistan's army, General Ashfaq Parvez Kayani—knew about such plans before the attack was carried out but did nothing to intercede. This alarming revelation confirmed complaints about the ISI's cozy relationship with the Taliban that U.S. soldiers on the front lines in Afghanistan had been expressing privately for years. According to the *Times,* proof of ISI involvement

> was based on intercepted communications between Pakistani intelligence officers and militants who carried out the attack, the officials said, providing the clearest evidence to date that Pakistani intelligence officers are actively undermining American efforts to combat militants in the region. The American officials also said there was new information showing that members of the Pakistani intelligence service were increasingly providing militants with details about the American campaign against them, in some cases allowing militants to avoid American missile strikes in Pakistan's tribal areas.

Within the ranks of the Pakistani military and intelligence services, support for the Taliban is not universal. Some units of the Frontier Corps have battled Haqqani's forces with courage and purpose. Indeed, more than fifteen hundred Pakistani soldiers have been killed fighting insurgents in the Tribal Areas, three times the number of Americans who have died in Afghanistan. But even as some Pakistani soldiers are losing their lives in a campaign against the Taliban and al-Qaeda, other Pakistani military units, as well as powerful factions within the ISI, are providing insurgents with money, weapons, and secret intelligence given to Pakistan by the CIA and the American military. In dozens of documented instances, units of the Pakistani Frontier Corps have shot at American forces across the international border.

Among the insurgent groups supported by the ISI, none has enjoyed the fruits of such backing more than the Haqqani Network,
which isn't surprising given that Jalaluddin Haqqani and the ISI have
maintained an intimate, mutually beneficial relationship that goes
back three decades. Presently that relationship is defined by a tacit
agreement between the Haqqanis and the ISI: if the Haqqanis restrict
their attacks to American, Afghan, and NATO targets, and refrain
from attacking Pakistani troops, Pakistan will refrain from interfer-
ing with the Haqqani Network.

The Pakistani ISI continues to assist Haqqani and other Islamist
insurgents for the same reason the American CIA once did: because
the *jihadis* function as a proxy army willing to bear arms against a
mortal enemy in possession of a nuclear arsenal with whom the government in Islamabad dares not wage war openly. In Pakistan's case,
that enemy is India (assisted by its close ally Afghanistan), which Islamabad considers at least as great a threat to its security as the
United States viewed the Soviet Union during the Cold War. As long
as Pakistan feels imperiled by India, it is unlikely to mount an effective campaign to eradicate the Haqqani Network, al-Qaeda, and the
Taliban from its Tribal Areas—an undertaking that would pose staggering challenges and tremendous risks for the current government in
Islamabad, which is widely acknowledged to be corrupt and incom-
petent, and has only a tenuous hold on the reins of power.

By staging hit-and-run attacks on targets in Afghanistan from
camps across the Zero Line in Pakistan, the Haqqani clan and its ilk
are using precisely the same strategy against the United States that
they employed twenty years ago to defeat the Soviets at the behest of
the United States. And in the long run, the insurgents may emerge
just as victorious as they did in 1989, because until Pakistan ceases
to give them sanctuary, it will be impossible for the United States and
its allies to defeat al-Qaeda and the Taliban by military force, regardless of how many soldiers the United States deploys to Afghanistan—
just as it was impossible for the Soviets to defeat the mujahideen
despite the overwhelming superiority of the Soviet Army.

If staying in Afghanistan is looking more and more like a no-win
prospect for the United States, so, too, does pulling out. Both options
are fraught with uncertainty, although the strife in South Asia is so

incendiary, and so thoroughly entangled with American security interests, that American soldiers are apt to be engaged in Afghanistan for years to come, if not decades. And if recent events are any indication, Americans are likely to be fighting and dying in Pakistan as well.

In July 2008, President Bush issued secret orders for U.S. Special Operations Forces to begin carrying out unilateral ground attacks in Pakistani territory without prior approval from Islamabad, marking a drastic shift in American policy and unleashing an outpouring of ferocious anti-American sentiment throughout Pakistan. The rationale for the new strategy was self-evident (the Pakistanis seemed unwilling to and/or incapable of eradicating enemy sanctuaries from their territory), but it was a very perilous gamble. Covert American action thirty years ago in this same corner of the world (which seemed then like such a good idea) is still yielding cataclysmic repercussions that were impossible to imagine at the time. Whatever near-term tactical advantage is gained by sending American soldiers over the Zero Line to fight al-Qaeda and the Taliban, it would be naive to presume such actions won't have unforeseen consequences thirty years hence, some of which may prove to be no less cataclysmic. Blowback, the CIA calls it.

As Bruce Riedel warned in an article titled "Pakistan and Terror: The Eye of the Storm,"

> Pakistan is the most dangerous country in the world today. All of the nightmares of the twenty-first century come together in Pakistan: nuclear proliferation, drug smuggling, military dictatorship, and above all, international terrorism. Pakistan almost uniquely is both a major victim of terrorism and a major sponsor of terrorism. It has been the scene of horrific acts of terrorist violence, including the murder of Benazir Bhutto in late 2007, and it has been one of the most prolific state sponsors of terror aimed at advancing its national security interests. For the next American president, there is no issue or country more critical to get right. . . .

In his 1992 best seller, *The End of History and the Last Man*, Francis Fukuyama predicted that the inexorable spread of capitalist democracy "would mean the end of wars and bloody revolutions. Agreeing on ends, men would have no large causes for which to fight. They would satisfy their needs through economic activity, but they would no longer have to risk their lives in battle." Fukuyama acknowledged that this rosy future would come with a slight downside, however: the emasculation of humankind. World peace would spawn "the creature who reportedly emerges at the end of history, the *last man*."

"The last man" was a derisive term coined by Friedrich Nietzsche in his overstuffed masterwork, *Thus Spoke Zarathustra*. In Nietzsche's estimation, according to Fukuyama, modern liberal democracies produced men

> composed entirely of desire and reason, clever at finding new ways to satisfy a host of petty wants through the calculation of long-term self-interest. . . . It is not an accident that people in democratic societies are preoccupied with material gain and live in an economic world devoted to the satisfaction of the myriad small needs of the body. . . . The last man at the end of history *knows* better than to risk his life for a cause, because he recognizes that history was full of pointless battles in which men fought over whether they should be Christian or Muslim, Protestant or Catholic, German or French. The loyalties that drove men to desperate acts of courage and sacrifice were proven by subsequent history to be silly prejudices. Men with modern educations were content to sit at home, congratulating themselves on their broadmindedness and lack of fanaticism.

Mocking these contemptible "last men," Nietzsche's Zarathustra famously declares, "Thus you stick out your chests—but alas, they are hollow!" Which prompted Fukuyama to label such milquetoasts "men without chests."

Given the current state of turmoil in South Asia, Africa, and the Caucasus, the onset of international peace prophesied by Fukuyama does not seem imminent. But his forecast about the ascendancy of the American wimp remains disturbingly accurate, according to the historian Lee Harris. In a polemic titled *The Suicide of Reason*, Harris argues,

The problem is not that Fukuyama is dead wrong; the problem is that he is half right. Unfortunately for us, the wrong half.

In the West, we are perilously getting down to *our* last man. Liberal democracy, among us, is achieving the goal that Fukuyama predicted for it: It is eliminating the alpha males from our midst, and at a dizzyingly accelerating rate. But in Muslim societies, the alpha male is still alive and well. While we in America are drugging our alpha boys with Ritalin, the Muslims are doing everything in their power to encourage their alpha boys to be tough, aggressive, and ruthless. . . . We are proud if our sons get into a good college; they are proud if their sons die as martyrs.

To rid your society of high-testosterone alpha males may bring peace and quiet; but if you have an enemy that is building up an army of alpha boys to hate you fanatically and who have vowed to destroy you, you will be committing suicide. . . .

The end of testosterone in the West alone will not culminate in the end of history, but it may well culminate in the end of the West.

Harris's dire conjecture certainly grabs one's attention, but it seems at least as far off the mark as Fukuyama's. Anyone who has spent time with American troops in Afghanistan or Iraq is bound to take issue with Harris's contention that the current generation of young men raised in the West suffers from a deficit of testosterone.

In truth, our society produces all manner of males, in proportions roughly comparable to those in Muslim (and other) societies: compassionate and cruel; leaders and followers; brainiacs and fuckwits; heroes and cowards; selfless exemplars and narcissistic pretenders. Patriotic zeal runs strong in the United States, and young Americans are no less susceptible to the allure of martial adventure than young males from other cultures, including fanatical tribal cultures. Decades from now, when the president of the United States declares yet another war on some national adversary, a great many men (and more than a few women) will doubtless stream forth to enlist, just as eager to join the fight as the Americans who flocked to recruiting offices during previous armed conflicts—regardless of whether the war in question is a reckless blunder or vital to the survival of the Republic.

If the United States' involvement in future wars is inevitable, so, too, is it inevitable that American soldiers will fall victim to friendly fire in those conflicts, for the simple reason that fratricide is part and parcel of every war. According to the most comprehensive survey of American war casualties (both fatal and nonfatal), 21 percent of the casualties in World War II were attributable to friendly fire, 39 percent of the casualties in Vietnam, and 52 percent of the casualties in the first Gulf War. Thus far in the ongoing conflicts in Iraq and Afghanistan, casualty rates are 41 percent and 13 percent, respectively. All these figures are conservative estimates, moreover; due to endemic underreporting of fratricide by the military, the actual percentages are unquestionably higher.

The possibility of falling victim to friendly fire seems to deter few men and women from enlisting in the Armed Forces, in any case. When one talks to soldiers on the front lines, most of them accept that fratricide occasionally comes with the territory; they view it as just one of many occupational hazards in their line of work. As an infantryman, Pat Tillman understood that outside the wire, bad things happen. But he was an optimist. Archetypically American, he was confident that right would usually prevail over wrong. When he swore the oath of enlistment in the summer of 2002, he trusted that those responsible for sending him into battle would do so in good faith. At the time, he didn't envisage that any of them would trifle with his life, or misrepresent the facts of his death, in order to further careers or advance a political agenda.

In *Thus Spoke Zarathustra*, Nietzsche introduced the concept of the *Übermensch*: an exemplary, transcendent figure who is the polar opposite of "the last man" or "men without chests." The *Übermensch* is virtuous, loyal, ambitious and outspoken, disdainful of religious dogma and suspicious of received wisdom, intensely engaged in the hurly-burly of the real world. Above all he is passionate—a connoisseur of both "the highest joys" and "the deepest sorrows." He believes in the moral imperative to defend (with his life, if necessary) ideals such as truth, beauty, honor, and justice. He is self-assured. He is a risk taker. He regards suffering as salutary, and scorns the path of least resistance.

Nietzsche, it is not difficult to imagine, would have recognized in

Pat Tillman more than a few of the attributes he ascribed to his *Über-mensch*. Prominent among such qualities were Tillman's robust masculinity and its corollary, his willingness to stand up and fight. Because Tillman's story conforms in some regards to the classic narrative of the tragic hero, and the protagonist of such a tale always possesses a tragic flaw, it might be tempting to regard Tillman's resounding alpha maleness as his Achilles' heel, the trait that ultimately led to his death.

A compelling argument can be made, however, that the sad end he met in Afghanistan was more accurately a function of his stubborn idealism—his insistence on trying to do the right thing. In which case it wasn't a tragic flaw that brought Tillman down, but a tragic virtue.

ACKNOWLEDGMENTS

I am deeply indebted to Marie Ugenti Tillman, whose contributions to *Where Men Win Glory* were beyond measure. Although other members of the Tillman family declined to be interviewed on the record for this book, I nevertheless owe profound thanks to Pat Tillman's parents, Mary and Patrick Tillman; his brothers, Kevin and Richard Tillman; and his uncle, Stephen Michael Spalding, for their relentless efforts to uncover the truth about Pat's death. Without their determination to hold the Army accountable, most of what is known about the fratricide and subsequent cover-up would never have been revealed. I am especially grateful to Mary and Kevin, who deserve most of the credit for bringing the truth to light. I encourage anyone who wants to learn more about Pat's life to read Mary Tillman's beautiful, searing book, *Boots on the Ground by Dusk: My Tribute to Pat Tillman*.

Thanks are owed as well to the numerous individuals at Doubleday, Broadway, Vintage/Anchor, and Knopf who have assisted me with this project over the past three years, most prominently Charlie Conrad, Bill Thomas, Steve Rubin, David Drake, Alison Rich, Kathy Trager, Sonny Mehta, John Fontana, Caroline Cunningham, Bette Alexander, John Pitts, Sonia Nash, Carol Janeway, Deb Foley, Rebecca Gardner, Jenna Ciongoli, Laura Swerdloff, LuAnn Walther, Marty Asher, Amy Metsch, Anne Messitte, Dana Maxson, Russell

Perreault, John Siciliano, Thomas Dobrowski, and Sloane Crosley. Thanks also to my agent John Ware, to Matthew Ericson for creating the maps, and to Ingrid Sterner for copyediting the manuscript.

Linda Moore, Bill Briggs, Becky Hall, David Roberts, Sharon Roberts, Pat Joseph, Bill Costello, and MaryAnn Briggs read early drafts of the manuscript and offered vital criticism.

The book benefited in crucial ways from conversations I had with Jade Lane, Russell Baer, Mel Ward, Brad Jacobson, Bradley Shepherd, Jason Parsons, Josey Boatright, Will Aker, the late Jared Monti, the late Abdul Ghani, Seymour Hersh, Paul Brookes, Ghulam Khalil, Michael Svensson, Abdul Khaliq, Mohammed Akram, Naim, Michael McGovern, Yar Mohammed, Zach Warren, Dennis Knowles, Ron Locklear, Eric Hayes, Scott Horrigan, Frank Adkinson, Allen Moore, John Hawes, Paul Fitzpatrick, Aaron Swain, Ehsan Farzan, Dominic Cariello, Mike Slusher, Alex Garwood, Christine Ugenti Garwood, Benjamin Hill, Jamie Hill, Brandon Hill, Túlio Tourinho, Réka Cseresnyés, Darin Rosas, Carol Rosas, Erin Clarke Bradford, Mike Bradford, Kemp Hare, Scott Strong, Dan Jensen, and Carson Sprott.

While conducting research in Afghanistan in 2006 and 2007, I received invaluable help from Ansar Rahel, Randy Kohlman, Franz Zenz, Eric Zenk, the late Joseph Fenty, John Breitsprecker, Tony Bennett, Paul Miovas, Mike Vieira, Ross Berkoff, Christopher Cunningham, Dan Dillow, Hunter Marksberry, John Garner, Matt Gibson, Franklin Woods, Derek James, Jorge Villaverde, Delbert Byers, Mike Howard, Paul Deis, Kevin Boyd, Thomas Marbury Jr., Jason Quash, Brian Serota, Dan Huvane, Matthew Cannon, Doc Devlin, Craig Westberg, Kevin Grant, Lawrence Willams, Brandon Peacock, Keith Macklin, Zach Schultz, Josh Renken, David Beebe, Daniel Linnihan, John Tierney, Mike Hanson, Tracy Less, Stephanie Van Geete, Matt Brown, Bradley Hubble, Todd Lowell, Elissa Hurley, Dan Bean, Ann Lockwood, Charlotte Hildebrand, Tom Baker, Bill Metheny, Cathrin Fraker, Ryan Woolf, Jason Sartori, Peter Parison, Roshan Karokhel, Ahmad Shah Sayeed, Baz Mohammed, Mohamed Azim, Abadkhan Akelzareen, Abdul Gafar, Shah Mahmad, Mohammed Sameh, Tayeb Haidari, Mohammed Zakirulah, Noor Aqa, Mohammed Amin, Hedayat Hedayatullah, Javid Nuristani, Shir Mohammed, Kobus Human, and Martin Venter.

For providing counsel and support over the long haul, special thanks to Mark Bryant, Tom Hornbein, Harry Kent, Owen Kent, Martin Shapiro, Nancy McElwain, Eric Zacharias, Sam Brower, Tom Sam Steed, Carine McCandless, Sean Penn, Eddie Vedder, Chip Lee, Brian Nuttall, Marilyn Voorhis, Drew Simon, David Wolf, Ashley Humphries, Eric Love, Josie Heath, Margaret Katz, Carly Hare, Leah Sullivan, Carol Krakauer, Karin Krakauer, Wendy Krakauer, Sarah Krakauer, Andrew Krakauer, Tim Stewart, Mel Kohn, Robin Krakauer, Rosie Stewart, Ali Stewart, Shannon Costello, Mo Costello, Ari Kohn, Miriam Kohn, Kelsi Krakauer, A. J. Krakauer, the late Ralph Moore, and Mary Moore.

NOTES

The following notes document the main sources for each chapter; they do not list the source of every quotation, anecdote, and fact. Passages throughout the book that refer to the ongoing American military campaign in Afghanistan (including the battle that claimed Pat Tillman's life), and to the politics, history, ethnography, geography, geology, and botany of South Asia, were informed in large part by research I undertook on the ground in Afghanistan in May and June 2006, and from December 2006 through February 2007. I spent most of that time in remote parts of Konar, Khost, Paktika, and Paktia provinces, where I accompanied troops from the U.S. Army's Tenth Mountain Division, Eighty-second Airborne Division, and Special Forces Operational Detachment–Alpha 773; U.S. Army National Guard Embedded Training Teams; the Afghan National Army; the Afghan Special Forces; and the Afghan Security Guard on numerous combat missions along the Pakistan border.

PROLOGUE

Details about the events of April 22, 2004, in the Spera District of Khost Province came from interviews and correspondence with Jade Lane, Mel Ward, Will Aker, Bradley Shepherd, Russell Baer, Josey Boatright, Brad Jacobson, and Jason Parsons, augmented by sworn testimony published in "Army Regulation (AR) 15-6 Investigation—Corporal Pat Tillman," by the U.S. Army Special Operations Command, Jan. 10, 2005; "Review of Matters Related to the Death of Corporal Pat Tillman, U.S. Army, Report Number

IPO2007E001, March 26, 2007," by the Inspector General, U.S. Department of Defense; "Hearing on Misleading Information from the Battlefield," preliminary transcript, U.S. House of Representatives Committee on Oversight and Government Reform, April 24, 2007; and "Misleading Information from the Battlefield: The Tillman and Lynch Episodes," by the U.S. House of Representatives Committee on Oversight and Government Reform, July 17, 2008. References to a July 2007 Associated Press article were based on "New Details on Tillman's Death," by Martha Mendoza, published on July 27, 2007. The reference to comments made by Ann Coulter was based on a column she wrote titled "2004: Highlights and Lowlifes," published in *Human Events* on December 30, 2004. The reference to Ted Rall was based on a comic strip he published on April 29, 2004.

CHAPTER ONE

My sources for the material about Pat Tillman's youth were *Boots on the Ground by Dusk: My Tribute to Pat Tillman,* by Mary Tillman; interviews and correspondence with Marie Tillman, Benjamin Hill, Jamie Hill, and Carson Sprott; the diaries of Pat Tillman; and *Fearless,* a forty-five-minute film about Tillman produced by Asylum Entertainment for the Outdoor Life Network. My main sources for the material about the Soviet-Afghan conflict were "The CIA's Intervention in Afghanistan," a 1998 interview with Zbigniew Brzezinski published in *Le Nouvel Observateur;* "Transcript of Bin Laden's October Interview," the transcript of an interview with bin Laden by Al Jazeera Television correspondent Tayseer Alouni in October 2001; *Ghost Wars: The Secret History of the CIA, Afghanistan, and bin Laden, from the Soviet Invasion to September 10, 2001,* by Steve Coll; *Charlie Wilson's War: The Extraordinary Story of How the Wildest Man in Congress and a Rogue CIA Agent Changed the History of Our Time,* by George Crile; *The Bear Went over the Mountain: Soviet Combat Tactics in Afghanistan,* edited by Lester W. Grau; *Afghanistan: A Military History from Alexander the Great to the Fall of the Taliban,* by Stephen Tanner; and "Soviet Air Power: Tactics and Weapons Used in Afghanistan," by Denny R. Nelson. The Francis Fukuyama quotation was taken from his essay "The End of History?"

CHAPTER TWO

My sources for the material about Pat Tillman's youth were *Boots on the Ground by Dusk*; interviews and correspondence with Marie Tillman, Ben-

jamin Hill, Jamie Hill, and Carson Sprott; and *New Almaden*, by Michael
Boulland and Arthur Boudreault. Details about Forward Operating Base Tillman, the Afghan Security Guard, and *Pashtunwali* came from research I conducted in Konar, Paktia, Paktika, and Khost provinces in 2006 and 2007,
which included interviews with Jared Monti, Aaron Swain, Dennis Knowles,
Ron Locklear, Eric Hayes, Ghulam Khalil, and Abdul Ghani.

CHAPTER THREE

My main sources were *Ghost Wars*; *The Looming Tower: Al-Qaeda and the
Road to 9/11*, by Lawrence Wright; *The 9/11 Commission Report: Final Report of the National Commission on Terrorist Attacks upon the United States*;
and *Afghanistan: A Military History from Alexander the Great to the Fall of
the Taliban*.

CHAPTER FOUR

My sources were interviews and correspondence with Marie Tillman, Benjamin Hill, Jamie Hill, and Carson Sprott; articles published in the *San Jose
Mercury News*; *Boots on the Ground by Dusk*; and *I've Got Things to Do
with My Life: Pat Tillman: The Making of an American Hero*, by Mike Towle.

CHAPTER FIVE

My sources were interviews and correspondence with Marie Tillman, Darin
Rosas, Mike Bradford, Erin Clarke Bradford, Kemp Hare, Scott Strong, and
Carol Rosas; and *Boots on the Ground by Dusk*.

CHAPTER SIX

My sources were interviews and correspondence with Marie Tillman, Darin
Rosas, Mike Bradford, Erin Clarke Bradford, Kemp Hare, Scott Strong, Carol
Rosas, and Dan Jensen; and *Boots on the Ground by Dusk*.

CHAPTER SEVEN

My main sources were *Taliban: Militant Islam, Oil, and Fundamentalism in
Central Asia*, by Ahmed Rashid; *Ghost Wars*; *The Looming Tower*; *The 9/11
Commission Report*; *Afghanistan: A Military History from Alexander the
Great to the Fall of the Taliban*; *On the Road to Kandahar: Travels Through
Conflict in the Islamic World*, by Jason Burke; *I is for Infidel: From Holy War
to Holy Terror: 18 Years Inside Afghanistan*, by Kathy Gannon; and "The

Making of Osama bin Laden from Saudi Rich Boy to the World's Most Wanted Man," by Jason Burke.

CHAPTER EIGHT

My sources were interviews with Marie Tillman; *Boots on the Ground by Dusk*; *I've Got Things to Do with My Life*; and "A Cut Above," by Tim Layden.

CHAPTER NINE

My main sources were interviews and correspondence with Marie Tillman and Réka Cseresnyés; *Boots on the Ground by Dusk*; *I've Got Things to Do with My Life*; "A Cut Above"; and articles published in the *Arizona Republic*.

CHAPTER TEN

My main sources were interviews and correspondence with Marie Tillman and Frank Bauer; *Boots on the Ground by Dusk*; *I've Got Things to Do with My Life*; and articles published in the *Arizona Republic*.

CHAPTER ELEVEN

My main sources were *Ghost Wars*; *The Looming Tower*; *The 9/11 Commission Report*; *Charlie Wilson's War*; *Afghanistan Cave Complexes, 1979–2004: Mountain Strongholds of the Mujahideen, Taliban & Al Qaeda*, by Mir Bahmanyar; and *Osama bin Laden: America's Enemy in His Own Words*, edited by Randall B. Hamud.

CHAPTER TWELVE

My main sources were interviews and correspondence with Marie Tillman, Benjamin Hill, and Brandon Hill; and articles published in the *Arizona Republic*.

CHAPTER THIRTEEN

My main sources were interviews and correspondence with Marie Tillman, Christine Ugenti Garwood, and Alex Garwood; the diaries of Pat Tillman; and *I've Got Things to Do with My Life*.

CHAPTER FOURTEEN

My main sources were the diaries of Pat Tillman; *The 9/11 Commission Report*; *Ghost Wars*; and *The Looming Tower*.

CHAPTER FIFTEEN

My main sources were interviews and correspondence with Marie Tillman and Frank Bauer; Supreme Court ruling 00-949, *Bush v. Gore*; "Conflicts of Interest in Bush v. Gore: Did Some Justices Vote Illegally?" by Richard K. Neumann Jr.; "My All-Pro Team," by Paul Zimmerman; *The 9/11 Commission Report*; and *Against All Enemies: Inside America's War on Terror*, by Richard Clarke.

CHAPTER SIXTEEN

My main sources were interviews and correspondence with Marie Tillman and Pat Murphy; "True Hero Athlete," by Gwen Knapp; *The 9/11 Commission Report*; *Against All Enemies*; *The One Percent Doctrine: Deep Inside America's Pursuit of Its Enemies Since 9/11*, by Ron Suskind; and *Angler: The Cheney Vice Presidency*, by Barton Gellman.

CHAPTER SEVENTEEN

My main sources were interviews and correspondence with Marie Tillman; *The One Percent Doctrine*; *Afghanistan: A Military History from Alexander the Great to the Fall of the Taliban*; *Special Operations Forces in Afghanistan: Afghanistan, 2001–2007*, by Leigh Neville; *Kill bin Laden: A Delta Force Commander's Account of the Hunt for the World's Most Wanted Man*, by Dalton Fury; *Messages to the World: The Statements of Osama bin Laden*, edited by Bruce Lawrence; *Jawbreaker: The Attack on bin Laden and Al-Qaeda*, by Gary Berntsen; *Not a Good Day to Die: The Untold Story of Operation Anaconda*, by Sean Naylor; "U.S. Special Operations Command 20th Anniversary History: 1987–2007"; "Excerpts from Usama Bin Ladin's 'Will' "; "The Long Hunt for Osama," by Peter Bergen; and "The Failing Campaign to Kill Jalaluddin Haqqani," by Marc W. Herold.

CHAPTER EIGHTEEN

My main sources were interviews and correspondence with Marie Tillman, Frank Bauer, Christine Ugenti Garwood, and Alex Garwood; and *Boots on the Ground by Dusk*.

CHAPTER NINETEEN

My main sources were interviews and correspondence with Marie Tillman and Túlio Tourinho; the diaries of Pat Tillman; and "Misleading Information from the Battlefield: The Tillman and Lynch Episodes."

CHAPTER TWENTY

My main sources were interviews and correspondence with Marie Tillman and Túlio Tourinho; and the diaries of Pat Tillman.

CHAPTER TWENTY-ONE

My main sources were interviews and correspondence with Marie Tillman, Russell Baer, Jade Lane, and Jason Parsons; the diaries of Pat Tillman; a transcript of the second Gore-Bush presidential debate held on October 11, 2000; *The One Percent Doctrine*; and *Fiasco: The American Military Adventure in Iraq*, by Thomas E. Ricks.

CHAPTER TWENTY-TWO

My main sources were the diaries of Pat Tillman; "Attack on the 507th Maintenance Company, 23 March 2003; An Nasiriyah, Iraq: Executive Summary," issued by the U.S. Army; "Misleading Information from the Battlefield: The Tillman and Lynch Episodes"; *Fiasco*; *Cobra II: The Inside Story of the Invasion and Occupation of Iraq*, by Michael R. Gordon and Bernard E. Trainor; " 'She Was Fighting to the Death'; Details Emerging of W. Va. Soldier's Capture and Rescue," by Susan Schmidt and Vernon Loeb; and "Iraq Media Guy Rebuilds Qatar at the Garden," by Ben Smith.

CHAPTER TWENTY-THREE

My main sources were the diaries of Pat Tillman; "Investigation of Suspected Friendly Fire Incident near An Nasiriyah, Iraq, 23 March 03," a report by U.S. Central Command; *Ambush Alley: The Most Extraordinary Battle of the Iraq War*, by Tim Pritchard; *Marines in the Garden of Eden*, by Richard S. Lowry; *An Nasiriyah: The Fight for the Bridges*, by Gary Livingston; *The Great War for Civilisation: The Conquest of the Middle East*, by Robert Fisk; *Generation Kill: Devil Dogs, Iceman, Captain America, and the New Face of American War*, by Evan Wright; *Cobra II*; and "A Deadly Day for Charlie Company," by Rich Connell and Robert J. Lopez.

CHAPTER TWENTY-FOUR

My main sources were Pat Tillman's diaries; "Investigation of Suspected Friendly Fire Incident near An Nasiriyah, Iraq, 23 March 03"; *Ambush Alley*; *Marines in the Garden of Eden*; *An Nasiriyah: The Fight for the Bridges*; *Generation Kill*; *Cobra II*; and "A Deadly Day for Charlie Company."

CHAPTER TWENTY-FIVE

My main sources were Pat Tillman's diaries; "Investigation of Suspected Friendly Fire Incident near An Nasiriyah, Iraq, 23 March 03"; "A-10 Friendly Fire Investigation Completed," a news release by U.S. Central Command; "CENTCOM Operation Iraqi Freedom Briefing 23 March 2003"; "Defense Department Briefing Transcript, 25 March 2003"; "Secretary Rumsfeld Media Availability En Route to Chile," a U.S. Department of Defense news transcript, Nov. 18, 2002; "Nine Marines Killed, 12 Soldiers Missing," a report by Fox News; "The Truth About Jessica," by John Kampfner; and "The Man Who Sold the War," by James Bamford.

CHAPTER TWENTY-SIX

My main sources were interviews and correspondence with Marie Tillman, Russell Baer, Jade Lane, Mel Ward, Aaron Swain, and Frank Bauer; the diaries of Pat Tillman; *Nuremberg Diary*, by G. M. Gilbert; *Osama bin Laden: America's Enemy in His Own Words*; and *Boots on the Ground by Dusk*.

CHAPTER TWENTY-SEVEN

My main sources were interviews and correspondence with Marie Tillman, Josey Boatright, and Réka Cseresnyés; Pat Tillman's diaries; and *Boots on the Ground by Dusk*.

CHAPTER TWENTY-EIGHT

My main sources were Pat Tillman's diaries; interviews and correspondence with Brad Jacobson, Bradley Shepherd, Jason Parsons, Russell Baer, Josey Boatright, Will Aker, Jade Lane, and Mel Ward; "Afghan Offensive: Grand Plans Hit Rugged Reality," by Syed Saleem Shahzad; "Army Regulation (AR) 15-6 Investigation—Corporal Pat Tillman"; "Review of Matters Related to the Death of Corporal Pat Tillman"; "Hearing on Misleading Information from the Battlefield"; and "Misleading Information from the Battlefield: The Tillman and Lynch Episodes."

CHAPTER TWENTY-NINE

My main sources were interviews and correspondence with Brad Jacobson, Bradley Shepherd, Jason Parsons, Russell Baer, Josey Boatright, Will Aker, Jade Lane, and Mel Ward; "Afghan Offensive: Grand Plans Hit Rugged Reality"; "Army Regulation (AR) 15-6 Investigation—Corporal Pat Tillman";

"Review of Matters Related to the Death of Corporal Pat Tillman"; "Hearing on Misleading Information from the Battlefield"; and "Misleading Information from the Battlefield: The Tillman and Lynch Episodes."

CHAPTER THIRTY

My main sources were interviews and correspondence with Brad Jacobson, Bradley Shepherd, Jason Parsons, Russell Baer, Josey Boatright, Will Aker, Jade Lane, and Mel Ward; "Army Regulation (AR) 15-6 Investigation—Corporal Pat Tillman"; "Review of Matters Related to the Death of Corporal Pat Tillman"; "Hearing on Misleading Information from the Battlefield"; and "Misleading Information from the Battlefield: The Tillman and Lynch Episodes."

CHAPTER THIRTY-ONE

My main sources were interviews and correspondence with Brad Jacobson, Bradley Shepherd, Jason Parsons, Russell Baer, Josey Boatright, Will Aker, Jade Lane, and Mel Ward; "Army Regulation (AR) 15-6 Investigation—Corporal Pat Tillman"; "Review of Matters Related to the Death of Corporal Pat Tillman"; "Hearing on Misleading Information from the Battlefield"; and "Misleading Information from the Battlefield: The Tillman and Lynch Episodes."

CHAPTER THIRTY-TWO

My main sources were interviews and correspondence with Marie Tillman, Alex Garwood, Christine Ugenti Garwood, Seymour Hersh, and Russell Baer; *Boots on the Ground by Dusk*; "The Hidden General," by Michael Hirsh and John Barry; "Final Autopsy Examination Report: Patrick D. Tillman," by the Office of the Armed Forces Medical Examiner; a transcript of an interview between Dr. Craig Mallak and a special officer from the Office of the Inspector General, Department of Defense; "Army Regulation (AR) 15-6 Investigation—Corporal Pat Tillman"; "Review of Matters Related to the Death of Corporal Pat Tillman"; "Hearing on Misleading Information from the Battlefield"; and "Misleading Information from the Battlefield: The Tillman and Lynch Episodes."

CHAPTER THIRTY-THREE

My main sources were interviews and correspondence with Marie Tillman, Jade Lane, Russell Baer, Bradley Shepherd, Mel Ward, Will Aker, and Seymour Hersh; *Boots on the Ground by Dusk*; *The Terror Presidency: Law and Judgment Inside the Bush Administration*, by Jack L. Goldsmith; *Torture and*

Truth: America, Abu Ghraib, and the War on Terror, by Mark Danner; *Chain of Command: The Road from 9/11 to Abu Ghraib*, by Seymour Hersh; "The General's Report," by Seymour Hersh; "Army Regulation (AR) 15-6 Investigation—Corporal Pat Tillman"; "Review of Matters Related to the Death of Corporal Pat Tillman"; "Hearing on Misleading Information from the Battlefield"; and "Misleading Information from the Battlefield: The Tillman and Lynch Episodes."

CHAPTER THIRTY-FOUR

My main sources were interviews and correspondence with Marie Tillman, Jade Lane, Russell Baer, Bradley Shepherd, Mel Ward, Will Aker, and Brad Jacobson; *Boots on the Ground by Dusk*; "An Un-American Tragedy," by Mike Fish; "Final Autopsy Examination Report: Patrick D. Tillman"; a transcript of an interview between Dr. Craig Mallak and a special officer from the Office of the Inspector General; "New Details on Tillman's Death," by Martha Mendoza; "Army Regulation (AR) 15-6 Investigation—Corporal Pat Tillman"; "Review of Matters Related to the Death of Corporal Pat Tillman"; "Hearing on Misleading Information from the Battlefield"; "Misleading Information from the Battlefield: The Tillman and Lynch Episodes"; "Information Regarding the Death of Pat Tillman," a news release by the Office of the Assistant Secretary of Defense; and "President Bush Discusses American Competitiveness Initiative During Press Conference," a transcript from the White House.

CHAPTER THIRTY-FIVE

My sources were interviews and correspondence with Marie Tillman and Mel Ward.

POSTSCRIPT

I gathered much of the material in this chapter during visits to Afghanistan in 2006 and 2007. In the course of my travels I spoke with Dennis Knowles, Ron Locklear, Eric Hayes, Allen Moore, Frank Adkinson, Scott Horrigan, Abdul Ghani, and Matt Brown. Other sources included *Counterinsurgency in Afghanistan*, by Seth G. Jones; "Afghan, Coalition Forces Disrupt Insurgent Network," by Timothy Dineen; "C.I.A. Outlines Pakistan Links with Militants," by Mark Mazzetti and Eric Schmitt; "Bush Said to Give Orders Allowing Raids in Pakistan," by Eric Schmitt and Mark Mazzetti; "Taliban Commander Is Face of Rising Threat," by Carlotta Gall; "India Vindicated by

Pakistan Charge," by Madhur Singh; "Right at the Edge," by Dexter Filkins; *The End of History and the Last Man*, by Francis Fukuyama; *The Suicide of Reason: Radical Islam's Threat to the West*, by Lee Harris; "Pakistan and Terror: The Eye of the Storm," by Bruce Riedel; and *Thus Spoke Zarathustra*, by Friedrich Nietzsche.

BIBLIOGRAPHY

"Army Regulation (AR) 15-6 Investigation—Corporal Pat Tillman." U.S. Army Special Operations Command, Jan. 10, 2005.

"A-10 Friendly Fire Investigation Completed." News release, U.S. Central Command, March 29, 2004. Release number 04-03-51.

"Attack on the 507th Maintenance Company, 23 March 2003; An Nasiriyah, Iraq: Executive Summary." U.S. Army.

Bacevich, Andrew. *The Limits of Power: The End of American Exceptionalism.* New York: Metropolitan Books, 2008.

Bahmanyar, Mir. *Afghanistan Cave Complexes, 1979–2004: Mountain Strongholds of the Mujahideen, Taliban & Al Qaeda.* Oxford: Osprey, 2004.

———. *Shadow Warriors: A History of the U.S. Army Rangers.* Oxford: Osprey, 2005.

Bamford, James. "The Man Who Sold the War: Meet John Rendon, Bush's General in the Propaganda War." *Rolling Stone,* Nov. 17, 2005.

Bergen, Peter L. "The Long Hunt for Osama." *Atlantic Monthly,* Oct. 2004.

———. *The Osama bin Laden I Know.* New York: Free Press, 2006.

Berntsen, Gary. *Jawbreaker: The Attack on bin Laden and Al-Qaeda.* New York: Three Rivers Press, 2006.

bin Laden, Osama. "Excerpts from Usama Bin Ladin's 'Will.'" *Al-Majallah,* Oct. 27, 2002. Translated by Foreign Broadcast Information Service. www.fas.org/irp/world/para/ubl-fbis.pdf.

Boulland, Michael, and Arthur Boudreault. *New Almaden.* Charleston, S.C.: Arcadia, 2006.

Bourke, Joanna. *An Intimate History of Killing: Face-to-Face Killing in Twentieth-Century Warfare.* New York: Basic Books, 1999.

Bowden, Mark. *Black Hawk Down: A Story of Modern War.* New York: Penguin Books, 2000.

Bryant, Russ. *To Be a U.S. Army Ranger.* St. Paul: Zenith Press, 2003.

Bryant, Russ, and Susan Bryant. *Weapons of the U.S. Army Rangers.* St. Paul: Zenith Press, 2005.

Burke, Jason. "The Making of Osama bin Laden from Saudi Rich Boy to the World's Most Wanted Man." *Observer,* Nov. 1, 2001.

————. *On the Road to Kandahar: Travels Through Conflict in the Islamic World.* New York: Thomas Dunne, 2006.

"CENTCOM Operation Iraqi Freedom Briefing 23 March 2003." News transcript, U.S. Central Command, March 23, 2003.

Chayes, Sarah. *The Punishment of Virtue: Inside Afghanistan After the Taliban.* New York: Penguin Press, 2006.

Chomsky, Noam. *Failed States: The Abuse of Power and the Assault on Democracy.* New York: Metropolitan Books, 2006.

"The CIA's Intervention in Afghanistan: Interview with Zbigniew Brzezinski." Translated by Bill Blum. *Le Nouvel Observateur,* Jan. 15–21, 1998. www.globalresearch.ca/articles/BRZ110A.html.

Clarke, Richard. *Against All Enemies: Inside America's War on Terror.* New York: Free Press, 2004.

Coll, Steve. *The Bin Ladens: An Arabian Family in the American Century.* New York: Penguin Press, 2008.

————. "Deluded." *New Yorker,* April 3, 2006.

————. *Ghost Wars: The Secret History of the CIA, Afghanistan, and bin Laden, from the Soviet Invasion to September 10, 2001.* New York: Penguin Press, 2004.

Connell, Rich, and Robert J. Lopez. "A Deadly Day for Charlie Company." *Los Angeles Times,* Aug. 26, 2003.

Coulter, Ann. *How to Talk to a Liberal (If You Must): The World According to Ann Coulter.* New York: Three Rivers Press, 2005.

————. "2004: Highlights and Lowlifes." *Human Events,* Dec. 30, 2004.

Crile, George. *Charlie Wilson's War: The Extraordinary Story of How the Wildest Man in Congress and a Rogue CIA Agent Changed the History of Our Times.* New York: Grove Press, 2003.

Danner, Mark. *Torture and Truth: America, Abu Ghraib, and the War on Terror*. New York: New York Review of Books, 2004.

"Defense Department Briefing Transcript, 25 March 2003." News transcript, U.S. Department of Defense.

Dineen, Timothy. "Afghan, Coalition Forces Disrupt Insurgent Network." News release, Combined Joint Task Force–82 Public Affairs Office.

Emerson, Ralph Waldo. *Self-Reliance and Other Essays*. New York: Dover, 1993.

Ewans, Martin. *Afghanistan: A Short History of Its People and Politics*. New York: Perennial, 2002.

Fearless. Produced by Asylum Entertainment. Outdoor Life Network. Oct. 22, 2005.

Filkins, Dexter. *The Forever War*. New York: Knopf, 2008.

———. "Right at the Edge." *New York Times Magazine*, Sept. 7, 2008.

Fish, Mike. "An Un-American Tragedy." ESPN.com. sports.espn.go.com/espn/eticket/story?page=tillmanpart1.

Fisk, Robert. *The Great War for Civilisation: The Conquest of the Middle East*. New York: Vintage, 2007.

Fukuyama, Francis. "The End of History?" *National Interest*, Summer 1989.

———. *The End of History and the Last Man*. New York: Free Press, 2006.

Fury, Dalton. *Kill bin Laden: A Delta Force Commander's Account of the Hunt for the World's Most Wanted Man*. New York: St. Martin's Press, 2008.

Gall, Carlotta. "Taliban Commander Is Face of Rising Threat." *New York Times*, June 17, 2008.

Gannon, Kathy. *I Is for Infidel: From Holy War to Holy Terror: 18 Years Inside Afghanistan*. New York: PublicAffairs, 2005.

Garamone, Jim, and David Mays. "Afghan, Coalition Forces Battle Taliban, Narcotics, Emphasize Training." Armed Forces press service, Oct. 19, 2007.

Gellman, Barton. *Angler: The Cheney Vice Presidency*. New York: Penguin Press, 2008.

George W. Bush et al., Petitioners v. Albert Gore Jr. et al. Supreme Court of the United States, no. 00-949, Dec. 12, 2000.

Gilbert, G. M. *Nuremberg Diary*. New York: Da Capo Press, 1995.

Goff, Stan. "The Fog of Fame." *CounterPunch*, Aug. 9, 2007. www.counterpunch.org/goff08092007.html.

Goldsmith, Jack L. *The Terror Presidency: Law and Judgment Inside the Bush Administration*. New York: W. W. Norton, 2007.

Gordon, Michael R., and Bernard E. Trainor. *Cobra II: The Inside Story of the Invasion and Occupation of Iraq*. New York: Pantheon, 2006.

Graham, Stephen. "Pakistan Vows to 'Weed Out' Pro-Taliban Agents." Associated Press, Aug. 1, 2008.

Grau, Lester W., ed. *The Bear Went over the Mountain: Soviet Combat Tactics in Afghanistan*. Washington, D.C.: National Defense University Press, 1996.

Grossman, Dave. *On Killing: The Psychological Cost of Learning to Kill in War and Society*. Boston: Back Bay Books, 1996.

Hamilton, Edith. *The Greek Way*. New York: W. W. Norton, 1993.

Hamud, Randall B., ed. *Osama bin Laden: America's Enemy in His Own Words*. San Diego: Nadeem, 2005.

Harris, Lee. *The Suicide of Reason: Radical Islam's Threat to the West*. New York: Basic Books, 2007.

"Hearing on Misleading Information from the Battlefield." Preliminary transcript, U.S. House of Representatives Committee on Oversight and Government Reform, April 24, 2007. oversight.house.gov/story.asp?ID=1242.

Hedges, Chris. "A Culture of Atrocity." *Truthdig,* June 18, 2007. www.truthdig.com/report/item/20070618_a_culture_of_atrocity/.

Herold, Marc W. "The Failing Campaign to Kill Jalaluddin Haqqani." *Cursor,* Jan. 18, 2002. www.cursor.org/stories/jalaluddin.htm.

Hersh, Seymour M. *Chain of Command: The Road from 9/11 to Abu Ghraib*. New York: HarperCollins, 2004.

———. "The General's Report." *New Yorker,* June 25, 2007.

Hirsh, Michael, and John Barry. "The Hidden General." *Newsweek,* June 26, 2006.

Homer. *The Iliad of Homer*. Translated by Richmond Lattimore. Chicago: University of Chicago Press, 1961.

Homer. *The Odyssey*. Translated by Robert Fagles. New York: Penguin Books, 1997.

Hosseini, Khaled. *The Kite Runner*. New York: Riverhead, 2003.

"Information Regarding the Death of Pat Tillman." Office of the Assistant Secretary of Defense (Public Affairs), July 31, 2007.

"Investigation of Suspected Friendly Fire Incident near An Nasiriyah, Iraq, 23 March 03." U.S. Central Command, March 6, 2004.

Jalali, Ali Ahmad, and Lester W. Grau. *Afghan Guerrilla Warfare: In the Words of the Mujahideen Fighters*. St. Paul: MBI, 2001.

Johns, Dave. "The Crimes of Saddam Hussein." *FRONTLINE/World.* www.pbs.org/frontlineworld/stories/iraq501/events_uprising.html.

Jones, Seth G. *Counterinsurgency in Afghanistan.* Santa Monica, Calif.: RAND National Defense Research Institute, 2008.

"Justice Scalia on the Record." CBS News, *60 Minutes,* April 27, 2008. www .cbsnews.com/stories/2008/04/24/60minutes/printable4040290.shtml.

Kampfner, John. "The Truth About Jessica." *Guardian,* May 15, 2003.

Keegan, John. *A History of Warfare.* New York: Vintage, 1994.

Knapp, Gwen. "True Hero Athlete." *San Francisco Chronicle,* May 4, 2004.

Kreager, Derek A. "Unnecessary Roughness? Youth Sports, Peer Networks, and Male Adolescent Violence." faculty.washington.edu/matsueda/UR2.pdf.

Lawrence, Bruce, ed. *Messages to the World: The Statements of Osama bin Laden.* London: Verso, 2005.

Layden, Tim. "A Cut Above." *Sports Illustrated,* Dec. 8, 1997.

Leeson, Francis L. *Frontier Legion: With the Khassadars of North Waziristan.* West Sussex, U.K.: Leeson Archive, 2003.

Livingston, Gary. *An Nasiriyah: The Fight for the Bridges.* North Topsail Island, N.C.: Caisson Press, 2003.

Lowry, Richard S. *Marines in the Garden of Eden.* New York: Berkley Caliber, 2006.

Mazzetti, Mark, and David Rhode. "Amid Policy Disputes, Qaeda Grows in Pakistan." *New York Times,* June 30, 2008.

Mazzetti, Mark, and Eric Schmitt. "C.I.A. Outlines Pakistan Links with Militants." *New York Times,* July 30, 2008.

Mendoza, Martha. "New Details on Tillman's Death." Associated Press, July 27, 2007.

"Misleading Information from the Battlefield: The Tillman and Lynch Episodes." Committee report, U.S. House of Representatives Committee on Oversight and Government Reform, July 17, 2008.

Naylor, Sean. *Not a Good Day to Die: The Untold Story of Operation Anaconda.* New York: Berkley Caliber, 2005.

Neiman, Susan. *Moral Clarity: A Guide for Grown-Up Idealists.* New York: Harcourt, 2008.

Nelson, Denny R. "Soviet Air Power: Tactics and Weapons Used in Afghanistan." *Air University Review,* Jan.–Feb. 1985.

Neumann, Richard K., Jr. "Conflicts of Interest in Bush v. Gore: Did Some Justices Vote Illegally?" *Georgetown Journal of Legal Ethics* (Spring 2003).

Neville, Leigh. *Special Operations Forces in Afghanistan: Afghanistan, 2001–2007.* Oxford: Osprey, 2008.

Nietzsche, Friedrich. *Thus Spoke Zarathustra: A Book for None and All.* Translated by Walter Kaufmann. New York: Penguin Books, 1978.

The 9/11 Commission Report: Final Report of the National Commission on Terrorist Attacks upon the United States. New York: W. W. Norton, 2004.

"Nine Marines Killed, 12 Soldiers Missing." Fox News, March 24, 2003. www.foxnews.com/story/0,2933,81921,00.html.

Oren, Michael B. *Power, Faith, and Fantasy: America in the Middle East, 1776 to the Present.* New York: W. W. Norton, 2007.

"Oversight Committee Holds Hearing on Tillman, Lynch Incidents." U.S. House of Representatives Committee on Oversight and Government Reform, 110th Cong., April 24, 2007.

Packer, George. *The Assassins' Gate: America in Iraq.* New York: Farrar, Straus and Giroux, 2005.

Piper, Joan L. *A Chain of Events: The Government Cover-Up of the Black Hawk Incident and the Friendly-Fire Death of Lt. Laura Piper.* Washington, D.C.: Brassey's, 2001.

Poole, H. John. *Tactics of the Crescent Moon: Militant Muslim Combat Methods.* Emerald Isle, N.C.: Posterity Press, 2004.

"President Bush Discusses American Competitiveness Initiative During Press Conference." White House, Office of the Press Secretary, Aug. 9, 2007.

Pressfield, Steven. *The Afghan Campaign.* New York: Doubleday, 2006.

Pritchard, Tim. *Ambush Alley: The Most Extraordinary Battle of the Iraq War.* New York: Presidio Press, 2005.

Rall, Ted. *The Cartoon,* April 29, 2004. www.gocomics.com/rallcom/2004/05/03/.

Rand, Jonathan. *Fields of Honor: The Pat Tillman Story.* New York: Chamberlain Bros., 2004.

Rashid, Ahmed. *Taliban: Militant Islam, Oil, and Fundamentalism in Central Asia.* New Haven, Conn.: Yale Nota Bene, 2001.

"Review of Matters Related to the Death of Corporal Pat Tillman, U.S. Army, Report Number IPO2007E001, March 26, 2007." Inspector General, U.S. Department of Defense.

Ricks, Thomas E. *Fiasco: The Military Adventure in Iraq.* New York: Penguin Press, 2006.

Riedel, Bruce. "Pakistan and Terror: The Eye of the Storm." *Annals of the American Academy of Political and Social Science* 618, July 2008.

Robinson, Linda. *Masters of Chaos: The Secret History of the Special Forces.* New York: PublicAffairs, 2004.

Scheuer, Michael. *Imperial Hubris: Why the West Is Losing the War on Terror.* Washington, D.C.: Potomac Books, 2005.

Schmidt, Susan, and Vernon Loeb. " 'She Was Fighting to the Death'; Details Emerging of W. Va. Soldier's Capture and Rescue." *Washington Post,* April 3, 2003.

Schmitt, Eric, and Mark Mazzetti. "Bush Said to Give Orders Allowing Raids in Pakistan." *New York Times,* Sept. 11, 2008.

Schroen, Gary C. *First In: An Insider's Account of How the CIA Spearheaded the War on Terror in Afghanistan.* New York: Presidio Press, 2005.

"The Second Gore-Bush Presidential Debate." Oct. 11, 2000. Commission on Presidential Debates. www.debates.org/pages/trans2000b.html.

"Secretary Rumsfeld Media Availability En Route to Chile." News transcript, U.S. Department of Defense, Nov. 18, 2002.

Shahzad, Syed Saleem. "Afghan Offensive: Grand Plans Hit Rugged Reality." *Asia Times Online,* March 20, 2004. www.atimes.com/atimes/South_Asia/FC20Df02.html.

Shay, Jonathan. *Achilles in Vietnam: Combat Trauma and the Undoing of Character.* New York: Touchstone, 1995.

Singh, Madhur. "India Vindicated by Pakistan Charge." *Time,* Aug. 1, 2008.

Smith, Ben. "Iraq Media Guy Rebuilds Qatar at the Garden." *New York Observer,* Oct. 26, 2003.

Smith, Gary. "Remember His Name." *Sports Illustrated,* Sept. 11, 2006.

Suskind, Ron. *The One Percent Doctrine: Deep Inside America's Pursuit of Its Enemies Since 9/11.* New York: Simon & Schuster, 2006.

Tanner, Stephen. *Afghanistan: A Military History from Alexander the Great to the Fall of the Taliban.* Cambridge, Mass.: Da Capo Press, 2002.

Tillman, Mary. *Boots on the Ground by Dusk: My Tribute to Pat Tillman.* With Narda Zacchino. New York: Modern Times, 2008.

Towle, Mike. *I've Got Things to Do with My Life: Pat Tillman: The Making of an American Hero.* Chicago: Triumph Books, 2004.

"Transcript of Bin Laden's October Interview." CNN.com/World. February 5, 2002. archives.cnn.com/2002/WORLD/asiapcf/south/02/05/binladen .transcript/index.html.

"U.S. Special Operations Command 20th Anniversary History: 1987–2007."
   U.S. Special Operations Command.

"Widow of Slain Marine Calls His Death 'Murder,' Denounces Killers for Not
   Following Rules of War." NBC 30 Connecticut News, March 26, 2003.

Wright, Evan. *Generation Kill: Devil Dogs, Iceman, Captain America, and the
   New Face of American War.* New York: Berkley Caliber, 2004.

Wright, Lawrence. *The Looming Tower: Al-Qaeda and the Road to 9/11.*
   New York: Knopf, 2006.

Zimmerman, Paul. "My All-Pro Team." *Sports Illustrated,* Jan. 3, 2001.
   sportsillustrated.cnn.com/inside_game/dr_z/news/2001/01/03/drz_insider/.

INDEX

ABOUT THE AUTHOR

Jon Krakauer is the author of *Eiger Dreams, Into the Wild, Into Thin Air,* and *Under the Banner of Heaven,* and is the editor of the Modern Library Exploration series.